T0312067

Technology Applied

Technology – love it or hate it – is a critical component for nearly every modern business.

To the business leader or aspiring business leader, the world of technology may sometimes appear to be confusing and obscure. The language and nuance of software, systems, and IT projects is often a barrier to effective communication between different parts of an enterprise at just the time when it's most needed – during a technology-enabled project that is seeking to deliver business benefit.

This book sets out, in clear non-technical language and with practical real-world examples, the essential background to different aspects of information technology (hardware, software, data, and interfaces); their latest manifestations, such as artificial intelligence and blockchain; and how they all combine into a technology project.

Most importantly, this book helps you, the business leader, understand the people behind the technology, appreciate their perspective and their motivations, and to enable you to ask the crucial questions that could transform your engagement to apply technology effectively

Technology Applied

A Business Leader's Guide to Software, Systems and IT Projects

Kevin Wooldridge
and Stephen Ashurst

Routledge
Taylor & Francis Group

A PRODUCTIVITY PRESS BOOK

First published 2025
by Routledge
605 Third Avenue, New York, NY 10158

and by Routledge
4 Park Square, Milton Park, Abingdon, Oxon, OX14 4RN

Routledge is an imprint of the Taylor & Francis Group, an informa business

ISBN: 978-1-032-44538-0 (hbk)
ISBN: 978-1-032-44537-3 (pbk)
ISBN: 978-1-003-37266-0 (ebk)

DOI: 10.4324/9781003372660

Typeset in Minion
by Newgen Publishing UK

KW Dedication
For everyone who has supported me through the authoring process, but especially for my wife and family who have had to put up with my absence (intellectually if not physically) and occasional spot quizzes on obscure technology facts.

SA Dedication
For Anthony and Isabella forever.

Contents

Preface

Technology applied.

These two words describe the world in which we live and work.

Technology is everywhere, constantly evolving, delighting (and frustrating) us.

There is, we also know, a significant amount of *theoretical* or *conjectural* or *speculative* technology out there. There must be: that's where the new tech comes from, right?

But what really matters is what technology does for us now, today, in the applied sense. Technology is the key component of the way we work, relax, travel and stay healthy ... without technology, *without tools*, humanity would not be the species we are.

So, tech is here to stay – and grow. But how many of us really understand the origin stories of business and organisation/enterprise technology? Especially in the world of work, business and administration ... where technology is ever more pervasive and yet often a closed-off world made up of mysterious, important-sounding but impenetrable acronyms; strange software code full of "bugs" and "hacks" and the whole thing intermediated by geeky people who we rely on as colleagues (especially when technology goes wrong) but who quickly lose us with their talk of *data* and *sprints* and *distributed ledgers*....

If you're a beginner in the world of work, a career business stakeholder, a junior or senior leader, a VP or SVP or EVP, the sponsor or senior responsible owner on a new project ... or if you're just curious to know where all this amazing technology came from and where it might be headed: this is the guide for you. There's even time for a few light-hearted references and tips for success.

With AI unleashed, and humanity the tool-user on the brink of epochal technology change, there has never been a better time to flex your reading habits and brush up on applied technology.

This is a great place to start, and we hope you learn from this book as much as we did in writing it!

Acknowledgements

As always, the authors are indebted to all of those who (directly or indirectly) have done the heavy lifting before us and provided a wealth of information in blogs, websites, books and videos. We couldn't have done this without you. If we've forgotten to mention you, that's on us – keep doing what you do.

We're also very grateful for all of the reviewers and idea-bouncers that we have been lucky enough to be able to ask for a steer during the course of writing. Again, if what we've written is somehow not what you told us, that's all down to us.

In particular, we'd like to thank Stephen Lindsay at Swift for his input, as well as Damian Fessey, Lori Costello, Vonna Komorowska, Mike Morris, David Elliot, John Harrington, Andrew Cook and Yiannis Karalis for their freely given time and expertise to review parts of the book.

A massive thank you to Vonna for bringing to life the various diagrams – genius.

And our thanks to Kris Mednansky at Taylor & Francis for her support and encouragement throughout the process.

If you're intrigued by the historical elements and would like to dig a little more, the authors would heartily recommend *Introduction to the History of Computing* by Gerard O'Regan which manages to cover the entire sphere of computing in a detailed yet engaging manner.

We'd also like to make a very positive point about Wikipedia. We've learnt a lot about technology, its history and its current state of play during the course of writing this book: we spent many days and weeks in libraries and in trawling various websites for information. We have invariably found Wikipedia to be a reliable initial "go to" site for a helpful overview of a given subject. As a free site, unfettered by adverts and clickbait, Wikipedia is something that should be respected and cherished. The authors have (and will continue to) make modest donations to support the site so that it can continue to provide information in a clean and reliable way. If you've ever used it for a similar purpose and have hitherto ignored requests for donations, we'd encourage you to think about what the alternative might be and to make a small contribution to its ongoing operation.

Finally, we'd like to thank all of the executives, business sponsors, steering committee members and stakeholders who, over the years, have contended with the curious world of technology and have stayed the course to deliver value for their organisations. Kudos to you. You inspired us to write this book and, with luck, it may ease the process just a little.

About the Authors

Kevin Wooldridge, after a mostly enthusiastic (and mostly successful) tilt at an Astrophysics degree, rather wandered into a career in financial technology (long before it was interesting enough to be branded as fintech). Initially cutting code in the languages of the day, he found his sweet spot as an interpreter between the worlds of business and technology. Since then, Kevin has spent most of his career drawing blobs and arrows on paper and screens and explaining them to a largely sceptical audience.

A keen rambler, board gamer and self-confessed foodie, Kevin fills his spare time trying to escape London for the distant idyllic hills and woodlands of the countryside (but always comes back for the food).

By day, **Stephen Ashurst** is an independent software writer and wealth tech consultant. By night, he is a fintech entrepreneur. Stephen did manage to get an undergraduate degree in PPE but failed Bar School miserably. Seeing the light, he quit law and turned his attention to the IT industry – a good move, for all concerned.

A resident of London, Stephen travels constantly for pleasure and work. But home is where the heart is. And so are family, friends, dogs and 3,000 books. Sadly, so is his kitchen, the site of varyingly successful cooking experiments.

Introduction

Any sufficiently advanced technology is indistinguishable from magic.

Arthur C Clarke

You're a business leader, a "captain of industry", confident in your abilities and assured in your vocational knowledge and expertise. But you have a problem. And in order to solve it, you've been drawn – perhaps somewhat unwillingly – into the world of technology.

You may have been involved in a tech project before, or maybe you've heard tales of woe from your colleagues. Bitter experiences of projects that overrun, projects that never deliver and systems that simply don't do what they need to. Shiny, exciting tech that either doesn't meet or vastly exceeds the business' needs. And all at huge expense (invariably more than predicted by the project team).

Or perhaps you are entirely new to the world of technology and tech-enabled projects.

Quite possibly, you're expecting magic to happen.

But it's not magic. It's technology.

There are rules, and there are limits. And knowing those rules – or at least understanding the principles behind them – can help you to stay within the limits of what is possible, what is achievable. This will enable you to manage both your expectations and the technology professionals who will be helping to deliver your solution.

There is no denying that the world is experiencing a period of technological revolution, and it will continue to do so for some years to come. While it may appear that the overall pace of technological change has slowed, that the boundaries of technology are being pushed back in ever smaller increments, the exploitation of those technological changes (such as recent innovations in distributed ledger technology – aka blockchain – and artificial intelligence – AI – and machine learning) will continue to evolve and mutate for decades to come. At times, quite dramatically.

As we exit the information revolution (or at least enter its endgame), we can see clear parallels to the industrial revolution that spread across the developing world of the late eighteenth and early nineteenth centuries. The key developments that drove it were the intricate machines that spun and wove cotton (with such gritty-sounding names as James Hargreaves' Spinning Jenny, Richard Arkwright's Spinning Frame and Samuel Crompton's Spinning Mule) alongside the steam engines of James Watt and Matthew Boulton that powered the dark satanic mills of the age. All of these inventions were present well before the expansion of industry and social change that characterised the industrial revolution. Those who achieved the greatest success were often those who adapted to the new technologies and bent them to a new application.

The same is true for the information revolution. The foundations have not only already been laid, but also most are already pretty long in the tooth. The microprocessor at the heart of every digital device has been around since 1958. Optical fibres were transmitting data when NASA went to the moon in the 1960s, and flat screens have been around in one form or another for the same amount of time. The technology is 60 years old – ancient by today's standards. And the first computer program? There are some who would argue that it's the oldest of the lot. The building blocks have been there for years.

The industrial revolution changed the face of industry (and landscapes) in Great Britain, Europe and America. The pace of change was dizzying. Business leaders risked ruin if they missed an opportunity to grow or exploit the latest technology or innovation.

Sound familiar? Do you feel like you're missing out if you aren't following the latest trends in agile, data science, blockchain and AI?

In the information revolution, hardware and software are the mighty machines of industry. Interfaces are the canals and rail networks. The technology professionals who work their magic are the engineers and inventors creating their visionary designs by lamplight. Data is both raw material and product.

We believe that there are lessons to be learnt from these parallels. We're not historians. We're not academics. We're certainly not technicians. Engineers perhaps. We are problem-solvers at heart.

And in solving those problems over the years, we've been amazed at how often the sponsors and senior business stakeholders of the projects with which we've been involved have either not fully understood (or executed) their responsibilities or have not engaged effectively with the project team. This cuts both ways. The project team (as we will see) are professionals, expert in managing change. They should be able to meet the business stakeholders more than halfway in terms of engagement. There's a mountain of books out there telling them how best to do that. But there are relatively few books written specifically for the business stakeholder.

For most business stakeholders, interacting with a project team, or with technologists in general, is a daunting prospect, outside of their comfort zone. Some just don't have the time. Some don't understand how the technology or project works. Some allow the technologists to take responsibility and make decisions that should really belong in the business domain.

Some have wildly unrealistic expectations of what technology can achieve, such as a belief that data will align with their world view or that two entirely unconnected systems will somehow "talk" to each other.

They expect magic to happen.

In this book, we hope to break down that magic. We're not bound by the rules of some mystical code – we're under no oath not to reveal our secrets. We're happy to do so – mainly because they're not really all that secret. Most of them are just common sense. But if it means that the next project runs just that little bit smoother, if the senior stakeholders – the business leaders – understand the principles and rules of effecting business change through an information technology (IT) project, then our time will have been well spent.

There's a wonderful story. You may have heard it.

A man is out standing in a field when he hears a voice from above him. "Hello", calls the voice.

The man looks up and sees a woman in a hot air balloon. "Can you tell me where I am?" she calls.

"Yes", he replies. "You're in the basket of a hot air balloon about twenty metres above a field".

The woman is silent for a moment, and then asks, "Are you in IT?"

"Yes, I am", says our man. "How could you tell?"

"Because", she says, "everything you told me is factually correct, but is of no value to me whatsoever".

The man is silent for a while, then asks, "Are you in management?"

"Yes, I am", replies the woman. "How did you know?"

"Because you were lost when we started this conversation and you're still lost, but suddenly it's all my fault".

This book doesn't contain all the answers. But it does contain a useful digest of relevant information, and it will help you, the business leader, ask some sensible questions of your IT experts (and have reasonable expectations of the answers) which may just help you see through the magic to an ordered business solution.

So, what is IT?

Like anything else, you could probably slice and dice it in a myriad of different ways, but we've chosen four essential building blocks of this IT magic:

- The hardware that creates an environment for it all to happen
- The software that creates the magic
- The data that drives it
- And the interfaces that keep it all connected.

Then we take a look at the risks that you might face. And this wouldn't be a book about technological change without a glance in the direction of the new kids on the block: distributed ledger technology in the form of blockchain and the seismic potential of AI and machine learning.

These components typically come together in a technology project, and we spend a fair degree of time on different kinds of projects and your role in them before also taking a look at the people that you may meet or need on the way.

For each of these components, we'll explore a little bit of history (because context is important), the current state of play, some plausible evolutions and, most importantly, what that means for you, the business leader.

Part bluffer's guide, part crystal ball and part checklist, this primer should give the business leader an insight into the workings, language and trends in technology and enable you to engage more successfully with your technology colleagues, enabling you to

- Make sure your hardware is appropriate for the task at hand
- Get the right software in the right way
- Manage and take responsibility for your data
- Make sure your interfaces allow data to move around your system and to and from the outside world
- Consider the appropriateness of a blockchain solution
- Know and mitigate your risks
- Work with AI, not against it
- Get the right people involved
- Put all of this into a project to achieve an outcome.

So.

What's your problem?

And how can you solve it by applying technology, through the execution of a technology project under your guidance and direction?

1

What's Hardware?

It is unworthy of excellent men to lose hours like slaves in the labour of calculation which could safely be relegated to anyone else if machines were used.

Gottfried Wilhelm von Leibniz

Computer says No.

DOI: 10.4324/9781003372660-1

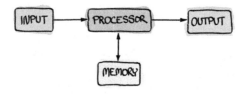

FIGURE 1.1
Hardware Components.

At the simplest level, a computer is made up of four components which together can be called the "hardware":

- *Input* – a way to get data into the computer
- *Processor* – the "brain" of the computer that will perform calculations
- *Storage* – where the computer will store data and programmed instructions
- *Output* – a means to get data out of the computer

Figure 1.1 shows how these components operate to produce an outcome.

These components have taken many forms over the years, from beads on wires (the abacus), dials and buttons, ticker tape and punched cards to the more familiar keyboard, mouse, screen, integrated circuit boards and ports of the modern computer. This schematic model was proposed by early computer scientist John von Neumann in 1945 (and is referred to as the "von Neumann architecture"[1]).

This chapter looks at business computer hardware: where it's come from and what it is now. We also extrapolate and consolidate that knowledge, to look at possible future trends.

The chapter ends with a "So what?" section, providing you – the business leader – with a range of questions that you could be asking yourself and your team about hardware before committing pen to paper on any hardware vendor contract.

WHY SHOULD I CARE?

As a business leader, you may not be choosing the hardware platforms that will run your organisation's software, but you could well be asked to support (or indeed pay for) the choices made about hardware by your technical teams. And while it may seem simple to choose whether an application will run on servers installed on your own premises or in the cloud, for example, there are other nuances about hardware – such as longevity and flexibility – that may influence that choice.

The digital age has its roots in the middle of the last century. The pace of change since then has been furious. There is now more computing power in your fridge than on the rockets that took humanity to Moon (the clock speed of modern micro-controller – the kind that tells your fridge to make a "ping" sound if the door has been open for too long – is 16MHz. The clock speed of the Apollo Guidance Computer that navigated men to Moon was just over 1MHz).

Although the rate at which business technology has advanced has been nothing short of miraculous, it has followed a path that was foreseen as far back as 1958, largely adhering to Moore's Law, a prediction that the processing capacity of integrated circuits would effectively double every two years; and Grosch's Law: that a doubling of the cost of hardware should increase hardware performance by a factor of four.

Understanding trends in hardware performance and longevity will be of great help when deciding which business equipment to use next, balancing initial costs against the ongoing cost of upgrading or maintaining your hardware.

HOW DID WE GET HERE?

Give a child a pencil and some paper and ask them to draw a computer, the chances are that what you will end up with is a picture of a screen and a keyboard.

It's what a computer has looked like for 50 years, give or take. Elements have evolved over time: screens and keyboards have become slimmer and more elegant; the mouse is a triumph of ergonomic design, fitting the palm of the hand like a second skin; peripheral devices such as floppy disc drives, dial-up modems and unsightly heaps of spaghetti cabling have come and gone. But the modern computer hardware really doesn't look too different from the chunky-keyed, flickering screen microcomputers that first appeared on the cluttered desks of electronics hobbyists at the start of the 1970s.

The hardware that powered those first computing devices was itself the culmination of 2000 years of collective human imagination, ingenuity and innovation.

Inevitably, the story of the mechanical calculating machine starts with those irrepressible inventors of the ancient Greeks, on the shores of the Mediterranean Sea. Or rather, beneath it ....

The First Known Computers: Playthings and Curios

The first known computer hardware was constructed sometime between 200 and 175 BCE. Analogue, rather than digital, it was an intricate mechanism of gears, dials and levers, known as a mechanical orrery (i.e. a model of the solar system), capable of mapping the motions of Sun, Moon and planets. It was sophisticated enough to account for eccentricities in the lunar orbit and was able to accurately predict both lunar and solar eclipses.

Such hardware was undoubtedly the marvel of its age, and it is believed that it was in the process of being shipped from Rhodes to Rome to be paraded by a victorious Julius Caesar when it met with watery misfortune off the coast of a small Greek island, Antikythera, from which it takes its modern name. There it lay for centuries until it was discovered by sponge divers and successfully recovered in 1901.

The Antikythera mechanism was a remarkable piece of hardware engineering, but it was not entirely alone in the ancient world, not least because we must assume that its creators must also have produced prototypes and upgrades that have since been lost.

In later years, the automata of Hero of Alexandria were famed for their complexity and wonder. Hero, who died around 70 BCE, invented a steam-powered engine called an *aeolipile*, a wind wheel and numerous theatrical devices including an entirely mechanical play controlled by drums and levers. These artefacts are also "hardware" and follow programmable actions just like modern computers.

In the ninth century BCE, during the so-called Islamic Golden Age of invention and creativity, three Persian brothers (Muḥammad, Aḥmad and Al-Ḥasan ibn Mūsā ibn Shākir) wrote the *Book of Ingenious Devices*[2] containing drawings and diagrams of around a hundred automata, mostly powered by water. Some of these devices had their roots in the ancient Greek Hellenistic period, but others were inventions of the brothers themselves, or modifications to add innovations such as cybernetic controls, feedback loops, one-way valves, and timing or delaying mechanisms.

But all of these devices, however ingenious, shared one common characteristic: they were hardware, yes, but served no direct "business" purpose. Automata were playthings and curios, designed solely to exhibit the genius of their creators, but of no day-to-day practical use. Automata would remain on the side lines of business, industry and commerce until the late Renaissance period in Europe and the accounting and mathematical advances of the seventeenth century.

After That: Adding Machines

The goal of eradicating human error in the process of making arithmetic calculations has existed for millennia. The abacus has been around, in one form or another, since the very earliest civilisations, spreading east and west from the Indus Valley to the South Pacific and the heart of Europe. Whether the abacus hardware was pebbles in grooves (the word "calculus" comes to us from the Latin for pebbles, *calculi*) or beads in frames, its basic concept changed little over 4000 years. As late as the mid-twentieth century, the abacus was still the most effective way to perform arithmetic calculations. A competition in 1946 between Japanese administrator Kiyoshi Matsuzaki using a soroban (a form of abacus) and US Army Private Thomas Nathan Wood using an electric calculator ended in a comprehensive victory (4–1) for the more antiquated device.

It took the genius of Renaissance-era mathematicians to begin to break the abacus' monopoly on calculation.

In 1617, Scottish landowner John Napier published his book on what he called *Rabdology*[3] – the use of movable, numbered rods to simplify the process of multiplication into one of addition. Napier's *Bones*, as they became known, could also be used for long division and the calculation of square and cube roots (with enough patience). Napier made other significant advances in the world of mathematics: inventing logarithms and proposing a form of binary notation (also documented in his tome on *Rabdology*). Napier's programmable artefact, the moving rods part of his hardware, was a notable first as hardware with a direct application.

In 1642 a young French prodigy, Blaise Pascal, built a mechanical adding machine to support his father's accountancy business. Pascal's calculator hardware, the *Pascaline*, deployed gears, wheels and numerical displays to master the complex operation of carrying forward results from one order to the next, as a dial clicked between nine and zero. Previous accountancy business machines, for example, had hardware that broke down when adding 1 to 999. The *Pascaline* could work in decimal or in bases 6, 12 or 20 (to support the French currency of the day, the livre) and could even handle subtractions by the use of the rule of nine's complement.

The nine's complement of a digit is that digit subtracted from nine. So, the nine's complement of three is six. Complements can be used to perform subtractions and other complex arithmetic. To subtract a smaller number from a larger, we can turn the larger number (the *minuend*) into nine's complement and add to the smaller number (the *subtrahend*), before converting the answer into its own nine's complement. To subtract 123 from 456, we convert 456 to nine's complement (543), add that to 123 and convert the result (666) into nine's complement to give 333. Try it!

Before being used for an operation, it was vital to reset the *Pascaline*'s hardware by setting all dials to nine and then adding one. This would invoke the carry mechanism across all the gears, setting the output display to zero. This "initialisation of variables" is still a fundamental step in software coding today.

The German philosopher and mathematician Gottfried Wilhelm von Leibniz took the *Pascaline*'s hardware one step further: adding a stepped drum and cog mechanism (a "stepped reckoner"), which would become the central hardware mechanism for calculating machines for the next 200 years.

Difference Engines and Arithmometers

It would be impossible to convey the history of computer hardware, even as briefly as we are doing here, without mentioning the "father of the computer", Charles Babbage. Babbage built his first difference engine in 1819 and was engaged by the British Government to build a larger scale version that would help to eradicate errors in the manually produced nautical and navigation tables on which the British Navy relied so heavily. Babbage made numerous attempts over 30 years to build first his difference engine and later an analytical engine that would do more than generate a sequence of numbers. Despite receiving many thousands of pounds of sponsorship from the Government, and becoming independently wealthy in later life, Babbage was never able to complete his more expansive works. This failure to construct working copies of his theoretical engines gave rise to accusations that Babbage's designs were flawed. However, two engineering projects in the late twentieth and early twenty-first centuries saw the successful completion of two Difference Engines, one of which is on public display in the Science Museum in London, and Babbage's drawings for the analytical engine are widely recognised as the first credible design for a digital computer.[4]

It wasn't until 1851 that the hardware of mechanical calculating machines became reliable, portable and simple enough to be mass-produced, allowing them to be installed in diverse business premises. Thomas de Colmar first patented his *arithmomètre* (arithmometer) in 1820, following an idea he had while Inspector of Supply for Napoleon's Grande Armée, a role that required a vast number of repetitive calculations. De Colmar's robust new hardware distracted him from his many other business ventures, but the improved calculator hardware was revealed to the public at the Great Exhibition in London in 1851 and went into production soon after.

For nearly 50 years, the arithmometer was the dominant commercial and business calculating machine hardware, operating without competition until the 1890s. Thousands of such devices were made, and the arithmometer hardware was distributed worldwide to businesses and governments. Reviewers noted that the arithmometer hardware could be "…used without the least trouble or possibility of error".[5] Complex addition, subtraction, multiplication and division operations could be successfully and accurately completed in a matter of seconds.

Manufactured Computers – At Last

By the twentieth century the arithmometer was finally overtaken by computer hardware made by other manufacturers, including Burroughs (initially known as the American Arithmometer Company). Large-scale commercial production of the arithmometer hardware was halted by World War I and never recovered.

The entrepreneurial spirit demonstrated by Thomas de Colmar was again shown, this time in Chicago in 1885, by a young works foreman called Dorr Felt. Financially constrained, Felt built his first calculating machine hardware – dubbed a comptometer – using such commonplace materials as a macaroni box, skewers, staples and rubber bands.[6] He took his idea to factory owner Robert Tarrant and together they set up the Felt & Tarrant Manufacturing Company to make and distribute comptometers for business use. Using a much simpler input mechanism of keystrokes (rather than the arithmometer's somewhat more complicated dials and sliders), the comptometer was fast and reliable and remained in production until the 1970s, when it was finally replaced by the electronic calculator.

But the man who probably did more than anything to advance the concept of the calculating machine hardware and bring it nearer to something we would almost recognise as a computer was a young German-American called Herman Hollerith.

While working at the Massachusetts Institute of Technology in 1882, Hollerith experimented with an electronic means of counting holes in punched cards. He reasoned that by defining a given location on each card to have a specific meaning (for example, whether a person was married or not) and then punching holes in the card to denote a positive or negative response, data could be stored and read by electronic means. Hollerith's new hardware meant that vast amounts of data could be collated and analysed far more quickly than by manual means.

Hollerith's patent for an electric tabulating system was granted in 1889, and his hardware was used for the 1890 census in the United States and in many countries across the world in the following years. Hollerith founded the Tabulating Machine Company in 1896 and continually improved his design, adding automated card feeders and a removable and programmable control panel to configure the machine to perform different tasks. In 1924, after a number of name changes and mergers, the firm was renamed as International Business Machines (IBM) Corporation.[7]

The First Digital Computers

The period between the Great Depression (1929) and the end of World War II (1945) saw rapid development of electronic computer hardware. Initially, many computers were analogue in design, for example, receiving and processing data across a range of values such as for gunnery calculations or tidal prediction, rather than designed to use data in digital form (i.e. expressed as a series of the digits zero and one). Hardware technology in this period was also still primitive by today's standards, using vacuum tubes and punched cards, requiring frequent rewiring and manual intervention.

But two key developments in the 1930s began to change all that.

First, in 1936, Alan Turing published his seminal paper *On Computable Numbers*,[8] where he set out rules for a hypothetical ideal computer, the "universal machine", that would be able to execute any conceivable program. Such hardware is now said to be "Turing complete".

Second, in 1937, George Stibitz built the first digital computer at Bell Labs in New York. For the first time, an electronic calculating machine based its arithmetic not on the direct value of a signal but on whether that signal was essentially a high value (a "1") or a low value (a "0"). The age of digital computing hardware was born.

Development progressed during the war in Germany (where Konrad Zuse built his fully digital Z3 in 1941) and also in the United Kingdom where Alan Turing's Bletchley Park "bombe" hardware was deployed to crunch huge data volumes to break the German military's Enigma code. This was a whole new level of hardware, but which still required crucial (and constant) manual intervention to optimise the number of variables being considered. Even more secret were the wartime Colossus machines whose existence was not acknowledged until 30 years later in the 1960s.

Soldiers, Scientists ... and Businessmen!

In 1945, the United States Army Ordnance Corps produced ENIAC (Electronic Numerical Integrator and Computer), the first fully programmable electronic digital computer hardware.

It's worth dwelling for a moment on the titan that was ENIAC. Looking back, the march of technological and hardware progress might seem inexorable, but the creation and operation of ENIAC really was a significant milestone that set the bar for all hardware to follow.

The hardware for ENIAC itself was colossal. It occupied a space equivalent to an entire office floor and featured tens of thousands of individual components (including vacuum tubes, diodes, relays, capacitors and resistors). It consumed so much electricity when running that it was rumoured the lights in Philadelphia would dim every time it was switched on. It led investors of the day to suppose that future computer hardware would be the size of small cities, requiring an army of attendants to supply an insatiable thirst for punched cards, or to constantly reprogram the device by moving cables from one location to another and setting and resetting vast arrays of switches.

But ENIAC delivered.

Its performance was measured at 500 FLOPS ("floating point operations per second") which may not seem very much, especially compared to the speeds of today's supercomputers which are now measured in petaflops (10^{15}) and more recently exaflops (10^{18} operations per second), but it meant that ENIAC could perform a gunnery calculation in 30 seconds that would take a human 20 hours to complete. This hardware effectively replaced 2,400 human beings. It was an efficiency dream made real.

ENIAC was itself soon replaced as the pinnacle of computing power. In 1951, EDSAC, developed at the University of Cambridge, became the world's first "stored program computer", hardware that enabled the computer's own memory to store operational parameters. For the first time in human history, hardware existed that fulfilled Turing's vision of a universal machine.

For most of the twentieth century, the development of computer hardware had been driven largely by government, military or academic endeavour. But in 1951, the world of business and commerce entered the fray.

After two of its executives saw both the ENIAC and EDSAC hardware in operation, the British food producer J. Lyons & Co. became the first commercial business to run an operational computer system. The Lyons Electronic Office 1 (or LEO 1, based on EDSAC) started operations in 1951. It was initially used to calculate the cost of bakery ingredients but later developed further to cover financial and payroll activities.

In the same year, ENIAC's direct successor UNIVAC became the first mass-produced business computer hardware, selling nearly 50 units globally. In 1954, IBM produced their first commercial entry, the IBM 650 Magnetic Drum Data-Processing Machine.

Hardware in Memory and Circuits

Further technological innovation followed swiftly to enable a second generation of business computer hardware. The introduction of magnetic memory, based on a technology first invented in 1928 by the German inventor Fritz Pfleumer, made for faster and more reliable data storage, while the invention of the silicon transistor replaced unwieldy, unreliable vacuum tube hardware. Mass-produced computers began to permeate the big corporations, with IBM selling or renting thousands of copies of its 704 and 709 series mainframes (named after the large cabinets that housed the central hardware and used to distinguish larger business machines from smaller desk-top devices).

Computer hardware technology took another huge leap forward in 1958 with the invention of the integrated circuit (independently by Jack Kilby at Texas Instruments and Robert Noyce at Fairchild Semiconductors). In hardware design terms, the integrated circuit enabled a vast number of transistors to be squeezed into a small space. This made the hardware more stable and vastly cheaper and quicker to manufacture. Kilby's initial circuits used the chemical element germanium, but Noyce's variant was made from silicon which proved to be more scalable.

The first computer built using silicon integrated circuits was the Apollo Guidance Computer (AGC).[9] The AGC hardware was installed by NASA in the command module and lunar module for the Apollo moon shots of the 1960s. It featured a numeric display and keyboard for input and output of data for use by the astronauts. This was hardware innovation that changed everything.

Over the next decade, manufacturers of integrated circuits achieved ever-greater degrees of miniaturisation, leading to near-exponential increases in computer processing speeds. In 1965, a semiconductor researcher named Gordon Moore was asked to speculate on the continuation of this trend. In a short article entitled *Cramming more components onto integrated circuits*,[10] Moore speculated that the density of integrated circuits would double every year for the next ten years. Ten years later, in 1975, he revised what was now referred to as *Moore's Law*, stating that the density would double every two years.

Remarkably, Moore's Law has broadly held true for several decades of the hardware industry, with computer processing power roughly doubling every 18 months. In many ways it has been a self-fulfilling prophesy, with the semiconductor industry setting out to match Moore's predictions year on year. Moore's Law will cease to apply to computer hardware development at some point, however, being subject to the immutable laws of physics and the limitations on miniaturisation due to the scale of the silicon atom itself.

But it is this inexorable drive to produce ever-tighter circuitry, embodied and quantified by Moore's Law, that has truly accelerated the hardware revolution. Without better, smaller, faster and cheaper hardware, computing capacity would have remained the purview of the large corporations and the military, scientific and academic worlds. Hardware evolution means there's many times more computing power in an everyday, mass-produced mobile phone than was available to the Apollo astronauts using the cutting-edge AGC in 1969.

A quote often attributed to Microsoft co-founder Bill Gates in the late 1990s went along the lines that if the automotive industry had kept pace with the gains in computer hardware efficiency, then "…we would all be driving $25 cars that got 1,000 miles per gallon". Regardless of the quote's provenance, 25 years later the comparative gains are even more remarkable.

Hardware … on Your Desk

The next (and arguably final) step change in computing hardware design came with the invention of the microchip or microprocessor.

It's hard to overstate the significance of the microprocessor as an enabler for the revolutionary changes that have taken place in the last 50 years. By bringing all of the components necessary for a central processing unit (CPU) into one chip, the microprocessor eradicated the need for separate units for input, output, processing and memory.

The first commercially available microprocessor, the Intel 4004, was introduced in 1971. By 1975, the first "microcomputer" – the Altair – was advertised in an electronics magazine as a kit for hobbyists. The Altair had a series of motherboards linked together and was programmed using a set of clumsy switches on a front panel. Three years later, Apple and Commodore had launched microcomputers that most of us would recognise today: a colour screen, a keyboard and even a floppy disk drive that would allow programs to be stored and transported from one machine to another. The Apple II also came bundled with software that most of us would find all too familiar: the first viable spreadsheet, VisiCalc.

Various other manufacturers followed with their own microcomputer hardware but the real game-changer was the soon-to-be-ubiquitous IBM personal computer. We still talk about a "PC" today, referencing the dominance that IBM enjoyed during the 1980s with their trademark "personal computer" hardware. The term was coined by IBM to allow them to distinguish their hardware from the raft of microcomputers available at the time. Bundled with Microsoft's DOS (disk operating system), the BASIC programming language, VisiCalc and a word processor, the IBM PC became the must-have accessory for the home or the office. Microsoft's mission statement of "a computer on every desk and in every home[11]" may have seemed a little far-fetched at the time but all the hardware elements were now in place to make that vision a reality.

IBM and its clones dominated the personal computer market, but Apple followed their own course, introducing innovations such as representing programs and data graphically on screen, controlled by the user moving and clicking something called a mouse. Some of these hardware innovations feel so natural to us now, and even more so to each new generation of "digital natives", but to the computer users of the 1990s, the ability to move, open and close programs on-screen using a piece of hardware, a plastic device at its side instead of typing obscure codes at a prompt, was genuinely a thing of wonder.

Hardware for data storage and transfer became more sophisticated too at this time. Internal magnetic disk drives became standard, along with removable disk drives for installing or transferring software and data between different personal computing machines.

The Distributed Computer

As the desktop computer became more and more ever-present in the office, the market for mainframe hardware began to dwindle, despite a continued increase in processing power. Hugely powerful, monolithic machines toiling away in dark, air-conditioned basements were gradually replaced with a new paradigm: client–server hardware. For 20 years the typical model for a business computer had been a central core with a number of dumb terminals distributed throughout the office acting purely as input and output devices. All the "work" was done in the centralised mainframe. Gradually, those terminals were replaced by workstations, each one a computer in its own right. Workstations, or active "clients" of the server, would send and receive data from the central core only as needed.

Advances in software and interface hardware also contributed to the downfall of the mainframe. Activities that once required a single brain could now be spread across multiple linked machines in parallel and for a fraction of the cost. But a small market for mainframe hardware would remain, as it does today, mainly in the form of large banks and financial institutions whose legacy software makes upgrading to alternative hardware configurations complex and risky.

The problem of using mainframes as servers was the fact that the original equipment manufacturers (referred to as OEMs), such as Hitachi, IBM, and Amdahl, tended to use their own, incompatible communication protocols. Users had to choose only one manufacturer and were then constrained to use only its hardware and software. Interaction between servers supplied by different manufacturers to provide a wider network of data exchange was impossible in practice.

With the advent of the first personal computers, businesses were able to move away from using a single OEM mainframe. Personal computers were quickly called into service as makeshift (and then permanent) servers, because of their greater interoperability. The native compatibility of personal computers working together enabled users to organise, configure and deploy a personal computer-based network.

Initially, these networked computers differed little from their desktop counterparts, but over time they became more specialised to their function. A computer designed specifically with large data storage capacity could function as a file server, or data warehouse, storing data and making it available to all users across a connected network. The development of the global internet spawned the need for telecommunications servers. Modern servers such as the IBM System x3850 are able to process hundreds of terabytes of information per second.

From Desktop to Laptop

At the end of the twentieth century and throughout the 2000s, miniaturisation and portability drove the computer hardware agenda.

It had long been the dream of hardware manufacturers to build a viable laptop device. But limitations in flat screen technology and battery life had made these impractical. The technological innovation for flat screens was already present before the end of the last century: the very first flat screen was built in 1958 and even the first OLED (Organic Light Emitting Diode) screen in 1987. But the demands of these early models for power and the level of definition that could be achieved made them unfit for a portable device. Early models were heavy, slow and had almost unreadable screens.

Something that looked like a modern laptop in hardware terms, the IBM ThinkPad, emerged in 1991. Technology and hardware continued to evolve including chips designed with a laptop's power consumption in mind, smaller and less demanding hard disks, more precise liquid crystal display (LCD) screens and batteries capable of holding and delivering more power.

By the early 2000s, the collective evolution of these technologies made it possible to mass-produce elegant laptop devices that didn't break your back every time you tried to pick them up and didn't break the bank to buy. Then technology took things a few steps further: solid-state drives took away the need for high-speed spinning disks and heavy cooling mechanisms, while wireless communication significantly reduced the number of inter-face ports needed.

In hardware terms, the personal computer had become a *portable* computer.

Handheld and Wearable Technology

The drive to create a laptop was fuelled by the desire to take all the capabil-ities of a desktop computer and make them portable.

But at the same time, efforts were underway to create something altogether different, building on the surge in popularity of mobile phones (themselves enabled by the miniaturisation of computer hardware) to create a portable – even handheld – device with the sole purpose of making and maintaining contact with colleagues and business partners.

During the 1980s, no self-respecting young entrepreneur would be seen without a Filofax in their hand – a ubiquitous accessory that brought a telephone directory, diary and numerous other paper-based planning tools together in one handy ring-binder.

With the miniaturisation of computer power, and the growing mobile phone industry and telecommunication networks, it wasn't long before the Filofax was replaced (almost overnight) by the personal digital organiser, or PDA. Starting in 1984 with the Psion Organiser, the next decade saw a flood of innovative mobile devices, including Palm pilots and the Nokia 9000, the first device to feature mobile connectivity.

The game changed in 1999 when Research in Motion (RIM) launched their BlackBerry device, which used a bespoke secure network to send and receive emails. To the security-conscious business, there was now only one choice to keep busy executives in touch while on the move. With its iconic screen design and keyboard-in-miniature, the BlackBerry in many ways represented the epitome of the dedicated communications handheld device.

Eight years later, in 2007, the landscape shifted again, this time in seismic fashion, as Apple launched the iPhone, followed just over three years later by the iPad. Their keyless touch screens and must-have elegance launched these devices into the global psyche, ushering in the era of mobile computing.

The seemingly unstoppable progression of Moore's Law has enabled microprocessors to be placed in ever smaller and more varied housings, while the evolution of the internet, the World Wide Web and wireless communication have enabled those myriad devices to communicate with each other. Suddenly, flat screens are everywhere – in your car, in aeroplane seats, in shops and supermarkets, on your wrist – and microprocessors are embedded in just about everything from your dog to the clothes you wear.

From Mainframe to Cloud

At the same time that manufacturers were struggling to create a truly portable computer to address the need for a mobile client, business innovators were creating a new paradigm to support the server side of the client–server architecture. Rather than house an organisation's mainframes and servers in data centres belonging to the business itself, suppliers of raw computing power began to offer the services of *cloud computing*.

Starting with Amazon Web Services (AWS) in 2002, followed by Google in 2008 and Microsoft Azure in 2010, the big players quickly established their operations. Using the now-ubiquitous internet and World Wide Web, a server could be placed almost anywhere in the world. Cloud providers were able to benefit from massive economies of scale, while businesses were able to use (and pay for) computing power only when they needed it.

WHAT DOES HERE LOOK LIKE?

With the advent of the personal computer, all the elements of the modern computer were in place. The computer of the 1990s is in reality no different from the computer of today.

The components themselves have shrunk and are, in nearly every respect, more functional and elegant than their counterparts of 30 years ago. Screens may have become thinner in the intervening years. The mouse may be replaced by a touchpad or even a touch screen. Interface ports may have been rendered less important, with the arrival of wireless communications. But the fundamental building blocks were now present:

- A microprocessor
- A data storage mechanism
- A keyboard
- A mouse
- A screen
- Interface ports.

Mainframes, too, have undergone evolution rather than revolution in the last 30 years. Faster and more adaptable, a mainframe computer today is little different, fundamentally, from the darkly brooding basement behemoths of the 1980s.

But businesses are no longer presented with a simple choice, as they were in the latter half of the twentieth century, of either hiring or buying their mainframe, setting it up in their headquarters and linking it to a set of desktops. Processing power now comes in all shapes and forms and can be located nearly anywhere in the world.

Business hardware today is designed to be flexible, interoperable and can be deployed for cost-conscious business goals. Moore's Law no longer means there has to be an arms race for hardware, where organisations are required to assume that investment today might require constant new investment and upgrades in order to keep pace with processing power tomorrow.

Hardware on Your Desk (or Kitchen Table)

Modern laptops are truly engineering marvels. High-quality flat colour screens; ultra-fast processing and large memory; stable and powerful Bluetooth and wireless broadband connectivity; interoperability via multiple ports of all descriptions and types; power from current and battery; a super-strong but thin composite cover; illuminated buttons and integrated camera, extensible displays onto external monitors and much more.

Screen resolution is crisp – 1920 by 1080 pixels is eight times what you would have got with a top-of-the-range Commodore Pet back in 1977.

Excellent battery life coupled with dynamic power-saving capabilities combine to support a mobile worker for almost an entire day without having to connect to a power socket. Modern wireless protocols mean that users can be online within moments of arriving at their workplace, which could as easily be a coffee shop or a kitchen table as an office.

And if you should want to anchor yourself to a desk for a day, a week or longer, the modern laptop has interoperability built in – a simple connection plugs the laptop directly into the local network. Add a larger, fixed monitor and you have a desktop workstation.

This interoperability is the superpower of the modern laptop. In the infancy of the mass-produced computer hardware industry, each manufacturer had its own designs for connections between the various hardware components, even across different models from the same manufacturer. Over time, each component has become standardised. The industry has finally reached the ideal state that whatever component you want to plug in, there's a standard socket and lead for it: mouse, keyboard, screen, headset: all are either wireless or through a standardised port.

The last bastion of manufacturer individuality, the power socket, appears to have finally fallen – the most modern laptops will simply plug into a USB-C lead (Universal Serial Bus) which provides a common standard for power, as well as for network connectivity. Finally, a desktop workstation can be universally available to all-comers with just one connection.

Hardware Everywhere

Much like the laptop, the modern handheld device seems to have it all.

Less than 20 years ago, manufacturers of handheld devices had to make choices – was it a camera or a phone? Was it a diary or an audio device? Should the device have keys or a touch screen?

All of these questions are now irrelevant. Just about every device has everything you might need, and the touch screen is ubiquitous (the last BlackBerry unit to carry a keyboard went out of production in 2016).

This versatility allows the modern mobile phone to be used for so much more than phone calls.

But there are limits, especially in a business context (unless your business is one that is centred around mobile technology). The busy executive or mobile employee can use their phone for voice calls, checking and sending emails and for checking the diary to make plans. And if your business has a specific need for a mobile application (such as confirmation of deliveries, or mobile point of sale applications), then of course, it's a no-brainer. But the phone is still not the ideal place to do anything more complex. Working through a spreadsheet, reviewing a legal document, even participating in a video call – none of these activities are improved by being executed through a handheld mobile device. Size of screen, the variety of commands that can be executed through touch alone, single-tasking – all are factors at play.

The argument is less strong for hybrid portable devices such as high-end tablets – these are essentially laptops in disguise.

As for wearable technology and the dramatic rise in embedded microprocessors and network connectivity in everyday items (known as the "Internet of Things" or IoT), again, unless such devices are the primary focus for your business, it is hard to see how such hardware would be useful. Fitting all of your employees with a tracker and motion detector to monitor their work patterns might sound like a good idea, but there are more sensitive and collaborative ways to gather such information without shattering the employer/employee relationship.

Hardware in the Data Centre

The first servers were simple repurposed personal computers. Those days are long gone.

The modern server is a modular marvel, mounted in standardised frames called racks. These rack-mounted servers are compact and easy to maintain with as few peripherals (such as screens and keyboards) as possible.

Blade servers take this concept even further. A server "blade" is stripped back to the bare minimum to save space and reduce power consumption. Each blade is mounted in a chassis or enclosure with multiple other blades: individually, each has the vital components to be considered a computer (such as microprocessors, storage and the connections between them) but many components such as power, cooling and networking are shared with other blades in the same blade system. The blade systems themselves can then be rack-mounted alongside other blade systems or rack-mounted servers.

To avoid interruption of service, most server racks come with their own uninterruptable power supply (UPS), either integral to the rack or alongside. Because rack-mounted servers are so tightly packed, they generate more heat than a standard computer, so cooling needs to be very efficiently managed. A large data centre will host multiple rows of racks of servers, typically arranged to facilitate airflow for cooling (allowing cool air to be supplied near the intakes and hot air to be extracted from the exhausts).

Rack-mounted servers are also often designed to be "hot-swappable", meaning that a faulty unit can be removed and replaced without interrupting processing – the server can be managed so that activity is routed away from the damaged component until it has been replaced. This configuration is ideal for data-crunching activities such as web hosting.

Hardware in the Cloud

Perhaps one of the most important developments of today's business hardware is the reduced requirement for businesses to buy or rent, install and maintain their own server hardware.

Server hardware is more important to organisations now than ever before. Regardless of the actual business being carried out, servers will process data for human resources (HR) teams, payroll, financial reporting, tax and other corporate activities. Deploying computing power through servers remains critical to every business. But businesses now have the option of how they own and deploy those servers.

Cloud computing provides businesses with the option of hosting their servers away from their own premises, choosing one or more cloud service providers to do the heavy lifting while they can focus on delivering business benefit through their software applications.

The cloud brings many benefits to an organisation, particularly if technology is not the raison d'être for the organisation itself (such as our old friends J. Lyons & Co in 1951). Typically, an organisation can expect to spend twice its initial outlay on hardware in supporting that hardware throughout its lifetime, in maintenance, upgrades and security costs, not to mention the expense of running and staffing a data centre. There can also be incidental costs, such as the lost business opportunity if an inadequately supported server fails and cannot be immediately replaced.

Cloud service providers offer an on-demand operational model, meaning that organisations only pay for computing power as they use it. For organisations with asymmetrical processing needs, this can be a further benefit. Rather than paying for and maintaining a hardware configuration that can cater for its peak demands but sits idly for the rest of the time, the organisation can effectively share hardware with other cloud customers, only drawing down processing power as and when required.

Cloud services are often broken down into one of three (sometimes four) service levels:

- IaaS – Infrastructure as a Service
- PaaS – Platform as a Service
- SaaS – Software as a Service
- BPaaS – Business Process as a Service (although this is less to do with the cloud itself and is more akin to a full outsourcing arrangement).

IaaS provides a hosting service for your software in a virtual machine – you are still responsible for the software, middleware and even the operating system. The service provider runs the machine for you, but you do everything else.

Examples of this sort of service are AWS, Google Compute Engine (GCE) and Microsoft Azure.

A PaaS provider goes one step further by hosting a virtual environment and operating system into which your software can be plugged.

Examples of PaaS providers include Google App Engine, OpenShift and SAP Cloud.

We will look at SaaS in the chapter of this book dealing with software. A typical example is Microsoft (Office) 365.

BPaaS is more akin to an outsourcing/offshoring arrangement. We will not cover this in this book.

Figure 1.2 shows the service level for each type of provider.

Another key distinction for cloud propositions is whether the cloud is public or private. Public clouds are more easily accessible and more flexible. Organisations whose security needs are more stringent due to data sensitivity or regulation may opt instead for a private cloud arrangement, which is more expensive but provides greater control.

Cloud providers are starting to offer hybrid cloud options offering a "best of both worlds" approach, providing higher security where necessary but also retaining flexibility and a "pay as you go" funding model.

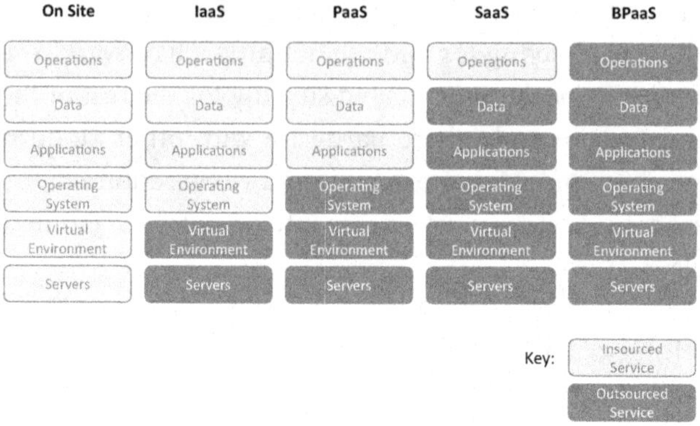

On Site	IaaS	PaaS	SaaS	BPaaS
Operations	Operations	Operations	Operations	Operations
Data	Data	Data	Data	Data
Applications	Applications	Applications	Applications	Applications
Operating System	Operating System	Operating System	Operating System	Operating System
Virtual Environment	Virtual Environment	Virtual Environment	Virtual Environment	Virtual Environment
Servers	Servers	Servers	Servers	Servers

Key:
Insourced Service
Outsourced Service

FIGURE 1.2
Service Levels Compared.

The Rise of the GPU

Since the first video games (including the now iconic arcade favourites such as Space Invaders and Galaxians), hardware manufacturers have struggled with the challenge of presenting fast, smooth graphics output to a screen. Whereas much of the work asked of a computer was more or less linear and interdependent in nature, a graphics display required thousands of independent parallel operations. As hardware (and its delivery into the home and the office) evolved, so have the demands and challenges of graphical output. Towards the end of the twentieth century, dedicated graphical processing units (GPUs) evolved to provide this service for desktop and eventually laptop computers.

These GPUs found a new use when first cryptocurrency mining and then language training for artificial intelligence (AI) models were found to benefit from massive parallelism. In modern server configurations, GPUs and CPUs are used in combination to provide both linear computing power and parallel processing.

WHERE NEXT?

KPMG, the management consultancy, produced a *Future of Hardware* report in 2022[12] with the following headline introduction:

These are pivotal times for hardware manufacturers. The COVID-19 pandemic accelerated trends in customer behaviour – such as a growing preference for as-a-service purchasing – and introduced widespread changes in workplace models.

Hardware continues to be used in new ways: in edge computing embedded in smart machines like robots and autonomous vehicles. Increasingly, suppliers compete on customer experience, making their products easier to buy, use, and upgrade. This has implications for how hardware companies go to market, source their products, and invest their capital.

Hardware players can thrive in this future by adapting business and operating models and becoming connected enterprises. As enterprises, with front, middle and back offices seamlessly connected, internal silos can be removed, data is freely shared, and companies can truly focus on customer needs.

The implications are clear: hardware itself is no longer a battleground for most modern businesses, being instead contested by the behemoths of the cloud era: Google, Microsoft, Meta and Amazon. Rather, competition will be focused on service providers and the experience they can give to their clients.

Marginal Gains for Laptops and Servers?

Like the modern mobile phone, it's hard to see (at least from a business perspective) exactly how the modern laptop can be, or even needs to be, improved. There could be lighter batteries and casings, and faster transfer speeds for wireless communications, but any gains in this area would be marginal at best. To the business user (and indeed any consumer), the choice of laptop is really one of personal preference in terms of screen size and features such as touch screens, against cost.

For servers, it's a similar story. Moore's Law will still be in effect, driving the capacity for computing power to ever-increasing heights, enabling ever more sophisticated and impactful applications. But at a practical level, these improvements largely pass us by. As the processing power speeds up, the amount of work we ask our computers to do seems to expand to fill that capacity. Those same complex applications that continue to make the business world more connected and visible need more graphics, more data, vastly increased security measures and more complex interoperability protocols than hitherto. Today's software simply takes up more brain power than the pioneering applications of yesterday.

The same could also be said for the various peripheral devices that we use to interact with our hardware. To the business user, it may appear that screens, mice and keyboards have also reached their logical zenith. Any future change will be incremental and potentially incidental.

Screens are readily available in all shapes, sizes, resolutions and degrees of flatness. The next step may be fully flexible, bendable screens or virtual screens projected onto your wall or table top by a laser device, but at the moment these are most likely to be expensive gimmicks or of limited use. Smart goggles may eventually replace screens, and the new breed of hybrid user that needs computer power at home or the office but not in between may favour a fragmented approach to their tech, with a docking station in each location and minimal hardware (literally just a box of microprocessors and solid-state storage with some USB ports) to carry in between.

Mouse design has come a long way since the earliest creations in the 1960s. Mechanical trackers such as the rollerball have been replaced by lasers and optical sensors obviating the need for a separate "mouse pad" and there is no need for a cable in a wireless world. The mouse is now available in many forms, with left-handed and vertical designs, static varieties and even mice shaped as pens. Not to mention touch screens and finger-pads. No doubt this variety will continue. But the function of a mouse is unlikely to change. With data and applications represented graphically on a computer screen, there will always be the need to select, move and open them along with any number of other operations. Experiments with voice control or motion-tracking are in their relative infancy: if you've ever been frustrated with your smart speaker or television making seemingly random choices based on your very clear instructions, you will cherish the precision that using a mouse brings. The mouse, or something very much like it, is here to stay.

Keyboards, too, will be with us for many years to come. We will leave aside any discussion on the merits of the QWERTY[13] keyboard layout compared to alternative configurations such as Dvorak and Colemak (which group the vowels and other more commonly used letters in the centre of the keyboard). It's true that the QWERTY layout was patented for typewriters in 1878,[14] making it contemporaneous with Thomas de Colmar and his Arithmometers, and there are undoubtedly more efficient ways that the keys could be distributed, but it is overwhelmingly the standard in Latin cultures, and in business it's rarely productive to go against the standard.

Imagine you're a keen data analyst rocking up for your new job at Data Analytics Corp. You sit at your desk waiting to show off your Mavis Beacon touch-typing skills when your team leader wanders over with a satisfied grin. "Here we use the FPUTNY keyboard, as we find that we achieve a 13.2% increase in productivity. It takes a little getting used to, but, once you unlearn all of your ingrained QWERTY mistakes, you'll find that … hey, come back …."

While higher typing speeds are possible with some alternative formats, speeds of 150+ words a minute are still quite possible on a standard keyboard. And which of us really needs to input data at those speeds? As with so many other facets of life, it's not how fast you type that matters, it's what you say. Sometimes less is more. And perhaps, like the mouse, the keyboard will gradually be used less as a primary means to get data into a computer: voice interfaces incorporating AI-driven language interpretation may take over that role. But no matter how sophisticated those models and mechanisms become, there will always be a need for fine tuning and precision.

If we strip back a computer to its basic components, it would indeed seem that each has more or less reached its zenith in terms of effectiveness and efficiency. Inputs (keyboard, mouse and wireless data) and outputs (screens and the same wireless data) are not going to materially change. The rest (processing and data) can be outsourced to a service provider who will manage whatever evolutionary changes take place.

Is it the end of the line for the computer hardware revolution? Perhaps.

There will be ever-faster machines, of course. Governments are pouring vast amounts of cash into research on quantum computers, which use quantum phenomena at the atomic level to store data in multiple states, promising an exponential increase in computing power. The very latest supercomputers are capable of terrifying speeds measured in teraflops and petaflops (trillions and quadrillions of floating-point operations per second, respectively). But as we have already noted, it is likely that for the vast majority of businesses such speeds will remain out of reach and any incremental improvement in processing power will be absorbed by increased software and security demands.

There will also be steps forward in terms of virtual desktops. Simulated screens through augmented reality are not yet commonplace, but headsets will eventually become sufficiently robust and reliable (not to mention comfortable) to be present in the office for those who need them. For job roles with a direct implementation of augmented reality (such as for an engineer who can view a real-world component overlaid with schematics or blueprints), this may happen far more quickly. But for a more administrative role, a virtual headset feels right now like a luxury or status symbol than a truly useful tool.

Cloud Wars

While the building blocks of cloud computing – the servers and network capabilities that support the vast data processing and storage facilities operated by the providers – may face a future of only gradual evolution, the cloud industry itself is still barely out of the blocks.

A Gartner report[15] at the end of 2022 confirmed an annual spend by end users on cloud computing in 2022 of nearly $500 billion, with that figure set to rise to nearly $600 billion in 2023. In 2020, the equivalent spend was around $250 billion. Estimates for 2030 top out at over $1.5 trillion.

With such a rich vein in prospect, cloud service providers are falling over themselves to capture market share, meaning that what may already make good sense from a business perspective will likely be sweetened further with beneficial deals to lock in your business.

The largest three providers (AWS, Microsoft Azure and Google Cloud Platform) account for over 60% of market share, with global coverage and hundreds of data centres between them.

As well as more volume, it's inevitable that more services will be incorporated into the provider's propositions, as current differentiators become commoditised. Providers will offer more nuanced offerings (such as hybrid cloud models) and additional service levels potentially adding further layers of abstraction between the end user and the servers that provide the computing power. Providers will also be challenging each other to meet (and surpass) net-zero carbon emissions as part of their green agenda.

Chip Wars?

The production of the semiconductors used in microprocessors is currently in a state of high tension.

Production is concentrated in a small number of nation states such as Taiwan and South Korea, impacted by COVID-19 and geopolitical tension.

While the silicon in a "silicon chip" is scattered all around in sand and rock strata, its extraction is time-consuming and complex, while the use of precious metals such as palladium, silver and gold as well as rare earth elements in chip manufacture makes the process hugely expensive.

The demand for chips has also soared, partly due to the COVID epidemic that restricted production, but driven also by the exponential rise in demand for processing power from cloud service providers, not to mention the IoT, data stores, blockchain nodes and the huge machinery required for AI training.

The supply chain for many of these materials is equally stressed, with the rare and precious minerals and gases required often located in difficult to reach or politically unstable regions.

It's unlikely that these collected tensions will ease any time soon, and the likelihood is that semiconductor production will be constrained, or even diminish, in time.

Mobile Technology – More, Not Better?

Some commentators opine that the smartphone, like the laptop, has reached its zenith. They say there are no more significant design advances needed or maybe even possible. All of the best features such as touch screens, biometric authentication, wireless capabilities and battery power are almost perfect. Foldable phones, voice-activated devices and seamless data backups? Tick.

But while the devices themselves may have reached the point of gradual evolution, their use is still in its infancy. A few years ago, who would have thought that access to your own organisation's network would be authorised using your own personal mobile phone? Or that you would be able to join a secure video conference with your colleagues while out jogging in the park?

With hybrid office and home working here to stay and a new generation of digital natives taking up the reins of industry, it's likely that business needs will push connectivity, efficient collaboration and productivity onto the next wave of devices. Mobile phones are not (yet) a collaboration tool. Anyone using the app version of collaboration software such as JIRA and Confluence, for example, will testify to that.

AI Technology

One area of hardware that will undoubtedly see a degree of change is in servicing the AI revolution (see Chapter 8). AI is currently very much a software solution both in terms of the training and production of large language models (LLMs) and in terms of its delivery to the general public (largely through web-based access to two or three global providers).

Inevitably in the decade to come, AI-specific hardware will be developed, ranging from GPU-like processors (also known as Intelligence Processing Units or IPUs) that are more closely aligned to the neural networks needed for LLMs to consumer devices better suited to the task. Think of a smart speaker that is designed with AI specifically in mind.

We may not all be sporting the latest "neural link" technology with thousands of metallic threads drilled into our brains, but it is inevitable that AI, still very much in its infancy as a technology, will have a significant impact in some way.

SO WHAT?

So, what does this all mean? How does the history (both ancient and recent) of computer hardware impact the decisions you need to make today? And how reliable is the crystal ball of trends in future hardware development?

You're probably thinking that it's really not your call. Of all of the topics in this book, the choice of hardware must be the one that falls most squarely in the domain of technology professionals, not business leaders. That's what you have an IT team for, right? And certainly, they will be making some strong recommendations to you. But as a business leader, as a sponsor for your IT project or perhaps the person paying for your desktop strategy, there are key questions you should be trying to answer before taking the word of your project team or procurement function that one hardware configuration is the right choice over another.

We can't tell you whether it's better for your organisation to run a mainframe on your own premises, or to subscribe to a cloud-based provider of computing power. Or whether you should ask your staff to bring in their own kit rather than rolling out an expensive new laptop to each of them.

But we can help you to form the right business questions to steer your IT team towards the best outcome for you.

In some of the other chapters of this book we have a raft of questions you should be asking yourself as a business leader.

But from a hardware perspective, we think there are only two:

- Who needs *access* to my hardware?
- Is hardware *central* and *critical* to my business or a utility to support it?

The answers to each of these questions will help you to decide on the best hardware configuration for your business need, or at least to understand and challenge your IT team's recommendations. The first question will typically influence your desktop strategy, while the second will help you to choose between siting hardware on your own premises, on the cloud or in some form of hybrid configuration.

Who Needs Access to My Hardware?

As with any tool, it's vital to understand who is going to use it. In the hands of a newly inspired DIY enthusiast, a hammer is a dangerous implement that can only lead to bruised thumbs and random holes in walls, whereas to a master joiner the exact same tool can be used to tease the most recalcitrant of nails into place. It's the same for computer hardware. Are the users informed experts or casual and occasional dabblers? Are their needs complex or relatively simple? As a community, are they mobile or static?

Users of Mainframes and Core Hardware

It's rare with modern hardware configurations that operators will be interacting directly with the core hardware itself. Gone are the days of crawling through a forest of cables plugging and unplugging things to effect changes in system behaviour. Usually, there will be a client–server interface so the operator will be using their desktop or laptop device to interact with a slew of applications that collectively manage business or technical operations.

As such, the user profile is probably not a factor in determining where your core hardware sits or how it is deployed.

If your business is so specialised that it does require such close attention, it's likely that you will want to deploy hardware in your own data centres for the operational flexibility and speed of response that affords you, but that is a specific decision outside the scope of this book.

Users of Desktop Hardware

The vast majority of business users will interact with computer hardware on their desk in the office, or more recently at home on the kitchen table, in the bedroom or the "dedicated" office space (which is all too often not quite dedicated enough to avoid the invasion of cats, dogs and small children into video conference calls at the most inconvenient times).

A study in pre-pandemic 2018 revealed that, on average, office workers spend almost 1,700 hours per year in front of their computer screens. That's over seven hours per working day. Any professional using a key tool for such a huge amount of their time would spend a great deal of time testing and trying different options before ensuring that the one they selected was the most perfect for the job. And yet, most of us will simply accept a poorly chosen option selected based on economic factors alone, in a configuration not ideally suited to the jobs we do.

Factors such as screen size, keyboard size, responsiveness and "feel", even the orientation of your mouse, can have a huge impact on the amount of work you can do in a day.

Let's start with screens – incontrovertible proof that smaller isn't always better.

With an ever increasingly mobile workforce, it may feel that giving your staff a 14-inch laptop is the way to go – it's light, easily stowable in a bag and can plug in anywhere. But those screens are so small – we're sure you've seen the down-trodden hordes of mobile workers, hunched over their tables in the corners of coffee shops or cafés, squinting at their laptop screens. And it's true that a lot of the work we do nowadays is conveniently packaged for screen-sized (and shaped) consumption. Presentations rather than papers, handily configured and colourful management information reports, even meetings are delivered to us in screen bytes.

A study[16] by University of Utah researchers concluded that there were significant productivity gains to be had from using larger monitors, or by using dual monitors side by side. Depending on the task, productivity gains ranged from 26% to 52% for a widescreen monitor compared to a single 18-inch configuration (with slightly lower gains for two standard monitors side by side).

So, it makes sense to use a large monitor wherever you can. The optimum solution is likely to be a workstation in the office with larger monitors to which your team can connect their laptops. If you support agile working and your workforce are as likely to be working from home as the office, it will almost certainly make sense to provide them with a monitor for their home configuration too, so at least they will benefit from twin screens. The cost of a monitor is only a few hundred pounds, so even if you buy two for each member of staff, their productivity gains will very quickly cover the cost (unless you're paying them substantially less than the living wage …).

It's a similar story for keyboards. A well-architected keyboard with responsive keys that allows the user to rest their wrists comfortably on the desk's surface will pay dividends in terms of speedier input, fewer mistakes and corrections, as well as less time spent in unproductive wrist-rubbing and finger-flexing. Gaming sites will go into great details about "switch travel distance" and "keyboard scan rate", and while these are less important in a business environment, we all like to see what we've typed appear swiftly and reliably on our screens.

And as for the humble mouse – while millennials may feel perfectly served by a drag pad on their laptop, it lacks the finesse and utility of a mouse. But again, there are plenty of bad mice out there. So while there's no need to go looking for the latest in ergonomic design, it's well worth investing a bit of time and research on getting a good, reliable wireless mouse for your workforce.

Is there a need for a desktop? Sometimes, even for the modern worker, mobility isn't everything. For emails and other simple tasks, a 14- or 15-inch screen may be fine, but to pick through 30 columns of data in a spreadsheet may become tricky. That doesn't necessarily mean that the business user needs a desktop as well as a laptop. For many, the best solution could be a laptop and a docking station – plug the laptop in and you have the best of both worlds.

It may not feel like a groundbreaking conclusion to recommend a docking station with a decent-sized monitor and ergonomically designed input devices. But remember to think about the users – if the need for desktop hardware is driven by simple operations such as reading and writing emails and participating in video calls, a laptop may be sufficient. But if more complex or bespoke software is employed, it may well be worth spending a little extra.

You may be tempted to flirt with a BYO ("bring your own") strategy where each employee uses their own sourced kit and links via a secure network to your corporate estate, but this will inevitably impact the compatibility and interoperability of your hardware. And ultimately you will want to be able to provide quick support to any problems your teams may encounter. By giving everyone the same hardware you will benefit from interchangeable parts and a menu of known issues and quick fixes to get your people back to work being productive as quickly as possible.

Remember, it's all about making those 1,700 hours per year as productive as you can.

Mobile Hardware Users

Unless your business deals specifically with mobile applications, it's unlikely that you have a choice to make in terms of mobile hardware.

In the past, organisations provided their employees with a corporate phone for security reasons, or to keep the employee's private details private. As a result, executives often had to contend with two or even three devices (private phone, corporate phone plus an organiser or some other device). In the modern world, neither of these are considerations. Corporate data can readily be segregated from private on the same device, and with everyone using VOIP ("Voice Over Internet Protocol"), there really is no need to give out your personal number in order to be available 24/7.

So the majority of corporate requirements can be met with the employee's own mobile phone.

In this case, BYO becomes a viable (and sensible) option.

Is Hardware Central to My Business or a Utility to Support It?

The answer to this question will determine your approach to the cloud.

It's a crucial question. But, luckily for you, it should be simple to answer.

If you're a bank or finance house running bespoke software on large mainframes, either in your own data centres of those of a facilities manager, then you are already incurring significant costs that you can't defer with a cloud option. Unless you need the flexibility of the cloud, you're likely to be better off doubling down on your investment in your data centre and housing your own hardware there. Even so, it may be that other benefits of the cloud mean that some of your non-core hardware requirements would be better suited away from your own premises.

If you're any other kind of business, there's a good chance that you would benefit from a cloud-based architecture.

There are a number of clear advantages, but also a few pitfalls for the unwary.

First and foremost, you only pay for what you use. If your processing demand is variable, you can draw on the computing power you need only when you need it. At other times, when you don't need the processing, you're not paying for hardware that is being underutilised. Furthermore, this elasticity is automatic, on-demand, without the need to request it through human interaction.

The flipside to this is that the on-demand pricing will scale as you use more power. If your business scales up, you may find your costs spiralling too. You need to be aware also of any hidden costs, such as fees to access data, especially if you breach your pre-agreed limits.

When comparing costs between cloud and on-premises hardware, remember to look at the total cost of ownership for your on-premises operation. There may be hidden costs such as energy and premises costs, staffing for your data centre, not to mention the cost of maintaining the hardware itself.

Setting up an in-house operation will be a much larger expense than taking out an agreement for cloud services. However, the upfront costs can be partially recovered as a capital expenditure as opposed to the running costs which will be operational expenditure.

Another benefit of the cloud is scalability. You can respond to increases in business quickly, often at the press of a button, without the need to source and install more hardware or upgrade your existing capabilities. This scalability is global, too, so if you find that you need more computing power in another region or continent, your provider will be able to respond to that demand far more quickly than if you needed to set up another data centre.

And with multiple data centres operated by the cloud provider, your business continuity and disaster recovery capabilities are increased. The provider would be able to switch processing to another data centre in the event of failure.

And a final caution about migration, either into, or away from, a cloud service provider. If your organisation has a complex technology estate and a large volume of data, this may take a significant amount of time (and cost) to migrate to the cloud, not to mention risk. This could have an impact if you wish to migrate from one provider to another, too. It's a significant undertaking and is not to be contemplated lightly. The use of a hybrid environment which combines on-premises infrastructure with cloud services might be a useful staging point, providing the ability to gradually migrate services and data into the cloud over a period of time.

On the face of it there are strong reasons to move into the cloud. But it is well worth taking the time to ensure that you are doing it for the right reasons, with the appropriate costs and benefits defined. It's also worth noting that not all cloud service providers are the same – look for the one that suits your business model the best.

NOTES

1 First Draft of a Report on the EDVAC by John von Neumann, 1945.
2 Book of Ingenious Devices by the Banū Mūsā brothers, c850.
3 Rabdologiæ by John Napier, 1617.
4 Introduction to the History of Computing by Gerard O'Regan, 2016, ISBN 978-3-319-33137-9.
5 The Gentleman's Magazine, and Historical Chronicle, for the Year 1857.
6 Introduction to the History of Computing by Gerard O'Regan, 2016, ISBN 978-3-319-33137-9.
7 *Introduction to the History of Computing* by Gerard O'Regan, 2016, ISBN 978-3-319-33137-9.
8 *On Computable Numbers*, Alan Turing, 1936.
9 *Introduction to the History of Computing* by Gerard O'Regan, 2016, ISBN 978-3-319-33137-9.
10 Electronics, Volume 38, Number 8, April 19, 1965.
11 www.computerworld.com/article/2534366/the-quotable-bill-gates--in-his-own-words.html
12 https://assets.kpmg.com/content/dam/kpmg/xx/pdf/2022/11/future-of-hardware.pdf
13 Or AZERTY/QWERTZ equivalents.
14 1878, U.S. Patent No. 207,559.
15 www.gartner.com/en/newsroom/press-releases/2022-10-31-gartner-forecasts-worldwide-public-cloud-end-user-spending-to-reach-nearly-600-billion-in-2023
16 Productivity, Screens, and Aspect Ratios, James A. Anderson et al, 2007.

2

What's Software?

The programmer got stuck in the shower because the instructions on the shampoo bottle said: Lather, Rinse, Repeat.

Anon

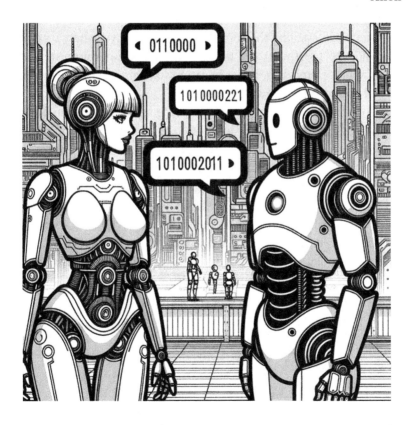

I'm non-binary....

DOI: 10.4324/9781003372660-2

Computers are vastly powerful machines, with more processing power today than in the wildest dreams of even the most optimistic of twentieth-century engineers. But while computers are fast and getting ever faster, they remain, essentially, idiots. Much like the programmer stuck in the shower, endlessly lathering, rinsing and repeating, a computer will blindly follow its coded instructions. If it's told to do something and not told to stop, it will get stuck in an infinite loop and continue processing forever.

That's why the old adage about "turning it off and turning it on again" works: the software running the computer has most likely got itself into a loop or is waiting for something that will never happen – by turning the computer off and then on again, the software starts again from scratch, hopefully, this time avoiding the sequence of events that led to the original issue.

These all-important coded instructions that tell a computer what to do (and what not to do) are called software. They could be defining the operating system (OS – telling the computer how to behave, where its devices are and how to use them). Or they could be an application, receiving, storing and processing data. The application software will tell the computer exactly what to do at any given time.

Modern software is very complex, involving hundreds or thousands (or even hundreds of thousands) of lines of code and thousands of variables. The more complex an application (and, more importantly, the more complex the process that application is required to support), the more software is needed to tell it exactly how to behave.

In this chapter we will look at software in its various forms and how the science of software engineering has evolved to deliver working applications that fulfil the needs of computer users across the spectrum.

But, most importantly, we will look, in the final section, at how you, as a business stakeholder, can have a direct impact on the complexity and cost of the software needed to run your business applications.

WHY SHOULD I CARE?

Invariably, in an Information Technology project, it will be the software that contributes most heavily to the project's cost and duration. It's almost certainly one of the key sources of errors and rework. Sure, you need computer hardware to run your code, and you need to understand your own data and how other systems and organisations use theirs, but it's the software that brings it all together as an operable system.

It's very rare that you will implement a technology project that has no software component at all. Even the most commoditised software (such as an email application) will have some aspects of configuration to control how it will behave in your own organisation. At the other end of the scale, you may find that software with the necessary capabilities for your business simply does not exist, and you will need to write it or have a third party write it for you.

So, it's vital that you, a business stakeholder in a technology project, understand how you can influence the cost and risk of that software element.

Can you make it cheaper by reducing the scope or scale of what it needs to do? Or by reducing the number of choices or conditions that it needs to interpret? Do you understand how changing your mind halfway through a project can lead to greatly increased costs to implement?

There are two very common (and potentially very expensive) mistakes made by project sponsors and business stakeholders.

The first mistake is to forget that "there is no magic". This mistake is often introduced as a question starting with the word "surely".

"Surely", says the eager business executive, "the system will automatically calculate the tax?"

"Surely the system will check that the part exists before allowing me to order it?"

"Surely the system will only allow the data's owner to see it?"

Questions of this type all hark back to our programmer in the shower (at the start of this chapter, in case you missed it). Unless the software has been specifically coded to add the tax, or check the part, or verify the access, the application simply won't do it. There may be good reasons for this – perhaps the software is used in multiple jurisdictions where different business rules apply, or maybe it's a requirement unique to your organisation.

But you'd be amazed at how many times senior stakeholders make assumptions about an application's capabilities, based purely on their own preconceived expectations rather than on extensively discussed and carefully documented business requirements which are then encoded into the application software.

The second mistake is to try to do too much in one go (trying to "boil the ocean", so to speak). Imagine that you fancy some eggs for breakfast. You open the fridge – no eggs. But you're OK, there's a store nearby. If you nip down there, you'll have time to buy a box of eggs, and you can still have your omelette done in time to start work. But then, while you're in the store, you spot some steaks for dinner, and some chips that will go nicely, as well as a couple of bottles of wine, and before you know it, you're doing the full week's shop. By the time you stagger home, laden with bags of shopping, the opportunity for breakfast has long since passed, and you've fallen foul of the perfection trap. The objective was to have a tasty breakfast. But the temptation to grab a few things for dinner at the same time led you astray and you failed to achieve your goal. Project people will tell you that "done is better than perfect" – and they are usually right. It's vital to have a clear goal in mind for the software that you are helping to shape – if you try to do too much, you may end up creating a behemoth that simply can't be delivered.

Avoiding these mistakes, among others, will help you to ensure that the software running your business applications has been appropriately tailored to your organisation's needs. Not too complex, but robust and reliable enough to get the job done. And hopefully delivered at the point that the business needs it to be delivered.

Knowing what software is, and how it needs to be written and tested, is a key factor in avoiding these pitfalls.

HOW DID WE GET HERE?

You might think that the development of software design and computer hardware would have been inextricably linked, each benefiting from breakthroughs in the other in a symbiotic spiral of innovation. But for much of human history, the two advanced independently. As we have seen, very early automata were simply machines capable of performing repetitive tasks or in some cases of responding to a feedback loop to exhibit some form of control. Meanwhile, logical and mathematical theory, which would later become the bedrock of computer programming and software engineering, developed at its own pace.

The two threads were not truly united until 1948.

Arguably, even the components of software were developed independently. At its simplest, software is an ordered set of machine-readable instructions that collectively perform various logical operations on defined machine-readable data.

Ada Lovelace is often cited as the "first computer programmer" and George Boole is credited with the definition of logical operators. But the foundations for digital processing were laid centuries before either of these digital innovators, in 1617, by a mathematician more famous as the invention of logarithms.

Software as a Concept

In the same publication[1] that he introduced Napier's Bones to the world, John Napier also put forward his theories of what he called "Rabdology". Using a simple mechanism of beads on a chess board, he proposed a form of binary notation that also simplified mathematical operations. He proposed that each square of the chess board be ascribed a value double that of the one to its right. So the first square represented the number one, the second square the number two, while the third square represented the number four and so on.

Referring to these as "numbers of a different kind", Napier demonstrated how fundamental mathematical operations could be represented by the movement of beads placed on the board. Adding two numbers together was simply a case of adding beads for both numbers to the relevant squares; whenever there were two beads on the same square, those beads were removed, and a new bead was placed on the square to the left (repeating this process if that square was already occupied). Doubling any number could be achieved by simply moving all the beads on the board one square to the left. And so on.

This may seem obvious to us now, but at the time it was revolutionary thinking and introduced two pivotal concepts still used today in software engineering.

First, Napier had defined a means to represent and use numbers in binary form. These operations are still at the heart of every digital operation today. A bead was either present in a square or it was not. The scale may have changed – there are billions of silicon transistors in every microchip – but each transistor is still fundamentally either on or off.

And second, he had conceptualised a digital (rather than analogue) approach to calculation. This mimicked (several centuries before the technology caught up) the first digital computer hardware of the 1930s (and every computer since).

It's worth dwelling for a moment on why these concepts are so important. When we say that something is digital, whether we know it or not, we are actually saying that it is binary.

Many of the first computers were analogue in nature. The value of something was directly defined by the strength of a signal or of a position on a gear wheel. This works well where the precise value of the output is not material. Think of a weathervane or a windsock. Their primary purpose is to indicate the direction (and in the case of a windsock, the strength) of the wind. If the indicated direction is a few points out, no one is going to mind greatly. But imagine if your laptop worked the same way when calculating your taxes. It's no good knowing that 20% of 98 is "roughly" 20. You need to know the exact answer. The problem with analogue mechanisms is that they lack this precision.

In binary (or digital) systems, the value of a variable is either on or off. This can be far more precisely defined. By combining a range of such variables (as Napier did on his chess board with beads), any desired number can be represented with absolute precision.

Napier is primarily remembered for his work on logarithms. As he himself put it in his *Wonderful Canon of Logarithms*,[2] "nothing is more tedious, fellow mathematicians, in the practice of the mathematical arts, than the great delays suffered in the tedium of lengthy multiplications and divisions". Napier demonstrated just how tedious mathematics could be by spending 20 years of his life writing out 90 pages of log tables.

But his lesser known *Rabdologie* treatise, published in the year of his death, with its neat solution to mathematical operations using what he called "location mathematics" – and the first documented reference to a decimal point – is perhaps far more enduring. It was the first step on the long road that led to digitisation and the software engineering we know today.

It would be another 200 years before the next significant steps were taken.

The first documentation of a computer program was by Ada Lovelace, a polymath, socialite and the only legitimate child of Lord Byron. Ada was steered towards mathematics by her mother who was hoping thus to avoid or delay the onset of madness that had consumed her illustrious father.

She corresponded with many scientists and creatives of the age including Charles Dickens and in particular Charles Babbage during the development of his analytical engine. In 1842, she worked on a translation of a seminar given by Babbage in Turin that had been documented in French by Italian engineer Luigi Menabrea. It is for this work that she is best remembered, adding copious notes, often in collaboration with Babbage himself. The paper published in 1843 included in an appendix an algorithm designed to run on the completed engine, to calculate Bernoulli numbers. The algorithm remained purely theoretical. Had the engine ever been built, however, it would have been effective, and Ada Lovelace is therefore often celebrated as the "first computer programmer".

Remarkably, she had also recognised the potential for a computer to do more than just calculate, suggesting such feats as the composition of music and drawing parallels with a loom's weaving of patterns with wool, inspired by the punched cards that were starting to drive Jacquard looms, automated weaving machines, in factories at the time.

Just a few years later, in 1854, the self-taught mathematician George Boole set out the fundamentals of logical operation that are still used today, bearing his name. The three operators in Boolean algebra (for variables x and y) are

- Conjunction ("AND") which is TRUE if both x and y are TRUE
- Disjunction ("OR") which is TRUE if either x or y is TRUE
- Negation ("NOT") which is TRUE if x is FALSE.

By replacing TRUE and FALSE with a 1 or a 0, respectively, Boole's logic can be represented digitally as logic gates, which can then be ordered to form an algorithm. See Figure 2.1.

These two pivotal concepts (binary numbers and logical operators) were to mature and develop at the hands (and minds) of generations of dedicated mathematicians and scientists, but it took the development of digital computer hardware to release their full potential.

Software as Hardware

Even then, the union of hardware and software wasn't immediate.

For a brief period, computers, even reprogrammable ones, carried their programs as a set of wires or switches that could be pulled or rewired to produce a different set of instructions and a different outcome.

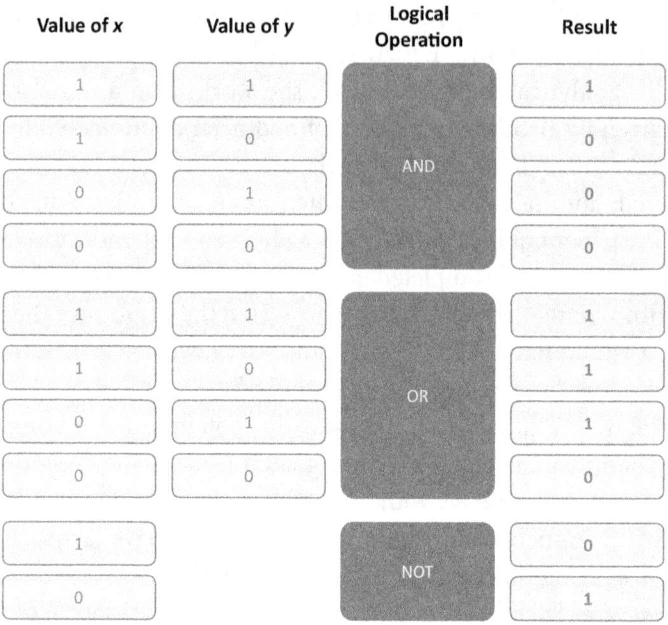

Value of *x*	Value of *y*	Logical Operation	Result
1	1		1
1	0		0
0	1	AND	0
0	0		0
1	1		1
1	0		1
0	1	OR	1
0	0		0
1			0
0		NOT	1

FIGURE 2.1
Boolean Logic.

ENIAC, the first programmable, electronic, general-purpose digital computer, managed its instructions through a series of plugboards and cabling. Once programmed, it could operate at speeds not possible in machines that read each instruction from a set of punched cards. It also allowed for "conditional branching", where an instruction would only be executed if certain defined conditions were met.

However, reprogramming the computer took days, if not weeks, and each new set of instructions had to be rigorously checked on paper before the programming team were allowed to effect the change by unplugging and plugging the thousands of wires into the plugboard.

ENIAC was programmed and reprogrammed by a team of women drawn from a pool of around 200 human "computers" at the University of Pennsylvania. Women had entered the technology workforce – calculating ballistic gunnery tables based on a complex set of variables and even more complex calculations – due to the labour shortages during World War II, ostensibly "freeing up" men for more skilled activities. When ENIAC was proposed to replace this human calculation with an automated digital one, it perhaps seemed natural that the women "computers" should in turn become the operators of the machine. Although the male engineers still got much of the credit, the women became experts in the machinery in their own right.

According to one such operator, Betty Jean Jennings,

> we spent much of our time ... learning how to wire the control board for the various punch card machines: tabulator, sorter, reader, reproducer and punch. ... Occasionally, the six of us programmers all got together to discuss how we thought the machine worked. If this sounds haphazard, it was. The biggest advantage of learning the ENIAC from the diagrams was that we began to understand what it could and what it could not do. As a result, we could diagnose troubles almost down to the individual vacuum tube. Since we knew both the application and the machine, we learned to diagnose troubles as well, if not better than, the engineer.[3]

It was Alan Turing who, in his 1936 paper *On Computable Numbers*,[4] first proposed the concept of a machine that stored within itself an algorithm defining the machine's behaviour. This concept of a "Turing Machine" remained purely theoretical until 1948 and the development of the "Manchester Baby" computer at Manchester University, the very first stored-program computer to hold software in electronic memory and execute it. The programming was very simple, comprising just 17 lines and a mere 8 different instructions. It set out to calculate the highest factor of the integer 262,144 by performing repeated subtractions (rather than division) and ran for nearly an hour.[5]

But at the end of those 52 minutes, the software produced the correct result (131,072), and a new era of digital computing was born.

Software as a Frontier

Initially, as for the Manchester Baby, new software was written specifically for each single machine or a single machine architecture. This software would take the most basic form, called machine code, and involved instructions directly to the computer's hardware. An example of this was the software written for the Apollo Guidance Computer (AGC) which was largely stored onboard in the form of a read-only solid-state memory involving wires hand-woven around magnetic cores, although a small number of commands could be overwritten by the astronauts using their display and keyboard interface (DSKY).[6]

But within a few years, several programming languages had been devised that could be transported from one machine to another, through the use of a compiler which turned simple written code into an executable program for each specific machine.

One of the first of these languages was FORTRAN (which stood for "Formula Translation" or "Formula Translating System"), written between 1954 and 1957 by John Backus, a programmer at IBM. Essentially a program to write programs based on a simplified instruction set including conditional branching and looping, the programming language was quickly adopted by the scientific community. Backus later stated

> Much of my work has come from being lazy. I didn't like writing programs, and so, when I was ... writing programs for computing missile trajectories, I started work on a programming system to make it easier to write programs.[7]

A plethora of languages followed. Within ten years, the core languages that would be used for decades and become the progenitors of all that would follow had been defined and published.

Many of them are still in use today, in one form or another.

ALGOL (Algorithmic Language) was first developed in 1958 by a committee of computer scientists (including Backus) at a meeting at the Swiss Federal Institute of Technology in Zurich. The original language was improved in 1960 (ALGOL 60), and although further changes were made in 1968, the 1960 version is deemed definitive. ALGOL introduced the concepts of code blocks (i.e. a grouped set of instructions that could be executed in isolation) as well as nested functions (functions defined within other functions and available only within the scope of the enclosing function) and parameterised procedures, all of which gave birth to the paradigm of structured programming (as opposed to a simple unstructured set of sequential instructions). British computer scientist Tony Hoare was moved to claim in his 1973 paper *Hints on Programming Language Design*[8] that

> the more I ponder the principles of language design, and the techniques which put them into practice, the more is my amazement and admiration of ALGOL 60. Here is a language so far ahead of its time, that it was not only an improvement on its predecessors, but also on nearly all its successors.

An indication of the proliferation of programming languages at the time can be inferred not only from the title of the paper, but also from the following statement contained within it: "According to current theories … every large scale programming project involves the design, use, and implementation of a special purpose programming language … specifically oriented to that particular project."

COBOL (common business-oriented language) was defined in 1959–1960 to be easily readable to the non-computer literate and to be self-documenting. In its original form, a language called FLOW-MATIC, it was devised by Grace Hopper who had been part of the team that developed the UNIVAC computer. Hopper was perhaps the first to see that while computers worked mathematically, human beings worked better with words ("[People] ought to be able to write their programs in English, and the computers … translate them into machine code") Rather than force the human beings to work mathematically, she proposed a compiler (called "A") that would automatically convert words into mathematical statements that the computer could understand.[9] Hopper was part of the team that matured FLOW-MATIC into the COBOL language. In theory, a COBOL program could be read and understood by a business user. It was a language written for businesses, not scientists, and it was quickly adopted by banks and other financial institutions. Significantly, it was designed by a committee not tied to a single manufacturer and is now standardised as part of ISO. COBOL is freely available to all and, although it has been largely replaced by the more complex languages that followed, applications written in COBOL remain in use across the financial world for core banking and financial software.

RPG (Report Program Generator) also began its life in 1959. It was developed by IBM as a means to help technicians transition from the physical programming required for their older tabulating machines (plugging and unplugging wires in a control panel) that ran in cycles (called machine cycles) to the new computers that processed files of information in a batch (called the program cycle) according to instructions held within a stored program. The concept of the program cycle heavily influenced the instruction set in the original RPG language. The computer would process a file of records, executing the program against each record. It was also constrained to the column format of punched cards. Various versions of RPG followed (notably RPG II in 1969, RPG III in 1979 and RPG IV in 1994), taking advantage of advancements in hardware and database design as well as more sophisticated programming methods. RPG is still in use on IBM mainframes today and is fully supported by IBM. Even the latest release includes a large amount of backwards compatibility (a key concept in software because the language itself is merely a tool with which to create operable programs written with significant effort and at great cost which could be invalidated by later language changes), so programs written in many of the earlier versions of the language will still run with little or no modification.

BASIC (Beginners' All-purpose Symbolic Instruction Code) was first released in 1964, after two college professors, John G Kemeny and Thomas E Kurtz, frustrated at the complexity of the available programming languages, sought a solution that would allow non-technical students to learn how to program. They designed BASIC with two key revolutionary characteristics: a simplified, text-based instruction set that could be easily understood by non-scientific students and the ability for users to share time on computer hardware in real time, thus avoiding the need to wait for the next available slot to see if their programming had worked. Users got immediate feedback. It was this time-sharing capability that made BASIC a modest success over the next decade, but it was the arrival of the micro-computer in the 1970s that really launched BASIC into ubiquitous use. When MITS (Micro Instrumentation and Telemetry Systems) launched the first microcomputer, the Altair 8800, in a hobbyists' magazine, entre-preneur Bill Gates called MITS saying he had a working BASIC interpreter for it. Between the call and the demonstration a month later, Gates and his partner Paul Allen worked furiously to produce both the interpreter and a simulator for the Altair. The demonstration was a success, their interpreter for BASIC became the standard and Microsoft was born. Already well-established, BASIC was a good fit for the new era of computing as it was small enough to fit in the tiny memories with which early microcomputers were furnished (the initial Altair version of BASIC comprised a total of 24 different commands and used only single letters for variable names to fit in 4 kilobytes of memory) and was simple enough to be usable by the untrained mass-market users that were suddenly exposed to the com-puter revolution. It quickly became the standard programming language: a version of BASIC was shipped as part of the read-only memory of nearly every microcomputer from the mid-1970s onwards. The use of BASIC began to decline towards the end of the twentieth century as computers became more powerful and more complex languages could be stored, but as the first real democratised programming language, its place in the history of software is secure.

MUMPS (Massachusetts General Hospital Utility Multi-Programming System) was developed in 1966–1967 at Massachusetts General Hospital for the purpose of managing hospital laboratory information systems. Developed internally following frustrations with an external vendor, the language contained (and still does, to this day) a number of quirky approaches. At a time when every program was single-threaded, essentially mimicking a batch process that ran from start to finish, MUMPS software was designed to run multiple processes at once. Memory was still a scarce commodity, so this multi-programming approach needed even more condensed terminology than other languages of the day: most commands could be written with one or two characters ("Q" for "Quit", or "S" for "Set"), and the language used interpretation rather than punctuation and reserved words to determine meaning, making programmers keen on truncated code with (unhelpfully) very few comments in their software. Additionally, the MUMPS database is hierarchical and multi-valued, with idiosyncratic access commands not used in many other languages. The upshot is that programs written in MUMPS tend to be very difficult to read to the uninitiated. Despite these limitations, MUMPS successfully penetrated the US hospital software market where it is still used extensively today, as well as being deployed within many retail and institutional investment solutions. A large amount of core banking software, originally built in the 1960s and 1970s and still running at the very heart of globally significant financial institutions, is based on a MUMPS core.

With the exception of BASIC, these early programming languages were used predominantly for big organisations to process large batches of data, but they do start to show a trend towards structured programming. In 1975, the British software consultant Michael Jackson (no, not that one) proposed a model for structured program design involving the codification of sequences, iterations and choices that could be made during the program's execution. JSP (Jackson Structured Programming) encouraged the programmer to plot out their software as a set of building blocks of such sequences and iterations before committing pen to paper (or finger to keyboard). Designed specifically for COBOL, the concepts of a structured approach matured and fed into the design of later programming languages.

Software for Computer Systems

Early computers were single-use machines, capable of running one program from start to finish. As computer hardware became more sophisticated with more peripherals to manage, part of the job of software became to allow the machine itself to operate – essentially to control the environment in which the actual applications would run.

This environmental control is the objective of an operating system.

An operating system (also referred to as simply an OS) is software that directly manages the computer hardware, software and peripheral resources. The software is often hard-wired into the computer's memory so that it is the first thing to load, allowing the computer to "bootstrap" itself into operation (a word derived from a nineteenth-century phrase denoting the impossible act of "pulling oneself up by one's own bootstraps").

The operating system as a concept began to appear in the 1950s, and as late as the 1960s, each new make of computer would typically be launched with its own bespoke software to govern its various core functions.

That began to change in 1970, with the launch of the mass-market microcomputer. The first portable operating system was CP/M (initially Control Program/Monitor and later Control Program for Microcomputers), which gained popularity across several microcomputer manufacturers.

CP/M was imitated and eventually completely replaced by Microsoft's MS-DOS (Disk Operating System) that was shipped with the IBM personal computer in 1981. The ubiquity of the IBM PC and its clones sealed Microsoft's place in the panoply of technology superpowers, but there was one more startling development to come.

As a response to the rampant success of the IBM PC and consequential dwindling sales of the Apple II PC, Apple launched the Lisa in 1983, along with a revolutionary operating system. Paired with a mouse, the Lisa allowed the user to view files and directories on-screen through a graphical user interface, and to move them around, even being able to "drag and drop" files from one location to another. Anyone who has grown up with modern computers and graphical interfaces will quite surely not understand the sheer incomprehension and amazement experienced by computer users of the day at this revelation, having been hitherto presented with only a blank screen and a single flashing cursor at which to start typing commands. The ability to visualise and control artefacts on the screen in two dimensions seemed nothing short of miraculous. The Lisa was followed by the cheaper Apple Macintosh which also included the same graphical approach.

Microsoft's response was Windows, launched in 1985. Initially an imperfect adjunct to MS-DOS, Windows was gradually improved over time, notably in 1990 (Windows 3.0) and 1995 (Windows 95 with its now infamous "Start" menu).

For mainframes and minicomputers, interoperability was less of a driver, with each manufacturer developing their own operating systems. An exception to this rule was UNIX, developed out of Bell Labs in the 1970s. Not tied to an individual manufacturer, UNIX became popular for research projects, ensuring that its usage grew over time.

It was in writing the core code for UNIX that two Bell engineers developed what is probably the most enduring of all programming languages, the root of nearly every modern language. The first version of UNIX was written in assembly language for a PDP-7 computer built by DEC (Digital Electronics Corporation). To make it portable, the designers, Dennis Ritchie and Ken Thompson, sought to develop a programming language that could be compiled onto different machines. Thompson had already written the programming language B, based on ALGOL. In 1971, Ritchie began improving B while Thompson started using and adapting it to write the UNIX core code for the more powerful and versatile PDP-11.

The result of their combined efforts was the C programming language (pronounced as in "see"), which Ritchie then set out in a seminal book, *The C Programming Language* (a standard reference still widely used today and one of the main reasons for the language's popularity) in 1978. C uses procedures and structures in a similar way to ALGOL, with a huge degree of flexibility and portability. Functions can return a value or no value, and a function can call itself ("recursion") to solve iteratively. The text is free-format (meaning that the positioning of the text on the page is not significant – just the order) allowing programs to be set out for readability to the human programmer. It is a compiled language, and the compiled code is easily portable between different machines. Although it can be used to program user applications, the main use for C was, and is, to write code for operating systems and embedded systems (such as in chip-controlled machinery). C became an ISO standard in 1990. It is still very widely used and is upgraded every few years (the latest version is C17 with a new version expected in 2024).

Software for Businesses

Until the mid to late 1970s, computer software (and hardware) was predominantly used in a strictly sequential way to execute an end-to-end process, applying a program from start to finish against a file of data.

In that decade and shortly afterwards, a number of factors (born of genuinely revolutionary advances in hardware, data and software) combined to transform the availability and operation of computer hardware and software from sequential batches producing defined sets of output files (on paper or on tape) for large organisations to real-time, event-driven, on-screen operations for just about everybody.

The first of these was the concept of the relational database in 1970, supporting non-linear access to data.

The second was the advent of the microcomputer and its subsequent evolution into the desktop personal computer such as the IBM PC and Apple II, hardware that almost any business could afford to buy and operate.

And the third was the arrival of the graphical user interface and the use of the mouse (and the left-click in particular) to create "events" in the computer's environment leading to an entirely new paradigm in event-driven processing.

SQL (Structured Query Language) grew out of the concept of a relational database (see Chapter 3) in the 1970s. Proposed by the inventor of the relational database, Edgar Codd, and developed initially by his colleagues at IBM, SQL was eventually released to market by Larry Ellison's Oracle as Oracle V2 (there was no V1), with other organisations following. SQL revolutionised data access and its commands became embedded in later programming languages. The revolutionary features of SQL (combined with the relational database design) allowed software programs for the first time to

- Specify complex predicates to retrieve (or update) data only where certain conditions are met. Predicates in SQL can become complex involving many attributes.
- Access data in sets rather than one record at a time. SQL allows a single database access command to retrieve (or update) all rows (records) on a table (file) that meet the criteria set out in its predicates. Before SQL, each record would need to be read one at a time in sequence from the file.

- Join multiple tables together. SQL includes the concept of a JOIN between two or more tables, with the nature of the join specified in the predicate. This even allows conditional access to data on one table depending on data in another (for example, retrieving only client data from table A where the client's address (in table B) is in a specified country. Joins can be inner (returning data only where it is found on both tables) or outer (returning all data in the first table joined with data from a second table if present). SQL also has the concept of NULL data (which is very different from zero or blanks) where, for example, there is no data to retrieve in a joined table.
- Directly update the data in the database. SQL provides the capability to directly manipulate data on the database itself, rather than reading the record into the program and amending it there. Before SQL, each record would need to be read in sequence from the file, amended according to the program, and written back to the file (or to an output file).

These features in combination allowed a program using SQL to be vastly simplified, allowing a single SQL statement to take the place of many lines of code to control loops, counters, conditions and data updates. SQL is an ISO standard "database language" (rather than a programming language per se).

Just as the relational model shook up database design and access, the concept of object-oriented programming (OOP) was about to revolutionise the world of software design. Although "objects" as concepts had been discussed for 20 years or so, and the progenitor OOP language Smalltalk had existed in some form from 1971, it took an article in the August 1981 edition of *Byte* magazine to introduce the concept to the wider community.[10]

OOP was a seismic shift in programming approach and it's worth taking a moment to understand why it's different. In a traditional software program, interactions are limited to files and records (or tables and rows in a relational model). In object-oriented design, everything is an object: it could be a file, a record in the file, an attribute, a variable or a function. In a graphical user interface (i.e. a screen-based environment), an object could be a window, a list of data or a button. Objects are invoked through a method, which is essentially a procedure or a function, a "message" to the object with an instruction (such as to "open" or "close") that may or may not return a variable (such as a status). Most (but not all) object-oriented languages define a class of an object (which sets out its characteristics), and the objects used in the program are instances of that class. Another key concept is that of inheritance, whereby a copy of a class or an object can inherit many or all of the characteristics of the parent class or object. Again, this is particularly helpful in a graphical user interface where a parent class can be defined for a clickable button and the actual buttons in the application are sub-classes derived from that one parent class. This ensures that all buttons in the application share a common "look and feel" and behave in a similar fashion.

Object-oriented design in its purest form affords many advantages, particularly in the context of graphical user interfaces, which experienced a surge in popularity in the 1990s, leading OOP to become the dominant method of the time. Objects can be updated in terms of their characteristics and behaviour without impacting the majority of the rest of the design, leading to reduced development and testing times and less risk of unexpected consequences. But it also has its drawbacks, focusing as it does on the data and objects rather than the processes. It is possible that much of the development in the 1990s was to put a user-friendly front-end screen onto an existing monolithic application that was already written in a more procedural language, so the object-oriented approach was the right one for the job at hand.

So, although the decade spawned a spate of object-oriented languages based on the progenitors Lisp (originally LISP, List Processing), Simula and Smalltalk, the more successful languages employed a blend of object-oriented techniques with more procedurally based elements.

The C++ programming language (named in true quirky tech fashion because ++ in C represented the "increment" operator and C++ was an increment to the original C) was designed by a Danish computer scientist called Bjarne Stroustrup between 1979 and 1985 at Bell Labs as an evolution of C, originally called "C with Classes". In its final form it introduced a number of object-oriented concepts to the essentially procedure-based C language. Stroustrup published his own definitive guide to C++ (*The C++ Programming Language*) in 1985, the same year as the commercial release of the software. According to Stroustrup[11] himself, C++ was designed to incorporate aspects of the Simula language supporting program organisation, to run quickly and be portable. These concepts developed into a set of principles by which Stroustrup allowed the language to evolve, the most notable of which were:

- C++'s evolution must be driven by real problems.
- Don't get involved in a sterile quest for perfection.
- C++ must be useful now.
- Every feature must have a reasonably obvious implementation.

C++ attracted criticism that it included too many features in an attempt to solve every problem. Most organisations would pick and choose which features to use, which tended to impact portability from one organisation to another and to reduce the readability (to the human eye) of the code. But it was massively successful, even so (or perhaps simply because of that versatility). It remains one of the top three languages in use today.

Visual Basic was Microsoft's response to the object-oriented and graphical user interface revolution. First released in 1991, it was intended to be easy to use with a shallow learning curve. Developers were able to create event-driven graphical applications by dragging pre-built components or controls onto a form, specifying attributes and actions for components and writing lines of code (or borrowing from runtime libraries embedded in the underlying Windows OS) where required for additional functionality. In theory, a developer could develop a simple application without writing much code. Visual Basic was entirely replaced by Microsoft in 2002 (renaming the original version as "Classic"), along with a fully integrated development environment (IDE) called Visual Studio. It retained its graphical drag-and-drop approach and is the primary language for developing applications for Windows.

Software as a Product – The First Business Applications

As information technology usage gradually bled from larger organisations to a much wider community of smaller businesses, the approach to computer and software usage changed from the bespoke to the more commoditised. While larger organisations may once have adhered to Tony Hoare's assertion in 1973 that every project needed a new programming language, many smaller organisations could not afford such developmental profligacy, especially when a small number of widely supported existing languages could be used to write applications. Businesses used COBOL, RPG, MUMPS, C/C++ and SQL to build their own systems. But as the numbers continued to grow, so too did the provision by third parties of ready-made business applications.

Two of the most familiar and enduring software applications saw their debut in 1979.

The first was pure software genius: the idea for a "killer application" so simple in hindsight that most of us probably wonder how businesses (and indeed civilisation) could possibly prosper in a world where it didn't exist – the humble spreadsheet, in the form of VisiCalc. Although its tenure in the world of business was brief (from 1979 to 1985), it arguably transformed the use and usefulness of computers more than any other single application.

VisiCalc was the brainchild of Dan Bricklin, a Harvard Business School student, who dreamt in 1978 of turning his simple calculator into a virtual display of multiple calculations using a mouse-like ball.[12] Using an Apple II and a gaming controller, Bricklin invented a calculator that worked in rows and columns, automatically updating the results in each cell based on a formula. His original name for the product was "calcu-ledger" because he didn't feel that people would understand what an "electronic spreadsheet" was. In the end, he and his friend Bob Frankston decided on "VisiCalc", short for visible calculator, and their company Software Arts was incorporated on January 2, 1979. By July of that year, VisiCalc was selling to small businesses who had discovered that they could replace hours of tedious calculation and recalculation with a tool that would automatically provide a result for every change made to a ledger. Initially, VisiCalc sold exclusively on the Apple II, and it was estimated that a quarter of Apple's sales in that year were for the software alone, described as "the software tail that wagged the computer dog". Sadly for Bricklin and Frankston, the era of the IBM PC spelt the end for their enterprise as VisiCalc was almost instantly replaced by Lotus 1-2-3 which ran on the newer, better hardware.

The year 1979 also saw the world's first word processors for the micro-computer, *WordStar* and *WordPerfect*.[13] Word processing was another "killer app" that encouraged businesses to dive into the world of computing and hastened the transition from hobbyists' microcomputers to the era of the IBM PC. Initial word processors were slow and what was seen on-screen was not what would eventually print (WYSIWYG – "What You See Is What You Get"), but the step change from hand-typed documentation to something that could be saved and edited was – again – transformational.

Slow to adapt to a Windows environment, these products were essentially replaced by Microsoft Word, along with Excel, as part of the Office suite of applications.

During the 1980s, Lotus (primarily with their 1-2-3 spreadsheet product) and Microsoft vied for dominance of the office software market. Lotus achieved startling success with 1-2-3 on the IBM PC, but gradually Microsoft (with Word in 1983, Excel in 1985 and PowerPoint in 1987) released challenger products. Eventually, Microsoft products were bundled pre-loaded with many of the IBM clones, and Lotus' presence in the market waned.

As businesses began to connect to the web, software applications became much easier to distribute, either as a loadable product or in some cases in a client-server model where the majority of the application remained centrally located with the vendor and the buying organisation loaded only a relatively light application to access the central product.

Software as a Community

Into the twenty-first century, programming languages and software design again transformed in the internet era. No longer the purview of a single developer, languages became freely available, open-sourced for everyone to use with vibrant communities to provide support, evolve the languages and collaborate on application development.

Linux is an operating system, initially written in 1991 by a Finnish university student Linus Torvalds with the help of some of his fellow students. Similar to UNIX ("UNIX-like"), but without any UNIX code, Linux uses an open license model: the kernel code is available for study and modification, which resulted in its use on a wide range of computing machinery from supercomputers to embedded and mobile devices (including Android phones) such as smartwatches. Linux has become the most popular operating system outside of the personal computer and laptop markets.

Java, initially developed by James Gosling at Sun Microsystems in May 1995, was derived from C and C++ but had the additional capability to be run on a "Java Virtual Machine" (JVM) – once complied, any Java application could run anywhere ("write once, run anywhere" or WORA). With the sudden explosion of web pages across the World Wide Web and the ability of web browsers to support Java "applets" (small applications), Java became the de facto standard for web-based programming. Sun released most of their code as open-source and free to use between 2006 and 2008. Java is maintained by the Java Community Process, whereby changes may be proposed as Java Specification Requests (JSRs) to be approved by an executive committee.

Python was conceived in the late 1980s and first released in 1991. It was developed by Dutch programmer Guido van Rossum when he was looking for a scripting language for a distributed operating system. Recalling an earlier language that he had worked on, ABC, van Rossum enhanced it to be more flexible, especially in the ability to use external procedures written in a different language (C, for example). ABC had been a competitor to BASIC, intended to help non-programmers understand and write their own code, and van Rossum intended Python to do the same. The language itself uses a simple, uncluttered syntax and promotes readability while not restricting programmers to a particular coding methodology. Software development communities tend to the quirky side, and the Python community is no exception. The language itself is named after Monty Python, and there are many light-hearted references to the show in its lexicon. Van Rossum himself was awarded the title "Beneficial Dictator for Life", as the overall arbiter of good practice, although the development of the language is governed by a steering council that approves PEPs (Python Enhancement Proposals). Not all of these are language-related: the governance and membership of the council is defined in PEP 13, for example, while PEP 20 sets out "The Zen of Python" including such aphorisms as

- Beautiful is better than ugly.
- Explicit is better than implicit.
- Simple is better than complex.
- Complex is better than complicated.
- Readability counts.
- Special cases aren't special enough to break the rules.

GitHub is not a programming language but a software development platform or IDE. It is cloud-based (www.github.com), allowing developers anywhere in the world to set up repositories to share, review and develop software in an open-source environment. Set up in 2008 by three entrepreneurs, the platform grew rapidly and was acquired by Microsoft in 2018.

Software developers can use GitHub to

- Set up a shared repository
- Store code and documentation there
- Collaborate with other developers who have access to the repository
- Create code branches (copies of existing code that are then amended) to test new developments or changes to existing programs
- Effectively manage version control of developing code branches
- Perform specific actions (such as pull, merge or fork) to manage code branches.

Software as a Service

Software as a service (SaaS) has grown as a licensing and delivery model with the continued expansion of the internet and the World Wide Web. In a SaaS model, software is licensed (usually directly from the software provider) on a subscription basis.

SaaS applications typically provide a fully commoditised service common to most businesses such as for email, document creation, accounting, payroll and human resources. The core application runs in the cloud and is accessed through a web browser, with no need for the user to download local software.

WHAT DOES HERE LOOK LIKE?

Software design and development has evolved beyond recognition in the last 40 years and will continue to adapt to the twin drivers of changing business needs and technological advances.

Even in the twenty-first century, the pace of change within the business software environment has continued. The mass appeal of web browsers and the internet, the creation from a standing start of voracious smartphone and tablet markets, and the growth of the Internet of Things (IoT), the advent of blockchain and the mass commercialisation of artificial intelligence (AI) have all driven the expansion of existing languages and the development of new ones.

Although fewer new languages were implemented in the last decade than in any two years in the 1990s, that doesn't mean that software design is standing still: far from it. The existing languages are now in the main sufficiently flexible and diverse that any given challenge can be met by adaptation or evolution. The benefits of standardised languages in terms of collaboration and a mobile workforce are also being realised.

On the other hand, sales of off-the-shelf or customisable applications for commoditised services are seeing steady growth (such as Microsoft Office suite which has seen approximately 20% growth for the last five years since its revision in 2018 or Salesforce which has seen similar growth over the same period).

The current landscape for software reflects the pressures on (and ambitions of) the information technology industry itself. There is a perception in business that software engineering and project delivery are inherently linked (even though this is not always the case), and therefore that high project failure rates, often as high as 70%, are partly or significantly the result of poor-quality software engineering design and deployment.

As a consequence of that thinking and regardless of whether this view is right, software engineering in the business and administrative environment today has a lower risk appetite, less desire for true innovation and fewer revolutionary or disruptive leaders than before (although this is arguably less the case in more practical environments such as in the agricultural and manufacturing sectors where there is a great deal of experimentation and innovation).

Add in the growing dominance of modern cloud-hosted, SaaS, mobile-first product designs and the rise of generative AI and distributed ledgers (blockchains) and we can start to make more sense of software fashions such as low-code/no-code, microservices, security as a priority and automation.

Software engineering is not a monolith, of course; and business needs constantly flex to meet changing demand and consumer preferences. The Agile Manifesto, a programming methodology prioritising iterative software engineering over more the cumbersome "waterfall" methods that had dominated the industry for decades previously, is a good clue to the "state of mind" of modern software engineering. Agile's four foundational principles are to favour

1. Individuals and interactions over processes and tools.
2. Working software over comprehensive documentation.

3. Customer collaboration over contract negotiation.
4. Responding to change over following a project plan

When software is personalised (using methods like Agile) and therefore made more intimate in order to satisfy the desires and requirements of the end-user and is deployed collaboratively, it takes on a very different character compared to the industrial and productivity-oriented software of before.

Languages

There really is a vast range of software languages. Some are purely speculative concepts, while some are practical but very purpose-specific. Most, if not all, bear idiosyncratic, not to say outlandish, names, from the mundane early groundbreakers (like FORTRAN, ABC, GEORGE and COBOL), through the microcomputer-driven expansion of the late twentieth century with its mixture of backronyms, pseudo-science and petulant humour (BASIC, PARADOX, Logo, B, C, Python and the emphatic Brainfuck – a truly crazy language with just 8 commands) into the twenty-first century with its playful exuberance (Genie, Elixir, Hopscotch, Crystal, Raku and Mojo to name but a few).

With so many to choose from, how can businesses decide what's the best one to help them solve their problems?

The reality is that nearly all of the hundreds of software development languages are simply not relevant in a business context. The vast majority of all software today is written in just a handful of languages (JavaScript, Python, Java, C#, C/C++, PHP and Swift).

- JavaScript: The darling of web developers for creating interactive and dynamic web pages. JavaScript is an interpreted language (meaning that it is not precompiled but is processed by the computer at run time) predominantly used in browser-based applications.
- Python: Versatile, intuitive language with a simple syntax, making it appealing to a wider community. It is increasingly used for AI, machine learning, data analytics and visualisation applications. Python is also an interpreted language.
- Java: Enterprise, compiled language that is run on a JVM. Its "WORA" concept makes it incredibly portable and versatile, particularly for web and mobile (Android) applications.

- C# (C Sharp): Developed by Microsoft and used extensively for software development in Windows environments. C# is a compiled language.
- C/C++: Used extensively for core application development. Many OSs (LINUX and other UNIX-like equivalents) are written in C, while Windows itself is written in C++. If you are writing a number-crunching application to run on a server, there's a good chance it will be written in C, while a "thin" client to be loaded onto a desktop or laptop might be written in C++.
- PHP: Scripting language used in website development, especially for servers.
- Swift: Apple's core programming language, based mostly on the C family. Initially used for all Apple development (on Macs, iPhones, iPads and Apple Watches), it is open-source and can also be used in other environments such as Windows or LINUX.

Figure 2.2 shows how each of these programming languages might be used, based on the type of application being built.

Generations of Software Languages

You may hear references to 3rd-, 4th- and 5th-generation software languages.

These generations are something of a misnomer – as we saw previously, many of the software languages derived quite quickly from their predecessors without being regarded as being from a "later" generation.

In fact, the generation of a language has less to do with when it was devised or the identity of its progenitors and rather more to do with the level of abstraction the language has when interacting with the computer.

- First-generation languages are defined to be the most basic means of communicating with computer hardware – binary machine code that is "written" by setting switches. This is not "human readable" and is specific to each individual machine.
- Second-generation languages use a form of assembly language that must be converted into machine code for the specific device on which

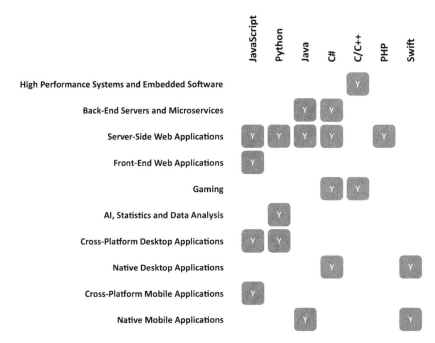

FIGURE 2.2
Application Languages.

it runs. Each operation is written as a line of code, but the syntax is crude and complex, making this an unlikely choice for software development.

- Third-generation languages are compiled or interpreted languages that are written by a developer. The software is converted to machine code either in advance (compiled) or at run-time (interpreter). Most software development uses third-generation languages (C, C++, C#, Java, Python and so on).
- Fourth-generation languages are not necessarily more sophisticated or complex than third-generation languages, but they serve a specific purpose, such as SQL for database access.
- Fifth-generation languages take the level of abstraction one step further, making the computer generate software to solve a specified problem, without the intervention of a software developer.

Software from later generations isn't necessarily "better". In fact, fifth-generation languages have yet to prove effective at problem-solving – it turns out that writing computer programs is pretty hard. There may be third-generation languages that are accompanied by large libraries of objects or code that may take away a lot of the repetitive work of software design and development, but – for now – a human developer is needed to align those libraries and hand-written code to produce the desired outcome.

Software Development Options

It may no longer make good sense (if it ever did) to design a dedicated pro-gramming language to meet your business needs, but it may well still be the right course of action to build and maintain your own software (with or without the help of an implementation partner). The less commoditised and more specialised your business needs, the more likely it is that you will not be able to find a software product on the market that delivers to your requirements, or there may be reasons why you want to have in in-house development capability, such as for flexibility or to meet a high pace of change.

On the other hand, if your need is for a commoditised corporate function such as payroll, finance or human resources, you may find that there is a vendor-supplied and maintained application that meets all of your needs (or closely enough that the additional cost of building it yourself is not merited).

Every organisation has the following options to procure the right software

- Developing custom applications
- Applications off-the-shelf
- Software as a Service.

Figure 2.3 shows (very) approximate relative costs for the high-level components of implementing and operating a software application for each of these options.

Each of these costs is explained in more detail below.

Developing Custom Applications

Developing, implementing and then operating your own code comes with significant costs, not all of which are immediately apparent.

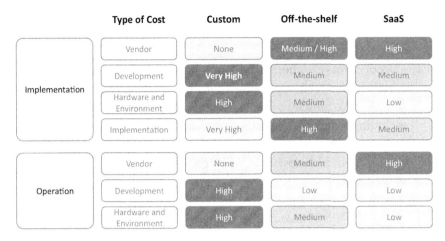

Type of Cost		Custom	Off-the-shelf	SaaS
Implementation	Vendor	None	Medium / High	High
	Development	Very High	Medium	Medium
	Hardware and Environment	High	Medium	Low
	Implementation	Very High	High	Medium
Operation	Vendor	None	Medium	High
	Development	High	Low	Low
	Hardware and Environment	High	Medium	Low

FIGURE 2.3
Software Development Option Costs.

Implementation

There are significant costs involved with implementing a new piece of software.

Vendor: The good news, of course, is that there's no cost to a software vendor to provide or develop software for you. You're doing it yourself!

Development: The flipside to the lack of vendor costs is that you will be paying a significant premium to run a project to develop the software yourself (see Chapter 7 for more information on projects). Setting up and running a project to build your software may include costs such as

- Project team costs – professional software developers don't come cheap, and you will need project or program managers, business analysts, testers and project officers depending on the size of your build. If this is a one-off (or significant expansion of your standing team) you may well end up paying a premium for contract professionals as well as 20% or more on top of an agent as a hiring fee.
- Implementation partnership costs – if you have your own home-grown pool of talent, that's great. But most sites will need to bring in specific expertise to help with the custom build and implementation.
- Stakeholder and subject matter expert costs – the project team can't work in isolation: they will need guidance and input from a range of senior stakeholders to subject matter experts to provide requirements and execute test scripts of user testing. Even if these business resources

are already part of your organisation, you may need to spend money to backfill your experts in their "day jobs" while they dedicate time to the development.

- Cost of mistakes – there is a reason that a software vendor will charge a high fee for their application: software design and development is complex; the finished product is the result of a great deal of hard work including a number of architectural dead-ends, misunderstandings, coding errors, data errors and numerous other mistakes. These are significant hidden costs that you are at risk of incurring if you decide to go it alone.

Hardware and environment: You will need computer hardware and software (OSs, development toolkits and project support software) to support your software development. For a self-build, you will need significantly more licenses for programming languages and software development kits, and you will also need more extensive testing facilities including defect management tools, such as JIRA.

Implementation: Even the implementation of your finished software is going to be more expensive for an in-house development. There are fixed costs that will apply regardless of how the software was built – you will need to train the operational team on the new product, swap out any existing software (perhaps migrating data from the old to the new as you do so), build the necessary monitoring and first-line response capabilities and so on. The more commoditised the product, the more artefacts will already exist to help you through this process. For a self-build, there will be no ready-made training materials for computer-based training, no existing data migration routines and no experts in the market who have done it all before and can help you to avoid the pitfalls.

Operation

Once the implementation project has been completed, there are still significant costs your organisation will have to bear in order to operate and maintain the software.

Vendor: Again, the good news is that there's no vendor demanding a license fee for the use or operation of the software – it's yours.

Development: Software, like the business that it serves, doesn't stand still. The software that you have built and implemented may need constant changes to meet the demands of your organisation. At the very least, the hardware and software environment on which it runs may evolve over time, with upgrades to servers and OSs: Each time this happens you will need to test and possibly amend your software to continue running. You will need to ensure that you have retained access to the necessary expertise to ensure that you don't end up with a business-critical software application that no one knows how to maintain. And just as for the initial development and implementation, there isn't a pool of experts on the market who will understand your software – you've built it so you need to make sure you can keep it going. One advantage, however (and it's a big one) of doing this all in-house is that you can adapt the software exactly how and when you need it, meaning you have the potential to respond swiftly to changes in your business or in the wider industry.

Hardware and environment: There are significant costs involved with maintaining an operational environment for your software. You may need a dedicated data centre or pay for cloud-based services for your production environment. Depending on the criticality of the software, you may need to additionally run and maintain a disaster recovery (DR) site, with regular testing and switching between the two sites. To support ongoing development and testing, you will need to maintain a development environment and a test environment for the different types of testing (system/integration testing, user acceptance testing, operational acceptance testing and non-functional testing) with all of the additional security measures required for these multiple environments to protect sensitive data.

Applications Off-the-Shelf

With a commercial off-the-shelf (COTS) product, the software vendor has already done a lot of the heavy lifting and will charge appropriately for that hard work, but that doesn't mean there are no activities for your organisation to take on.

Much of the additional costs involved in implementing and operating an off-the-shelf application will depend on the level of customisation your business needs. As always, the more commoditised a product, the less cost there is to implement and run it. For an application that is the same all the world over (such as for word processing or email), some simple local customisation may be all that's needed (file locations, security preferences and so on). For a more specialised business application (such as one that manages sales or financial operations), there will be more local impacts, such as regional tax or other business rules that need to be defined.

Implementation

There are significant costs involved with implementing a new piece of software, even if the vendor will bear some of these.

Vendor: Depending on the level of customisation you ask for, there may or may not be any need for the vendor to adapt the product to suit your business needs. In this case, the only cost you will pay the vendor is the initial fee for their application. But be wary of claims that software will work "out of the box". The more complex the business that is served by the application, the more customisation may be required.

Development: With an off-the-shelf application, there is naturally less software development to be done, but you will still need an implementation project to customise and install the software:

- Project team costs will be lower as you will not need nearly so many software developers and less testing.
- Stakeholder and subject matter expert costs – the implementation must still be supported by the rest of your organisation, just as for an in-house build. You still need to understand the requirements and make sure that the software does what you need it to do.
- Cost of mistakes – although there is still the opportunity for mistakes (notably, selecting the wrong vendor or the wrong product!), it can be hoped that more basic software development errors can be avoided in a product that has already been largely written by the vendor and is in live operation elsewhere in other organisations.

Hardware and environment: You will still need some hardware and software to support any customisation and implementation activity. You will also need to ensure that your testing capabilities and defect management tools are aligned (or are compatible) with those of the vendor.

Implementation: For an off-the-shelf product, although you will need to support some of the same fixed costs as for an in-house build – training, rolling out the software, data migration, building a monitoring and support infrastructure and so on, there will be more available artefacts to help you, whether supplied directly by the vendor or available from a community of existing users.

Operation

Operating and maintaining the software will incur a cost for an off-the-shelf product, too.

Vendor: The vendor will (most likely) charge a license cost or use some other means to ensure that they are recompensed for the intellectual property they have developed.

Development: Just as for an in-house build, vendor-supplied software will need to evolve either from a business perspective or to continue to function in the operating environment. Depending on the deal you are able to secure from the vendor, some of this ongoing development may be incorporated into the license fee, some of it may be shared across their user-base, and some of it may be chargeable to your organisation directly (needless to say, it's very important to understand this as part of the commercial discussions you have with the vendor). As the vendor will be responding to multiple needs across its client base, it may be that any specific needs you may have will be deemed lower priority than industry-wide changes and you may have to wait longer than you would like for changes to be made. It's also an important factor in selecting your vendor that they have the necessary resources and commitment to continue to support the ongoing development of the software in the years to come.

Hardware and environment: Aside from needing to support ongoing development of the application itself, your organisation's operational hardware and environment costs are likely to be similar for a vendor's product as for one you have developed in-house.

Software as a Service

As with an off-the-shelf product, in a SaaS model, the software vendor will normally already have a completed product available to meet your business needs. But, again, there may be customisation and other activities that will require input from your organisation to fully implement and operate the product.

Implementation

There are significant costs involved with implementing a new piece of software, even if the vendor will bear some of these.

Vendor: As for the off-the-shelf approach, implementation costs to the vendor will depend on the level of customisation you ask for, plus any one-time cost to buy the application itself.

Development: As for the off-the-shelf approach, development costs will be lower than for an in-house build, but there will still need to be some project team and stakeholder or subject matter expert costs.

Hardware and environment: The vendor should bear much of this cost, save for any changes to the "client" hardware that your teams will use to interact with the core product that will be developed by the vendor. You may find that it's easier to use the vendor's own testing and defect management tools.

Implementation: There will inevitably still be training costs and quite possibly roll-out and data migration costs, but you should benefit from the vendor's own expertise in implementing their software in other organisations. Monitoring and support may also be part of the SaaS deal, and you may not need to grow this capability in your organisation.

Operation

The SaaS model has the biggest impact during operations.

Vendor: The vendor will charge a fee that may be transaction-based, license-based or derived from some other business factor.

Development: As for the off-the-shelf product, in a SaaS model, the cost of any ongoing development will be mixed: some will be included in the license fee, some will be shared across the user-base, and some of it may be chargeable to your organisation directly. It's likely that this model will be even less agile than the off-the-shelf approach in terms of meeting the changing needs of the business.

Hardware and environment: The vendor will be hosting and operating the application for you as part of their fee. You will have some responsibility for ensuring that your own environments can connect to those of the vendor.

Choosing the Right Development Option

Your choice of which software development approach to follow for a particular business need is unlikely to be taken in isolation. You may already have sufficient development capability, and the current project is just one more item for the work stack. The need itself may be so commoditised that the SaaS option is inherently obvious, or there may simply be no products on the market that meet your needs. Or you may find exactly the right solution for part of your business problem, but it needs to be integrated with the other components of the solution as well as with the rest of your hardware and software estate such as your client relationship management (CRM) application or to a data repository where you gather your business information for analysis.

The decision will always be a nuanced one – there is no "right" or "wrong" answer in the majority of cases. But, unless your organisation is in the business of designing software, the following principles may be of help in reaching it:

- Buy before build – unless there is an over-riding reason to build your own software, in general, it is always better to buy a product that serves the correct purpose than to build a new one.
- Adopt not adapt, and favour configuration over customisation – if you are buying a product from a vendor, the less you have to change it the better. This will both simplify the initial build and also ensure that the operating product is easier for the vendor to maintain, which makes it cheaper for you. That doesn't mean that you need to compromise your business needs – but you can try to focus on the output of the product rather than how it is achieved and adapt your own internal process to accommodate how the software product has been designed.
- Reduce complexity (also known as KISS: "keep it simple, stupid") – the more options you try to retain in your operations, the more forks there are in the logic and the more expensive it is to write, run and maintain. Try to identify any unnecessary complexity in your requirements and remove it or simplify it where possible.
- Solve the problem – does the software actually solve a business problem? Too often, software is bought by organisations after a slick sales pitch, or when technology teams implement a shiny new toy, in either case without really considering the problem that the new software solves. And even if it does solve a problem, is it one that needs to be fixed? Right now?
- Know your unique selling point (USP) – what is it that your organisation delivers to its clients that defines it and separates it from its competitors? If the software will form an intrinsic part of that specific

part of your organisation, you may well feel that it is something over you wish to keep a tighter control than you would have when buying software externally from a vendor, whereas a more commoditised product may benefit from a SaaS arrangement.

Low-Code and No-Code (LCNC) Options

Software development capabilities have been evolving for over 50 years, since the first FORTRAN and COBOL programs of the 1950s. While the choice before businesses remains essentially "buy or build", in recent years, there has been a trend towards build options that automate the programming process, supporting the "citizen developer" (a non-engineer who develops applications or capabilities for a business using dedicated development platforms rather than by coding in a programming language) with graphical click and drag-and-drop software design tools.

These build options are called "low-code" and "no-code" (LCNC).

Both low-code and no-code platforms support the development of applications by allowing users to drag and drop a range of pre-defined objects (such as screens, buttons, labels and fields) into a development area and defining their characteristics and behaviour as well as any workflow needed to move from one part of a process to the next. In a low-code platform, the user may be required to write a number of lines of code (in a defined language) to customise how the object will behave. In a no-code platform, not even that step is needed (with the detriment that a no-code application will be less configurable than one designed using low-code).

There are many advantages of using low-code or no-code:

- Citizen developers – the first major advantage of citizen developers is that there are a lot of them compared to fully trained software developers: just about anyone can have a go at designing an application to support a process.
- Rapid development – with no laborious coding and testing to perform, developing applications using low-code or no-code development tools can produce results far more quickly than traditional software development approaches.
- Accurate solutions – because the application is designed by the business users who will be using it, there is less opportunity for

requirements to be lost or confused. The citizen developer will build exactly what is needed.

- Flexibility – with easy access to the development platform, business users of the application can quickly respond to changing needs or perceived flaws.
- Accessibility – LCNC solutions can be built for almost any process. Something that simply wouldn't warrant a traditional software delivery project can be achieved quickly with an LCNC application, bringing increased automation to all layers of the business.

As you might expect, there are also disadvantages, namely

- Poor performance – the executable code that is the output of LCNC platforms is not optimised to be efficient, secure or scalable – it's unlikely that organisations would choose to develop external, client-facing high-volume applications using this approach.
- Loss of control – with democratised development, there is a very real risk of a loss of control of what is being developed by whom and for what purpose – this can lead to undocumented applications, key person dependencies, duplication and version control problems.
- Poor user experience – the citizen developer may not always consider the user when designing the applications leading to a poor or confusing user experience
- Undocumented products – there's a risk that the citizen developer doesn't fully document the new applications or the processes that they support, keeping it all in their head. This creates a key person dependency and a risk for the organisation if the author leaves or moves roles.

Again, as for the choice between build and buy, there will be nuances as to whether a low-code/no-code build option makes sense. But as part of a controlled and varied approach to business automation, LCNC provides a credible option to supplement enterprise-wide, professionally developed software applications.

In many respects, this is not a new choice. The use of spreadsheet macros is rife in some (arguably most) organisations, with exactly the same benefits and drawbacks of LCNC – quick manipulation of data for reports and business information, with the downside being a proliferation of undocumented and unsupported pseudo-applications. LCNC simply makes the applications significantly prettier (and more user-friendly) than a spreadsheet macro.

Key Concepts in Software Design

In order to better appreciate the impacts that business drivers have on software design, it is useful to understand some of the building blocks that make up an application.

Some of the most important programming and design concepts are as follows:

- Iteration
- Subroutines
- Conditionals
- Structured programming
- Data types
- Input and output
- Object orientation and event-driven programming
- Exception-handling.

Iteration: One of the most important constructs in programming is the iteration or loop. From the very earliest mainframes processing a stack of punched cards, the ability for the computer to circle around and start again on the next record was crucial. Loops still feature in large numbers of programs, especially those featuring heavy data processing such as overnight updates and reports. In designing an iterative process, the programmer must

- Decide where the loop needs to start
- Decide what instructions to include within the loop and
- Decide the conditions to exit the looped process (such as when the loop has executed 50 times or when the last record on a file has been processed).

Loops can be nested so that one iteration is contained within another.

The precise commands will depend on the syntax of the programming language. Some common constructions include the WHILE loop, where the code specified in the body of the loop will execute "WHILE" a condition is true and a FOR loop where the loop will execute until the specified condition is true (another well-known "programmer-in-the-real-world" gag involves a programmer being told by her partner "While you're at the shop, get eggs" – she never came back).

The most critical part (and most common error) when coding an iteration is to correctly identify and manage the end condition. As for our programmer going to the shops, it's important to avoid an infinite loop or a loop that simply never executes because the end condition is already satisfied.

Subroutines: Sometimes it helps to write code that doesn't simply execute line by line. In early programming languages, it was helpful to write a section of code that could be invoked from the main logic (a subroutine). As programming languages became more sophisticated, it became possible to call the same subroutine with different parameters to produce a different result and eventually to build and access a library of existing procedures with either shared or isolated data attributes.

Depending on the programming language, these subroutines may also be called functions, procedures or methods, with subtle differences in behaviour.

The most important common attribute of these structures is that once the invoked subroutine has been executed, the flow of the program returns to the point where the subroutine was called.

Conditionals: A conditional statement in a computer program allows the programmer to introduce a decision into the logic. A conditional is typically defined as IF (condition) THEN (instruction). If the stated condition is true, then the software executes the conditional instruction(s).

In early languages, conditional statements were primitive (IF/THEN), but more sophisticated commands developed as languages matured. IF/THEN/ELSE allows a choice of commands, depending on whether the condition is true or not. Later languages support CASE statements, where a range of conditions can be specified, each with a resulting instruction.

This ability for program logic to branch depending on the state or value of its data is perhaps the key concept that turns computers from simple automata that execute a series of defined commands into digital assistants, machines capable of evaluating and responding to different stimuli.

IF you've got the concept of conditional branching, THEN go on to the next paragraph, ELSE go back to the top and start again. See what we did there?

Structured programming: Structured programming was an attempt to bring these three fundamental concepts together in a way that promoted readability and re-usability. The structured program theorem (broadly credited to a 1966 paper by Corrado Bohm and Giuseppe Jacopini, *Flow Diagrams, Turing Machines and Languages with Only Two Formation Rules*) states that any computable function can be expressed as a combination of three specific control structures:

- Sequence – executing one subroutine followed by another
- Selection – conditionally executing one of two subroutines
- Iteration – repeatedly executing a subroutine as long as a condition is true.

While early programs tended to be largely linear in nature, comprising merely a list of instructions, as the breadth and complexity of programmatic commands increased, a need was identified to adopt a structured approach to prevent programs from becoming unmanageable. The particular villain of the piece was the "GO TO" or "GOTO" command which simply redirects the execution flow of the program to a new line rather than the next one in the sequence. This differs from a subroutine which, once completed, returns to the point in the logical flow whence it was invoked. The GOTO command was vilified in an open letter[14] by early programming guru Dutch computer scientist Edsger W. Dijkstra, who noted that it was an "invitation to make a mess of one's program".

Dijkstra also noted that the programmer's involvement stopped when the code became live which is an understandable view, albeit one flavoured by the typical programs of the day which were perhaps more one-use. The real benefit of a structured approach comes when the same code needs to be maintained by a programmer other than the original author – the simpler the logic of the code, the easier it is to understand and enhance or fix at a later stage. In most instances, particularly in a business context, 50 lines of ordered, structured code is better than 10 lines of genius, but impenetrable, logic.

Data types: Ultimately, it is the job of software to interact with data. With the exception of the very simplest of programs, the purpose of executing the code is to take some existing data and to either amend it, generate new data from it or expose it in some way (such as to a screen or in a report). Data can be fixed within the program (such as a parameter that defines how the program should operate) or it can be a variable – accepting the result of a calculation or an input from an external database.

Most software languages require that data be structured into a number of data types. These data types constrain the values of data that can be held and also define how that data can be used.

Typical data types include

- Integers – any integer, which in some languages can be positive or negative (so for example, a 32-bit integer can range from −2,147,483,648 to 2,147,483,647)
- Floating point – an integer with an associated exponent (which denotes where the "point" is placed
- Strings (or characters) – text
- Booleans – binary data that is "true" (one) or "false" (zero).

Depending on the programming language, different data types can be subject to different operations. For example, strings can be manipulated in ways that do not make sense for integers (you might want to concatenate "John" and "Smith", but you wouldn't typically want to concatenate 123 and 1,000), whereas integers can be incremented (such as when being used as a counter for a loop).

Setting the correct data type for a variable can be crucial in making sure that the program uses the variable appropriately.

It's also something to be aware of when providing data to software engineers as part of a business project. Just because some of your data looks like a number, you can't always assume that it will behave as such. Dates and identifiers are particularly problematic. Dates can look like numbers but don't behave in the same way. For example, incrementing a date has specific rules: 20231231 plus 1 is 20240101 (always remember that a computer is a very fast idiot – unless you tell it that it's a date, it may give you 20231232). There is additional complexity in conversion between different formats. And identifiers or references that are purely numeric can cause issues when operated on programmatically, especially if there are leading zeroes involved to pad the number out to the right length.

Input and output: As well as manipulating data within a program, it's important to get data into and out of the program. Early input and output mechanisms were punched cards and printers. Later, programs would read records from files stored on magnetic tape, outputting a similar file of amended or derived data as a result.

With the introduction of the relational database, data access became far more sophisticated, supported by dedicated data access languages such as SQL. Modern software has to cater for a massive range of inputs ranging from mouse clicks, physical manipulation, real-time data from other applications or smart devices, as well as a range of relational and non-relational databases (also known as "NoSQL" databases) as well as outputs including screens, other applications and data files in a vast array of formats.

Object orientation and *event-driven programming*: With the advent of graphical interfaces came the seismic shift of software programming from linear, file-based processing to event-driven software that responded to user interaction. Applications in a business environment now typically follow one of two paradigms:

- Transactional applications where data and other screen processing is driven by an event on a screen such as a user pressing a key or clicking a mouse or by the receipt of a single small message from another application or device (also known as OLTP – Online Transactional Processing)
- Analytical applications where data is typically received as large files or retrieved from a database as records and processed sequentially (also known as OLAP – Online Analytical Processing).

Exception-handling: With so much complexity in terms of different commands, complex structures and hundreds of data variables of different types, as well as external data sources to manage, it's no wonder that software has a tendency to fail, especially during the early stages of testing. As well as logic errors (where the developer or designer has made a mistake), there can also be environmental errors, such as where a program finds itself locked out of a data source or where data is simply not in the right place or in the expected format.

In such cases, it's always better if the software application can fail safely rather than just collapse without warning, or even worse, carry on doing what it thinks it has been told to do. Quite apart from the fact that this limits the damage that can be done by a "rogue" application, it allows the state of the program at the time of failure to be recorded so that the issue can be properly analysed after the event and the root cause of the error can be fixed.

Most programs will operate with some kind of exception-handling logic in place, especially when reading or writing data externally to the program's environment. If an operation fails, the normal logic of the program is interrupted to execute a safe close down and recording of the error. This exception-handling is the only time that structured programming techniques can be sidestepped, although always with care to avoid expensive unexpected shutdowns.

The failed launch of an Ariane 5 rocket carrying millions of dollars' worth of satellite equipment in 1996 was identified as being due to an erroneously invoked exception that unnecessarily halted part of the rocket's guidance controls, causing the mission to abort. Ironically, the software itself was to control the rocket's speed on the way to the launch pad, rather than in flight.

Program Design – An Example

So how might all these concepts come together in an application? What are the things an application developer might need to think about when designing their software? We believe that an understanding of these concepts and how they influence program design, even at a simple level as shown here, will help you as a business leader to organise your thinking and define your requirements more clearly and in a more immediately applicable manner for your software developers.

Let's imagine that you're a software developer, part of a team that's been given the task of designing an application to build a shopping list for a regular weekly shopping trip.

First, let's assume that you have a perfect set of requirements from the business analysis team and that your users are certain about what they want in the application and how they want it to behave. See? We've already moved a long way from a typical scenario where software developers often have incomplete requirements and inconsistent stakeholders.

Let's first think about the inputs and outputs of the application. It needs to understand the date and time and who the user is – all of these can be inherited from the operating system as the application is started up.

The application will be on-screen, with all of the inputs and outputs that go with it. The user will move the mouse or tab between fields to select different products and then click to add them to the list. The application will need to manage these interactions, as well as posting the necessary data to the screen for the user to see.

As the user adds items to the list, the application will need to access an external database provided by the shop showing a picture of the product as well as a short description, its price and availability. If the requirements call for a balance check on the user's bank account, that data will need to be obtained through a call to some open banking software.

Finally, the application will need to save the user's finished list to the database and then allow them to print it out to take with them to the shops.

What data might our application need? The user's name and credentials, for sure. Their date of birth, perhaps, to allow them to buy age-restricted products. Maybe the requirements allow the user to specify some preferences to be applied when building the list. These data will need to be loaded at run time when the application starts up.

The graphical interface requires a vast amount of data: every window, field, button and label on the screen will need to be defined in terms of location, size, colour and behaviours. This part of the application might be developed using low-code, so that windows, buttons, and other screen artefacts can be easily defined using a drag-and-drop interface.

The shopping list itself has data associated with it. When was it made? Is it complete? Has it been printed off for use? How many items are on the list? What was the total cost?

Then there's the data for each item in the shopping list. Each item will need a unique code to identify it, some text description (how many characters are you going to allow?), a selected quantity and a unit price. Each product needs a number of flags against it to record allergens and other factors that might apply such as whether it is vegetarian or vegan in nature. Maybe there's a requirement to flag an item that's on special offer at the shop. Do these items need to be shown in a separate part of the screen to draw the user's attention to them?

Then there's the execution of the program to think about. There will be some activities that the application will need to complete every time it's started, then it will drop into an event-driven mode waiting for user input.

On start-up, the application will need to load system and user data and establish a connection to the outside world to get product data. What happens if that connection can't be established? We can't sit waiting for-ever – the application will need a time limit and then drop into offline mode. Then, the application will need to retrieve and display the user's latest or incomplete list to the screen, looping round each item in the list to get any necessary product data and then display it in the next slot on the screen.

Once the initial screen is displayed, the application will sit waiting for an event, which might be a user input (such as selecting a product, adding or reducing the quantity desired, resizing or closing a window or even exiting the application). Standard operations may be simple to program with a low-code tool, but the more specific events such as selecting a product will need a sequence of activities to be programmed such as retrieving the product data for display and adding the item to the shopping list.

Finally, the developer must think about how the application might be terminated. The program can't simply stop. Are there checks to perform? What data might need to be saved? The window needs to be closed down on screen and the environment tidied up neatly so no unwanted data is hanging around in the computer's memory.

And once the team has finished the application, it needs to be launched – making sure that it can connect to different environments and run on different computers and devices with different operating systems, as necessary.

Even then, the team's work is not over. The first users have got their hands on your application – there are bugs to fix and improvements to make. If the software hasn't been structured well and hasn't been documented prop-erly, how will the team know what needs to change?

Even in such a simple scenario, with clear requirements and an undemanding application, you can see that there are so many things that a software developer needs to think about. There's a lot that can go wrong. Your role as a business stakeholder is to help the development team by being clear on your requirements and to make sure you don't make their lives difficult by changing your mind.

The Rise of DevOps

It is this inextricable link between the development of software and its oper-ation in a production environment that has led to the concept of DevOps, literally the concatenation of Dev ("development") and Ops ("operations").

It is an approach that emphasises collaboration between the development and operations teams in order to streamline the software delivery lifecycle.

This collaboration is facilitated (and largely automated) by platforms such as Microsoft's Azure DevOps which provides tools to support the planning, coding, testing, deployment and monitoring of software with the goal of improving productivity and consistency, while reducing the incidence of errors. The DevOps cycle encourages continuous improvement through regular, small releases of software updates rather than large, monolithic updates.

The DevOps lifecycle involves a super-team executing a continuous loop of the following activities:

- Planning: identifying drivers for change and future needs
- Coding: small changes to code are made to meet the requirements
- Build: the disparate bits of code are put together as a release candidate
- Testing: testing of the applications through user acceptability testing, operational testing and other forms of testing
- Release: the software is deployed into the operational environment
- Deployment: the built application is published to the user community
- Operation: the DevOps team looks after the operational code and related hardware configuration
- Monitoring: observation of user behaviour and the effectiveness of the application to drive future change.

The DevOps culture includes a dedicated team to support software through its life (not just during its development) using collaboration tools and dashboards to rapidly and safely manage business-critical applications. This culture necessarily takes time (and money!) to implement and bed in, but the results tend to be faster code deliveries that are safer and more secure for the organisation, providing the capability for the business to quickly flex as needed.

Hello World!

Just as a bit of fun, here are all of the programming languages featured in this chapter, demonstrating the same very simple program, namely the printing of "Hello World!".

FORTRAN

```
C      Hello World in Fortran

       PROGRAM HELLO
       WRITE (*,100)
       STOP
100    FORMAT (' Hello World! ' /)
       END
```

ALGOL

```
'BEGIN'
       'COMMENT' Hello World in Algol 60;
       OUTPUT(4,'(''('Hello World!')',/')')
'END'
```

COBOL

```
       * Hello World in COBOL

***************************
IDENTIFICATION DIVISION.
PROGRAM-ID. HELLO.
ENVIRONMENT DIVISION.
DATA DIVISION.
PROCEDURE DIVISION.
MAIN SECTION.
DISPLAY "Hello World!"
STOP RUN.
***************************
```

RPG

```
// Hello world in RPG IV version 7.1

dcl-s wait char(1);

dsply ( 'Hello World!') ' ' wait;

*inlr = *on;
```

BASIC

```
10 REM Hello World in BASIC
20 PRINT "Hello World!"
```

MUMPS

```
; Hello World in Mumps-M
w !,"Hello World"
```

C

```
/* Hello World in C, Ansi-style */

#include <stdio.h>
#include <stdlib.h>

int main(void)
{
  puts("Hello World!");
  return EXIT_SUCCESS;
}
```

C++

```
// Hello World in ISO C++

#include <iostream>

int main()
{
  std::cout << "Hello World!" << std::endl;
}
```

VisualBASIC

```
REM Hello World in Visual Basic for Windows

VERSION 2.00
Begin Form Form1
  Caption        =   "Form1"
  ClientHeight   =   6096
  ClientLeft     =   936
  ClientTop      =   1572
```

```
ClientWidth     =    6468
Height          =    6540
Left            =    876
LinkTopic       =    "Form1"
ScaleHeight     =    6096
ScaleWidth      =    6468
Top             =    1188
Width           =    6588
Begin Label Label1
  Caption         =    "Hello World!"
  Height          =    372
  Left            =    2760
  TabIndex        =    0
  Top             =    2880
  Width           =    972
End
End
Option Explicit
```

Java
```
// Hello World in Java

class HelloWorld {
  static public void main( String args[] ) {
    System.out.println( "Hello World!" );
  }
}
```

Python
```
# Hello world in Python 2
print "Hello World"
```

SWIFT
```
// Hello world in Swift

println("Hello, world!")
```

With thanks to www.helloworldcollection.de.

WHERE NEXT?

Software design and practice will continue to evolve, with commoditisation, collaboration and personalisation as key themes.

A lot has been written about generative AI, and the potential this has on changing the way software will be designed and used. There are edge cases for possible interactions between generative AI and software design that fill the human mind with thrill and dread in equal measure (*Terminator*, anyone?), but the reality is likely to be more prosaic.

Generative AI, in whatever circumstance it might be used, still has to cope with one of the iron rules of computer science, GIGO: garbage in, garbage out, as depicted by Charles Babbage in his *Passages from the Life of a Philosopher*[15]:

> On two occasions I have been asked, "Pray, Mr. Babbage, if you put into the machine wrong figures, will the right answers come out?" … I am not able rightly to apprehend the kind of confusion of ideas that could provoke such a question.

The antidote to our fever-dream AI panic might indeed be rooted in this practical answer. Software must have requirements clearly stated before anything can be coded. And requirements are a uniquely human attribute: after all, it's emotions (rather than logic) that give rise to desires, hopes, ambitions, grief, despair etc., and it's from here that requirements arise. Emotions are not intelligence but feelings. Our view is that requirements, therefore, need a sensual creator and are unlikely to come from generative AI, which looks for patterns and aims to copy and expand on them.

The so-called "Internet of Things" (IoT) provides a useful clue as to how software might be significantly changed in the next decade. By synchronising all devices fully (not just at the cloud drive or browser level, for example), there is scope for better and more all-pervasive collaboration between software, meaning that interoperability becomes ever more important. Creating that interoperability will be a challenge, as it is with humans speaking different languages. But a universal software that all applications can use on any database would be a significant step forward.

So where might software, its design and perhaps more importantly its availability from vendors either as a product or as a service, be going in the years ahead?

Software as a Partnership?

There has been a continual shift in software development away from the businesses that eventually use it.

The initial spate of new languages in the late twentieth century was replaced by businesses using common languages to build bespoke software. Then a range of visual software products to meet commoditised needs such as accounting and office administration were marketed first as products and latterly as a service.

Where next?

First, software applications can last for a long time (many banks and financial institutions still rely at their core on applications written 60 years ago), and this inertia can mean that the pace of change of software in these organisations is naturally inhibited.

Second, we can expect the range of business services that fall within the commoditised sphere to increase. From generic products such as emails and word processing, the scope of globally available all-pervading products has increased to include financial systems, human resources and client relationship management (CRM) systems. In addition, standardised workflow tools can be bought off-the-shelf and then tailored by business users to serve their own specific needs.

Third, as more complex business needs are met by the SaaS model, the relationship between the supplying and consuming organisations will necessarily become one of partnership rather than simply software provision. For these more tailored applications, the simple rollout across the market of updates which need to be accepted in order to continue to use the product will be replaced by collaborative software implementations between the software vendor and their long-term client, the impacted business.

And finally, software applications themselves will become more modular and flexible, with a range of individual applications that can be configured and deployed as needed by the consuming business. There is a risk, of course, that this very flexibility will lead to a proliferation of requirements, with modules being implemented that would previously have been included only in the "nice to have" vein. It will be incumbent on business sponsors and users to be self-police and ensure that the organisation only takes on a software product that enhances its capabilities at an affordable cost.

These factors all combine to suggest that software changes in most organisations will be more likely if the software service providers take a more partnership-oriented role than hitherto. For all but the most commoditised of products, rather than seeing each business as an opportunity to maximise short-term profit, vendors and service providers should look to become genuine partners to organisations, ensuring that modular, configurable products are made available that align more exactly to the client's needs.

More Collaboration across the Enterprise

The recent rise of integration and collaboration tools such as DevOps and GitHub will continue, particularly given the commensurate rise in remote working following the COVID-19 pandemic. The concept (and tooling) of DevOps in particular, with its focus on integration between development and operations, will continue to become embedded into organisations to bring development and operations closer together.

For many years, the paradigm of software delivery being entirely separate from the operation and monitoring of the production application has led to a schism between the application development teams and the rest of the business. By ensuring that a single, dedicated team supports the entire development lifecycle throughout, organisations can encourage all participants to share at all times in the responsibility of managing their software.

This will inevitably help business users to be more connected to the software development process, which will in turn encourage a simpler and more direct approach to requirements definition. The continued interaction between the users and designers of the applications will lead to a shared responsibility.

Software for Business Users

With DevOps, software developers will move closer to business users in a combined team that manages applications throughout their lifecycle, not just during development.

The corollary will also be true: business users will move closer to software developers by learning new skillsets such as SQL and Power BI. While these capabilities don't require a full appreciation of programming (such as the components of structured programming such as sequencing, selection and iteration), they will inevitably enhance the business user's appreciation of the structure, relationships and quality of their data, which, as we have seen, is a fundamental component of good coding.

This familiarity with both the underlying data and some of the logical structures and techniques required for creating SQL commands or Power BI dashboards and reports can only help during discussions with technical professionals as part of any further development of the applications used by the business.

The Rise of the Citizen Developer

This movement of business professionals towards a "self-serve" mentality will also manifest in the growth of LCNC platforms, creating a hybrid role of business application developers from the business teams themselves, so-called citizen developers.

Initially, organisations would do well to ensure that these enthusiastic amateurs are closely supported by technology professionals to ensure that a degree of rigour is applied. Applications should only be attempted that add value and each should be fully documented and centrally logged to avoid duplication of effort. Each application should have a clear owner who is responsible for its upkeep, with a defined succession plan in place should the owner move on or leave the organisation.

It will also be important to ensure that these applications form part of the overall data strategy of the organisation, and that data – especially personal data – does not sidestep the rigorous controls required by increasingly demanding regulation.

The platforms themselves will inevitably support this drive towards increased control, ensuring that they support relevant security and compliance requirements. Platforms will also become more sophisticated, incorporating AI and machine learning to make the process of application design easier and more intuitive.

Platforms will also become easier to integrate with the rest of the technology estate, with communication and data protocols to support easy extraction of data and workflow links to other "mainstream" applications.

The use of low-code and perhaps especially no-code for proof-of-concept development, or prototyping will also grow. Business users will be able to create working mock-ups of the applications they envisage, before passing the working model to professional developers to build using full-stack development tools and methodologies.

On the other hand, smaller organisations may be able to fully support their bespoke application development needs with LCNC platforms, avoiding the costs of professional development teams entirely.

SO WHAT?

How does this impact you, the business leader?

What are the calls that you will be asked to make about software development? What influence can you have over the technology professionals in your organisation?

Well, for a start, you almost certainly need to get more involved with the decisions they are already making on your behalf. What software is your organisation already supporting and developing that may or may not be aligned with your business goals and strategies? Is the business fully represented on projects developing its own future technology estate?

As with the other chapters in this book, the questions that you need to ask yourself (and other key stakeholders in your organisation) are nuanced: there is probably no right or wrong answer (with the possible exception of "should we design our own programming language?" to which the answer is almost certainly "no").

But answering – or at least considering – the following questions may help to ensure that your organisation follows a prudent path when buying or building applications.

Questions to ask *before* buying or building new software:

- Do I really need new software?
- Is my business need unique?
- Is there an available software product that meets my needs?
- Is customising or building software within the core competency of my organisation?

Questions to ask *when* buying or building new software:

- Who is choosing the software?
- Can I simplify the scope of the software?
- Can I reduce the complexity of the software?
- How customisable is the software (and how customisable do I need it to be)?
- What happens when things go wrong?
- How easy is it to maintain the software? (regular updates, code branches, scalability etc.)
- Do I have an operating model in place to support my new software?

Do I Really Need New Software?

This is the key question.

Now, you might be a startup or a business that is branching out into new territory. Software might be a fundamental part of your growth strategy. That may give you a clear need.

But in the vast majority of cases, software is bought or built to replace existing applications. Here is where organisations really need to examine their motivations and drivers.

Too often, existing software is replaced when in fact it's not the software that's the problem. It might be data quality that's the real issue or the other applications that surround the software you're looking to replace. Or it might be your processes or controls in the teams that use the software.

Is there even a problem that needs to be solved? Many an executive attending a conference or trade show has had their head turned by a shiny piece of computer kit and a flashy application accompanied by the polished patter of the vendor's best salesperson (which really does happen – a lot). But just because there is newer (and quite possibly better) software out there doesn't mean that your existing software doesn't do the job.

Replacing software is risky and expensive. It's not like replacing a car, where you can simply turn up in the old model and drive off the forecourt in a gleaming new convertible. Not only does the new software have to link to the rest of your technology estate, but you will also need to get data out of the old software and into the new as well as train your team on its use and upkeep, to mention just a few of the potential burdens on top of the cost of the software itself. If there's a "car on the forecourt" analogy, it would be that you need the car to tow a caravan, so you must first hook it up, and there's a whole bunch of camping gear in the boot that you need to transfer from the old car to the new. And maybe the new car has a manual gear-change so you need to learn how to drive again.

Before you commit to this vast drain on your organisation's time and money, consider whether you have a real problem that needs to be fixed, and fixed now, and whether there are alternatives to software development. You might also consider

- Upgrades to your existing software – is the vendor about to release an upgrade that will fix your current issues? Upgrading (rather than replacing) will come in at a fraction of the cost with a much lower risk.
- Training for your users – are you sure you are using the existing product to the best of its capabilities? Maybe the problem is in your use of it and not in the software itself.
- Fixing your data – all too often it is data that's the real cause of issues – is the data arriving into the system from upstream applications? Can they be fixed to provide better data? Can applications be linked with interfaces to automate the propagation of data around the system and eliminate re-keying errors? A few simple data quality checks might address the vast majority of your data issues and allow you to focus on the real problems rather than bringing in new software that will face exactly the same problems with poor data quality.
- Delaying the software build – is this a problem that needs to be fixed right now? All organisations have a capacity to absorb change: how much else is going on in your world at the moment? Is this going to be the project that breaches your capacity and throttles the motivation and energy of your change professionals as well as your user community?
- Building supporting applications – you may be able to build some supporting applications (using low-code platforms or business intelligence software such as Power Apps) that allow you to streamline or fix your processes. These could be workflows that automate handoffs between teams (rather than emails which can be mistyped or forgotten), simple form-based applications that allow data to be input in a structured way, process automation tools that can extract data from one location and structure it for input into another application

without the need for human intervention or reports that help to high-light where there are backlogs or bottlenecks.

Only after you've looked into all of these options and you determine that you will still have a problem, should you think about buying or building new software.

Simple, isn't it? But you'd be amazed at the sheer number of organisations that overreach themselves with a technology change agenda that they just can't deliver, for software that they simply don't need.

Is My Business Need Unique?

Some businesses are truly unique or operate in a narrow field of competitors. There aren't many NASAs out there, or Metas or Googles.

These organisations will have highly specialised, unique needs.

But most organisations don't operate that way. Most businesses can iden-tify many similar organisations as themselves whose needs are aligned or even exactly the same. Accountants, solicitors, hospitals, retail – each will have processing needs that are similar for all competitors, at the most basic level. What differentiates them is how that service is delivered, not the soft-ware that enables it.

If you've identified that new software is needed, it will help to under-stand whether that software is something that will provide your business with a unique advantage over its competitors, or whether it simply enables the business to function, in a similar way to your competition. For a retail business, supply chain management, while critical, may not be anything more than an enabler, whereas the quality of the corporate website is likely to be a differentiator for customers. Unless, of course, you believe that your unique advantage lies in a fully automated supply chain management pro-cess using distributed ledgers and AI – in which case, crack on.

The more unique your business, or the particular part of the business that will be served by the software, the more likely it is that you will need to build your own application rather than be able to find an off-the-shelf product.

But even then, you need to be very sure before you commit to the self-build route. Just because you think that the website is a unique point doesn't mean you can't buy one off-the-shelf and customise it with your own graphics and style – it might be just as unique as if you had built it yourself, at a much-reduced cost.

It's worth taking the time to identify what is truly different about your business or its needs before deciding to meet those needs through a software build. And once you've identified what it is about your business, or this particular part of your business, that's special, challenge yourself again. Is it so special that it's worth spending a lot of money on bespoke software to deliver or support it?

Is There an Available Software Product That Meets My Needs?

So you've decided you need some software, and you've challenged yourself on whether you are fulfilling a commoditised or a specific need. But even for standardised requirements, there simply may not be the right software product out there.

Or worse, there may be two similar products that each meet your requirements, and you need to choose between them.

How do you go about proving that the software product fits your needs?

For the near-ubiquitous highly commoditised need, there are likely to be large numbers of reviews and opportunities to view the software, and choosing between multiple options may simply be a question of cost or compatibility with your other software.

Where the need is less generic, there may be key differences in the functional support for your requirements between different vendors' software packages. There may also be technical or security thresholds that one or other application does not meet.

It may be difficult to compare these different products objectively. You may be more familiar with one of the products than another. It's very easy for confirmation bias to creep in – the subconscious reinforcement of your existing preference. But does that mean it's the right tool for your organisation? Can it fit in with your other applications? Is cost more important than functionality? Which vendor is more suitable for your organisation?

The way to resolve these and other questions fairly and objectively is through a process that almost no one enjoys: the Request for Proposal, or RFP. You could write a book about the RFP process (in fact, a lot of people have), and we can't go into all of the detailed nuances here. What we can do is highlight what's important in the process from a business perspective.

Most of the books you might find are written from the viewpoint either of the project team conducting the RFP or of the vendor in responding to it. What value can the business stakeholder add – what are the key questions that you need to ask and how should you interpret the results?

A good RFP should cover broadly the following areas:

- Functional fit
- Technical suitability
- Vendor health
- Implementation capability
- Commercial
- Community and environmental considerations.

Functional fit – does the software do the job? This is often the initial focus of attention. And, of course, it matters that the software does what you need it to do: otherwise discard it from the process. The project team will launch into an exhaustive – and exhausting – function point analysis for that very reason. But with your help, that functional analysis needn't take up a disproportionate amount of time. With your help, the team can zone in on the two or three key features that will really make a difference to you, your colleagues or your clients. Take the time – think about what matters. Which features are purely "hygiene" (an issue if they're not present, but not a differentiator)? Which features have the "wow" factor? Do this analysis up front, and then be clear to the project team. They are looking for this guidance and will be grateful for it.

Technical suitability – does the software fit into your technical estate and meet your technical and security criteria? Just like our old friend George Boole, this is really a binary question. Either the product will fit into your world, or it won't. It's a bit like downloading an Android app for an Apple iPhone – some things just won't work. This one is probably better left to the technologists ....

Vendor health – can the vendor supply and support the software? This criterion is all about the vendor or supplier of the software. What's their track record like on delivering or implementing? Who else in your line of business has implemented their software and how did it go? Or is doing so now, taking up more of the vendor's precious resources? How financially and organisationally secure is the vendor? These are important questions – the project team will be relying on you for your knowledge and understanding: they aren't the experts in the field – you are. You may have used the software at another organisation or know a close and reliable contact elsewhere who uses it now. Does it actually work? You will know which organisations are similar to your own. The project team don't know any of these things. Although the vendor will have provided data in their response, your relevant knowledge will be invaluable in picking out where there may be inaccuracies or omissions.

Implementation capability – both for the vendor and your own organisation. At first sight, these may not seem to be areas where you can add value. But remember that the project team don't have the history and experience that you have in the business. You may be able to provide useful input from other sites where the vendor has implemented (or tried to implement) the same software. In terms of your own organisation's ability to implement, it's important to not just focus on the software itself, but the organisational and operational change that goes with it. How ready are your colleagues to adopt the new working practices? How will team structures and individual roles need to change? Is the product intuitive or will there need to be comprehensive training provided? Your input and insight on these topics will be crucial.

Commercial – total cost both of the implementation and of operating the software plus other terms and conditions. Sometimes, it all comes down to cost. As with other factors, it's important not to focus exclusively on the software. What incidental costs might the business need to bear? On the other hand, are there costs that the business has currently that would be avoided with one product over another? You can help the project team ensure a like-for-like costing, avoiding the egregious mistake of comparing apples with pears.

Community and environmental considerations – in many ways the most important criterion but also the hardest to evaluate. How aligned is the vendor with your organisation? Are its goals and aspirations heading in the same direction? If you're looking to expand into a market that the vendor is planning to get out of, it's not likely that your long-term relationship will prosper. Is there a community of users who can help you through your implementation and operational journey, or are you going to have to go it alone? The project team will look to you to corroborate what the vendor is telling them.

Is Customising or Building Software within the Core Competency of My Organisation?

Finally, in trying to decide whether to buy in your software or build it yourself, it's worth asking whether such engineering really falls within the competency of your organisation. If you have an army of developers and project professionals raring to go, and the budget to sustain them in the years ahead as they support your native product through the inevitable operational incidents and market-driven changes, then building may be the right option for you.

If you will need to source in a development capability and find yourself reaching for the "Project Management for Dummies" 2024 edition, you may want to look again at one of those vendors and their not-quite-fit-for-purpose products that would probably do the job you need perfectly well.

Who Is Choosing the Software?

It's really important that the right people are in the chair to make the eventual choice of the software (regardless of whether you are building or buying).

A common perception in organisations is that the technologists get to choose the software, and they want to do exciting, shiny innovation. The actual business need is "boring", and the tech guys just aren't interested in that.

Ultimately, the choice should be down to the business sponsor, but the wise sponsor will take advice from the relevant teams. Technology teams can advise on technology aspects such as data security and ease of integration. Project teams can advise on implementation and expected ease of configuration and build. You and your business colleagues can consider ease of use and perhaps some wider context such as strategic partnerships.

If any of these teams identify a clear red flag, then you need to listen to them. But otherwise, a nuanced view (perhaps aided by a logically designed scorecard) is the best way to reach a decision.

Can I Simplify the Scope of the Software?

You've decided that you have a problem and that you need a software product to resolve it. Great. But whether you're building or buying, you need to make sure that the scope and scale of the solution is appropriate to the original problem. Just like our shopping example above, you need to know when to stop. If your problem is solved by a dashboard or a report, build the report and leave it at that. If your problem is solved by adding one module to your existing office management suite, don't end up adding three or four modules, or replacing the whole suite with something newer and shinier.

As a business leader, it's up to you to help the project team to understand how much is enough.

Even if your eyes are fixed on a longer term goal, can you get there in stages? Is there a minimum viable product (MVP) that will release efficiency or growth benefits for your organisation, which then might give you the room to attack the next phase? It's a win–win scenario.

The agile approach to project delivery can really help here – with iterative, incremental builds allowing you (in theory at least) to stop at any time with a viable piece of software that works within the rest of your operating model to solve all or part of your problem.

Can I Reduce the Complexity of the Software?

As well as reducing the scope of the solution (do less), you can be instrumental in reducing its complexity (do it more simply).

We've seen that one of the key constructs in programming is the conditional clause – every branch in the logic adds complexity. It may feel like the right thing to do to keep options open when defining your requirements, but life becomes easier for everyone in the project team if you are able to identify a single logical path.

Try to reduce the number of data fields needed: every variable has to be defined, populated and stored – if it's never really used for anything, it's just taking up space in the software and time in the project.

This is a tough challenge – often you won't realise that you've over-engineered a process until it's too late – the screen looks too cluttered, or the report is too messy, or the project is simply taking too long to implement. Ask yourself early on where you can remove complexity and stick to it.

How Customisable Is the Software (and How Customisable Do I Need It To Be)?

If you're buying a product, you may need to make some changes so that it works in your organisation. These might be regional or local requirements, or it might simply be that the software allows for different ways to achieve an outcome (maybe through workflows or with different data sets).

It may be an important factor for you to understand just how easy it is to customise in this way. Many software products can now be tweaked through low-code amendments – dragging and dropping stages in a process or creating new data fields.

If you're going to customise the software heavily, this may be a factor that helps you decide which product to buy.

But should you be customising at all?

What's so special about the way that you and your organisation perform a process that means you need it to be done differently from all the supplier's other clients? Before you customise, think about whether the native out-of-the-box solution is good enough.

Every customisation takes you further away from the standard product that the vendor supports – it takes time and effort to customise and test, and then takes time and effort again when the software needs to be upgraded a year later.

If in doubt – don't.

What Happens When Things Go Wrong?

When designing software, it's all too easy to focus on what should happen when everything works. Your project team will call this the "happy path", and they should also be encouraging you to think about what happens when things go wrong.

Time spent on identifying and catering for these "unhappy paths" (or better yet, preventing them) is never wasted and will yield untold dividends in terms of time and user experience when the software is in operation.

Applications or systems can fail for a vast number of reasons – a component of the underlying hardware could fail, or one piece of software may not find the data it needs to start up, or the software could simply have a bug in it that causes downstream applications to crash. A lot of the time the system behaves exactly how it should, and the "error" lies with the user: PICNIC ("problem in chair, not in computer"). This could be down to training or a "fat finger" issue where the user knows exactly what to do but does the wrong thing by accident.

Ideally, every possible error needs to be catered for using software exceptions – each of which costs time and money to design, code and test.

These could be preventative checks (such as validation on input fields or consistency checks on data before the user is allowed to press the "Next" button) or detective controls (such as error-handling in each application and in the interfaces between different applications, timeouts when a procedure call gets no response from the invoked application or database, or next-day reports that search the database for inconsistencies and omissions).

It's not necessarily your job to cover all of these (the more technical cases should be standard fare for your developers or even managed by the software or operating system itself), but you do need to think about the more common errors, especially where user input is involved. You know the data, the processes and the teams of users (or at least you are representing their interests on the project) – where are the mistakes likely to creep in? It's always better to prevent an error from happening than to manage the consequences, so think about validation on each user operation, or designing the interface so as to reduce the likelihood of errors. Good design will eradicate a number of likely errors without the need for exceptions – think of a door that opens away from you and says "Push" but is still fitted with a handle, enticing you to try to pull the door open (error).

So, have a think: which data fields might be inherently confusing or complex (such as a reference or an identifier)? Where do the team currently make the most mistakes? Is it obvious to the user which fields on a screen are mandatory? Are the labels meaningful and helpful? Can you add tips or other text to help explain what the user should do next?

And what about those error messages? How many times have you seen messages like "Field missing", or "Unknown Error" or "Fail: 56X#0032" flashing on the screen and having no idea what's gone wrong or how to fix it? Frustrating, no? Building a library of meaningful, contextual error messages that are helpful to the user is critical, and your input could be vital.

And for every error, there needs to be a process to recover from it. The more technical failures might need a technical response (rebooting a server, replacing some parts) but other errors, especially data errors, are likely to need remediation by the application's users. Again, your knowledge of the business will help here: who's the right person to identify and analyse the errors in each case, and who is the right person to fix them? Should this be a "hit squad" dedicated to corrections of all types, or should the issue be routed back to the original perpetrator to clean up their own mess? These are business decisions, and that's on you as the business stakeholder.

How Easy Is It to Maintain the Software?

Very little stays the same in the world of technology. Your shiny new product will soon be blowing out a candle on its first birthday cake, and it will be time to update it. This may be to cater for an operating system upgrade, or it may be that the product itself needs to be uplifted to meet external demands. You may even have requested some changes to it yourself, to enhance the process.

Maintaining software is hard.

Often, these updates will need a project all on their own, with problem statements, requirements-gathering, development, testing and implementation.

So before you decide which package to buy or build, make sure that there is a clear roadmap and that the vendor (or your own internal development team) will support you through future changes, with documentation, training guides and most importantly a clear change process.

It's worth understanding the cycle of change and discussing with the vendor (or your own team) whether that's appropriate. Some products have annual or quarterly scheduled changes only (with the option of "hot fixes" for dramatic incidents between these dates). Other products operate a rolling and continual program of change with multiple tiny software updates every day.

Do I Have an Operating Model in Place to Support My New Software?

Finally, before you allow the new product to become operational, you will need to make sure that the operational teams are ready for it.

If you've built customised software yourself or with an implementation partner, this is where DevOps (or an approach like it) really helps, as operational teams are involved throughout the development process.

Regardless, your project team should be making sure that they are ready to hand over support for the new application(s) to the operations teams.

As a business leader, you can help the teams understand the parameters of this support. What volumes are you expecting? Can you phase the uptake of the software to give the teams a "soft landing"? What processes do you see as having the most risk of error or failure? Do you need to provide extra training or arrange for "floorwalkers" to be on hand in the first few days of operation?

By thinking about how and when the software will be used, you can help to smooth the transition from a development and implementation project into a perfectly running machine, where application and operational terms work in perfect harmony.

NOTES

1 *Rabdologiæ* by John Napier, 1617.
2 *Mirifici Logarithmorum Canonis Descriptio* John Napier, 1614.
3 *When Computers Were Women* by Jennifer S Light, 1999.
4 *On Computable Numbers* by Alan Turing, 1936.
5 *A History of Manchester Computers* by Simon Lavington, 1998.
6 *Introduction to the History of Computing* by Gerard O'Regan, 2016, ISBN 978-3-319-33137-9.
7 *Introduction to the History of Computing* by Gerard O'Regan, 2016, ISBN 978-3-319-33137-9.
8 *Hints on programming Language Design* by CAR Hoare, 1973.
9 *Women of Wisdom: Grace Murray Hopper* by Lynn Gilbert, 2012.
10 https://archive.org/details/byte-magazine-the-next-step-article-march-1989
11 *Evolving a language in and for the real world: C++* by Brian Stroustrup, 1991-2006, Texas A&M University.
12 www.bricklin.com
13 *Computerworld*, August 1999.
14 A Case against the GO TO Statement, published as *Go-to statement considered harmful* in 1968 by Edsger W Dijkstra.
15 *Passages from the Life of a Philosopher* by Charles Babbage, 1864.

3

What's Data?

Information is the oil of the 21st century, and analytics is the combustion engine.

**Peter Sondergaard, Senior Vice President and
Global Head of Research at Gartner, Inc.**

Data is like garbage. You'd better know what you are going to do with it before you collect it.

Mark Twain

Jonathon took his data cleansing responsibilities very seriously.

DOI: 10.4324/9781003372660-3

Data, it seems, is everywhere. Ubiquitous. All-pervading.

Data about you and me; data about our money; data about our television viewing habits or our musical or literature preferences; data about where we've been, how we got there, who we spoke to, what we said and what we did.

There's even data about data.

Half a century ago, at the birth of the information technology industry, data was a precious resource – vital to make the machinery function, used (and stored) only sparingly. This sparsity gained brief notoriety at the turn of the century with the "Y2K bug" or "millennium bug". Both names are misnomers. The root cause of the problem was the representation of any given year as a two-digit number (YY) as opposed to four (YYYY) to save space on databases and in messages. Many computer programs were coded to perform a calculation on the assumption that the missing two digits were a 1 and a 9. These programs would start to produce unreliable results as soon as those two digits could be a 2 and a 0 for a twenty-first century date. So the issue was triggered by the change to a new century – the fact that it was also the turn of the millennium was coincidental. And strictly speaking, a bug is a software or coding error, whereas the problem at hand was a design compromise knowingly employed to save space (but arguably the "centennial compromise issue" wouldn't have sold as many newspapers). Since then, the capability to store, transport and process data has grown exponentially. Data no longer constrains design and its usage has expanded well beyond the boundaries of its original purpose to drive software applications, becoming a valuable resource in its own right.

Data is king.

Knowledge is power.

It's worth noting that these are not the same thing. Knowledge and data are not synonymous. Some would argue that they aren't even directly related or adjacent to each other – that there's a step in between: information.

The DIKW pyramid ("data, information, knowledge, wisdom") is a useful construction to help explain these differences. It proposes a hierarchy with data at the lowest level, leading to information, then to knowledge and finally to wisdom at the apex.

Data can be seen to be pure facts. There is no extrapolation or context involved. A transaction on a ledger for the sum of £500 three days ago is data.

Information begins to supplement the raw data by making it meaningful. The fact that the ledger represents a bank account and the transaction is a debit represents information.

Knowledge begins to form a context around the data and may involve extrapolation, patterns or draw from other data or information that is external to the datum itself. The fact that the bank account in question is your own joint account that you share with your partner, and the debit represents a purchase in a shop you know you didn't visit on the date in question are both matters of knowledge.

Wisdom is perhaps the most elusive and subjective of all – the critical decision as to exactly what to do with the knowledge that has been gathered. Is it wise to confront your partner on the purchase in question? That's something that only you can decide....

The value of data increases the further up the DIKW pyramid you travel.

Another way to think about the difference between data and information is to imagine your favourite book reprinted but drastically rearranged so that every single letter is placed in alphabetical order instead of forming words, sentences and chapters as originally set out. The reprinted book contains exactly the same data as the original but is worthless as a source of information (or indeed joy).

In an IT context, data is often assumed to be that which can be *stored*, *transported* or *used* electronically. It's worth bearing in mind that this is only part of the data story: not only is there data that sits outside the digital domain, there is also the interpretation applied to the collective well of data, its extrapolation into information, knowledge and eventually – with luck – wisdom that really matters.

This chapter takes a look at data and how it is stored, passed around and used in modern technology contexts.

There's a short analysis of its history, and the current state of play. Data maturity is still very low in most organisations. Accordingly, there's a great deal of potential for future growth and innovation.

As usual, the chapter draws to a close with some key questions that you, as a business leader, should be asking about your data, your management of it and its value to your organisation.

WHY SHOULD I CARE?

Data has become a commodity – it is both the raw material and the product of the machinery of the information revolution.

As a business leader, *you own your data*, so it's vitally important that you understand just how valuable (and vulnerable) it is.

Without reliable data, your applications won't work as expected. As more and more processes are automated, the accuracy and completeness of your data – as well as establishing who owns and manages it and who resolves data issues – will become ever more critical to business operations.

And as valuable as your data is to you and your organisation, it may be even more valuable to those outside it. It's equally important to be able to protect your data from those who seek it through nefarious means as it is to manage it and package it for those who might be able to use it in partnership or through a commercial relationship.

Used properly, your data will help you to develop more efficient processes, better define your target markets or ideal consumers or products. But use it improperly, and you may fall foul of a host of layered and increasingly complex regulations that seek to ensure data is kept, transmitted and used appropriately and safely.

There's still a great deal of mystery about data. Terms like "big data", "data science", "data analytics" and "data governance" are all relatively new and many are used somewhat interchangeably.

As a business leader, and potentially a key stakeholder on an IT project that will either rely on existing data or change how it is gathered, stored, transported or used, it would be helpful for you to understand data and data management.

HOW DID WE GET HERE?

Almost since there has been conscious thought, humans have felt the need to record data.

Data itself, of course, has been around a good deal longer – the light from distant quasars is billions of years old, reaching back to the birth of the universe, and every photon contains a wealth of data for those with a mind (and the wherewithal) to look.

But only a tiny portion of those early records remain available to us today.

Ancient Data – Sticks, Stones and Bones

The first known data stores date from the Palaeolithic era: bone tally sticks, discovered in Africa and central Europe. The Lebombo bone (around 40,000 BCE) is a baboon's fibula carved with 29 notches. The Ishango bone (around 20,000 years later) appears to have tally marks carved in columns.

Cave paintings, again in Africa and Europe from the same era, could very well have been a means to record data. By representing those animals that are good to hunt and kill, the ancient painters perhaps sought to pass information to their descendants, along with markings that may denote the passage of Moon to indicate the seasonal nature of the herds.

Henges of stone, arrayed to align perfectly with the midsummer and/or midwinter sun are complex data stores, recording the passage of the days, months and years. The earliest found to date, Warren Field in Scotland, dates from around 8,000 BC, pre-dating Stonehenge by about 6,000 years.

The first recorded writing was also in stone, recorded by citizens of Sumer in Mesopotamia, the fertile land between the Tigris and Euphrates rivers. Sumerian cuneiform and Egyptian hieroglyphs (3,400–3,100 BC) were carved in tablets (stele) of stone or clay.

But if we are talking about stone, and about data, there can be only one winner – possibly the most famous of all, the Rosetta Stone. Inscribed in 196 BC with an edict from King Ptolemy V to be housed in a temple on the banks of the Nile Delta, the stone was reused as building material for a medieval fort on the coast near the town of Rashid (Rosetta) and was eventually discovered in 1799 by Pierre-François Bouchard, a French officer in Napoleon's Grande Armée. Crucially, the edict had been carved into the stone in three languages: Ancient Egyptian hieroglyphic and Demotic scripts, along with Ancient Greek. Data is valueless without meaning, and it was the existence of the third text, in the well-studied Ancient Greek, that allowed scholars to eventually unlock the meaning of the Egyptian hieroglyphic and Demotic languages. The Rosetta Stone truly was the first data dictionary. Thankfully, Bouchard recognised its importance and arranged for it to be transported to Cairo for study.

Data as the Written Word

For centuries, the most common form of data storage was in the written word, mostly as religious texts or books, such as the Bible or the Koran, or historical documents. With manual translation and even duplication in the same language, inevitably errors crept in.

An example that clearly demonstrates the potential for divergence in written works is the Anglo-Saxon Chronicle. The chronicle is believed to have originally been a single document written in the ninth century to record the history of the Anglo-Saxon peoples from the fall of the Roman empire through to the reign of King Alfred the Great and beyond. Copies were made and carried to different parts of England, whereupon they began to diverge by drawing on local events and other lost texts. Nine copies now remain (although sadly not the putative original version). No single copy is definitive, and there are many discrepancies between different accounts of the same events.

The split tally stick was one ingenious innovation that sought to address this issue. A technique common across medieval Europe was to carve notches in a plane of wood to represent a transaction, then split the wood lengthwise so that both halves carried the same information. Both parties could take away their own half of the record, secure in the knowledge that (due to the unique graining of the wood) only one stick would be a perfect match for their own, and that should the other party seek to gain advantage by carving additional notches, these could be identified as they would only be present on one half of the record.

Split tally sticks were so trusted as a source of data that they became ingrained into the mercantile practices and even language of the times. In the United Kingdom, they were accepted as a form of currency ("wooden money") and were used extensively to record the paying of taxes and the issuance of government debt, right up until the end of the eighteenth century. Even then, they had one more decisive role to play.[1] A veritable mountain of stored tally sticks had built up in the basement of the Palace of Westminster that housed the British parliament. The stash of sticks was protected under law until the last beneficiary of a recorded debt had died. The Clerk of Works, one Richard Weobley, was finally tasked with their destruction in 1834. Deciding to burn them in the palace furnaces, Weobley failed to account for the fact that the furnaces were designed to burn coal, not tinder, and the resulting fire burnt down the Houses of

Parliament. The event was not without its up sides. The fire and smoke that cast such an ethereal light across the Thames was captured by the foremost artists of the day including J. M. W. Turner (who viewed the fire from the south bank and also from a boat on the river) and John Constable (sitting in a carriage on Westminster Bridge). The resulting loss of centuries of accumulated public records led to the commissioning of the Public Record Office in Chancery Lane (a big "win" for data governance), and the destruction of the official weight measurements caused the government to finally rationalise from two systems two one, favouring avoirdupois over troy (henceforward only used for gold). And the new Palace of Westminster, completed in 1870, with its gothic styling and including the clock tower most commonly referred to as Big Ben, has since become one of the most iconic buildings in the world and is a UNESCO World Heritage Site.

Another way to avoid copy errors was introduced in the form of printing. Wooden block printing originated in China in the seventh century and spread to Europe, but it was the introduction of the moveable type printing press in 1439 by Johannes Gutenberg that sparked the first information revolution as books and pamphlets printed using his metal types and oil-based inks swept across Europe.

Although data was now more reliable and could be copied and transported accurately, it was still limited to the written, or printed, or even carved word.

It took the voracious thirst for automation brought on by the industrial revolution some 400 years later that would lead to the first attempt to store and use data in any other way.

Data to Drive Machinery

The manufacture of patterned textiles using a draw loom had been slowly evolving for centuries. With the increase in speed brought about by steam-powered machines, manual methods of weaving no longer met the demands. A French weaver and merchant named Joseph Marie Jacquard, following earlier work by some of his contemporaries, invented the loom that bears his name in 1801. The Jacquard loom used a chain of punched cards to control the heddles of the loom to weave a pattern into the fabric. Following a few improvements, Jacquard's looms began to be sold throughout France and eventually around the world.[2]

Crucially, the data needed to create the woven pattern was *stored* in the punched card sequence, which could be reliably fed to the loom.

This innovation was reused nearly a hundred years later by Herman Hollerith and his punched card tabulating machines. Although Charles Babbage postulated the use of data input into his difference engine using punched cards, there is no evidence to suggest this was ever done. Hollerith, on the other hand, immediately found a use for his tabulating machines in the collation of data in the American census of 1890.

Hollerith had been involved in processing the data for the tenth census in 1880. His experiences (which he described as "barbarous") led him to believe that "some machine ought to be devised for the purpose of facilitating such tabulations".[3] For the 11th census he proposed to capture census data on cards, with punched holes in specific locations representing data such as gender, age (to be captured as two digits), race and literacy. To support these punched cards, he devised a keypunch machine (to facilitate input and increase data accuracy), a card sorting machine and a tabulating machine that could count the number of cards that met each criterion.

By the 1920s, as Hollerith's Tabulating Machine Company was on its way to becoming International Business Machines (IBM), punched cards of different shapes and sizes were in common use. In 1928, IBM introduced a standardised format with 80 columns and 10 rows. This format influenced the design of early ("green screen") computer monitors which were restricted for many years to 80 columns of characters.

With the rise of computer hardware manufacture and the increased use of computational power throughout the next 50 years for industry and finance, punched cards soon became ubiquitous and were enshrined in the public consciousness as being inherent to information technology. They were still in use towards the end of the twentieth century for data storage and execution, until threatened and eventually utterly replaced by magnetic storage media.

Around the same time that Hollerith was rolling back the digital data frontier (digital because a hole was either cut or not cut in the card at each location), advances were being made in analogue recording techniques. Thomas Edison had first presented his phonograph in the United States in 1877, the same year that French poet and inventor Charles Cros had demonstrated his paleophone in France. Both machines used a needle to record sound waves in a medium that could then be used to etch a copy into a disc or cylinder. The initial creations were crude and unreliable (although to the unexpecting audience, the sound of a human voice or tune captured in machinery must surely have been quite startling – most particularly when Edison first unveiled his invention in the office of the *Scientific American* journal with "very few preliminary remarks" before turning the crank "and to the astonishment of all present the machine said: 'Good morning. How do you do?' "[4]).

Because the needle faithfully recorded the sound's variations as it cut the recording medium, these inventions were analogue in nature rather than digital. In early devices, recordings would last for only a few plays, and until the arrival of vinyl in the 1930s, phonographs were curiosities with low take-up in industry or in popular culture.

Digital data storage, on the other hand, spent a few decades in the limelight in the early twentieth century after American inventor Edwin Scott Votey gave the world the first automated piano player, the Pianola, in 1896. Powered by bellows, the pianola played tunes pneumatically by blowing air through a series of holes in a continuous feed of punched paper. Pianolas became popular, with many makes available and thousands of tunes stored on paper rolls, which came in multiple different sizes with a varying spacing for the holes. In a precursor to modern open source arrangements and in pursuit of standardisation, a group of American manufacturers met in New York state in 1908, at the so-called Buffalo Convention, to agree a standard width and spacing for the rolls, after which the majority of pianolas were able to play the same roll of music. A strangely elegant device, the pianola was unable to see off both the Great Depression and the arrival of the vinyl record, and production stopped in 1929.

Data in Databases

While computer hardware was in its infancy in the mid-twentieth century, there was no need for large, connected databases. If a particular machine was responsible for applying credits to a bank account, it simply loaded transactions on punched cards or magnetic media and processed each one in turn. The application would read each record, process it and write the results to an output file to be processed by the next application, or stored.

But as the computers became more sophisticated, the tasks they were asked to perform became more intertwined. Suddenly, it mattered that the accounts in question belonged to people, who in turn had ages and addresses and spouses and children. A more structured approach was needed.

Initial attempts were flawed. In the 1960s, IBM championed a hierarchical data structure consisting of parent and child entities (with each parent able to have multiple child entities). This seems to work for simple data (each person has one or more accounts, and each account has one or more transactions) but falls down if the data structures are not rigidly hierarchical: joint accounts, for example. In this case, what's needed is a database that reflects the real relationships between the data entities.

The concept of a *relational database* was first introduced by an IBM computer scientist, Edgar Frank Codd, in his 1970 paper *A Relational Model of Data for Large Shared Data Banks,*[5] where he asserted that "future users of large data banks must be protected from having to know how the data is organized in the machine". He devised 13 rules (known, perversely, as Codd's twelve rules, numbered 0 to 12) to define the behaviour of such a database, notably rules 1 and 2 which stipulated that data must be represented logically in tables, and that each datum can be located ("guaranteed to be logically accessible") using a combination of table name, primary key and column name.

To satisfy these rules, Codd introduced the concept of *data normalisation*. This is the process of ensuring that each datum is represented singly and uniquely in the database, defined by a primary key. Think of our account structure above. The primary key for a bank account is typically a combination of the account number issued by the bank, and something that identifies the bank itself (in the United Kingdom, for example, the primary key of a retail bank account would be the combination of the bank's sort code and the account number). Now, imagine that we want to record on our database that each bank account has an owner. We might imagine that the identity of the owner could be recorded as a datum on a table relating to the account. But what about a joint account? It would have two owners, each of whom could have multiple other bank accounts. In this case we would need to create a new table to link each account to each owner.

In Figure 3.1, we can see that in a hierarchical model, the joint account behaves differently as it has multiple owners. In the relational model, the relationship between the clients and the accounts is recorded in a separate *account owner* entity, meaning that the joint account is just the same as the singly owned accounts.

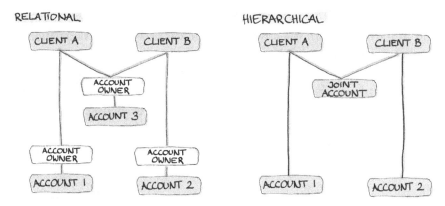

FIGURE 3.1
Relational vs Hierarchical Database.

Codd's 1972 paper, *Further Normalization of the Data Base Relational Model*,[6] defined what is now the widely accepted standard for data normalisation, referred to as "third normal form". To achieve first normal form, a database table must always contain the same number of fields. Second normal form requires all attributes in the table to provide facts about the primary key of the table, while third normal form requires all attributes to not provide facts about any other primary key elsewhere in the database. In short, every attribute must provide facts about "the key, the whole key, and nothing but the key" (often suffixed with "so help me Codd").

Data normalisation remains a pivotal concept in database design.

Codd also championed a new way of accessing and updating data – using a query language (which he called Alpha) that could update multiple table rows at a time rather than the laborious read-process-write approach of sequential processing.

Eventually convinced of the value of a relational database, IBM took Codd's ideas and created their DB2 relational database and Structured Query Language SQL/DS query language, but not before other organisations (notably Larry Ellison's Oracle but also Sybase and eventually Microsoft) began to build and market their own relational databases and versions of *SQL*. The language was originally to be called SEQUEL (apparently standing for Structured English QUEry Language and a pun on the similar QUEL language designed by rival Ingres) but was renamed as SQL due to a trademark issue. SQL (which later came to mean Structured Query Language) is often still pronounced "sequel" today.

As computer hardware and peripherals became more sophisticated, and in particular with the advent of graphical user interfaces, relational databases were adapted slightly to the new object-oriented approach (explained more fully in Chapter 2). Tables of data could now be organised into "objects" which could represent business data such as accounts or more abstract data such as an on-screen window or even just a button on a screen. Each object could have associated data but also procedures which could be invoked by software to perform functions (such as opening or closing a window or when the user clicked a button).

Data for Analysis

Data analysis as a formal process, along with data architecture and design, didn't really come into being until the late twentieth century when random access memory began to replace sequential processing.

One notable exception and early pioneer of data analysis was John Graunt, a London haberdasher and milliner in the seventeenth century. With his friend Sir William Petty, Graunt studied the weekly Bills of Mortality, gathered and published by each local parish. In his 1662 work *Natural and Political Observations Mentioned in a Following Index and Made upon the Bills of Mortality*,[7] Graunt published his findings in data tables and used statistical analysis to draw conclusions about life expectancy, as well as the profligacy of the plague and other diseases such as rickets. Graunt was the first person known to use data analysis techniques in this way and is often cited as the father of demography.

But in a technological sense, for most of the twentieth century, data was the poor relation to hardware and software development, being largely used in an unstructured way or as a linear input to a sequential procedure. But with the arrival of the relational database, and the accessibility provided by SQL and its kin, data started to have a life of its own – to be independently available outside of the software processes it had been designed to feed.

To understand how data and its storage transitioned in 50 years or so from the merely linear to the overwhelmingly ever-present, it might help to look at how its usage evolved in that time. To do this, let's imagine an organisation that is in the business of making and distributing sweets and other candy confectionery.

As we've seen, data's main role prior to the relational database was to drive specific sequential processes. For our sweet company, this would perhaps involve some parameters to control automated machinery on the production line, and perhaps some rudimentary staff records to power the monthly wage run.

With the relational database and associated query languages came the ability to construct management reports and more complex processes. The sweet company would now be able to maintain a database of ingredients to track supply and demand. Specific reports could be written to provide information on stock levels, as well as the popularity of certain brands or sweets. But these reports would take time and effort to write, usually needing dedicated project resource. The reports themselves would be inflexible once written – if an executive of the organisation wanted to view the data in a different way, which simply wasn't an option.

Often, the reports were slow to produce. A pure relational database might be a great way to store data, but it isn't always easy to find the data you're looking for to put in a report. So, the normalised databases were often denormalised again, gathering useful data into a separate index or reference table – this added an overhead in storing the data, but meant reports could be produced more quickly.

It was this ever-increasing demand for different types of reports that drove the evolution of data management. Think of our sweet manufacturer. The buyers need to know inventory levels and rates of consumption. The production chief needs to know whether the production lines are functioning efficiently. The sales team need to know when, where and by how much sales fluctuate across regions, by season and by other factors. The marketing team may even want to know if red sweets sell better than blue sweets. All this information can be gleaned from the underlying data, but each report would need to be specifically written, with the potential need for additional indexing on the data.

More flexibility was needed. The door was open to business intelligence and the multi-dimensional array, or data cube.

In their 1997 paper, *Data Cube: A Relational Aggregation Operator Generalizing Group-By, Cross-Tab, and Sub-Totals,*[8] Jim Gray et al proposed the storing of data in multi-dimensional arrays, calling them data cubes, or just cubes. Crucially, the paper explains how data is aggregated at the lowest level and can be rolled up as needed for specific reports.

For our sweet manufacturer, each sale of sweets could be stored in an array with the following axes (although the term "cube" suggests only three dimensions, there is no logical limit to the number of dimensions that could be used. Many texts use three dimensions for simplicity – we've chosen to show four dimensions just to prove a point):

- Time
- Geography
- Sweet type
- Sales team

Every sale would add data to the correct data cube for the various parameters. To build a report of all sales over time, the latter three axes could simply be rolled up into a single value for each point on the time axis. Alternatively, a more complex report could build a picture of each sales team's performance for each type of sweet, by month, year on year.

The role of the data analyst started to become critical, not just in getting data out of a database, but also in devising how to slice and dice the axes of the array to be most meaningful to the organisation and its executives. More importantly, if the need for data extracts changed, reports could be written quickly (often without the need for dedicated project professionals) to interrogate the data already present in the array. And by combining multiple data sources into a single dashboard view, on-screen reports could provide busy business users with a vast amount of data in a single glance.

Then only limit, it seemed, was access to more data and the capability to structure it for subsequent retrieval.

Unstructured Data

And that's where the internet stepped in. Suddenly, from the late 1990s onwards, organisations had access to (and storage for) ever increasing amounts of data from not just within their organisation but externally as well. This data was gathered from all of these disparate sources in unstructured form: what is now referred to as "big data". Reporting tools became more sophisticated at trawling through vast amounts of data, picking out only what was relevant. And the internet also provided greater capacity to store data (in the cloud), so it became cheaper to collect and hold different kinds of data, and to make connections between that data that may not have been available previously (for example, payroll records for the sales team could now be easily linked to sales performance figures, perhaps adjusting for seasonal trends).

Having access to so much data was great of course. Remember that data is king. Data is the base of the DIKW pyramid: it underpins everything else and is the first step on the path to wisdom. But it created a new problem – where could it all be stored?

The answer was a *data warehouse*, a vast digital library where all of the data needed by an organisation could be stored and retrieved as needed. Data would first be extracted from the various sources into *data lakes*, which could contain the same data extracted from multiple sources both internally and externally. From the lake, this data could be extracted, filtered, transformed into an enterprise-wide model and loaded into the data warehouse for analysis by data scientists and others.

The data in the lake was raw and unhomogenised, leading to a new concept of an unstructured (or "NoSQL") database.

The concept of a carefully crafted relational database, while not replaced, was supplemented by these massive NoSQL databases and vast data lakes.

Data in Pictures

With so much data, it can become hard to pick out what's relevant.

Data visualisation was not a new concept, but the sheer scale and complexity of data available, and the tools to gather and analyse it led to an explosion of data visualisation techniques.

A Scottish engineer and economist, William Playfair, is credited as one of the first proponents of data visualisation. He invented the bar chart (to show trade data) in 1786, and the pie chart (showing the geographical distribution of the Ottoman Empire) in 1801.

Florence Nightingale used a form of pie chart called a rose chart (where the amplitude of the segment is proportional to data on one axis, while the size of the segments angle is proportional to data on a second axis) to illustrate the causes of mortality in the British army in Crimea, and in particular how few of those deaths were due to wounds received in battle.

But one of the most stunning early data visualisations – in 1869 – was the brainchild of Charles Minard, a French civil engineer. Minard sought to demonstrate the disastrous march on Moscow by Napoleon and his Grande Armée. Eschewing a simple replication of the data, Minard chose to show

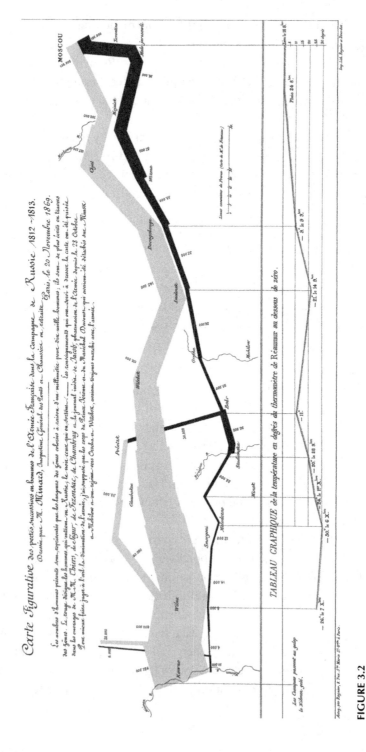

FIGURE 3.2

Charles Minard 1812 Campaign Infographic.

multiple axes, such as the size and position of the army over time on both the outward and return legs further supplemented by the falling temperature in the winter months. The result (see Figure 3.2) is a masterpiece of infographics: the key data is viscerally represented, reinforced by the elegance of the presentation. It is still revered today as a "gem", "the best statistical graphic ever drawn", and one of the "best three charts in history" (Florence Nightingale's Crimea chart and John Snow's Cholera Map in 1854 being the other two [9]).

As with many of the topics in this book, the means to visualise data began to change rapidly in step with the growth of computer technology in the 1960s and 1970s. As well as being regarded by many as the founder of data science, with his advocacy of "experimental data analysis", US mathematician John Tukey foresaw the use of computer technology to produce graphical displays of data. The following decade, Edward Tufte wrote the seminal work, *The Visual Display of Quantitative Information*,[10] still a scholastic reference at many universities. Tufte noted that the purpose of a graphic should be to communicate complex ideas with "clarity, precision, and efficiency" and to allow the viewer to make comparisons by making large data sets coherent.

As data, analytics and graphics have become more sophisticated, data visualisation has grown exponentially. Bar charts and pie charts are now part and parcel of everyday life, but some visualisation has been elevated to an art form. The reader is encouraged to look at books such as *Data Sketches: A journey of imagination, exploration, and beautiful data visualizations* by Nadieh Bremer and Shirley Wu for some truly breathtaking and thought-provoking graphics.

WHAT DOES HERE LOOK LIKE?

Of all the topics in this book, data is the domain where change is likely to have the most pressing impact on the business landscape. As we will see elsewhere in this book, hardware, software, interfacing and project methodologies are plateauing in terms of the rate of change. Blockchain and artificial intelligence (AI) are exciting opportunities, demonstrating dynamic expansion, but haven't yet had a significant impact on the majority of organisations.

But data is changing now: rapidly expanding in usage and depth, transforming how organisations do business, and presenting both a risk and an opportunity as a valuable commodity.

So, let's take a moment to look at the world of data today, before we consider where it might be heading and what that means to you, the business leader.

We'll start with one of the most fundamental aspects of business data – who owns the data? There should be no surprises here – *you do!*

Data Governance

One of the most common mistakes made by business stakeholders in an information technology context is to believe that someone else has the responsibility for their data. Your IT infrastructure can only ever be an enabler for your data – the person who owns it is you (or one of your business colleagues). Think of your IT infrastructure as a notebook – if you write something down on the page, you'd never expect the notebook to take ownership for it. Just because you have an IT team supporting your infrastructure – and project teams responsible for managing change – does not mean that they are suddenly responsible for your data.

Data governance as a formal discipline is relatively new. Its key objective is to ensure that the data within an organisation is managed appropriately, with an identified owner who is responsible for its quality (and any remediation necessary to improve that quality).

Many organisations have discovered that their data is disjointed, poorly maintained, duplicated, inconsistent or simply not available to those that need it. Against this backdrop, recent data regulation requires organisations to be responsible for their data, particularly any client or personal data they may hold. Ideally, an organisation will follow best data governance practice for the resulting benefits of having reliable, accurate, consistent data wherever it is needed throughout the enterprise, rather than because it is mandated by regulators and governments, but the impact is much the same.

Data governance bibles such as the DAMA DMBOK (The Data Management Association *Data Management Body of Knowledge*) will break the discipline down into segments as shown in Figure 3.3.

As well as covering data architecture, modelling, quality and security, a fully rounded data governance function will ensure that data is sourced appropriately (including from external data providers), is stored and

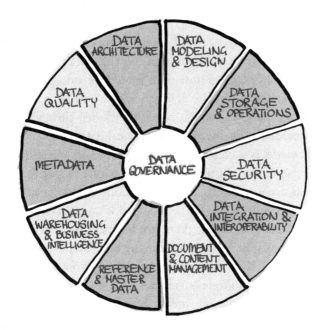

FIGURE 3.3
Data Governance.

warehoused safely and is moved between different applications safely and securely.

Data governance practices may vary from one organisation to another. Some organisations will operate a formal approach whereby a data steward will ensure each and every datum is managed appropriately and procedures are documented (such as who manages the data, what it is for, who can view it and how long it must be kept), while other organisations may apply a less rigid structure.

At the very least, every organisation should have a clear policy about its governance of data. As a business leader, you should know what data is within your remit, and what data you need from elsewhere in order to fulfil your role.

Data Architecture and Models

Data doesn't just happen (or it shouldn't). Just like you'd never build your house without setting out a blueprint, you shouldn't allow your IT systems and processes to create and use data without a clear plan. And in many ways, data architecture is more important: you can quickly see that a house is built poorly – rooms will be shaped inappropriately for their function, or cracks may appear in the walls. In data, you won't see the cracks until it's too late!

Data architecture describes how data should be stored, processed and transported across the enterprise. It is typically presented as a set of models ranging from the purely business semantic model, through logical and physical data models to realisation as a physical database.

A *semantic model* is a conceptual model of the organisation's data and how it is all related. For example, a bank's semantic model would include such entities as accounts, branches, transactions and account-holders. It's a crucial first step – if the business can't agree what an account is and how it relates to an account-holder, then any business process is doomed to fail. This may sound glib, but there are many organisations where this distinction is not clear. How does an account differ from a portfolio? If an account is opened for multiple currencies, is it one account with multiple positions, or multiple accounts? And as we saw earlier, if there are complex structures such as joint accounts, then these can be more easily identified and mapped at the semantic level than later in the process.

A *logical data model* is the next step after the conceptual model. Here, the data is analysed and organised into relational (or object-oriented) structures, following appropriate normalisation rules for the enterprise. The logical model doesn't concern itself with where or how the data will be stored – it focuses purely on the data as an abstract concept.

A *physical data model,* on the other hand, takes the logical model and applies some hard, physical, pragmatic realities to it. Where is the data going to be stored? How big are the data tables going to get? Do they need to be split or partitioned? How quickly (and how) does data need to be accessed? How is it to be transported?

A physical model may also begin to look at which applications will be supplying the data and using it, which introduces another key concept of data architecture: *data mastery.* As important as it is to understand who owns the data within an organisation, it is crucial to know how that data is injected into the system: is it received from an external agent, from a client or third party, or is it typed or scanned in by members of an operational team ("data stewards")? As you'd expect, in a properly architected system, data is only ever input once – the application where this happens is the "master" of the data. Data may be physically replicated elsewhere across the enterprise for ease of access (remember, this is a physical model), but these are copies or slaves of the master data. At no time should slave data be updated directly by a person or an application.

The physical model may also begin to explore how data will be transported from where it is mastered to where it is needed. Again, the model will look at practical considerations such as whether the data is needed in real time or as a file, and the volume and frequency of data transport.

Finally, the data architecture will define the physical *databases* that will house the data. Depending on the scale and scope of the enterprise, there may be many such databases: for different applications or for multiple instances of the same application, or copies of the entire database for development and testing as well as live operations.

Not all applications will treat a given logical datum in the same way. It's important to know that what's called by one name in one application may have a different name (and even maybe a different size and shape) on another application. And each application may have a different use for the data. Remember the Rosetta Stone? Each organisation needs an equivalent of the Rosetta Stone to record what data is needed in the system, and how it is maintained and used. This is the *data dictionary*.

Every organisation should have a data dictionary. It should contain every data entity, attribute and primary key in the enterprise. It should explain how the data is input and validated, stored, transported and used in every application. It should note the different names and formats across different applications and identify a business owner, data quality and integrity checks to be performed, and how the data should be disposed of. The data dictionary should be cherished, lovingly updated, and read avidly by every executive, business user and technician in the organisation.

Sadly, this is rarely the case. Some organisations (arguably, not even "most" organisations) will have some form of embryonic data dictionary, perhaps the by-product of a past development project, that is no longer maintained and has become static. Most organisations will have some application-specific data dictionaries (perhaps supplied by the application vendor), but these will not be enterprise-wide.

Data Quality

American scientist Paul R. Erlich famously coined the phrase "to err is human, but to really foul things up you need a computer".

This is harsh. A computer is only as good as its programming and its data, both of which are ultimately supplied by humans (for now, at any rate). It may be true that a computer, working much faster than a human and massively in parallel, can amplify data errors to catastrophic proportions, but the ultimate root cause remains the mistype or plain old dumb data input by a human being.

Errors can occur in at least two ways: faulty software can take good data and produce incorrect results (which are then stored as data). Or the data can be incorrect in the first place. Faulty software can be screened by testing (and by live incidents) and fixed – once corrected, the software should function as planned. But data errors, especially when caused by user error, can keep occurring. *Data quality* is the process of identifying such errors, by comparing actual data held (and used) within a system to the stated ideal, the "golden copy" of the data. It is also the process of correcting existing errors and preventing further erroneous input.

There are broadly three kinds of data error that are common in organisations: data omissions, data integrity errors and data replication errors.

Data omissions are simply cases where data is not present that is required. Maybe a financial system needs to know the client's date of birth, but this has not been captured.

Data integrity errors can occur within a single application or across the enterprise. A data integrity error occurs when two related data attributes contain conflicting values. For example, a client may be marked as being a United Kingdom resident, while their main address is outside the United Kingdom.

Data replication errors occur as data is transported or duplicated in different applications across the enterprise. This happens most frequently where data is rekeyed manually in the different systems, rather than being automatically replicated by internal messaging. If a client's name is "David" but this is mis-keyed in one application as "Dave", there is a replication error.

Depending on the level of data quality in an organisation, it may not be possible to identify and fix all instances of errors. Some errors are simply annoying, while others can cause processing errors. In the case above, it may not matter that in one system the client's name is recorded incorrectly, while an incorrect residency status may lead to an inaccurate tax calculation with detrimental impact for the client and the organisation.

An effective data quality programme needs to

- Identify and classify data quality issues
- Prioritise issues based on the impact on the client, the firm or other third parties
- Design and implement a remediation programme for the data
- Make necessary process or system changes to minimise or prevent future occurrences.

It's not always easy to prevent data errors from creeping in. Even something as simple as a data omission may not be trivial to prevent: if the input process allows for partial input, or the specific attribute is only needed for certain cases, it may not be possible to add validation to the data capture process. However, systemic validation at the point of input remains the preferred mechanism to prevent data errors. In a properly architected system, which adheres to sound data mastery principles, the validation is needed in only one application (where the data is mastered), and the data is transported reliably throughout the enterprise thereafter. In reality, of course, most of these "downstream" applications will in any case apply their own validation to ensure that the data they receive and use is fit for purpose. But if the data is properly validated at the point of entry, these data integrity and fault-tolerance checks should find no further issues. The tightest validation should be applied at the start, when the data arrives into the organisation's sphere of control.

This also applies to data integrity: if there is a field that could be derived (rather than input), then there is no opportunity for a conflicting value to be manually entered. In the residency case above, the United Kingdom residency flag could be derived by the application based on the data in the primary address.

If data needs to be remediated, it's better if this can be done in an automated fashion. Data replication errors can be fixed in this way. But data omissions and integrity errors can often only be corrected by returning to the original source of the data and recapturing it (for example, ringing up the client to ask them for their date of birth or to confirm their main address). In this case, you as a business leader may need to get involved in the management of the remediation programme. Remember, it's your data.

Data Consistency – The Atomic Commit

A key concept in the world of data management is the atomic commit.

Imagine that you are running a computer application that will update a set of records. What would happen if the application gets halfway through the process and then hits an issue and falls over? Other applications that come along and read the data, or screens that allow the business user to view the data, have no way of knowing that the job is only half done. They may make decisions based on half-complete data.

This issue is solved with the concept of a database transaction – a logical transaction that spans all of the updates that need to be done at once. Once the transaction is started, as each object or row or file record is updated it is locked to all other applications and the lock stays in place until the final update, after which the application ends the database transaction with a commit statement. If the updating application hits an issue, the database transaction will be rolled back as if nothing had happened.

In this way, the updated data is said to be subject to an atomic commit.

Atomic commits can also be performed on a distributed database, so that data in different locations can be updated in a synchronised way. This involves a number of database transactions coordinated in each location: either all are committed or all are rolled back.

Data Security

Your data is valuable: to you, to your clients, to your competitors and to those with malicious intent. You wouldn't let just anyone spend your money, and you need to protect your data in the same way.

Luckily, the CIA is here to help. No, not that one. CIA in a data security context stands for:

- Confidentiality – ensuring that only authorised people have access to data.
- Integrity – ensuring that data is accurate and consistent.
- Availability – ensuring that data is available to those who need it.

Data security has both an inward-looking and an outward-looking lens.

Inwardly, you need to ensure that your data is available only to those people in the organisation who need to use it in the execution of their duties. Furthermore, you need to make sure that you only hold data for as long as is necessary, not just from a regulatory perspective but also because unnecessary data takes up space in your storage and has an impact on the time it takes to access the useful data all around it.

You will need to protect your data from both deliberate and accidental acts by your employees. Deliberate acts might include the following:

- An employee sending proprietary materials to their private email address (such as internal documentation), even if innocently to work on while at home
- A curious employee searching through a customer database for information on clients
- A disgruntled employee deliberately removing or amending data on a database
- A disgruntled employee copying data to take to their next place of work (this could be client data or it could be operational data such as documented procedures, specifications and the like).

Accidental acts that might threaten your data include the following:

- Accidental mis-keying of data by a user (either the wrong data for the correct record or the right data for the wrong record)
- Erroneous updates to a live system by a user thinking they are using a test version of the application
- Accidental sending of data to the wrong external recipient (e.g. by email)
- Loss of a laptop or other equipment.

Outwardly, an organisation needs to ensure that data is protected from a vast number of threats, the landscape of which has been vastly widened by the proliferation of the internet and cloud-based services.

Your organisation should have a rigid data security policy (following the global ISO 27001 standard for information security) that dictates how data can be protected from both internal and external threats, accidental or otherwise. This will cover classification of documentation, standard checks before sending emails, passwords and other credentials, and security on your laptop or other devices.

But what can you, as a business leader, do specifically to support your colleagues in the data and information security team?

First and foremost, you can ensure that data within your area of responsibility is fully documented in the data dictionary, with a clear description of what the data is, who can use it and what it can be used for.

Second, if you are asked to contribute to the design of a process, make sure you are clear about the data as much as the process itself. How critical is the data? How does it arrive? How is it input into the system, and how reliable is that part of the process? Do you need to think about independent validation: "four eyes" checking where a colleague will approve the input or even "blind re-keying" where a colleague also inputs the data and the application compares the two entries? Most applications support role-based access that can be configured to your organisation's needs – it's important to consider this early in the project lifecycle, and to ensure that access is continually monitored in live operations.

Similarly, when designing a process, it is key to make sure that an audit trail is recorded of any data changes, and that this is easy to retrieve and examine. Many audit trails (especially in older systems) can be as simple as a sequential record of every change made, which can be very difficult to retrieve after the event. Audit trails are critical as a detective measure to verify who has made changes to data within applications. That only works if the audit trail can be interrogated by date, user and type of data.

Finally, you should be clear about how and when the data needs to be available. How critical is the data to the operation of the business? What would happen if the applications were unavailable for an hour, a day or longer? What data would you still need in order to conduct business? What data can the organisation simply not afford to lose? Answering these questions will help your technical colleagues build appropriate strategies around backups and disaster recovery, making sure that your data is protected and available as required.

If you are involved in a project to configure, develop or improve one or more software applications, you may be called on to help test the finished product, usually as part of user acceptance testing (UAT). Data plays a huge part in testing and can take two forms. In some tests, you may be able to use entirely fictitious data, running tests for a Mr M. Mouse or a Mrs Jane Doe. But quite often, you will need to run tests using data that has been copied from live operational systems. This could be because there is a range of data that would be impossible to replicate manually, or because the project specifically requires the testing of migrated data (to prove that data moved from the old application to the new behaves as expected). There is a risk that people who would not normally have access to live data can see the copy data in the test system. If the data is sensitive, your organisation's data security policies may require the data to be automatically obfuscated before it can be used in this way. While this protects the data (and ultimately the client or third to whom the data relates), it can make testing more complex if the obfuscation routines manipulate the data to the extent that it is meaningless or prevents useful testing. For example, if every client in the test system is renamed Mr F FFFF by the obfuscation routine, and is given a date of birth of October 1, 1970, any test that is driven by the client's age will be invalidated, and you will not be able to tell the clients apart. Obfuscation is useful in protecting data (and there's less chance that a user accidentally logs on to the live system thinking at it is a test system as the data will appear very different) but too much obfuscation and homogenisation of data can lead to testing issues. As a business leader, you can help to influence the obfuscation routines by identifying sensitive data and proposing appropriate ways it can be obfuscated but still support the necessary testing.

Regulation

Regulation, and in particular data privacy regulation, has risen dramatically over the last few years, as governments seek to protect individuals from the misuse of their private data.

The European Union's GDPR ("General Data Protection Regulation") was enacted in 2016 and has become the basis for data privacy laws in many other jurisdictions.

The regulation runs to 99 clauses and nearly 80 pages, but in essence it sets out the rules by which organisations can hold and process personal data in terms of:

- "Lawfulness, fairness and transparency"
- "Purpose limitation" – data shall be collected only for specified, explicit and legitimate purposes
- "Data minimisation" – data shall be adequate, relevant and limited to what is necessary

- "Accuracy" – data is to be accurate and kept up to date
- "Storage limitation" – data to be kept for no longer than is necessary
- "Integrity and confidentiality" – data shall be processed in a manner that ensures appropriate security, including protection against unauthorised or unlawful processing and against accidental loss, destruction or damage.

The regulation also sets out the concept of a "data subject", being an identified or identifiable natural person, and requires the data subject to have given consent for the use of their data (unless processing is necessary for contractual or legal reasons or is in the individual's or the public interest). It also sets out the rights of the data subject to have access to their data.

Two other parties identified in the regulation are the "data controller", being the organisation that has responsibility for holding and processing the data, and a "data processor" which may be an outsourced third party or a cloud-based application that processes the data on behalf of the controller.

As a business leader, you may be called upon to ensure that the data rights of individuals are protected in your organisation's applications and processes.

Aside from client data held and processed in applications, there are two less obvious categories of data that fall within these regulations:

- Personal data about non-clients
- Personal data held in unstructured form outside of the organisation's applications.

Individuals other than clients who may be covered by such regulation include your colleagues, individuals working for third parties or partners, or any other individual. So data held in your organisation's HR (human resources) application needs to meet the criteria set out by the regulation just as much as data held in your CRM (client relationship management) application.

Data held in unstructured form is also often overlooked. If you record a file note about a client and store it in your own local filing system, this remains personal data and is subject to regulation.

Big Data, Data Analytics, Data Science and Business Intelligence

The world of big data and its related sciences and disciplines is still relatively new. Prior to the advent of the internet, more data was stored in analogue form than digital. From around 2002 onwards, digitally stored data gained the ascendency, with the amount of data accelerating at an exponential rate.

In 2023, for example, it is anticipated that the world's collective networked technologies will generate around 120 zettabytes of data. In 2010, the number was a lowly two zettabytes. A zettabyte is 10^{21} bytes, equivalent to about 300 trillion copies of *War and Peace*. The vast majority of this data deluge is in the form of videos and social media, but there is also a substantial growing contribution from the Internet of Things (IoT).

When used in context, "big data" means more than just a large database. If you are an online retailer, you may have a database of tens of thousands of customers, their email addresses, their marketing preferences and so on. That could be considered to be a big database. But "big data" is typically characterised by the volume of data, the speed at which it is gathered and the variety of structured and unstructured formats. Collectively, these are sometimes referred to as the "three Vs":

- Volume – collecting data from a variety of sources, including transactions, smart (IoT) devices, industrial equipment, videos, images, audio, social media and more
- Velocity – the growth in the IoT is transforming data collection from an asynchronous process into data streams that must be handled in real time
- Variety – usable data now arrives in all types of formats – from structured, numeric data in traditional databases to unstructured text documents, emails, videos, audios, stock ticker data and financial transactions.

Big data would include every click made on your website by every visitor, whether a customer or not. It would include every purchase transaction (and every incremental step for every transaction from ordering through to delivery), every contact made with every supplier. It will include data not directly related to your business such as staff data (time spent in the office, holidays and other time off taken) or data about the business premises.

This data is gathered by a myriad of means and deposited into a data lake, a formless soup of raw, unrelated data.

Prominent data analyst Stephen Few's Perceptual Edge website[11] offers this wisdom on its front page:

> We are overwhelmed by information, not because there is too much, but because we haven't learned how to tame it. Information lies stagnant in rapidly expanding pools as our ability to collect and warehouse it increases, but our ability to make sense of and communicate it remains inert, largely without notice.
>
> Computers speed the process of information handling, but they don't tell us what the information means or how to communicate its meaning to decision makers. These skills are not intuitive; they rely largely on analysis and presentation skills that must be learned.

Data analysis is the discipline of trawling through the data lake looking for meaningful data and in particular where there is a causal relationship between two or more sets of data. This mining process, looking for nuggets of information in a vein of data, can be improved by data scientists, who will help to spot patterns in the data, and perhaps make recommendations for additional data or different forms of data to be captured in the lake.

Once the data analyst has identified, retrieved, filtered and sorted the data, the resulting business intelligence can be presented visually using a range of techniques.

Few notes the following eight types of metric for data visualisation:

- Time series (the value of a datum over time)
- Ranking (related data ranked in ascending or descending order)
- Part-to-whole (ratios such as pie charts)
- Deviation (such as observed differences to a theoretical or expected norm)
- Frequency distribution (the spread of a variable over ranges of time)
- Correlation (comparison between two or more related variables showing cause and effect)
- Nominal comparison (showing unrelated values for comparison such as sales by region)

- Geospatial (showing the spread of a variable by geographical location).

As with any industry experiencing such dramatic growth, a range of tools have evolved in parallel, from those developed specifically for the data scientist to others more suited to business users. The most common are set out below.

Hadoop is an open-source collection software utilities that can be deployed on a network of computers to perform analysis involving massive amounts of data. It works by splitting files into large blocks and distributing them across a series of nodes. Each of the nodes then processes its own package of data in parallel. Hadoop comprises two main capabilities: a storage component, Hadoop Distributed File System (HDFS), and a processing component (which uses a distributed algorithm known as MapReduce). Initially released in 2006, Hadoop is used by many of the largest data-heavy organisations in the world including Amazon (AWS), Meta and Yahoo; usage is most common in the United States.

Kaggle is both a data science platform and an online community. It enables users to explore and build data sets and models in a collaborative environment with other data scientists and machine learning engineers. Founded in 2010, Kaggle was acquired by Google in 2017.

SQL, the grandaddy of relational database query languages, is as relevant today as ever. With its ability to perform set functions, access to multiple tables with a single statement through "joins" and the updating of data directly in the database without needing to retrieve it first, SQL gives the user a wealth of capabilities for data analysis and manipulation. SQL has a vast range of applications, from being embedded in software applications to its use as a stand-alone data analytics tool (provided that the data in each case has been structured into a relational database). Even a small amount of SQL knowledge allows the operator to perform very powerful searches and data updates, making SQL something many non-technical personnel use on a regular basis, especially if their role involves some form of statistical or data analysis.

Python. While most professionals would agree that the best programming language for the data analyst is SQL due to its simple database communication, another programming language, Python, may be a better option for other data analysis functions such as analysing, manipulating, cleaning and visualising data. It uses a human-readable notation including keywords in English rather than complex-seeming punctuation marks and encourages simplicity. The first version of Python was released in 1991.

Power BI or *Tableau.* As a business leader, you might not expect to get involved directly with Kaggle, Hadoop or Python (although you could definitely dabble in the latter to good effect). You may get your hands dirty with SQL – being able to construct a structured relational database of the subset of data from your organisation's data lake and then performing your own queries on it to build statistical models or to produce management information may be really valuable to you. But your go-to tool should be an interactive data visualisation and business information tool such as Power BI (released by Microsoft in 2015) or Tableau (launched in 2003). These platforms enable business users to convert various formats of data into coherent, visually immersive and interactive outputs.

Finally, let's hear it for *Excel.* There's a secret about business information that very few people will mention: business users don't really want to build fancy dashboards and interactive charts that they can slice and dice. They'll ask for them, of course: they're cool and trendy. But most of the time, they'll ask for the raw data as well, "just dropped it into an Excel file". Excel remains the most widely used tool for data analysis. It supports searching, complex filtering, deduplication, pivots, macros and formulas, and even basic data mining. The citizen developer from Chapter 2 is almost always going to be a power Excel user first – let's call them a "citizen analyst".

Data Formats

We couldn't leave a chapter on data without a quick nod to the often-confusing world of data formats. These may be dropped into conversations by your project team or data analysts and each has its own advantages and disadvantages. If you already know your JSON from your YAML, please feel free to skip to the next part. If not, the following (albeit non-exhaustive) list may help you.

- PDF (Portable Document Format) – a software-independent unstructured format for text and graphics files, displayable on any device regardless of hardware and operating system. Although the data is unstructured (compared to say a relational database or a comma-separated values [CSV] or JavaScript Object Notation [JSON] file), the file itself contains a complete description the document, including the text, fonts, vector graphics, raster images and other information needed to display it.

- CSV – probably the most simple and common way to exchange structured data, the CSV format uses commas to separate each sequential text value. Data is stored in tabular form as plain text, with each line representing a single data record. Importantly, the attribute name for each datum is not explicitly set out in each record: it is either assumed from the position of the data (e.g. the fifth column is "name") or is more often contained in a header row that identifies the attributes in the correct sequence. The delimiter does not necessarily need to be a comma, and sets of double quotes can be used to contain data that includes the delimiter character or for other reasons of clarification.

- JSON – pronounced like the name Jason, JSON files contain attributes and values in pairs. Although designed for use with the JavaScript programming language, JSON is an open-source format that can be used with any application. A range of data types are included, including text, numbers, Booleans (true/false) and arrays of data.

- XML (Extensible Markup Language) – a standardised file format using special characters ("markup") to create structures such as tags for section names and attribute names. XML supports all Unicode characters including non-Latin text. Data definitions are set out in schemas.

- YAML – another markup language similar to XML but with simpler syntax and no schema definitions. It is often used for the transmission of documentation due to its ease use. YAML is compatible with the JSON format but has some additional features such as comments and extensible data types.

- XBRL (eXtensible Business Reporting Language) – a business-oriented markup language that allows text documents to be tagged for semantic meaning, ensuring that all parties viewing the document can extract structured data from it as well as ensure that they have fully understood the semantic meaning of a given datum. Each XBRL instance contains the business facts being reported along with a collection of taxonomies (called a Discoverable Taxonomy Set [DTS]), providing metadata about these facts.

- BLOB (Binary Large Object) – a term coined in the mists of time (from a data management perspective) in reference to the 1958 Sci-Fi B-Movie *The Blob*, to reference a large unstructured item of data. Some modern programming languages allow manipulation of Blobs.

WHERE NEXT?

As with hardware and software, the basic building blocks of data were in place relatively early in the information revolution. Relational databases and even data objects were in use well before the turn of the century, along with *SQLs* to interrogate them. The mechanisms by which organisations store, access and analyse data haven't changed greatly in the last decade or so.

What has changed dramatically is how organisations use data, both storing and accessing it in ever greater quantities.

How will those trends towards big data, better governance, deeper and more widespread analytics and visualisation continue, and how will regulators respond?

Bigger Data

Global data generation is going to continue to grow exponentially, driven mainly by social media and the IoT, certainly for the next few years.

Some drivers for data growth appear to have reached a plateau. For example, according to recent reports, the number of emails sent and received per day worldwide in 2023 is approximately 350 billion, representing only a 4.3% increase from the previous year (333 billion), a trend that is expected to continue. And, according to Statista,[12] there are an estimated 6.3 billion smartphone users globally (out of an 8.1 billion population), a number that has grown by about 5% each year for the last five years. The rate of smartphone ownership per capita has stayed broadly static in that time. Gone are the days of 20–25% growth.

But in the world of business and finance, it seems that the collection and analysis of big data has only just begun, and while this represents a small proportion of the world's current data generation, this trend will push the pace of data growth for some years to come.

One way to track data growth is through the size, number and location of data centres that hold and process the data.

There are approximately 8,000 data centres globally.

The United States is home to a third of these, with Germany (6%), the United Kingdom (5.7%) and China (5.5%) the next in line. Of the eight biggest data centres in the world, the top two are in or near Hohhot in China (China Telecom's Data Centre sprawls over 10 million square feet, while China Mobile's comes in at nearly 8 million square feet), while five are in the United States, ranging from Nevada and Utah to Georgia.

Non-European countries such as Canada, Australia, Japan, Brazil and India might expect to begin catching up to the leaders over the next decade. Further, many existing data centres are at risk of being out of date – the average age of data centres globally is nine years, whereas Gartner estimates that data centres over seven years old are at risk of being obsolete.

Vacancy rates (i.e. the proportion of a data centre's capacity that is unused) are falling across the globe, and rates of construction are increasing by 5–6% annually.

Data centres already account for about 4% of global energy consumption.

One consequence of these numbers might be that with data-generation growing at an exponential rate and capacity growing at a slower, more linear, rate, the demand for data capacity may start to outstrip supply, with cost and availability consequences.

Formal Data Governance

Formal, structured data governance in organisations is relatively recent and in many cases has been implemented in a disjointed or piecemeal fashion.

Perhaps the biggest trend in the next few years will be a mind shift from data governance being an "IT" problem to its being the responsibility of the whole organisation. In particular, the role played by business and operational leaders in owning and managing their data will become more and more accepted, and the data teams will be able focus on the analytical roles they are paid to do rather than spending their time beating the drum for improved governance to an unwilling audience.

Increasingly, organisations will find the budgets to strengthen their data governance, classifying and mapping their existing data while also ensuring any new projects treat data as the pivotal and precious resource it is, rather than an afterthought.

With the likelihood of deeper and wider data regulation, organisations will be required to manage their data more reliably and be able to provide evidence of this more quickly to regulators.

Most importantly, data governance will need to be seen not as a response to heavier regulation but as a self-fulfilling end in itself – not just to have better data (and better control of that data) but to be able to enact business more effectively as a result.

Organisations can expect to see more complex and complete policies on data usage, alongside a stronger data governance team with real power to ensure compliance with policies. As a business leader, your role as the data owner will become stronger and more specific. You will be expected to know your data and take an active role in ensuring its quality, consistency and security.

More Sophisticated Data Warehouses

The first data warehouses were typically held in the organisation's own data centre, often being simply the result of taking overnight backups of the operational systems. Warehouses would grow organically as technology projects – impacting parts of the overall system – built feeds into the data warehouse almost as a byproduct.

As the use of data warehouses matured, and organisations began to see them as the rich, untapped vein of minable data that they are, they began to be moved off site into the cloud. Data lakes were added as a staging point where big data could be collected before being transformed into a single canonical data model for the organisation and loaded into the warehouse.

As data begins to exist and thrive in its own right, these organically grown stores may need to be amended, and in some cases pulled apart and rebuilt from scratch, in order to properly accommodate the data needs of the organisation.

Domain-specific data warehouses may come into being, where local data can be used more appropriately, away from the rest of the firm's data (especially where there may be sensitivities as to who can access the data).

Another relatively new concept is the "lakehouse", a cross between a data lake and a data warehouse. Following on from the simple fact that data storage is cheap whereas computation is expensive, the trend is towards more agile stores of data, allowing analytics to take place nearer to the data source.

More Involvement in Data Analytics

For many organisations, data analytics is still very much a sideshow, hiding in the wings, while the "proper" business of the organisation is played out on centre-stage. But with organisations having to deal with ever-increasing volumes of data, and the demand for tighter controls and more defined responsibility from the regulators, analytics will become a critical tool for most organisations.

Data quality remains a key issue – in order to cleanse data, it must first be located and identified, then analysed for inconsistencies and errors. Data owners will play a significant role in that process, and even more so in the design of plans to cleanse and remediate the data.

But alongside these corrective measures, business users will be encouraged to use data to benefit the organisation. Once the data you have is reliable, you will be able to use it to direct your business more effectively. Your data analytics colleagues will be making more use of tools like Python and Hadoop as well as taking advantage of seismic industry advances in AI and machine learning to spot emerging trends or identifying poorly performing business areas. AI and machine-learning, in particular, will revolutionise the speed with which data can be analysed, providing the opportunity for analysis of live data in real time. Instead of being able to review last month's sales figures, you will be able to see sales data as it happens (or even before it happens) and make real-time decisions using the most relevant data (although arguably you can do that now with currently available tools, but the collective surge of analytics and business capabilities will make this more achievable).

Your own involvement is likely to be through a more user-friendly interface such as Power BI, Tableau or via the more mundane Excel (and possibly SQL if you're feeling super keen). Whereas once the production of this business intelligence required months of work with a project team to produce (something like) the desired reports, business users will be encouraged more and more to "self-serve" using a range of data analytics tools.

There are huge advantages in a self-service environment. Only you really know what you are looking for – and while you could explain that to a data analyst who can then write a report for you, it may not be immediately obvious or successful, needing constant tweaking and aligning. As the report-writer yourself, you can flex as necessary to get to the data (and the outcome) you want.

Ubiquitous Data Visualisation

Have you ever been blown away by a presentation? Admired the way the presenter has encapsulated the key message in a simple graphic?

Imagine the audience's reaction to the first ever pie chart displayed in 1801 by William Playfair, or to Florence Nightingale's rose chart in 1857.

In the modern era, it's almost impossible to spend a day without seeing some kind of data visualisation, whether it's a line chart for stock market value, a bar or pie chart showing market share or audience numbers, or a more sophisticated infographic showing some kind of distribution over time or location like a weather chart.

So, if you want to get that "wow" factor and really get your message across simply and effectively, your data visualisations are going to have to be something special that sets them apart from the daily norms.

Many applications provide ready-made visualisation tools such as bar charts and pie charts. These are standard tools and still work really well for more mundane presentations such as status reports or regular updates. But for that one-off, career-critical or pitch-clinching presentation, it will become more and more common for organisations to use dedicated data visualisation tools.

Data visualisation tools provide users with an easy way to create visual representations, especially when dealing with large data sets that could include millions of data points. There are many different tools available on the market, but the best share a number of common features:

- Ease of use – the best tools are intuitive and are supported by excellent documentation and tutorials.

- Data import – being able to handle huge sets of data is important. The very best tools can even handle multiple sets of data in a single visualisation.
- Variety of visualisation – the best tools can output an array of different chart, graph and map types, in both a static image and as interactive graphics.
- Cost – as you'd expect, there is a wide range of costs, from freeware to the very high-end professional tool. If the tool has a high price-tag, it's worth ensuring that its capabilities justify the cost.

Wider Data Regulation

In the years since GDPR was enacted in Europe, privacy laws have continued to be enacted elsewhere across the globe, with an increase in regulatory enforcement.

In the United States, GDPR-like privacy regulations are (or will soon be) in effect in a number of states, notably California. Comprehensive privacy laws are currently under consideration by several other state legislatures and there is some discussion of federal privacy legislation. The American Data Privacy and Protection Act (ADPPA) would have set limits the collection, processing and transfer of personal data without express consent, but was not voted on by the full House of Representatives.

GDPR-like laws have also been enacted in various other countries, including Brazil and China, with changes expected in Australia to align to GDPR including the right to be forgotten.

But there are many regions, notably, developing economies, that do not have adequate consumer protection in place yet. The United Nations Conference on Trade and Development reports that in as many as 52 countries, data was not available regarding their privacy protections "suggesting that online consumer protection is not being fully addressed".

Regulators will also need to adapt to advances in technology, especially in the field of AI.

Fines in recent years have varied from region to region but can be generally expected to increase over time. Regulators have targeted a range of industries: predominantly technology companies but also organisations in the retail, telecom, energy, healthcare and professional services industries, among others. Organisations should also expect regulators to continue to enforce the law across a range of industries. While regulators may remain open to reducing fines if the organisations involved can demonstrate steps they are taking to mitigate the harmful effects of data breaches, it is unclear how forgiving regulators will be in the coming years.

As more privacy regulations are enacted globally and as regulators step up enforcement of the GDPR and other existing laws, it's vital that organisations continue to make privacy a priority. This includes ensuring corporate governance supports privacy protection.

The regulatory frameworks presented by the GDPR and other laws make clear that senior management must play an active role in managing data privacy rather than delegating responsibility.

Recommendations for organisations to prepare for stronger regulation might include data mapping exercises to determine how information and data flow through organisations, both digitally and physically, the implementation of data classification policies enhanced data governance practices and the tightening of information security.

SO WHAT?

Data is one of the fastest changing aspects of the information revolution at the moment. What does that mean for the business leader?

For most organisations, the key trend will be the movement of data into the mainstream (unless your organisation is purely data-driven, in which case that's possibly already the case). What are the questions you should be asking, of yourself and your data governance teams, in order to support this transition?

Questions the business leader should ask are as follows:

- What's the data maturity level of my organisation?
- Do I know and understand my data?
- Is my data reliable?
- Who has access to my data?
- What can my data tell me?
- How can I use infographics effectively?

What's the Data Maturity Level of My Organisation?

Before you can do anything personally in the data domain or domains that belong to you, it's worth evaluating the data maturity level of your organisation as a whole. If the organisation itself is more mature, you will find that your job of data ownership becomes a lot easier, as you will have support from above and around you.

Assessing data maturity is something you could do yourself, or you can bring in an external consultancy to do it for you.

Maturity assessments will typically place your organisation on a scale from 1 to 5 and will look at data governance (do domain owners know that they own their data and understand what it is), data architecture (is data designed into the organisation's applications or simply allowed to land where it falls), data quality (how often do data quality issues cause problems for the organisation, and what levels of control are there) and data management (how is data input, amended and removed from your business and its systems).

The reality is that the vast majority of organisations will find themselves at the lower end of the scale.

But the first step to enlightenment is self-awareness, as they say, so the very act of performing a formal or informal maturity assessment is a step in the right direction.

Do I Know and Understand My Data?

This is the key question for the business leader from a data architecture point of view.

Do you know your data?

Do you know where it comes from, and how it is stored, transported and used? What specific purpose does it serve? How significant is the data? What downstream processes – whether automated or manual – does it govern? Are you collecting data you don't need? Are you missing data that you do need?

Do you know every data attribute? Do you know where that data attribute sits relative to the rest of your data? Do you know its primary key and entity? That's not to say that you need to know all of the aspects of data architecture and be able to recite third normal form verbatim, but you do need to understand which data belongs to which keys.

Do you know the semantic meaning of every datum? Is it written down? Is it clear to everybody in the business what that datum is, what it represents? Is there a similar attribute that could cause confusion? Are there two widely accepted sets of data that are in fact the same?

You should be able to answer all of these questions.

You should have a data dictionary that sets out, for every attribute:

- What it is called
- What it's used for
- How it is collected and by what system or process
- Where is your master data or "golden copy"
- Whether and how it gets updated
- What validation needs to be applied
- How the datum is used by downstream processes (manual or automated)
- Who can see or use it
- Any business rules that apply
- How it is transported around your system and externally
- Any regulatory aspects
- How long you need to keep it for
- How it is disposed of

Remember that this is at the level of the logical model: you're not expected to know exactly what the datum is called on every system and the mechanics of how it is physically transported and held. But you should know its label name on screens, for example, and whether these differ across systems.

And you should at least understand how the logical model is mapped to physical data fields in tables and on databases.

Is the same logical datum being mapped onto two different physical fields? Or are two unrelated logical data being squeezed into a single physical field? This happens more than you might expect and is referred to as "overloading" by data architects. It tends to happen as systems evolve over time. If a new datum is needed to control a business rule in an existing application but the organisation doesn't want to bear the expense of adding and managing a new field when there is an existing field that's "no longer used", the temptation exists to simply "repurpose" the existing field for the new use. Other examples are identifiers that are somehow meaningful, such as a product identifier that starts with a specific letter indicating the manufacturer: in this case, if a new manufacturer takes over the production, the data will be misleading. This overloading isn't always so obvious and it is a common trap in database design. Every datum should be placed in its own discrete physical attribute wherever possible.

You may wonder if this is your responsibility at all? Surely, it's up to the data team to define these things? But remember, you are the owner of the data: the data architects merely seek to model the data that you help to define. You should find that your organisation's data architects are only too happy for you to step up and take on your responsibility to help define the data landscape. It will make their modelling job a lot easier if they have a data owner who really recognises the need and is willing to take the time to understand their data.

Is My Data Reliable?

If understanding your data from an architectural perspective is critical, so too is knowing how reliable your actual data is in the real world. The most perfect logical model will fall down if the data within it is flawed.

Do you know where your data comes from? For every attribute and primary key in your model? Where and how does it enter the organisation? Is that a reliable source? Is data collection automated or does it involve some manual input by a member of staff? What validation is applied to the data at point of entry? Is that enough? Can the data be amended, and if so by whom and in what circumstances? Is the data replicated across multiple systems? Can it be independently amended and become out of kilter?

In an ideal world, all of your data would be sourced reliably and remain in pristine condition throughout its lifetime. But in reality, you will inevitably have many data quality issues and need to focus on the most important ones. So, you need to understand what impact these data quality issues have on your organisation, and how significant they are.

If your organisation can bear the cost of a permanent rolling data quality programme, then any operational issues caused by bad data can be fed into that programme, analysed and prioritised accordingly. Again, it's vital that this prioritisation is completed with your input and direction. The data quality programme itself cannot be the arbiter of what is most important to the organisation: it needs the considered view of the business sponsors and stakeholders. If no permanent programme exists, at the very least you should ensure that there are regular reviews of operational incidents, identifying those where data is a root cause, and lobby for the appropriate remedial steps to be taken.

Key causes of poor data quality include the following:

- Data entry errors – where data is manually input by humans, errors will occur. Humans are fallible, get distracted, fail to read correctly, mistype, or type in the wrong place. Wherever possible, seek to eradicate the human factor by getting data to be sourced automatically. In the case of client data, try to get the client to input the data directly (such as into a web portal or through an app).
- Data integration and transformation errors – where data is passed around your systems, even by automated means, it can become corrupted. Where two systems have inconsistent data formats, converting from one format to another can introduce errors (even simple transformations such as one data field being longer than another, leading to truncation of the data).
- Lack of an authoritative data source – in a database that's distributed over a number of systems, such as with a reporting database, even if data errors are identified and fixed, if the data is not fixed at source, the problem will persist. This also applies to derived data where some automated process takes raw data and calculates a result of some sort – in this case fixing the data isn't going to end the issue; you'll need to ensure the erroneous process is also corrected.
- Data storage and accessibility issues – even if your data is correct, if it can't be accessed by the person (or application) that needs it, it may as well not be there. Or if it's freely available to everyone in the organisation (especially if that access allows anyone to update it), it may quickly become corrupted.
- Data governance and ownership issues – an inevitable consequence of poor data governance is poor data quality. If the data is not owned by the business, with clear rules and responsibilities, well-documented and properly architected, there will be little control of data throughout the organisation. Remember the mantra – as a business leader you own the data, not the IT team.

It's unlikely that you will ever have perfect data. A simple mantra is "you're never done on data". You will always need to prioritise the most impactful quality issues, and the rate of change of business rules, software, operational users and other factors means there is always opportunity for something new to go wrong. But don't beat yourself up: identify the biggest issues, prioritise those and don't sweat the small stuff.

Who Has Access to My Data?

Your data is valuable. In the wrong hands it can open up your organisation to malign intent. This can impact your business' reputation or damage your clients directly. Even internally and, presumably, unintentionally, allowing unfettered access to your data to the wrong parts of the business can have dire consequences. There may be confidentiality issues (imagine if all HR records were made available to everyone in the organisation including salaries, records of grievances or disciplinary actions), or the data may be accidentally updated or even wiped.

Some data, by its nature, must be more stringently restricted for regulatory or legal reasons. Data breaches, even internal ones, can have serious consequences for your organisation.

Strong data governance will help, here. Knowing, for each datum, exactly who should be able to see it and update it – and through which applications – will help to define what access controls you will need.

Another benefit of strong data governance is a clear policy on data archiving and deletion. Once data is no longer required (and this may be a matter of regulation), it can be archived or deleted. The sooner it can be removed from live systems, the better: first, it no longer clutters up your live databases, saving time and space, and second, there is no chance of it being used or updated erroneously by your operational teams, or of its being included in live business intelligence outputs providing a misleading slant on your business trends.

Where data is needed in test systems, anonymisation and obfuscation will help protect data from unauthorised viewing and accidental updates.

Another hidden risk of unauthorised access lies in any unstructured data that you or your operational teams may have recorded. File notes, spreadsheets, working copies of client reports and any other material stored in directories on the organisations filing systems may be freely available to be viewed by those who would not normally have access to the data through structured channels (applications and formal processes).

Unstructured documentation should never be part of your formal operational processes, but if they are, you should ensure that such copies are temporary and are destroyed as soon as possible.

Where data is sent to external agencies through authorised channels, control of those channels must be a formal part of your information security policy. Any changes to external data destinations should be carefully controlled.

What Can My Data Tell Me?

As a business leader, you probably already receive a regular set of reports and management information, telling you how your part of the business is faring.

But is there other data you could be using? Data about your clients. Data about your team. Data about the products you are selling (and those you are not). Data distributed across time or geographically. There really is no limit, and as we have seen, there are plenty of tools available to extract and interpret data.

There may be data that would have been useful, but the project team didn't have capacity to deliver, or simply got prioritised into the next decade. If you have your own capability (through Power BI or SQL) to build your own extracts and reports, you may be able to get one step ahead and identify trends before your competitors (whether external or internal).

How Can I Use Infographics Effectively?

Once you've extracted the vital data and identified the trends, how can you use it effectively to transform the business?

In some cases, a simple bar chart or pie chart may do the job, but often you will need to make the right impression on senior leaders to persuade them to spend their precious budget on the changes you are proposing. In those cases, it may be worth spending a little extra time (and money) producing a commanding infographic or data visualisation.

A picture may tell a thousand words, but the impact of a well-designed data visualisation can multiply that many times.

NOTES

1   *The Day Parliament Burned Down* by Caroline Shenton, 2013.
2   *Introduction to the History of Computing* by Gerard O'Regan, 2016, ISBN 978-3-319-33137-9.
3   An Electric Tabulating System by Herman Hollerith, 1889.
4   *Scientific American* July 25, 1896.
5   A Relational Model of Data for Large Shared Data Banks by Edgar Frank Codd, 1970.
6   *Further Normalization of the Data Base Relational Model* by Edgar Frank Codd, 1972.
7   *Natural and Political Observations Mentioned in a Following Index and Made upon the Bills of Mortality* by John Graunt, 1662.
8   *Data Cube: A Relational Aggregation Operator Generalizing Group-By, Cross-Tab, and Sub-Totals* by Jim Gray et al, 1997.
9   Worth a thousand Words, *The Economist*, October 2013.
10 *The Visual Display of Quantitative Information* by Edward Tufte, 1983.
11 www.perceptualedge.com
12 www.statista.com

4

What's an Interface?

The idea is that the content is the interface, the information is the interface, not computer-administrative debris.

Edward Tufte

Like most users, Frank was getting pretty fed up with predictive text....

 DOI: 10.4324/9781003372660-4

"Mr. Watson, come here, I want to see you".

With these somewhat prosaic words, on March 10, 1876, Thomas Watson (assistant to Alexander Graham Bell) became the first recipient of an electronic message conveyed directly from one user to another in real time. Watson himself later wrote: "Perhaps, if Mr. Bell had realized that he was about to make a bit of history, he would have been prepared with a more sounding and interesting sentence".

Thirty-two years before that, Samuel Morse sent the more momentous – apocalyptic, even – message "What hath God wrought" over 44 miles of telegraph cable between Washington, DC, and Baltimore using a code of long and short electrical pulses.

These early pioneers could have hardly comprehended how, not even 180 years later, it would be possible to connect any two points on the globe (and beyond) at any time and that the messages relayed over this almost infinite network would include voice, text and data between people, computer systems and an ever-growing array of devices such as watches, clothing and kettles.

The modern business will use hundreds of applications, possibly thousands, each performing its own specific functions. But what really transforms a business is when all of the applications *talk* to each other. Imagine if you could write a document using word-processing software, or you could send an email, but not both. Or if you could record a client's contact details in your customer relationship management (CRM), but then had to manually hand write every letter (OK, so that still happens and more often than you might think). Interfaces are the glue that holds all of these different applications together.

In this chapter we look at interfaces, both between applications and externally to other organisations, as well as the inexorable rise of the internet and the World Wide Web, through Web 2.0, Web 3.0 and beyond.

And, as usual, we'll be looking at what that means to you, the business leader – what you need to know and do to make the best use of the interface technology available now and in the future.

WHY SHOULD I CARE?

Think of a world without interfaces.

Think of trying to run your business in such a world. No data coming in: no emails, no orders, no payments. No data going out: no invoices, no product catalogues. And no data moving between the different applications in your organisation.

No Google.

Interfaces are the glue that holds all of your applications together and exposes them to the outside world. Without interfaces, computers would have remained curiosities – standalone calculators for big corporations and playthings for hobbyists. It was only by connecting those calculators to the outside world that the banks and financial institutions started to see real business benefits in having them. And it took the internet to really transform the humble PC into the world-dominating essential it is today.

It's easy to think of an interface as sitting squarely in the technology domain. It's just wires and sockets, right? Or transmitters and receivers. But that would be selling it short, like thinking of a movie as being just pictures and sound. A good movie will inspire you, excite you and make you laugh or cry. It's the content that matters. A well-designed interface may not invoke the same emotional levels as a good rom-com, but the same is true – it's the content that matters, not just the tech.

Interfacing is about three things:

- The technological capability to *connect* two (or more) "end points" – places where messages start and end or are sent and received;
- An agreement between the sender and receiver(s) as to how to encode the *meaning* of the message into data that can be transmitted; and
- A means to *safeguard* the contents of the message from prying eyes and those with malicious intent.

So, in an organisation that is dependent on sending, receiving and cycling meaningful data securely around its technology domain, your business is utterly dependent on the quality of its interfaces.

It means you, as a business leader, should really understand how they work and the role that you can play in making them more effective.

HOW DID WE GET HERE?

Mankind has flirted with telegraphy (or long-distance messaging) for millennia, and, bizarrely, much of that communication was digital in nature. A warning beacon, lit to pass news of an invasion along a chain from one station to the next, was essentially binary – either it was lit or it wasn't. Smoke signals are much the same. In the fourth century BC, the Greek scholar Polybius popularised a form of code by representing the letters of the alphabet in a 5 by 5 grid: each letter could be spelt out by the positioning of torches in sequence.

Semaphore, using flags , torches or other visual signals, was heavily used in military manoeuvres and for conveying commands over long distances. Napoleonic France championed the Chappe telegraph, invented by Claude Chappe in the late eighteenth century, a system of pointers and pulleys atop a vast network of towers stretching across continental Europe. At sea, flags were flown from masts and rigging to achieve the same end: Admiral Nelson's "England expects that every man will do his duty" before the Battle of Trafalgar in 1805 was broadcast from the HMS Victory to the rest of the fleet by a sequence of 12 combinations of up to three flags each (Nelson was convinced by his signaller John Pasco to change the message from "England confides…" to "England expects…" simply because "expects" was a defined word in the code and needed only one combination of three flags, whereas "confides" would need to be spelled out individually, letter by letter). One of the most famous uses of flag semaphore was on the cover of the 1965 Beatles album "Help!", where the members of the band were depicted seemingly spelling out the album title in semaphore using their arms. Sadly, in a triumph of style over substance, what they're actually saying is "NUJV".

It wasn't until the mid-nineteenth century, amid a spate of innovation, that an electrical telegraph was designed that could encode a message, transmit it across a meaningful length of cable without a significant loss of signal and then convert it back into a readable form at the far end.

Once the technology was in place, the coders and cryptologists took their turn.

Interfacing with Dials, Dots and Dashes

The decades that preceded the first commercial telegraphs in 1838 were filled with technological innovation as the dawn of the electronic age spawned a myriad of possibilities. At the same time, the advent of the railways created a very real need for more reliable, instantaneous communication than had been possible with purely optical methods.

Inventors and visionaries applied their ingenuity to the task. Static electricity was replaced by voltaic cells, or permanent magnets were spun by hand to generate an electrical current to send signals down wires to a receiver that had to produce its own energy to detect and amplify the signal. Baron Schilling von Canstatt proposed the use of binary digits (or "bits") to transmit data, while Carl Friedrich Gauss and Wilhelm Weber used an induction coil and a permanent magnet to send messages across the rooftops of Göttingen in Germany in what is widely regarded as the first use of an electric telegraph. Keys and dials were used to select the characters to send, while a range of solutions for displaying the message to the recipient was used from sparks and needles to pith balls hovering above 26 electrostatically charged wires.[1]

The invention of the electromagnet by William Sturgeon in 1825 was the key catalyst for change and in particular caught the attention of one Samuel Morse, a painter travelling back from Europe to America in 1832. Intrigued by the concept of a telegraph, Morse sought the aid of scientists Joseph Henry and Leonard Gale and fellow inventor Alfred Vail. Two key breakthroughs were made: the first was the invention of a system of relays that would periodically boost the electrical signal while the second was the development of a set of codes that would allow messages to be sent along a single wire. In January 1838, Morse and Vail demonstrated their single-wire electric telegraph in an ironworks in New Jersey, sending a signal through 2 miles of cable.

Across the Atlantic, an English pair of inventors, William Cooke and Charles Wheatstone, had already patented their own version of the electric telegraph in 1837, having started on the path slightly later than Morse. Their version used a range of smaller batteries to produce a more sustainable current down six wires to control two needles.

Both teams benefited from the very existence of the railways they were to serve: the tracks connecting the major industrial and commercial hubs provided an ideal thoroughfare alongside which to lay the cables and wires necessary to carry the electrical signal between those very same locations (Morse even briefly experimented with sending signals down the tracks themselves). Cooke and Wheatstone laid their cables between Paddington station in London and West Drayton along 13 miles of the Great Western Railway, eventually switching to two wires and one needle when extending further to Slough, while in 1843 Morse laid his single cable along 38 miles of the Baltimore and Ohio Railroad between Washington, DC, and Baltimore.

The Cooke and Wheatstone system used a needle to point to the transmitted letter, whereas the Morse system used Morse Code, a series of dots and dashes (or short and long signals also called "dits" and "dahs") to represent each letter, which was initially printed to a ribbon. Ultimately, the cost of the extra wiring required to control the needle became a barrier and the Morse system eventually won the day. By 1850, just six years after Morse had sent his famous "What hath God wrought" message from Washington to Baltimore, over 12,000 miles of cable had been laid across the states of America.

Because Morse's telegraph transmitted each character in turn, causing a stylus to make a mark on the slowly feeding ticker tape, he designed his code to be as succinct as possible. Initially, the code included only numbers, but this was later expanded by Vail to include the 26 letters of the alphabet. Vail used a set of printer's type to identify the most commonly used letters and to these he assigned the shortest sequence of dots and dashes (the two most frequently occurring letters E and T are represented by a single dot and a single dash respectively). By shortening the sequence for the most common letters, Vail's innovation promoted quicker telecommunication – although the equipment of the day limited transmission to around 30 characters a minute, later operators were able to decode messages at an astonishing rate, many averaging over 60 words per minute (while the fastest Morse code operator ever officially recorded was Theodore Roosevelt McElroy at 75.6 wpm in 1939).

Vail's original code was adopted in America, but a rival coding became the standard in Europe, leading to a period of confusion, especially once the first transatlantic cables were laid in 1866. The European coding (modified by the German Friedrich Gerke) was more resistant to distortion over such distances and became the dominant format internationally. With the invention of radio transmission (initially called "wireless telegraphy") at the end of the nineteenth century, the international version of

Morse Code became more common and was finally adopted globally at the International Radiotelegraph Convention in London in 1912.

Although planned beforehand, the convention was influenced by the sinking of the *RMS Titanic* earlier that year and by the much-publicised delay in the arrival of local shipping to rescue survivors from the disaster. There were many factors that caused that delay, but it's not clear that the use of two variants of Morse Code was one of them. In fact, with the benefit of hindsight, the communications failures experienced on the night were typical interfacing issues.

The Titanic was outfitted with a Marconi telegraph that used longwave radio signals known to have a short effective range. The two Marconi-employed telegraphists (Jack Phillips and his assistant Harold Bride) were run ragged by constant requests to send trivial "Marconigrams" on behalf of Titanic's well-heeled passengers. When he received a message from the radio operator of the nearby *SS Californian* saying that it had encountered ice, Phillips testily responded "Shut up! I am busy". When disaster hit, Phillips at first sent a distress code common amongst the Marconi radio operators: "CQD" ("Seek you", "Distress") before switching to the newer "SOS" call. Radio traffic was awash with ships seeking clarification and amateur radio operators, messages were relayed ineffectively and the *Titanic* itself became the bottleneck, able only to either send or receive a single message at any one time. And the nearest available ship, the *SS Californian*? Upset by Phillips' earlier request to "shut up", the radio operator had switched off his set and gone to bed.[2]

In modern terms, these various failures could be categorised in terms of technology, security and content. The technology was flawed and largely untested, with a number of single points of failure. The message channels were open and insecure, allowing non-critical traffic, both in terms of the spurious "Marconigrams" and the amateur or unrelated shipping traffic creating noise that impeded the signal of the distress call. And finally, the content itself was confused – no single standard existed at the time, and the "CQD" call was ignored by some nearby ships as they did not recognise it.

Once Morse's telegraph became operational, innovators began to explore ways of making the technology more accessible. In 1846, the inventor Royal Earl House patented the first printing telegraph, which linked two piano-style keyboards – each with a spinning typewheel – by cable. The wheels were mechanically synchronised so that whenever a key was pressed at the sending station, it activated the wheel at the distant station just as the corresponding character moved into position to produce typed text.

By 1857, a number of small telegraph companies were in operation and merged to form one large corporation: the Western Union Telegraph Company.

In 1874, the French inventor Emile Baudot, in developing his own printing telegraph, noted that Morse Code wasn't well-suited to automation due to the uneven length of data required for each letter. Baudot introduced a five-bit code which could be more reliably interpreted by the receiving machinery. Baudot's keyboard used five piano keys (two for the left hand and three for the right) which operators would press in turn: the pressed keys would be locked until the machinery cycled round with an audible click (the "cadence signal"), telling the operator that they could press the next combination of keys to send the next letter. Operators had to keep up with the machinery and keep to the cadence. The rate at which bits are sent across an interface is still measured in Baud (one bit per second).

Improvements were made to Baudot's machine in 1901 by the inventor Donald Murray, who conceived the idea while working at the Sydney Morning Herald. Murray's system allowed the operator to punch a paper tape using a typewriter-style keyboard, and it was the tape that was then used to transmit the message. This mechanism was much easier on the human operators as there was no longer a direct connection between the keyboard and the transmitter. To manage the formatting of the typed message at the receiving end, Murray introduced further innovations: a "shift" code that switched the meaning between letters and figures, and a number of control characters (also known as "format effectors"), including the CR (Carriage Return) and LF (Line Feed) codes.

Murray sold the rights for his machine to Western Union who gradually replaced all of its Morse telegraphs with the new "teletypewriters".

Throughout the early part of the twentieth century, the telegraph, and in particular the telegraphic printer, underwent a steady stream of improvement and refinement, until by the mid-1920s there were multiple purveyors of devices (such as those of the United Kingdom's Creed & Company), all of which featured a typewriter-style keyboard, the capability to print a page of transmitted text at a rate of tens of words per minute.

These developments reached their conclusion (in the mechanical era at least) in the telex (TELegraph EXchange) machines and related networks that arose in the mid-1930s. Carried by thousands of miles of undersea cables that enshrouded the world, telex machines provided a global, digital communication channel, albeit one that was painfully slow by today's standards and which needed human beings at either end to input and read the messages themselves.

Interfacing with Voices

In 1874, a number of parallel advances in an attempt to create what was called a "harmonic telegraph", with inventors Elisha Gray and Alexander Graham Bell both working on enabling the transmission of sound.

Thomas Watson, Bell's assistant, recalled later[3] how Bell had described his vision:

> I have never forgotten his exact words; they have run in my mind ever since like a mathematical formula. "If," he said, "I could make a current of electricity vary in intensity, precisely as the air varies in density during the production of a sound, I should be able to transmit speech telegraphically." He then sketched for me an instrument that he thought would do this, and we discussed the possibility of constructing one.

A few months later, in June 1875, while attempting to fix what seemed to be a stuck reed in their experimental equipment, Watson inadvertently plucked the reed which caused Bell, from the next room, to yelp in surprise.

> That undulatory current had passed through the connecting wire to the distant receiver which, fortunately, was a mechanism that could transform that current back into an extremely faint echo of the sound of the vibrating spring that had generated it, but what was still more fortunate, the right man had that mechanism at his ear during that fleeting moment, and instantly recognized the transcendent importance of that faint sound thus electrically transmitted.

Bell and Watson had, almost by mistake, invented the first telephone (although this is possibly the most disputed "first" in the history of scientific invention, with other claimants including the Italian Antonio Meucci in 1854, German Johann Philipp Reis in 1861, Elisha Gray who filed a patent on the same day as Bell, and even Thomas Edison).

The pair worked on their device in two attic rooms, leading to the famous instruction from Bell to Watson in March 1876 to "come here". Bell was fierce in his desire to commercialise his invention, with public displays often involving Watson being asked to sing to a remote audience.

More innovation followed: at first, telephones were hard-wired in pairs, directly connecting two fixed locations with no mechanism to alert the recipient to an incoming call, requiring them to sit by the phone all day. Watson experimented with signalling devices involving the striking of hammers and ringers, while Hungarian Tivadar Puskás is credited with the invention of the telephone exchange and switchboard by 1887.

Bell and his financiers initially offered to sell their patents to the Western Union Telegraph Company for the sum of $100,000, but the president of the company believed that the telephone was merely a toy. Thomas Watson later opined that "two years later the Western Union would gladly have bought those patents for $25,000,000".

The Bell Telephone Company was created in 1877 quickly becoming one of the powerhouses of American, indeed global, telephony and research. Two days before the end of the century, it transferred its ownership to its own subsidiary, American Telephone & Telegraph Company (AT&T). AT&T briefly bought a controlling share in Western Union (which withdrew early from the telephony business in favour of the telegraph) in 1909.

It is curious to note that, in the early part of the twentieth century, the telephone – which, although electronic, was essentially an analogue mechanism – rose to completely dominate global communications, with the digital electronic telegraph relegated to a very distant second best.

It took the invention and popularisation of the computer to decisively reverse that trend and for digital communication to become not just dominant but universal.

Interfacing with Computers

The first computer-to-computer interface was built by AT&T for the United States Air Force air defence initiative, SAGE (Semiautomatic Ground Environment) in the 1950s, to link the various dispersed radar stations to the command centres in real time. Digital radar images needed to be converted into an analogue signal, sent down the phone lines and then converted back into a digital signal so that it could be interpreted by the IBM supercomputer at the local Direction Centre or Control Centre.

In fact, SAGE used IBM AN/FSQ-7 computers in each of 23 Direction Centres, and IBM AN/FSQ-8 computers at 8 Combat Centres. Each computer was built with 2 "sides" which were swapped regularly, making 62 computers in total. The conversion process of modulating the digital data into an analogue signal and then demodulating it back to digital gave the interface device its name: a "modulator-demodulator" or modem.

AT&T worked on a commercial version of this device, and in 1958 the first spark of the internet was struck with the release of the Bell 101 modem, soon followed by the Bell 103 in 1963, capable of transmitting data at speeds of up to 300 bits per second over standard phone lines.

As the IBM System/360 mainframe drove business computer usage through the ceiling in the mid-1960s, AT&T modems were on hand to allow those businesses to connect their systems to each other.

But the limitations of using the public telephone network soon became apparent. A lot of time was wasted waiting for the connection to be made between the two computers on the line – a few seconds only but even at the low transfer speeds then possible this was a significant delay. And to make matters worse, the networks would apply a minimum chargeable duration for each call (usually 3 minutes) – fine for a human-to-human call but fiendishly expensive for two computers that could get their business done in seconds.

These issues were solved with the concept and implementation of dedicated *packet-switching* networks.

Between 1962 and 1966 a collection of visionaries conceived and implemented the fundamental building blocks of the modern *internet*. Central to this process was ARPA (later DARPA), the US Advanced Research Projects Agency. J. C. R. Licklider, the first director of the Information Processing Techniques Office (IPTO) at ARPA who had worked extensively on the mechanics of "time sharing" or the use of one large mainframe computer by several users at different typewriter-like terminals, dreamt of an "intergalactic" network of connected computers. He inspired his colleagues to implement his design, and in 1965, Ivan Sutherland and Lawrence Roberts successfully connected two computers directly to each other, using time-sharing to allow each computer to access the other. Elsewhere, two computer scientists, Paul Baran in the United States in 1962 and Donald Davies in the United Kingdom in 1965, independently proposed the concept of sending data in packets, or blocks, over a distributed network of connections rather than via a single line. Davies, in particular, was inspired to look for an alternative transmission protocol by his realisation that information exchanges between computers were significantly more "bursty" than those between human beings. In 1966, Davies suggested the term "interface unit" for what we would today call a router: a device that would split, distribute and reconstruct the original message from the packets.[4]

A successor to Licklider as director of IPTO, Bob Taylor, took the idea of a galactic network and applied it to ARPA's many distributed communities of research teams. He believed that the "next thing to do was obvious": connect the teams working across the country,[5] building on Baran's and Davies' ideas of a packet-switching network. Although initially favouring a "star" formation with a central router, the team eventually hit upon the idea of a number of distributed, smaller routers that would collectively govern the switching of packets to their correct destinations.

ARPANET, and the internet (albeit at a very limited scale), was born.

Managing this new form of distributed computing required a revolutionary way of communicating. It was different from anything that had preceded it. There was no single complete connection across the network: packets of data had to be passed from host to host without waiting for a reply, possibly multiple times through multiple paths, with a way to track undelivered packets and resend them. A "Network Working Group" was established and set about the task of devising such a protocol. In 1974, the working group proposed the first version, the Transmission Control Program (TCP), and a few years later this was further split into the TCP that governed the creation of the packets and the Internet Protocol (IP) that managed their distribution across the network (collectively known as TCP/IP). An upgraded form of this protocol is still the governing protocol of nearly all internet traffic today.

In the United Kingdom, Davies, challenged by the extraordinary cost of physical data storage, had created a local area network (LAN) of smaller minicomputers distributed across the laboratories of NPL (the National Physics Laboratory) connected to a single "file server" that alone was connected to the expensive disk drives. The LAN became a practical reality for industry at large when, in 1974, Robert Metcalfe and David Boggs, working for Xerox Palo Alto Research Centre (PARC), published a paper setting out the Ethernet networking protocol. In 1979, DEC and Intel joined forces with Xerox to standardise the Ethernet system for everyone to use.

The first specification by the three companies called the *Ethernet Blue Book* (known as the "DIX standard" after their initials) was released in 1980.[6] The DIX standard typically featured a yellow-coloured "backbone" cable running throughout a building, with smaller co-axial cables at intervals to connect to workstations. The large cable became known as the "Thick Ethernet" and had a speed of 10 Mbps. IBM's solution was the token ring network, which passes data in small packets called tokens in one direction around a ring of network nodes until each token arrives at its intended destination.

Packet-switching, too, became more sophisticated, with the X.25 protocol introduced in 1976, becoming the network protocol of choice for banks and other financial institutions, especially for ATMs (automated teller machines).[7]

Meanwhile, modems were still the main method for transporting data from one computer to another, over the public telephone networks. Transfer speeds rapidly increased in pace, from a mere 300 baud (bits per second) in 1963 to 9600 baud in 1991, then leaping to 56,000 baud in 1996 using technology invented by Brent Townshend (who rather cleverly elected not to use his invention to produce modems but rather licenced it to manufacturers at $2.50 per device, making him a multi-millionaire almost overnight). Just as it seemed that the limit had been reached for forcing data down a wire designed to carry the modulations of the human voice, Bell labs created the technology to use bandwidths wider than those used by the human voice (what we now call broadband) and the concept of a digital subscriber line (DSL). Speeds further improved by the introduction of an *asymmetrical protocol* that leveraged the fact that most users wanted to receive more data than they sent. By 1998, an ADSL modem would allow transfer rates nearly 30 times faster than a standard 56k modem.

Interfacing with Meaning

The world of digital communications was poised to engulf the planet speeds of megabits per second would soon be possible, and with the invention of the World Wide Web, more businesses, more people and more computers than any of these revolutionaries could ever have imagined would soon be passing data around the globe in unfathomable quantities.

But what could they possibly all have to say to each other?

And, more importantly, how could they make sure that the data, once delivered, could be read and used by the receiving machine?

To answer that question, we have to go all the way back to 1833 and our dear old friend Morse Code, with its dits and its dahs. First improved by Alfred Vail and Friedrich Gerke, then adapted for more reliable communication by Emile Baudot and Donald Murray, the codification of characters for printing on telegraphy machinery remained largely unchanged between 1901 and the early 1960s.

Once again, it was the advent of large-scale computer technology that triggered a spate of innovations. In order to send and store complex data (rather than just human-readable text messages), it was necessary to use more than just the 26 letters of the English alphabet and a few format effectors permitted by the five-bit code. Computer manufacturers began to use a range of codes from six bits to nine bits or even more, including IBM who introduced their Binary-Coded Decimal Interchange Code (BCDIC) based on the formats used in their punched cards (including such considerations as reducing the number of combinations that would cause two holes to be next to each other on the card, weakening its physical structure).

In 1961, a committee of the American Standards Association (ASA, which later became ANSI, the American National Standards Institute) began to develop the American Standard Code for Information Interchange (ASCII). ASCII used seven bits instead of the five used by Baudot's and Murray's codes, allowing for 128 characters, but also introduced a number of other computer-friendly features. The letter characters were arranged in numerical order, meaning that an alphabetical sort could be achieved simply by sorting the data numerically. Moreover, the upper and lowercase letters differed only in the setting of bit six (zero for upper case, one for lower case), meaning that a sort routine could ignore that bit and sort independently of the case.

ASCII was immediately accepted by nearly all of the world's computer and communications companies, except of course IBM, who initially continued with their own standard. For their soon-to-be-world-beating System/360 machines, IBM introduced the Extended BCDIC or EBCDIC, which uses 8 bits per byte (the smallest addressable unit of memory, made up of 8 or more bits) and can represent 256 characters. IBM's misfortune was that, apart from their own use of EBCDIC in their mid-range and mainframe computers, it never really caught on. Not to be completely outdone, IBM eventually adopted the ASCII code but extended it by using an eighth bit so it could represent 256 characters (called "Extended ASCII").

The two formats were incompatible with each other and were both still limited in the number of characters they could assign (ASCII had no character for the cent, despite being an American standard, EBCDIC lacked a number of punctuation marks, while neither code could cater for diacritics such as umlauts or accents or indeed almost any non-Latin character sets).

These limitations were eventually addressed in 1988 (although legacy issues will remain in any computer system that relies on these codifications - in 2019, a European bank fell foul of Article 16 of GDPR in Court of Appeal of Brussels because it was unable to correctly represent a client's name that included an umlaut; the bank's ultimately unsuccessful defence rested on its use of IBM AS/400 machinery that still used EBCDIC as its character codification). Spurred on by the microcomputer and personal computer adoption rates across the globe, employees at Xerox (Joe Becker) and Apple (Lee Collins and Mark Davis) collaborated to draft a proposal for an "international/multilingual text character encoding system" – Unicode. Originally using 16 bits (now 32), Unicode provides the capability to represent over a million different characters including all global "living" languages as well as emojis.

But it's one thing to be able to agree on which combinations of digits represent which characters. It's another matter entirely to send messages from one computer to another where those characters can be correctly interpreted.

Inevitably, from a business perspective, one of the first commodities that can be digitised is money. It's intangible, with no intrinsic value: the coin in your pocket is representative; it only has value if your counterparty will accept it. Money is fungible (meaning that it doesn't matter which particular coin you have) and is very easy to represent digitally – all you need is a currency and a value. The downside to this is that money is also relatively easy to steal, especially during its most vulnerable moments when it is being transferred from one place to another.

Equally inevitably, therefore, it was the financial institutions of the world that first came to realise that for any kind of commercially viable communication between their respective computer systems to work, they all had to "speak the same language" and exchange messages in a secure way. If sending Bank A believes that it has instructed a transfer of £1,000 but receiving Bank B believes it has received $1,000 and both banks update their own local records accordingly, or Bank B does not receive the message at all, the respective accounts will not reconcile and financial confusion will ensue.

To fully automate business processes between institutions, transactional data needed to be exchanged electronically in a form that could be processed by machines. The data needed to be precisely defined in terms of meaning (*semantics*) and provided in a consistent format (*syntax*). Most importantly, both of these needed to be agreed upon and understood by all the actors participating in the process. Financial messaging standards arose as a byproduct of the first attempts to use computer technology to automate financial business, such as domestic payments. Initially financial messaging standards were largely domestic in scope (e.g. the UK BACS standard, Standard 18), but as the requirements of business became increasingly international, the industry responded by forming explicitly international institutions with a standards-setting remit. The best known is probably Swift (Society for Worldwide Interbank Financial Telecommunication), which was founded in 1973 on three pillars: a secure network for financial message exchange; a global community of financial institutions that agreed to participate in business transacted on the network; and formal standards used to describe precisely the business messages exchanged on the network, to avoid ambiguity and enable automation.

As financial messaging standards-setting evolved from a domestic to a global concern, existing international standardisation bodies – notably ISO – were engaged by the industry to provide the mechanics and governance framework required to move from proprietary standards to international open standards, freely licensed for use by any community with a development and maintenance process that is open to participation from any user of the standard.

For over 50 years, Swift has been the driver for, and in many cases the curator (as ISO's registration authority) of, international messaging standards for the financial industry (first for banks and then from the 1990s for other financial institutions such as global custodians, depositories and fund managers). Key to this role has been the clarity with which it is able to encourage collaboration between banks around the world whose natural inclination is to be fiercely competitive. This is equally true of ISO which has encouraged collaboration for over 50 years with its collections of (industry-funded) technical committees, sub-committees and working groups to produce a raft of published standards for a wide range of technologies and industries.

It's also instructive to see how standardisation of data meaning and message syntax has progressed:

- In 1964 – characters: codification of character sets in ASCII (ISO 646)
- In 1991 – data fields: codification of fields to be used in financial messages for the securities industry (ISO 7775)
- In 1999 – messages: codification and standardisation of securities messages to be exchanged between financial industry participants (ISO 15022)
- In 2004 – message definition: standardisation of a process to create open-source standardised messages for the financial industry (ISO 20022).[8]

Standardisation didn't stop with financial messaging, though. As computing power increased exponentially and data storage became almost infinitely cheaper, it became possible to digitise more than just financial records and textual data. Standards for the conversion and transport of other digital media followed, fuelled by unparalleled demand from the burgeoning online community:

- GIF (Graphics Interchange Format) in 1987 for the transport and storage of images and short animations, pioneered by CompuServe, a provider of online services
- JPEG (which stands for Joint Photographic Experts Group) in 1992 for images
- PDF (Portable Document Format) also in 1992 for text and image documents, pioneered by Adobe
- MPEG (which stands for Moving Picture Experts Group) in 1993 for film and music files.

These innovations and developments, the results of an incalculable amount of time and effort from the industry participants involved, enabled and promoted the exchange of data through formalised channels: defined files and messages. But what of the more mundane day-to-day communication between (or within) organisations? What about the need to simply communicate in an unstructured way – to *talk*? To most, if not all, business users of computers in the modern world, connectivity means email.

The very first email (as we would understand it today) was sent in 1971 across the ARPANET network by Ray Tomlinson using a protocol that would eventually become known as FTP (File Transfer Protocol). But, as the internet was still in its infancy and unavailable to most computer enthusiasts, another mechanism had to be found for those who really needed to keep in touch. Stranded in Chicago by a storm in 1978, two such hobbyists (Ward Christensen and Randy Suess) had the opportunity to collaborate on an idea they had been developing. A few weeks later the first computerised bulletin board was launched, called – appropriately enough – CBBS ("Computerized Bulletin Board System"). Members would use their modems one at a time to dial up and post messages to the board or read what others had posted.

The Simple Mail Transfer Protocol (SMTP) was implemented in 1983, evolving out of the ARPANET FTP to send messages, followed by the Internet Message Access Protocol (IMAP) in 1986. SMTP is still used for sending mail today, while IMAP provides interoperability between mail providers with different protocols (Gmail and Outlook have their own proprietary protocols for retrieving mail).

During the 1990s, email became more and more prevalent, often introduced into businesses in phases – first internally over each organisation's LAN and then in time over the internet to and from external organisations.

In 1998, even Hollywood got involved, with the blockbuster romantic comedy *You've Got Mail*. If you've ever wondered at the pace of change during the information revolution, it's worth taking a look at the technology in use in this film. Arguably the revolution itself was done by the time it came out: all the building blocks were in place. And yet the tech used in the film seems incredibly primitive to the modern viewer. It's slightly unnerving to realise that it was made only 26 years ago.

And although the revolution may have been over, the full impacts were about to be felt ... by almost everyone.

Interfacing with ... Everyone

So, hang on, you might be thinking. You've got this all wrong. You're telling me the internet was invented in the 1970s? What about Sir Tim Berners-Lee? What about CERN? What was there left for him to do in 1991?

As we've seen, an interface is a combination of the physical capability to connect two (or more) interested parties, be they human or machine (let's call them endpoints) and the information, or data, that is passed between them (hopefully with the same meaning to the recipient as intended by the sender).

The internet may have been born in 1971 when ARPANET was officially declared operational. But there was still plenty to do. Other networks (such as France's CYCLADES, the United Kingdom's JANET and the US National Science Foundation's NSFNET) using other network protocols were implemented around the world, and slowly these networks were seeking to connect to each other – "internetworking", so to speak.[9] For the next 20 years or so, there followed what is sometimes referred to as the "Protocol Wars" as different methods of connectivity vied for supremacy (because if you want to connect every computer in the world to each other, it stands to reason that they all have to – at some point – agree on how it's going to be done). A theoretical standard was approved by ISO in 1984, the Open Systems Interconnection model (OSI model). However, TCP/IP was the internetwork protocol that was actually being implemented by technology and telecommunications companies, and by 1989 it had become the de facto standard.

What Sir Tim Berners-Lee did in 1991 was to combine this growing global internet with the means to embed a file location into text that could be viewed on a page: hypertext.

The idea was not entirely new.

The visionary scientist Vannevar Bush provided a foretaste in his prophetic 1945 essay *As We May Think*.[10] He proposed a device called a *memex* (or "memory extender").

A memex is a device in which an individual stores all his books, records, and communications, and which is mechanised so that it may be consulted with exceeding speed and flexibility. It is an enlarged intimate supplement to his memory.

It consists of a desk… the piece of furniture at which he works. On the top are slanting translucent screens, on which material can be projected for convenient reading. There is a keyboard, and sets of buttons and levers. Otherwise it looks like an ordinary desk.

> Wholly new forms of encyclopedias will appear, ready made with a mesh of associative trails running through them, ready to be dropped into the memex and there amplified.

Aside from the references to microfiche, this bears an uncanny resemblance to the desktop internet-connected PCs of the late 1990s and 2000s.

Working at CERN (the European Organization for Nuclear Research) since 1988, Berners-Lee noted that visiting scientists would struggle to share their data or their documents, even though they were stored in their own networks, connected through the internet. He proposed a mechanism whereby every page could be given a unique address (a uniform resource locator or URL) using the newly available internet domain name system (DNS). This URL could then be coded into hypertext. He developed the Hypertext Markup Language (HTML) for this purpose as well as the Hypertext Transfer Protocol (HTTP) to manage the request by the user to view the target page. He initially used his own very basic browser called ENQUIRE, written in 1980, on his local workstation as a web server. Using a mouse to click on hypertext would recall the linked page from anywhere on the internet and display it on the user's screen. With this one server, the World Wide Web was born on December 20, 1990 and announced to the world in August of the following year. By November 1992, the web comprised 26 servers.

Dominance was not guaranteed: rival mechanisms existed such as Minitel in France and Gopher in the United States. Gopher briefly threatened to become the leading method of interacting with the web until its owners (the University of Minnesota) decided to licence their product in 1993, while in response CERN made their software freely available as open-source.

Third parties began to write their own browsers: Mosaic, briefly, before Netscape Navigator grew to a position of dominance, followed by Microsoft's Internet Explorer (which was based on a version of Mosaic).

Berners-Lee left CERN in 1994 to work at MIT (Massachusetts Institute of Technology) and set up the World Wide Web Consortium (W3C) to improve the quality of the web and to promote open-source protocols.

The first popular online directory on the web was Yahoo! Founded in 1994 by college students David Filo and Jerry Yang as "Jerry and David's guide to the World Wide Web", the website started as simply a list of pages that the two friends found interesting. As their interests grew, the list became too long so they broke it down into categories and subcategories and was renamed as the Yahoo! Directory. Although completely outgunned by "web-crawler" directories in later years, the human-edited Yahoo! Directory persisted until the end of 2014.

The final barrier to the commercialisation of the web was removed in 1995. The US National Science Foundation's NSFNET had provided the backbone of the internet but operated under an Acceptable Use Policy that limited its use to educational or research activities. In 1995, NSFNET was closed down, and the web was open for business.

Entrepreneurs quickly realised the value of being able to reach paying customers anywhere in the world, and some of the biggest web success stories were among the early adopters of the technology. Amazon and eBay both started trading in the same year. Google started as a college project called "Backrub" in 1996 when Larry Page devised his concept of a web crawler that would identify and categorise linked pages on the web.

These companies, and others, launched initial public offerings (IPOs) in the late 1990s, fuelling what would become known as the dotcom boom.

It's not the purpose of this book to analyse the collective madness that engulfed the world in that period. But it is worth noting in passing that much of what transpired was utterly predictable and the result of very simple business or investment principles.

Companies that prospered tended to have a clear vision and instigated sound business practices. Those that foundered tended to suffer from poor business management or flawed execution. Take webvan.com: the idea and the vision were sound, but the company grew its physical assets too quickly under pressure from investors to seize first mover advantage. The company went bust having built a billion dollars' worth of warehouses and with a fleet of shiny new trucks, but not enough suppliers or customers. Another widely publicised failure was Boo.com: its plans for rapid expansion relied heavily on investment (which dried up as the dotcom bust took hold), and its revolutionary graphics required broadband download speeds at a time when most consumers were still dialling up through their modems.

Investors got burned by the bust for the same reasons that they saw ludicrous paper profits during the boom. The web was both the cause and the subject of this collective folly: amateur investors in their droves got caught up in the social bubble, egging each other on to invest in stocks that had little more than a website to their name. Buying stocks had never been so easy – one click of the mouse button and money disappeared from your credit card and you were the proud owner of 25,000 shares in completelyuselessITcompany.com. No stuffy stockbrokers to get in your way or to suggest that you instead put your hard-earned cash into a "safe" stock like a bank or a utility. Firms themselves got caught up in the hype, seeking investment based on untenable valuations and projections.

In the end, the collective greed and herd mentality of these first democratised investors led to the inevitable bust: in late March and early April 2000, technology stocks lost on average a third of their value (between March 24th 2000 and April 14th, the Nasdaq 100 fell 33% from 4804 points to 3217.5) – some lost it all.

But the internet, the web and the tech stocks were not out of the fight – the sector was wounded but still viable. Those products with a sound business model recovered, and prospered, aided by the next technological revolution in interfacing – mobile data.

The capability for wireless mobile phones had existed since the invention of the radio by Marconi at the turn of the twentieth century, although early models were hampered by the available physical technology, such as with the United Kingdom's "System 1" where units had to be housed in the boot of a car while the Swedish equivalent weighed in at 40 kg. Bell Labs in the United States started looking into a cellular network and by 1978 had solved the issue of seamlessly transferring calls between cells as the caller moved around. Although the first automated network was the Nordic Mobile Telephone (NMT) system launched in 1981, Bell soon followed with the Advanced Mobile Phone System (AMPS) that became the basis for cellular networks around the world. Handsets remained expensive and heavy, but popularity began to grow (helped by some starring roles in Hollywood such as the chunky Motorola Dynatac 8000X – aka "the brick" – in *Wall Street* in 1987). Devices became smaller (and lighter), the obligatory antenna became incorporated into the phone's casing, while screens and keypads became more sophisticated with more features. The invention of the SMS (Short Messaging Service) in 1992 added an entirely new use case for mobile telephony (the first SMS message was sent on 3rd December 1992 when Neil Papworth, a developer, sent a text – "Merry Christmas" – to Richard Jarvis, a director at Vodafone, who was enjoying his office Christmas party). Suddenly, it was possible to contact anyone anywhere, even if they weren't able to pick up the phone. SMS caught the zeitgeist at the end of the millennium – mobile phone ownership in the industrial world climbed rapidly from around 15% in 1996 to nearly 50% by the turn of the century.

But it was when the cell networks were augmented with the capability to transmit data that the mobile phone really came into its own. Although second-generation (2G) networks were digital in nature, they did not have the bandwidth for significant data transport and had limitations on the size of data that could be transported (initial SMS messages were restricted to 140 characters each). With GPRS (General Packet Radio Service also called 2.5G) it was possible to connect to the internet using the standard internet protocol. With a serendipitous leap forward in flat-screen technology, mobile browsing became possible.

First the Blackberry (the must-have accessory for the busy executive in the noughties) followed quickly by the iPhone in 2007, the internet – and the World Wide Web – opened up to everyone, everywhere, no matter what they were doing.

Meanwhile, data speeds across copper wires had continued to increase over dedicated DSLs. As the web-hungry public looked to consume more and more data, cabling technology had to increase at greater than exponential levels. *Fibre-optic* cables (which bounce light pulses from end to end, using the principle of total internal reflection to turn corners with no loss of signal) were able to connect digitally at speeds of thousands of megabits per second. Although more expensive than copper wiring, the advantages of fibre are legion. In addition to the higher bandwidth, there is almost no loss of signal over long distances and no interference from other lines as there is with electromagnetic transmission through copper wiring.

At almost the same time as digitally enabled networks, two other technologies that had been in development for some time began to gain traction: *Bluetooth* and *WiFi*. Both are short-distance radio (wireless) protocols: WiFi (developed from a frequency hopping protocol invented during World War II by Hollywood actress Hedy Lamarr) effectively converts a LAN into a wireless network while Bluetooth enables point-to-point connectivity between two devices (such as a headset and a phone).

With the combination of mobile data or broadband connections to the public internet and local wireless connectivity in the form of WiFi or Bluetooth, it was suddenly possible to seamlessly connect a website to a free-standing laptop, a headset or even wearable tech such as a smartwatch, at a data transmission speed undreamed of by the early pioneers.

Interfacing for Businesses

While the internet and the web gave the public new avenues of entertainment and created untold commercial opportunities for a raft of new business ventures and organisations, the mechanics of how those businesses themselves interfaced their own systems internally and connected to the outside world was also being transformed.

Internal connectivity of workstations to servers remained typically in the domain of the LAN, via Ethernet (and later WiFi), whereas the technology to link different applications (between different servers and even different organisations) made steady progress.

As businesses began to move away from monolithic, enterprise applications and began to operate on multiple smaller interconnected apps, the need to seamlessly connect these applications became more critical just as the number of different possible connections became increasingly diverse. Part of the process of building or buying an application from a vendor necessarily began to include consideration for how easy it would be to connect that application to the rest of the technical estate, through an application programming interface (API).

Similarly, a range of dedicated languages and applications to support connectivity became part of the standard technology toolkit available to organisations seeking to build their own connections.

External communications also became more standardised, either via dedicated data lines or over the public internet. Regulatory and financial authorities began to publish defined message sets for regular reporting, using standardised methodologies such as ISO 20022.

The modern tech-savvy business has a range of options for both internal and external connections between applications and other organisations.

WHAT DOES HERE LOOK LIKE?

The modern technology architecture for an organisation can involve hundreds of applications, the majority of which need to communicate with at least one other component. At the very least, you may have applications for CRM and marketing, HR and finance, email and office productivity, plus any number particular to your organisation's specific business. These applications may be on site, in a data centre, in the cloud or they may even be owned and operated by a third party. All of these disparate applications need to be connected seamlessly, effectively and securely.

As we noted at the start of this chapter, interfacing is about three things:

- The technological capability to connect two (or more) endpoints
- An agreement on how to encode and convey meaning in a message
- A means to safeguard the contents of the message.

In addition, the global connectivity provided by the World Wide Web presents particular opportunities to reach a wide target audience, be that a prospect, an existing client or any other interested party.

Network Topology

Networks for businesses are a bit like the desks and chairs of your office furniture.

You never stop to think about how important they are, but you'd notice pretty quickly if they're not put together properly.

Like any piece of architecture, there is a structure to a network.

The TCP/IP protocol defines four layers for the transporting of data from one application to another:

- *Link* layer – the lowest layer in the protocol, this governs the movement of data within an individual network
- *Internet* layer – the sending of data from one network to another
- *Transport* layer – establishes and maintains the connection between the two host systems
- *Application* layer – the generation of the data by the source application and its reconstruction by the target application using protocols such as markups in HTML.

Imagine that you are writing a letter to a friend. You draft the letter by hand, including a number of in-jokes and personal references that only your friend would understand (this is the application layer). But you end up writing so much that the letter no longer fits into a single envelope. You split the letter into two bundles and place them in envelopes marked "1" and "2" (the transport layer). You then stroll to the post box and post your letters (link layer). The sorting office routes the letters to your friend's address (internet layer), and the postman delivers both envelopes (link layer). Your friend sorts the two envelopes so as to read the letter in the correct order (transport layer). Finally, your friend read the letter, enjoying the personal references that only they will understand (application layer).

Similarly, the OSI model remains a reference standard. It defines seven layers: physical, data link, network, transport, session, presentation and application.

The *network* itself is a collection of *nodes*, which can be a computer server fitted with a network interface (the component that allows a computer to connect to a network, such as an Ethernet card and associated Ethernet port), various repeaters, hubs and switchers which collectively pass the network traffic along the network, bridges between networks and firewalls which are really just more servers on the network with specific responsibilities for running security software.

Connecting all of these nodes are cables, which come in many shapes and sizes. Choosing the wrong cabling, just like choosing the wrong hardware for your network nodes, may have an adverse impact on your business. Some rooms or floors may have a large number of workstations that need lots of data, whereas cabling to connect two remote data centres may need to be both fast and durable, resistant to cold (and bulldozers).

There are several main types of network cables including coaxial, shielded twisted pair (STP) and unshielded twisted pair (UTP) cables, as well as fibre optic cables. The type of cable dictates the speed of data transmission through it as well as its durability. Coaxial cables have a conducting core that transmits data, surrounded by an outer insulating jacket. Twisted pair cables are simply pairs of insulated copper wire twisted together, typical in Ethernet cables.

Modern networks are often either WiFi or use Ethernet (RJ45) or USB-C connectors.

Message Patterns

Applications can talk to each other in real time through something called an API. A given application (or computer program) may define an API that allows other applications or programs to access it, to pass or extract information or to instruct the application to perform a function. Applications may connect to each other directly or through another type of program called *middleware*.

For non-real-time communication, such as the passing of sequential files for overnight batch processing, applications use the FTP over the internet or the secure FTP (SFTP) which also encrypts the transported data. In this case, the sender and recipient will need to have separately agreed on the file formats, syntax and semantics.

Connectivity between different applications can vary enormously. Factors such as the volumes of traffic across the interface, the speed with which (or indeed if) a response is required, the criticality of the activity and its level of risk will all need to be taken into account when designing and implementing each and every interface.

It is helpful to take a common approach to interfaces that need similar treatment, and many organisations will create a number of architectural and message *patterns* that describe how the various interfaces need to behave.

Middleware is the term used by technologists to talk about the software that sits between two (or more) other applications. Wikipedia[11] very usefully describes middleware as "the dash in client-server, or the -to- in peer-to-peer". There's no particular magic here – it's just software that needs to be developed and tested like any other. There are dedicated middleware applications and programming languages that support the specific needs, but it's still just software. Typical problems resolved in middleware include:

- Enrichment – messages that need extra data to be added between source and destination
- Translation – messages with data that needs to be converted from one format to another between source and destination
- Validation – messages with data that needs to be validated en route, so that it can be received by the target application (for instance where the validation in the receiving application is more stringent than in the source application)
- Filtering – identifying and removing messages that are not required by the target application
- Logging – ensuring that all interfacing activity is recorded (for audit and exception processing)
- Exception-handling – to cater for cases where messages go astray, don't arrive or contain invalid data.

Generally, middleware of this nature is part of an asynchronous message exchange. This means that the sending application will not wait for a response.

One of the goals for middleware (or indeed for any interface) is that it should be *stateless*. This is a key concept – whenever the middleware receives a message to process (whether that is to translate it, validate it or simply pass it on to its destination), all of the information needed by the middleware should be included in the message itself or be possible to derive or obtain based on the data in the message. If the middleware needs to know additional data, or context, then it is deemed to have state or to be stateful. If an interface has a state (i.e. it remembers data or information from one execution to the next), there is an additional complexity in that the applications need to ensure that the same instance of the middleware is used each time. Typically, and especially for large volumes of transactional data, many copies of middleware are running at any one time, each picking a message from the top of a queue to process – this is only possible if the exchange is stateless and the middleware application can start to process based only on the data in the message it has selected.

Another key consideration for message design is whether the applications involved are to be tightly coupled or loosely coupled. Tightly coupled applications may be linked by what is called a "point to point" interface with minimal (or no) middleware to adapt the message from one format to another. Such links are more difficult to break at a later date if one or another application needs to be replaced, but the interface itself is simpler. Loosely coupled applications may be linked by other means such as a "publish and subscribe" mechanism where a message is sent to a central location and is then broadcast out to any applications that have requested it, or even through a database where the sending application writes the data to a central database, which can then be referenced by requesting applications. Loosely coupled applications are much easier to break apart and replace.

Applications can also be linked in a more dynamic way, with one application requesting information (or instructing an activity) from another as and when it needs it. This is called a remote procedure call. The called application could be a monolithic server application, a micro-service or even a desktop application. Procedure calls are typically performed synchronously. This means that the calling application will wait for a response to its request before continuing.

Popular middleware applications and related technologies include:

- FTP/SFTP – (Secure) FTP is a messaging protocol that governs the movement of files of data. A given file may contain many messages. In this protocol, the file is not transformed in any way – what is sent is exactly the same as what is delivered to the target.
- BizTalk – Microsoft BizTalk Server is a set of middleware applications that provide message broker and monitoring services as well as the application of message translation and business rules. An organisation's developers can write code for BizTalk applications using Microsoft Visual Studio.
- Apache Kafka – is an open-source real-time data streaming platform, based on publish and subscribe architecture. The application receives data from "producers" at the point that the data is committed and stores it so that "consumers" are able to read it.
- MQ – a message queuing middleware application designed by IBM. MQ stands for "message queue" and the protocol essentially involves messages being placed in a queue by one application, while another application is able to take the top message from the queue to process it.
- JMS – the Jakarta Messaging API is a queue-based messaging protocol for Java applications. It can be point-to-point or publish and subscribe.
- REST (Representational State Transfer API) – an API for building web services.
- SOAP – a protocol for the exchange of messages (typically XML) to invoke web services.

There's a lot of technology to take in there, and we've really only scratched the surface. The world of interfacing applications is rich and diverse. Understandably so: in many organisations, especially where software products are bought and customised, the main activity for an in-house programming team is to link them all together.

But what's the business angle? Where can you, the business leader, add value? From a business perspective, the main factors that influence interface design are as follows:

- *Sender and recipient(s)* – who is sending the message and who is receiving it? Is this just an exchange between internal applications, or does it involve an external party? This will help to determine the nature of the connection required such as over dedicated cabling or the public internet.

- *Process flow ("passing the baton")* – it's important to know what function the message plays as part of a wider process: is control of the process being handed over to the recipient (passing the baton), or does the sending application retain control and continue with the process flow (keeping the baton)? This factor essentially determines whether the message is a synchronous "request-response" or an asynchronous one-way pattern.
- *Volume* – how many messages will there be? The technical architecture will be very different for a scenario where 10,000 messages might be expected per day (or per second) compared to just one message a day or even a year (or, in the case of some exception messages, never).
- *Urgency* – does the message need to be received and processed immediately? Can there be some delay? Can the message be parked or buffered and processed overnight?
- *Criticality* – different from urgency – what's the importance of the message? What happens if the message gets lost and isn't received by the other application?
- *Risk/Security* – what happens if the message is intercepted? Does it contain proprietary or damaging information?

Let's take a look at how these factors could combine to influence interface design for a financial institution that provides stock prices to its users online and then allows them to make trades on those stocks.

We'll look at three messages and their interfaces:

- The financial institution publishing the stock's price to all of its clients
- A client instructing a trade on the stock
- Daily reconciliation between the financial institution and the asset's custodian.

First, publishing the price. This is a high-volume interaction that must be received and processed in real time by any of the institution's clients who are logged on at the time, via the public internet. It's a simple message containing an indicative price, and while it would be unfortunate if it went astray, there is nothing particularly proprietary about the price – this is market information and will in any case change in the next few moments.

In terms of criticality, that's low, too – if the client doesn't get the message this time around, they will see the new price when it's refreshed in a few seconds' time. This message can be sent as a broadcast from the institution's applications; no reply is required.

Second, the client trade. This is neither low volume nor high volume. You wouldn't expect every client to be trading every second, but you would hope that many of your clients would place a few trades every day. It's also likely that you would want to process the trade in real time so that the client gets the best price for their trade – as close as possible to the indicative price you displayed to them earlier. This is a critical exchange – you don't want to lose this message, and you also want to be sure that all parties confirm its receipt. Most likely, the application on the client's phone or desktop has locked the client out while waiting for a response. This is a request-response protocol.

Finally, the daily reconciliation between the institution and its custodians. This is high volume activity but in a single burst at the end of each day. There's no great urgency – as long as the message is received and processed by the end of the day. This could be a batched file of data sent each evening by FTP across a secure channel – this is sensitive information and you certainly don't want it falling into malicious hands.

As a business stakeholder potentially involved in the design of a message pattern, your key responsibility is to be clear on these business drivers so that the right message patterns can be designed and implemented (see Figure 4.1).

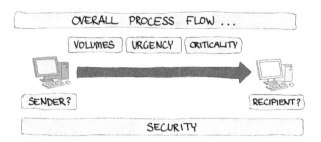

FIGURE 4.1
Business Input into Message Design.

Meaning and Format

A messaging protocol will define the rules for communication between two or more participants in a message exchange. It will ensure that the message reaches the intended recipient(s).

But for the message to be meaningful, the recipient must be able to understand the message content. To do this, both sender and receiver(s) must agree on two things:

- The syntax (format) of the message – how the different data fields are ordered, and whether they are mandatory, optional or conditional
- The semantics (meaning) of the data in the message – what a given datum actually means or represents.

Let's take a look at a very simple message: the SOS in Morse Code.

The agreed syntax is that dots are indicated by short signals and dashes are indicated by long. The syntax would also include how long a pause should be left between each pulse, each letter and each word.

The semantics would dictate that an S is represented by three dots and an O by three dashes. Furthermore, there would need to be an agreement that "SOS" itself has a significance beyond its three simple letters.

Syntax and semantics can easily be agreed bilaterally between the sending and receiving party, or even unilaterally if one party is writing both the sending and receiving application. The advantage of such an approach is that the messages can be simple and quick to encode.

But, as the undoubtedly apocryphal African proverb says, "if you want to go fast, go alone; if you want to go far, go together".

If you want more than one other party to understand the messages you send or want to receive, then you need to define the syntax and semantics and (just as importantly) write it down and publish it. This is typically what is called an API.

And if you really want to make sure that everyone can send, receive and understand the messages, then you need to make that API an open standard.

As we saw previously, message definition in the financial industry matured over time from the definition of characters to data fields, to messages and finally to the definition of a standard for the creation of messages. For web services, the syntax and semantics of the procedure call must be fully understood by both the calling and called applications.

Why are standards important?

Think about this the next time you go shopping or want to buy a drink at the bar. You'll pay for your goods or your libations with a credit card, pressed against a point-of-sale device. You'll probably barely even notice the transaction, perhaps a slight beep from the machine as it authorises your payment.

But think what's happened:

- The device has read your card details from the chip embedded in it and identified the card issuer
- The device has contacted the issuer and validated the card
- The device has sent the transaction to the issuer
- The issuer has responded to confirm that the payment is valid.

Imagine if every card, card issuer and point-of-sale manufacturer had defined a different set of rules (including syntax and semantics) around how this data should be stored and extracted and how the messages should be exchanged. Instead of that simple press-and-forget transaction, both you and the flustered shop assistant or mixologist would need to perform a complex dance of trying different cards against different machines until (by luck) one of the combinations worked. By then, you'd need another drink!

Card issuers don't compete on the quality of the messaging they receive and send from point-of-sale devices. They compete on interest rates, benefits and, in some cases, levels of market acceptance for their product. So, they collaborate and agree on a set of messages that will accomplish all of that data exchange in the same way, regardless of which card and which machine is being used.

Not all industries benefit from the standardisation that has been implemented by the credit card companies (who have collectively moved to a set of ISO 20022 messages that govern transactions, reconciliation, fraud and other card-related functionality). In many cases, there are no such standards, while in some there are competing standards (an oxymoron, perhaps, but one of the great things about standards is that there are so many of them). Or an older standard may have been replaced by a new one.

As always, there's money to be made from inefficiency. Tech companies will provide translation software that either automatically translates messages from one syntax to another in-flight or provides organisations with the capability to match data fields from one syntax to those in another, with translation and business rules to be applied in the process.

One of the concepts in networking is referred to as "the last mile". In a physical network, this is usually taken to mean the final connection to the customer's house or office, which is often older and less sophisticated than the rest of the network. A network passes data at the speed of the slowest network member so it is often this "last mile" that acts as the choke point on customer's access speeds.

There's a similar issue with the semantic meaning contained in the messages that are carried by the network. Ultimately, data needs to be represented on screens, or read by a human being, and it is here that many mistakes are made most frequently. Data can be mistyped or mis-read, or two different people may simply understand the same data in two different ways (especially prevalent where human beings fulfil different but related roles and are inclined to view the data from different perspectives).

While each organisation individually may have a robust data architecture and data governance framework, the meaning across organisations can differ. A significant part of any standardisation discussion is devoted to ensuring that the semantic meaning of the data messages is clear and agreed upon across all parties. Often, as a byproduct of such standardisation, disparate processes can become harmonised towards a common approach, to the general benefit of the industry.

One other process that can reduce errors in understanding is by ensuring that written text is tagged with a clear digital representation of its meaning. The eXtensible Business Reporting Language (XBRL) is an open-source framework for categorising and digitising business information, such as in company annual reports. Key fields in the text can be tagged with semantic meaning (which is also defined in a separate schema) so that its meaning is clear to all. The XBRL tags can also more easily be exported and digitally consumed than the original text.

Security

The modern business network isn't just about cloud hosting and resilient access for a distributed network of users such as those in the office, in offices in separate geographies, those working in a hybrid way and/or travelling.

Modern business networks are required to support all of the above securely, reliably and durably via VPNs, private clouds, colleague broadband (at different speeds) and on the basis that colleagues may deploy their own variable equipment on operating systems that may be obsolescent, insecure or even unsupported.

Coordinating a network for all types and locations of users brings new challenges for modern business network managers. Above all, security, reliability, durability and performance of the network must be the focus of strategy.

See Chapter 6 for more on risks and security.

Web and Mobile Interfacing

The internet is your shop window to the world. Used properly, it will allow you to reach customers wherever they are.

But we're not here to tell you how to do that.

Your web strategy is your own.

But where we can help you is in understanding some of the mechanics and terminology that your IT teams will use in the design of a web interface.

The way that the World Wide Web works hasn't materially changed since its invention by Tim Berners-Lee in 1991. An application called a *web browser* (such as Chrome, Safari or Edge) running on the user's computer will send a request across the internet to a web server identified by its *URL*. The web server will reply with data to the user's browser. The data in this message contains everything the web browser needs to build the page for the user.

Specifically, the data retrieved includes combinations of the following:

- *HTML* – a text document that includes the text to display on the web page plus a wide range of special tags ("markup") that control how the text appears on-screen, such as the font, displaying in title case, or in bold, or in a particular colour. HTML may also include the definition of a form for the user to fill in to send data back to the web server for processing.
- *Cascading Style Sheet (CSS)* – similar to an HTML text document, but separating the definition of the style from the text content, allowing the same style to be applied to multiple sets of content.

- *JavaScript* – small applications written in the JavaScript programming language that are executed by a JavaScript engine incorporated into the browser itself. JavaScript applications allow for dynamic activity on a displayed web page such as animations, popups and up-front validation of data keyed into a form by a user.
- Various *multimedia* files such as images, sounds and videos.
- *Cookies* – data sent by the web server and stored by the browser on the user's computer to record progress or the contents of specific fields such as logon credentials, name, address etc.

Your involvement in the design process for web pages (as well as those for mobiles, tablets, watches and so on) will most likely be to discuss the content of forms for the user to complete or in drafting or agreeing text for the user to view. You may discuss wireframe mockups with a designer before a developer produces the HTML script to produce the real thing (it's possible for this all to be done through low-code tools, but the output as yet from such a process is unreliable so developers will typically still write the scripts from scratch).

You may be asked for your opinion on the User Interface (UI) or User Experience (UX). These are not the same thing. The UI is all about the web page itself – what does the user see, what can they click and where do they input their data? The UX goes beyond those elements and embraces the entire interaction the user will have while using the website. The UI could be great (neat layout, clear instructions, very clickable buttons), but if the UX is poor, the user will become bored or disaffected. A poor UX could result from the overall processing flow, poor validation at the web server or just an outcome that's not what the user expected. Imagine if you were trying to buy tickets to an event – the website itself could be slick and efficient (UI), but at the end of the process it's not clear which tickets you've bought, and you don't receive an email or other notification to tell you. That's a poor UX. If you're asked to provide a view, try always to think about the whole process and not just what's on the screen at any one time.

It's also worth remembering that browsers run on all kinds of devices: desktops, laptops, tablets and mobile phones. Even on watches. The UI and UX will need to be carefully considered for each format and may well be very different on a smaller device. Organisations are increasingly basing their UI/UX designs on "mobile first", recognising that users typically spend significantly more time on their mobile phones than on a desktop device.

WHERE NEXT?

Similarly to the domains of computer hardware and software, it may seem that the revolution is over for networks and network usage. Cabling, fibre optics and wireless connectivity have reached the point of evolutionary change, while data and message standardisation is well entrenched as a collaborative enterprise to produce industry-wide efficiencies. Network security will continue to dance in lockstep with the cybercriminals.

But what about the World Wide Web? While the raw mechanics are unlikely to change any time soon, the way the web is used – if not in its infancy – is still very much in its teenage years, and although it's hard to say exactly where it's headed, we can be sure it's going somewhere interesting....

Room for Improvement on Wireless...

While the underlying technology may not be as rapidly transforming, there are plenty of strong evolutions in the world of wireless connectivity.

Elon Musk's Starlink network of satellites has brought ubiquitous broadband connectivity to whole regions of the globe that were previously dark.

The rollout of 5G networks is set to revolutionise various sectors, including agriculture, by offering faster, more reliable and more responsive network services. With high-speed data transfer, low latency and higher reliability, these networks will support growth in the use of autonomous machinery, connected machines through the Internet of Things (IoT), as well as the use of drones for reconnaissance and monitoring large areas.

At the other end of the scale, beacons are small, battery-powered devices that continuously broadcast an identifier using Bluetooth Low Energy (BLE) technology. These devices enable very localised effects. As a smartphone or other device enters the range of the beacon, applications are able to use the beacon's unique identifier to display specific messages or trigger specific actions on the device. These could be used in shops to promote specific products, in museums to display information about a specific exhibit and so on (as if your phone had seamlessly scanned a QR code).

Faster Cables and More Efficient Network Protocols

The speed at which data can be forced down copper and fibre cables has increased almost beyond measure since the first days of the dial-up modem and will continue to rise as more inventive ways are found to compress or modulate data.

But faster networks don't necessarily mean faster work. A variant of Parkinson's Law applies: just as "work expands to fill the time available", so data size expands to exercise the available network capacity. Modern applications and the data they exchange are more massive than their twentieth-century predecessors. The simple act of loading a web page involves vast amounts of style data and markups, as well as JavaScript applications and media files.

In terms of physical cabling, there is a great deal of inertia in the existing network infrastructure. It will take some years for any new standard to become the norm, as networks are gradually replaced. The USB-C standard was finalised in 2014, but it is only relatively recently that the USB-C connector has become widely enough used to have reached the tipping point of popularity, to the extent that it is starting to replace previous USB standards among others. Thin enough to be used in mobile devices, but with data speeds up to 10 gigabytes per second and carrying a usable power supply to boot, the USB-C will soon become the go-to connector for the office.

Network protocols will continue to evolve to remove network latency and other inefficiencies. The TCP uses a range of congestion control algorithms to manage bottlenecks and other causes of traffic congestion over the internet and these are under constant revision. In addition, QUIC ("Quick UDP Internet Connections") is a new protocol with a leaner approach to splitting data into packets and recombining it than TCP/IP and has a more effective method of dealing with the delivery failure of an individual packet. QUIC is already implemented (invisibly to most) in many browsers.

On the other hand, the Recursive InterNetwork Architecture (RINA) is a proposed alternative to TCP/IP that advocates a recurring inter-process protocol to achieve scale rather than specialised protocols in each layer. According to the authors of a 2023[12] paper on the subject,

> driven by the requirements of the emerging applications and networks, the internet has become an architectural patchwork of growing complexity which strains to cope with the changes. Moore's Law prevented us from recognising that the problem does not hide in the high demands of today's applications but lies in the flaws of the Internet's original design. The Internet needs to move beyond TCP/IP to prosper in the long term, TCP/IP has outlived its usefulness.

The rise of the IoT is also pushing IPs towards leaner and less demanding mechanisms. The Constrained Application Protocol (CoAP) has been specifically designed for "constrained devices" such as wearable tech. It can be used for communication between devices on the same constrained network or between constrained devices and other standard internet nodes.

More Glue between the Apps

For a medium-sized business or larger, it's likely that you will need to use a range of business applications, for CRM, HR, accounting and finance, as well as those specifically for business use such as your CRM.

As more and more of these business functions are commoditised, and more software becomes available off-the-shelf to service those needs, the more you will need integration between them. Quite often, you will want to be in charge of that integration, whether for security reasons or simply because there is no ready-built integration between the applications themselves.

Where organisations in the past might have retained a software capability to write their own applications, this effort is likely to turn towards integration using middleware applications and languages.

While many of the applications will be presented by the vendor as having an "adaptor" to connect to other commonly available applications, quite often these adaptors are of limited use or don't meet your organisation's security requirements. Even as the level of commoditisation grows, it's unlikely that a given organisation will have exactly your combination of applications across the board, so some customisation will be needed.

Such interfaces are trending towards real time, rather than the batch processing more typical of older installations. Real-time interfaces are fast but also require increased availability and scalability to maintain service levels in the face of any increases in load.

Semantics and Syntax

The gradual growth of standardised messages will continue. As more and more organisations across different industries become more adept at identifying the commoditised, collaborative opportunities afforded by messaging standards, freeing them up to focus on the competitive space, standards will surely follow.

The financial industry had a head start, as financial networks preceded the internet by several decades. But, as Stephen Lindsay of Swift notes, that is both a blessing and a curse. "Today we still live with much of the legacy of the early days", he says.

"Standards first created in the 1960s and 1970s are still in use and institutions need to manage a patchwork of domestic and international standards that, because of the way they evolved, can use incompatible terminology, data types, codes and conventions. A trivial example – the party receiving funds in a payment transaction can be designated the Beneficiary (Swift MT), the Creditor (ISO 20022), the Payee (Fedwire), etc. and can be represented by various identification schemes, from simple name and address to a variety of domestic and internationally issued identification codes. Institutions have had no choice but to deal with this complexity, and technology providers have developed sophisticated data transformation and mapping tools to enable them to do so."

"The reason these standards persist is because changing an entrenched industry standard is hard. Not so much from a technology standpoint; more because of the coordination effort required to get all users of a standard to switch in a way that does not disrupt current business processes. Further challenges include persuading institutions of the business case for change (because new investment will typically be required from every participant); and the need to coordinate with other standards changes that might be happening at the same time."

"Right now, ISO 20022 is replacing a number of local and international proprietary standards for payments, for RTGS, local instant payment schemes and for cross-border. ISO 20022 is around 20 years old. It has taken the industry this long to reach this point, and much still remains to be done."

"ISO 20022 will bring richer data and interoperability benefits – enabling a smooth transition of data between cross-border and domestic (most cross-border payments originate of terminate in a domestic market infrastructure) – and allowing market participants to rationalize and streamline technology and business processes. But it's a long game."

Trusted interlocutors, such as Swift, have a role to play in the enabling of messaging interoperability. Translation tools cannot just convert seamlessly from one message standard to another but can store the original message in its existing form, ensuring that data is never lost even if the translation requires some form of truncation.

Lindsay sees value in this approach. "Early days, but if [it] proves successful it could remove the need for coordinated industry migrations by allowing early adopters to adopt something new (rich ISO 20022, or API technology, for example) and benefit from the investment, without requiring every other participant in the process to do the same at the same time."

Web Connections

If you can, take a look at a web page from 15 years ago or even longer. It looks pretty basic by today's standards, right? But if you look at one from ten years ago, it's really not so different from today. Stylistically, as well as the level of sophistication of content, web pages haven't really changed much and aren't likely to in the near future.

And the fundamental concepts of URLs in text hyperlinks allowing web pages to be linked to each other haven't changed since 1991.

But how we interact with web pages has changed dramatically in the last few years and is almost certainly on the brink of a revolution.

The variety of devices that connect to the web has grown exponentially. While the original concept was for desktop PCs to access web pages, the accessibility of mobile data coupled with smartphones (and in particular the iPhone and its clones) accelerated the growth of internet usage in a totally unexpected way. Apps for social media, music and video streaming, goods and food delivery are now more likely to be accessed on a mobile device than on a desktop. And the IoT will continue that trend.

Meanwhile, the current superpowers of the internet (Meta, Alphabet and Microsoft among others) are busy creating the Next Big Thing: the metaverse. The vision of the metaverse is a permanently connected virtual world where people will interact with each other through avatars. It's not a new concept, but the technology to date has been lacking. Arguably, it's still not quite there – virtual reality (VR) headsets are still heavy, bulky, unreliable and in some cases uncomfortably warm. And battery technology hasn't yet provided a solution that allows for fully wire-free access for any length of time. But once these hurdles are collectively cleared (as inevitably they will be), the virtual world will be a potentially lucrative and immersive place to do business.

Whether it's for more effective coworking for a distributed workforce (imagine participating in a virtual meeting with colleagues in a virtual meeting room, and then, on leaving the room, bumping into another colleague's avatar in a virtual corridor) or for meeting and accessing clients in a virtual marketplace, the metaverse will provide untold opportunities for collaboration at distance.

It remains to be seen just how effective these virtual interactions can become. Presently, there remains no substitute for a physical, face-to-face meeting: only in the presence of another person are you able to access the full range of non-verbal cues, including foot-twitching, leg-crossing, hand-wringing and other off-screen activities. Furthermore, the importance of silence as a conversational technique is often underrated. On a video call, it seems that participants feel that silence is a void to be filled. Face-to-face, silence has more impact – it has a presence of its own. Silence can often be your friend, encouraging others to share more intimately than perhaps they would have done amid the noise of their colleagues. These are all challenges that the VR headset is unlikely to address on its own.

But, just as the internet itself provided untold opportunities, and the advent of the smartphone lent a new impetus to online business, the metaverse, in all its forms, is likely to once again expand our capabilities in new directions. The key thing, as always, will be to maintain a clear view of the problems that need to be solved. Adopting technology and innovation for its own sake will be less effective than identifying a genuine and material problem that such innovation can solve.

SO WHAT?

Interfacing has many aspects, and it governs how all of our other technology connects. At the start of this chapter, we invited you to think about how you might run your business without interfaces – even if you had the fastest computers with the biggest, crispest screens, unlimited data storage capacity and state-of-the-art software, if you can't link it all together and – more importantly – reach your customers or collaborators, it's really not going to do the job.

Some aspects of interfacing are, we'll admit, deeply technical. But while you may not need to understand how the interfaces are working, you should be clear on what it is delivering to you and whether it's appropriate.

And on the less technical aspects, there are many ways that you, as a business leader, can get involved and ensure that the interfaces you have within and beyond your organisation are as effective as possible, giving your business its best chances to thrive.

So, what are the questions the business leader should ask:

- Is my physical network appropriately scaled for my business?
- Do I have an overarching view of my business applications and the interfaces between them?
- Am I clear on the business drivers for each and every interface?
- How can I help to drive the standardisation of message flows for my industry?
- Am I clear on the problems or opportunities that might be solved by more effective web interaction?

Is My Physical Network Appropriately Scaled for My Business?

"I've had to turn off my camera – I'm working in the office today".

Along with "Sorry, I was on mute", this has become one of the tropes of the post-lockdown virtual office environment. Office networks that before the pandemic were perfectly adequate for file-based traffic suddenly had to deal with an upsurge in real-time video. Because, ironically, even when co-located in the same office, people now tend to video call instead of having a physical meeting.

It will be some years before these office networks are suitably upgraded to support this increased demand.

Your technical teams won't be ignorant of this limitation, but it is worth taking a look at your overall networking requirements and ensuring that the next installation of the network takes into account how it will be used.

Are there rooms or areas that will need a higher bandwidth than others? Training rooms? Or does your modern open-plan office have collaboration spaces where people will typically gather together in physical meetings, meaning that it needs less network coverage than elsewhere? Do you have a lab that's investigating VR technologies, with a commensurate leap in bandwidth requirements?

Helping your technical teams gauge the likely network needs of each part of the office may help you and your colleagues to stay better connected (and on camera!) for longer.

Do I Have an Overarching View of My Business Applications and the Interfaces between Them?

Now this one might sound as though it's getting a bit technical.

Surely the IT department has an architect of some sort who draws all of the necessary boxes and lines?

Well, if that's true, then great. Find their desk (or their virtual desk), go and have a chat and get them to walk you through the whole thing. Better yet, get it printed on a single sheet of paper (go big – even if this means getting it done commercially), nail it to a wall and ask the architect to walk you (and everyone) through it.

And if it's not true, then it's even more important that you have this view (or that someone does – but it's better if it's you).

For very large organisations, this might be a bit of a stretch – but in that case break it down and at least make sure you have the view for your own area of responsibility. And if you're the CEO of a large organisation, make sure someone on your team is on the hook to understand this stuff. It's important – and it's not just "tech".

It's fine to stay at a high level – you don't need to know every detail about every interface. But you should know enough to be able to answer the next question for most of them (and certainly the most critical ones).

Understanding how all of your business applications hang together and are supported by your (probably in-house built) integration software will help you to understand when there are issues, be they due to data loss, data integrity, bottlenecks or other delays.

These pictures aren't static either. You should make sure that, within your organisation, the architectural picture is updated for every change project that impacts one or more of the applications or interfaces. And you should refresh your understanding from time to time to ensure you have the latest view.

As a business leader, you may be asked to opine on new applications or on projects to link one or more applications. Knowing how these will fit into the overall structure is a key component of those decisions.

Am I Clear on the Business Drivers for Each and Every Interface?

For every interface in your organisation (at least for every interface that has a business component), you should know what it's doing, as well as why and when, although you may not need to know exactly how the interface works.

What you should know

- *Who* – the source and target applications and what they do. Understanding where the data has come from, and where it's going, is crucial to the overall understanding of the interface.
- *What* – the data contained in the interface. This doesn't need to be at a detailed level but should give you a broad idea such as "customer data" or "product data".
- *When* – whether the interface is real time or batched in some way for later delivery. "When" could also be taken to represent how often the interface is used – what are the volumes of traffic involved?
- *Why* – what's the purpose and criticality of the interface?

This information will help you to understand the interface topology and how information is distributed around your organisation's applications and data stores.

While you're at it, you should understand the monitoring and exception-handling of each interface. Who is monitoring it and how – what's the escalation when something goes wrong? Is it clear which issues are purely technical and which have a business perspective? The more critical the interface (such as real-time, transactional interfaces), the more stringently it should be monitored and any issues addressed.

How Can I Help to Drive the Standardisation of Message Flows for My Industry?

There may already be existing interface standards for your industry or that may be a logical next step. Either way, the huge collaborative effort needed to propose, agree and implement industry standards doesn't happen by itself. It needs the input and commitment of dedicated industry professionals.

Professionals like you.

By now, you should be clear that interfacing is about so much more than the technical connectivity between host systems. Especially from your perspective as a business leader, it's all about the data. Technology will change faster than underlying business needs.

Data drivers should be decoupled from those of format and protocol, enabling new network technology to be introduced with minimal disruption to the industry. For example, global adoption of the ISO 20022 standard is really about embedding ISO 20022 data definitions into organisations' applications and data management processes. Data that today might be exchanged as messages across a bespoke secure network might be conveyed tomorrow by exposed APIs across the public internet. But the fundamentals of the business transaction – who is requesting what action from whom – will remain largely the same. Flexibility is critical. Industries will need the flexibility to switch flows, deploy new formats and protocols and scale up and down in line with changing business needs.

So even if you don't really understand how the networking aspect of it all works, the business and data drivers are very much down to you. If, by your efforts and those of like-minded industry colleagues, you can bring disparate messaging needs together as a single commoditised flow that can be used by all, then the industry as a whole will benefit, allowing you to focus on improving those aspects of your business that are genuinely competitive.

Am I Clear on the Problems or Opportunities That Might Be Solved by the Internet?

We've seen that web interaction (and other connectivity) is probably one of the most volatile and adaptable components of the modern technology universe. How, where and when your customers and colleagues can interact over the internet are subject to polarising swings as the next piece of "must have" technology is rolled out.

In such a situation, it's probably impossible to predict what any given organisation should adopt or even to drive forward.

So we're not going to try.

Instead, it's worth bearing in mind some principles (that in fact are common to all IT endeavours). These are all essentially versions of the programmer's mantra: "if it aint broke, don't fix it":

- Just because there is something shiny doesn't mean that you need to get involved. VR headsets may look space-tech and exciting, but is it really practical for your colleagues or clients?
- Is there really a problem that needs to be fixed, and if so, is there a simpler way to fix it? If client satisfaction is going down, is the right solution to provide an expensive chatbot with a cute avatar on your website or to fix the distribution problems that have caused the issue in the first place?
- If the pace of change is high, is it worth investing time and money into a solution in that space? If you elect to provide VR headsets to your entire team so they can attend meetings together in cyberspace, you can be sure that a cheaper, lighter and more reliable headset will have been introduced before your first meeting.

That being said, there is plenty of fertile ground and scope for innovation in physical industries such as farming and manufacturing, leveraging the improvements in networking (such as 5G) and both localised and ubiquitous network devices.

NOTES

1 *Introduction to the History of Computing* by Gerard O'Regan, 2016, ISBN 978-3-319-33137-9.
2 *"Unsinkable": The Full Story of the RMS Titanic* by Daniel Butler, 1998.
3 *The Birth and Babyhood of the Telephone* by Thomas A. Watson.
4 *Proposal for a Digital Communication Network* by DW Davis, 1966.
5 historyofcomputercommunications.info
6 www.computerhistory.org/collections/catalog/102740417
7 *Introduction to the History of Computing* by Gerard O'Regan, 2016, ISBN 978-3-319-33137-9.
8 www.iso.org
9 *Introduction to the History of Computing* by Gerard O'Regan, 2016, ISBN 978-3-319-33137-9.
10 *As We May Think* by Vannevar Bush, 1945.
11 https://en.wikipedia.org/wiki/Middleware
12 *Recursive InterNetwork Architecture, Investigating RINA as an Alternativeto TCP/IP (IRATI)* – Grasa, Bergesio, Tarzan, Trouva, Gaston, Salvestrini, Maffione, Carrozzo, Staessens, Vrijders, Colle, Chappel, Day and Chitkushev.

5

What's Blockchain?

Whereas most technologies tend to automate workers on the periphery doing menial tasks, blockchains automate away the center. Instead of putting the taxi driver out of a job, blockchain puts Uber out of a job and lets the taxi drivers work with the customer directly.

Vitalik Buterin

Sally was far from convinced about this new "distributed ledger"….

DOI: 10.4324/9781003372660-5

This seems like a good point in the book to talk about blockchain.

Before we get any further, we need to make something very clear: *Blockchain is not the same as crypto.*

Blockchain is an innovative distributed ledger technology (DLT) that has built rapidly on the capabilities provided by the internet coupled with fast and ubiquitous distributed computing power. It combines computer hardware, software, data and interfacing to allow communities of users to interact in a decentralised way: making decisions and operating collectively and collaboratively rather than being subject to a central orchestrating entity.

Cryptocurrencies are just one (and happened to be the first) way of using this new concept to exchange data and value. There are many more.

Think of blockchain as a highway, and crypto as a bunch of flashy red sports cars tearing along the road. But there is plenty of other traffic on the road too: trucks and transports from every industry, delivering value quickly and securely.

Although we talk about "the blockchain", there are in fact many thousands of independent *blockchain networks*. Each network is formed from a number of *nodes* (computers). Each node runs software that enables it to link to the other nodes in the same network through the public internet, and each node keeps a local copy of the *entire blockchain* as data, updating it as instructed by other nodes. New transactions are validated by one or more nodes (following an agreed *consensus* protocol) and formed into blocks: new *blocks* are periodically added to the end of the *chain* (and of course these new blocks are also shared with all the other nodes in the network). Data in the blockchain is *secured cryptographically*, ensuring that existing data cannot be tampered with or altered without adding a new transaction to the end of the chain.

This sharing of the entire database between all the nodes on the network is the fundamental difference between blockchain and more traditional ways of managing and sharing data.

What does it mean in practice? Let's take a very simple model of a cash network involving four participants, illustrated in Figure 5.1:

- Traditionally, the participants would have used a bank as a central body to route and validate payment instructions. The bank's centrally managed database would be the "source of truth" for the participants'

TRADITIONAL CASH NETWORK

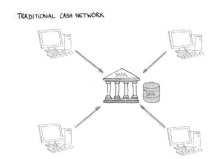

BLOCKCHAIN NETWORK

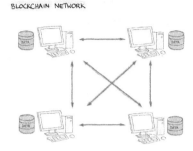

FIGURE 5.1
Example Blockchain Network.

cash positions and each participant would need to contact the bank to find out their current cash position.

- In a blockchain network, there is no central bank. Participants pass cash to each other in peer-to-peer transactions which are validated by other participants in the network through a consensus mechanism. There is a single source of the truth which is replicated and distributed across the entire network.

As we will see, it was this goal of disintermediating banks and other trusted third parties that led to the creation of the first blockchain – bitcoin – and the bitcoin cryptocurrency.

Cryptocurrencies since then have had something of a tarnished reputation, and because of its crypto origins, blockchain has typically been viewed hitherto with distrust and distaste by core industries. But blockchain itself is not the same as crypto, and in its purest (mechanical) form, it represents the logical next step in the democratisation of data. Branded as "Web3" or "Web 3.0", a new generation of the World Wide Web is emerging, embracing concepts such as democratisation and decentralisation, built upon blockchain technology, tokenisation and artificial intelligence (AI).

After a saunter through the entwined history of blockchains and cryptocurrencies, we set out some of the key mechanics of blockchain, along with some of its other potential applications. As always, the final section contains some questions that you, the business leader, should be asking about your organisation to determine whether or not you could benefit from this new and exciting technology.

WHY SHOULD I CARE?

You've no doubt heard the tale of the emperor's new clothes.

Two knavish types pretend to weave a set of magnificent new robes for an emperor, telling him and his court that the clothes are invisible to the unintelligent. Not wanting to be seen as stupid, the courtiers all pretend that they can see the non-existent robes. When the emperor dons them for a procession, the crowd are not fooled, being less vain and haughty than the emperor and his courtiers.

The story of blockchain might seem to be a bit like that.

For a start, it seems to be inextricably interwoven with the story of cryptocurrencies, seen as risky investments by most and as the work of dark forces by many.

And secondly, it has perhaps the aura of something that the technologists have invented – the story hasn't come from big businesses adapting their approaches but from some amateurs or hobbyists working in garages (although it's worth noting that many of the richest people in the world started out as hobbyists in garages).

Blockchain might appear to be something that we want to believe has value rather than something that actually does: a "solution looking for a problem".

But blockchain really does have the power to change the face of businesses the world over.

The distributed ledger is a natural evolution from the internet. Rather than connecting lots people to one set of data, why not distribute that data and make it visible to all? And rather than have one organisation that is responsible for defining what that data should be, why not implement a world-wide consensus algorithm so that the distributed ledger itself is a single source of the truth?

Quite simply, a properly architected and democratised blockchain network removes the need for the "trusted parties" that have habitually operated in a central capacity between two transacting parties (such as how, in a cash transaction using a more standard "off chain" model, a bank is needed between the buyer and the seller to ensure that the buyer has – and transfers – the necessary funds to the seller).

It's worth investing some time in understanding the power of blockchain and what it might be able to unlock in your business or your industry.

HOW DID WE GET HERE?

Blockchain and distributed ledgers began life in obscurity. Papers published to describe the bitcoin network, the complex software written to control it and the first known transactions on it were all perpetrated by someone known only as Satoshi Nakamoto, a name more shrouded in mystery and secrecy than any Agatha Christie novel.

Quite literally, you couldn't make it up.

Ledgers

Ledgers themselves, of course, are nothing new.

The first ledgers hail from the very earliest of civilisations in Mesopotamia and the fertile lands of the Tigris and Euphrates rivers where trade between city states flourished. Use of these ledgers later spread to Egypt and Greece, and throughout the Roman Empire.

The Tang dynasty introduced the first double-entry ledgers to manage their complex trading arrangements with multiple cultures along the Silk Road.

Islamic requirements to account for indebtedness and to perform complex calculations for inheritance led to Muhammad ibn Musa al-Khwarizmi's ninth-century work *The Compendious Book on Calculation by Completion and Balancing*.[1] His book introduced a concept of balance and "restoration" (*al-jabr* – from which we get "algebra"), leading to the construct of an equation where the components on the left-hand side are balanced by the components on the right-hand side. It's from al-Khwarizmi that we get the word "algorithm".

Europe lagged behind due to the use of Roman numerals which made calculations difficult. The adoption of Arabic numbers led to an explosion of arithmetic and the art of double-entry bookkeeping was introduced in the banking families of Italy in the twelfth and thirteenth centuries. Luca Pacioli recorded these practices in his book *Everything about Arithmetic,*

Geometry and Proportion.[2] Written in Italian vernacular (rather than Latin or Greek), this influential tome popularised Arabic numerals and spread double-entry accountancy practices throughout Europe.

For hundreds of years, movements of money and goods were recorded in ledgers across the globe. Almost all of these ledger entries were made in relation to one of the following:

- A good or a commodity – that had intrinsic value
- *Specie* money – where the value of a coin was derived from its constituent commodities (such as gold, silver and copper)
- *Representative* money – often issued as paper or promissory notes that guaranteed a value of a specific commodity that had been set aside and held in reserve.

The Bank Charter Act of 1844 gave the Band of England the right to issue bank notes that could be redeemed either for gold or equivalent bank credit. From 1931, the Bank no longer redeemed their notes (or bank credits) in gold.[3] The United States followed in 1971 as part of the "Nixon shock" of financial measures taken to address rising inflation, bringing to an end the Bretton Woods system that linked international currencies to the price of gold. Paper money was now being issued globally in a form that didn't necessarily relate to a quantity of a commodity. *Fiat* money's only value is derived from the issuing authority, which requires absolute *trust* from the recipient of the issuer's good standing and ability to so redeem.

Almost all electronic financial transactions globally are effected in fiat currencies. Or they were – until the arrival of a new dynamic in 2008 – the distributed ledger.

Distributed Ledgers

In their book *Blockchain Applied*, Stephen Ashurst and Stefano Tempesta define blockchain as a reboot of ledger technology that hadn't changed in several hundred years.

Research into distributed ledgers, cryptographic currencies and proof of work (PoW) began in the late 1980s and 1990s including the publication of papers by a collection of computer scientists including Nick Szabo, Wei Dai and Hal Finney. In 1991, research scientists Stuart Haber and W. Scott

Stornetta pioneered the time stamping of digital documents so they could not be backdated or manipulated.[4]

In October 2008, following the global economic crash, the hitherto unknown name of Satoshi Nakamoto was associated with an extraordinary paper *Bitcoin: A Peer-to-Peer Electronic Cash System*,[5] which was posted to a cryptography mailing list. Not only did the paper set out the proposed mechanics for a cryptographic distributed currency, it also railed against the iniquities of the traditional banking system and "the inherent weaknesses of the trust based model".

Satoshi put forward a solution for an "electronic payment system based on cryptographic proof instead of trust, allowing any two willing parties to transact directly with each other without the need for a trusted third party", as shown in Figure 5.2.

A few months later, in January 2009, Satoshi created the first bitcoin *block* and released the source code for the bitcoin *network* (approximately 31,000 lines of code). Three days after that, Hal Finney – who had downloaded the software – became the first recipient of bitcoin (10 in total) in a transaction sent by Satoshi.

Gradually, interest in this strange new form of money grew. Initially worth less than a cent, bitcoin's value grew, too. On May 22, 2010, programmer

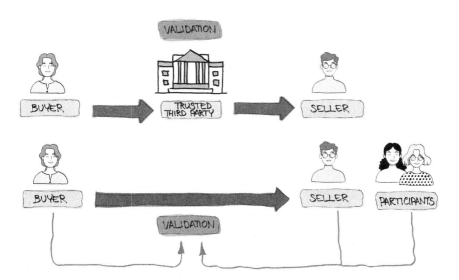

FIGURE 5.2
Trust in a Financial Transaction.

Laszlo Hanyecz paid 10,000 bitcoin (worth well over $250 million today) for two delivered Papa John's pizzas. By the end of the year, 1 bitcoin was valued at $0.30. A year later, over $4.

But by then, Satoshi Nakamoto had disappeared. To this day, the identity of this mysterious coding genius and economic rebel is unknown. A reporter for The New Yorker, Joshua Davis, wrote an article in 2011 having pursued a number of clues as to Satoshi Nakamoto's identity and having interviewed a number of cryptography experts. None were able to pinpoint Nakamoto's identity or would admit to being him (or her, or them). They did acknowledge Satoshi's expertise in cryptography and in coding in C++, the language used for the original bitcoin program. With Satoshi's departure, stewardship of the Bitcoin Foundation was passed to others, leaving them to manage the fledgeling network's development.

Bitcoin started to hit news headlines, mainly due to its use in the shadiest areas of the web and its meteoric rise in value. But while the currency itself attracted a great deal of attention, the mechanism behind it – the *blockchain* – remained in the shadows, known and understood by only a few.

The bitcoin program written by Satoshi allowed anyone to join the network. The computer running the program would become a node on the network, able to propose transactions and compete to validate each block of transactions, solving a cryptographic puzzle to do so. The successful node would be rewarded with more bitcoin in a process known as *mining*. As bitcoin rose in value, the rewards for solving the puzzle rose as well, and more and more participants joined the network, some with significant computing power. Vast server farms, containing stack upon stack of graphics boards – uniquely suited to solving the cryptographic puzzles – were built by avaricious bitcoin miners.

Oscar Wilde said that imitation is the sincerest form of flattery: bitcoin wasn't the only cryptocurrency for long as individuals and communities sought to replicate its success.

In October 2011, following a number of other forays, the next successful currency to launch was Litecoin. The source code for Litecoin was derived from that of bitcoin, with a shorter block duration and using a different hashing algorithm.

Others followed, mostly derivatives of the bitcoin source code: Namecoin, Peercoin, Primecoin (which uses prime numbers in its consensus mechanism), Dogecoin (initially a satirical joke) and even Titcoin (a cryptocurrency intended for the "adult" industry).

Distributed Processors

But it was the launch of the Ethereum network in 2015 that transformed the blockchain from being merely a cryptocurrency mechanism into a truly innovative business infrastructure. Vitalik Buterin was a 21-year-old maths prodigy who had been writing for an on-line publication called *Bitcoin Magazine* following his "bitcoin moment" (an experience reported by many as an epiphany so strong as to manifest physically) in 2011. Unlike most others, Buterin was able to see beyond the prospect of immediate financial gain from cryptocurrency speculation, grasping the vast potential of the blockchain. And he realised that bitcoin and its derivatives were too constrained by the original source code to realise that potential. He resolved to start again from scratch. He built a new network – Ethereum – that would create a *distributed virtual machine* through fully Turing-complete executable code implemented as transactions on the blockchain. Instead of centrally creating a solution for each business case in turn, these "smart contracts" allowed the community of users to solve their own business cases however they chose by building software that could be distributed to every node. Instead of just democratising currencies, it was now possible to democratise any business that uses a ledger, be it stocks and bonds, mutual funds, real estate or even supply chains.

The cryptocurrencies and their wild ride continued to grab the headlines: price fluctuations, tumbling records, fortunes made and lost, frauds, conspiracies and manipulation. High-profile failures of crypto exchanges, including Mt. Gox in 2014 and FTX in 2022 with criminal charges and eye-watering liabilities, tore gaping holes in the industry's reputation, causing deep concern among global regulators.

But, in the background, Ethereum and its derivatives made genuine progress towards the realisation of the distributed application platform, the Ethereum Virtual Machine (EVM).

Not that this progress was without hitches. The code was not flawless, and occasionally code upgrades introduced new flaws. These flaws (or the exploitation of them by criminals) would cause blocks to be added to the chain that were either incorrect or contained criminal transactions. Very rarely, the cryptocurrency community acted to eradicate these blocks, by returning to the last "good" block and rebuilding the chain from that point, without the erroneous transactions. This remediation created "forks" in the chain. In 2013, a "soft fork" occurred when an upgrade to the bitcoin code introduced an error that temporarily created two chains; the code was withdrawn and the "longest" chain became the reference chain. In 2017, bitcoin experienced a "hard fork", as the community disagreed on the best way to implement changes to increase network efficiency. The currency (and the blockchain) split into two chains from that point, the majority continuing along the bitcoin chain, while the dissenters used a different chain, renamed Bitcoin Cash. In 2016, due to a large theft on the Ethereum network, the community decided to revert to the last block before the theft occurred; the Ethereum chain continued from that point. This, again, was a hard fork, as the un-reverted chain continued as Ethereum Classic.

Blockchain technology has been with us for just a few years. In that time it has grabbed the headlines for all the wrong reasons, but as industries begin to explore the mechanism itself, seeing past the noise of cryptocurrencies, it presents perhaps one of the biggest transformation opportunities for businesses since the arrival of the World Wide Web.

WHAT DOES HERE LOOK LIKE?

What exactly is blockchain and why is it potentially so transformational?

While there's quite a lot going on "under the hood", there are really only three significant things you need to know about blockchain that will help you understand whether you have a problem that it can solve.

First, it is a *distributed digital ledger.*

A distributed digital ledger is a store of information that is shared throughout a network. Information is recorded in a series of transactions, but the crucial difference is that it is replicated and synchronised throughout the network without fail. The network is often decentralised too, thereby creating a resilient and robust environment to store information. For those who have access to the network every transaction is accessible to view, and they have the certainty of knowing that the transaction information is the same across the network. This is sometimes referred to as "a single source of the truth".

Second, it is *immutable*.

Information stored on the distributed digital ledger cannot be updated, reversed or deleted as it is cryptographically secured. Only new transactions can be added.

And third, *decentralised applications* (DApps) can be deployed on the blockchain.

Programs known as smart contracts allow transactions to invoke business logic held within them. Transactions created by distributed applications can access multiple smart contracts to perform business activities to fulfil business processes and ultimately create a business capability.

A blockchain secures data in a distributed and immutable manner ensuring earlier transactions are never able to change. This has the potential to massively reduce (or even remove) the need for many reconciliation and audit processes. The transfer of balance values or change in ownership of assets is always in real time. You can apply business logic to new transactions with extreme efficiency ending the need for time-consuming processes. This extreme efficiency allows for new business processes to be possible. Processes that once took weeks to conclude involving many parties can now occur within the time to create a single block. Just these three components together open up some very disruptive business opportunities.

Let's take a look under that hood….

What Is a Blockchain and How Does It Work?

A blockchain is a distributed digital ledger where transaction information is stored securely in sequential blocks that are cryptographically chained together. The transaction information is immutable but is readable to any entity that has access to the blockchain.

How each blockchain generates these blocks depends on its architecture. In general terms though, this is how it is done:

- The blockchain network either choses or incentivises a computer, called a node, to validate transactions waiting to be included in the next block of the blockchain.
- This node selects a group of unconfirmed transactions and applies a set of validation rules to each transaction in turn, this is known

as the consensus mechanism. While these rules can vary between blockchains, they all involve applying a cryptographic algorithm to confirm the authenticity of a transaction. All nodes know the consensus mechanism, ensuring that any node chosen to validate a transaction will always generate the same result or any incentivised node has the ability to solve the cryptographic problem.

- After the original node validates a number of transactions, it notifies the other nodes on the network.
- Each node then confirms the original node's result using the consensus mechanism.
- Once the rest of the network agrees, the block is added to the blockchain.
- This validation process generates a unique cryptographic hash value which is then used to validate the transactions in the next block.

This linking of blocks through the hash forms the chain hence the name blockchain. The network repeats this process for each new block.

Blockchain Program

First and foremost, a blockchain is a computer program that defines how all the components of the blockchain network will behave. In the case of bitcoin, that computer program was written by Satoshi Nakamoto, while for Ethereum it was Vitalik Buterin. For these early pioneers, the source code was freely distributed, and others could join the blockchain network by simply running the program.

The program sets out the operating parameters of the blockchain network: the size of the blocks, what constitutes a transaction, the hashing algorithm (the puzzle) to be used to validate blocks, and how consensus is to be achieved. For Ethereum and later blockchains, the program also defines the syntax and commands that can be used for the smart contracts. When new versions of the blockchain source code are released and implemented, the blockchain begins to behave in a different way from that point on (as happened on the bitcoin network when an error in the new code caused a temporary "soft" fork in 2013 while a more fundamental change in 2017 created two networks which shared a common chain until that point).

Members of a community can participate in a blockchain network by compiling and running the program on a connected computer (usually via the public internet), turning that computer into a node on the blockchain network.

Being a node on the blockchain network allows the computer to discover and communicate with other nodes on the same network, send, receive and store blockchain data, execute and validate transactions (contributing to the consensus mechanism of the network and receiving rewards).

Blocks and Data

The first blockchain network, bitcoin, was designed specifically to send and receive digital cash, validated and secured cryptographically (hence the name cryptocurrency). Cash was sent and received in transactions, and transactions were built into blocks. As each block was validated, the hashed contents of its constituent transactions were stored in the block header. Satoshi allowed for blocks in the past to be condensed to save room, keeping just the hashed data. Every node on the blockchain network stores a local copy of the database for the whole of the chain. Currently, the bitcoin database takes up over 500 gigabytes of storage (on every node in the network), and is growing in linear fashion, as new blocks continue to be added approximately once every 10 minutes.

Other networks have been implemented with different rules about block sizes and frequencies. The Ethereum database is already larger than that of bitcoin, despite starting four years later.

The Importance of Trust – Or Lack of It

Satoshi Nakamoto designed the bitcoin network as an alternative cash platform to one that was "trust based". In Satoshi's own words, "what is needed is an electronic payment system based on cryptographic proof instead of trust, allowing any two willing parties to transact directly with each other without the need for a trusted third party".

Why is trust a bad thing, you might ask. The main problem with electronic cash (i.e. cash that has no physical form) is that a malicious agent can try to spend the money twice. This can't happen with physical coins or paper notes (regardless of whether they are specie, representative or fiat money) – once you've given the physical representation away, you can't do it again. For electronic money using a trust-based system, a trusted third party intervenes in every transaction between payer and receiver, ensuring that each quantum of cash is only spent once. But the problem with this trust-based system is that the third party can unilaterally make decisions and reverse its own records (quite possibly with good intentions). Satoshi's vision stretched to a fully peer-to-peer cash system where there was no "trusted third party": trust was, instead, achieved through cryptographic problem-solving and consensus.

The bitcoin blockchain network provides this trust as follows:

- As a transaction is introduced, it is broadcast to all nodes on the network. Each node collects these new transactions into a block.
- Each node works on solving a cryptographic problem as a "PoW".
- When a node finds a PoW, it updates the block to record the result and broadcasts the block to all nodes.
- Nodes accept the block only if all transactions in it are valid and not already spent.
- Nodes express their acceptance of the block by working on creating the next block in the chain, using the hash of the accepted block as the previous hash.

The trust is achieved by a consensus of "honest" nodes all agreeing that the longest sequence of blocks (categorically defined by the hashed data within them) is the correct path.

How Transactions Work

It's also important to understand how transactions work in the blockchain.

A transaction represents an instruction to perform an action that will change values on the ledger. Initially, transactions were simply a means to send coins (such as bitcoin) from one wallet to another, but following the introduction of smart contracts, transactions can also be used to initiate any of the smart contract's functions.

The transaction is initiated by the submitting node and will typically include the following elements:

- A *unique identifier* assigned to the transaction, often represented as a hash value. This serves as a reference to the transaction and can be used to track and verify its status on the blockchain.

- The *wallet addresses* for the sender and the recipient.
- Any *transaction data* – the details of the transaction, which can vary depending on the blockchain network and the reason for the transaction.
- A *digital signature* – a cryptographic signature generated by the blockchain software to verify the authenticity and integrity of the transaction.

Once a transaction has been generated, it is written to something called a memory pool (also known as a "mempool") and is copied to all nodes on the network. Each node will add the new transaction to the block it is currently building – once that block is complete, the node will begin to solve the cryptographic puzzle to verify the whole block.

Depending on the consensus mechanism in use for that particular network (see below), one or more nodes will attempt to verify the transactions in the block (which includes ensuring that there is a sufficient coin balance in the sending wallet's account to effect the transaction). Regardless of the consensus mechanism, one node will be successful in validating the block and will add it to the end of the growing chain of blocks. This data is then circulated to all nodes in the network.

If any other nodes have attempted to validate a block at the same time as the successful node (possible depending on the consensus mechanism), the unvalidated blocks become orphaned and the constituent transactions are returned to the memory pool for inclusion in a later block.

Figure 5.3 shows the process flow for a blockchain transaction.

Ledger Models

There are two fundamental models for tracking quantities on blockchains (whether that be cryptocurrencies or some other tokenised asset). These are the unspent transaction output (UTXO) model or the account model.

As implemented by bitcoin, UTXO tracks the unspent currency available to a given wallet address. If you have received 20 currency units in a transaction and have spent 18 of them, you have 2 left. The UTXO model treats each transaction as discrete: there is no concept having an "overall total" of currency.

In the account model on the other hand, such as is used by Ethereum, the blockchain manages an overall total for each account. This involves a

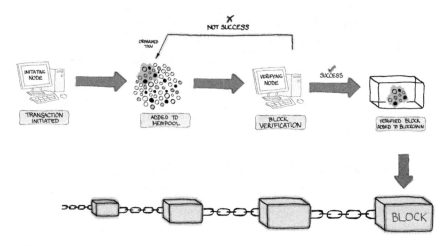

FIGURE 5.3
Blockchain Transaction Flow.

processing overhead but is essential to the operation of smart contracts which are implemented as accounts.

What Is Consensus and How Does It Work?

Consensus protocols are designed to address the challenge of achieving consensus in a decentralised and trust-less environment, where multiple participants may have conflicting interests or may be prone to malicious behaviour. By following the consensus protocol, participants can agree on a single version of the truth and maintain the integrity of the blockchain.

Consensus protocols are a critical component of blockchain technology, as they enable multiple nodes within a decentralised network to agree on the validity of transactions and the state of the ledger. The consensus protocol determines the rules that nodes must follow in order to validate transactions and add new blocks to the blockchain. There are several types of consensus protocols used in blockchain technology.

Here are some of the most common mechanisms.

PoW: PoW is a consensus protocol used in the bitcoin blockchain network, where nodes compete to solve complex mathematical problems to validate transactions and add new blocks to the chain. The first node to solve the problem earns a reward of cryptocurrency for their effort. The data in the block is cryptographically hashed with a trial value (called the "nonce"), and if the resulting string meets certain criteria (such as having a specified number of sequential zeroes at the start), then the puzzle is deemed to have been solved. The node's success in completing the puzzle is the "proof" that it has done the necessary "work".

Periodically the application checks how long blocks are taking to be created: too quickly and it will implement a "difficulty bomb", increasing the complexity of the cryptographic problem to lengthen the time taken to create each new block (and vice versa when block times are increasing too much).

The amount of computing power (often referred to as hash power) used to solve the cryptographic problem is a demonstration of network strength and adoption as more work is being used to solve the cryptographic problem to obtain the reward.

Proof of Stake (PoS): PoS is a consensus protocol that is used in several blockchain networks, including Ethereum. In a PoS system, specific nodes are selected to validate transactions and add new blocks based on the amount of cryptocurrency they hold, rather than performing computational work.

PoS requires nodes to obtain and stake a significant amount of the blockchain's native coin for the opportunity to create new blocks and support the blockchain consensus. A node that creates a new block receives the blockchain's coin as a reward.

The number of nodes actively supporting the network consensus is a sign of network strength and adoption as more entities are aligning their self-interest to the blockchain's success by staking more of the blockchain's native coin.

Delegated Proof of Stake (DPoS): DPoS is where specific nodes are selected to validate transactions and add new blocks based on the number of votes they receive from other network participants.

Practical Byzantine Fault Tolerance (PBFT): PBFT is a consensus protocol which enables nodes to reach consensus even in the presence of malicious actors or faulty nodes. This protocol involves a three-phase process of request, prepare and commit to ensure that all nodes agree on the validity of transactions and new blocks.

Proof of Authority (PoA): In PoA, the integrity of blockchain is managed by a small group of trusted members, known as validators. Only these validators are given the right to create new blocks and validate transactions.

Proof of History (PoH): PoH involves keeping a record of the timing and sequence of operations on the blockchain. This allows the network to verify the time and order of events without having to rely on the participation of multiple parties.

Proof of Elapsed Time (PoET): PoET works a little like a lottery. Each node is given a random waiting time. The one whose waiting time ends first gets to create the next block and add it to the blockchain. This mechanism is more energy-efficient than PoW as it needs less computing power.

Coins and Gas

The first blockchains (such as bitcoin) were created purely for the transfer of cryptocurrencies, a type of digital coin that operated and was accepted only on that network.

The coin for the bitcoin network was bitcoin (BTC). For the Ethereum network, it was Ether (ETH).

These coins became known as cryptocurrencies, and, for a few years, the coin was more in the public eye than the network behind it. Starting with the Ethereum network, however, blockchain networks became capable of supporting other tokenised assets, through the use of smart contracts. More on that later.

The key takeaway, though, is that although coins are used by the networks in performing their activities, they are no longer the only purpose of transactions in many (or even most) cases.

For a transaction to be committed to the blockchain, a transaction fee (often known as gas) must be paid to the node that validates the transaction. In the vast majority of blockchains, this fee is paid using the blockchain's own native coin.

The size of the fee is determined by a number of factors, including:

- The computing power needed by the node to action the instruction – the more computing power needed (usually related to the complexity of the related smart contract) the greater the fee the node will seek because there is a finite amount of computational power that can be used for each block.
- How busy the blockchain is when the transaction is sent – there is a finite amount of computing power than can be used for each block

and with a high demand for power the chosen node will pick those transactions with the highest fee-to-power usage ratio.

- How much the sender is willing to pay to ensure their transaction is validated. Senders of high-value or high-priority transactions will often be willing to pay a larger fee (which may delay the execution of transactions during busy periods).

Mining

One of the most confusing concepts in the cryptocurrency world is that of mining. The explanation of mining is often bundled up with the explanation of blockchains as a whole, and people are led to believe that it is integral to the mechanism.

Mining was introduced as part of Satoshi's bitcoin paper, but it is far from being a fundamental component of the distributed ledger mechanism.

Blockchain works as a trust-less peer-to-peer mechanism because the participating nodes all contribute to the verification of blocks, through the consensus mechanism. The idea behind mining is that the successful node – the one that solves the cryptographic puzzle – receives currency as a reward. This additional currency becomes available to the owner of the node to spend on the network. Bitcoin, for example, generates new currency every 10 minutes. As part of Satoshi's original program, this mining process is limited and the reward mechanism will stop when the number of bitcoins in circulation reaches 21 million.

Imagine a group of scientists, each with a notebook, gathered round a screen that's displaying a logical problem. Each scientist is trying to solve the same problem. When one of them does, she shouts out the answer. All the other scientists immediately write it down in their notebooks and turn the page. The screen shows the next problem (which includes the answer to the previous problem) and each member of the group starts to try to solve it. Every notebook contains the same chain of solved problems, each of which includes a reference to the previous problem's solution.

Mining is really just the same as allowing the successful scientist who solves the puzzle to collect a cookie from a jar (other incentives are available). Once the jar is empty, the scientists will need to be incentivised in some other way (such as through transaction fees – "gas" – as explained above).

Not all networks provide this reward, as we will see later.

Public and Private Keys

Unless you're a keen cryptographer in your spare time, the concept of keys may be new to you, but it is one of the most important concepts in blockchain. The keys are generated cryptographically, which is where we get "cryptocurrency".

Keys are generated in pairs:

- A *private key* which is 64 characters long
- A *public key* which is 128 characters long

The public key is generated directly from the private key using a one-way process. It's not possible to recreate the private key from the public key.

The private key and public key can be combined cryptographically ("hashed") to generate a wallet address (the result of the hash function is shortened to 40 characters and then prefixed with 2 additional characters to make a 42-character long wallet address). Note that one public key and private key pair can generate many wallet addresses this way. The terms "public key" and "wallet address" are often used interchangeably but they do technically mean different things.

Transactions (from a wallet) are signed with both the public and private key, as shown in Figure 5.4. The act of signing a transaction proves that the sender has control over the private key and is used by the blockchain to confirm the transaction has been sent legitimately. The private key should always be kept secret and secure (preferably off-grid) as without it, transactions cannot be sent from the corresponding wallet address.

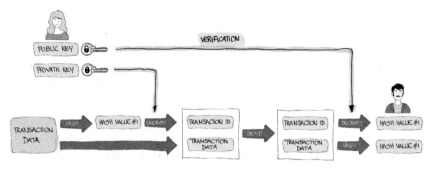

FIGURE 5.4

Cryptographic Keys in Transactions.

For additional security it is possible to have multiple private keys linked together thereby requiring at least a majority of private keys to sign each transaction. This kind of security for a wallet address is known as multi-signature or multi-sig security.

The relationship between the two keys is important. Because of the mathematical derivation of the public key from the private key, it's possible to validate that the digital signature used in the transaction was indeed derived from the sender's secret private key by using only their public key which can be derived from the sender's wallet address.

The private key is vital to the security of the blockchain. Each person's private key should be kept very safe and secure: many people keep it off the grid completely, written down and locked in a safe. In the early days of bitcoin-mania, there were numerous stories of lost hard drives containing the private key that would unlock billions of dollars' worth of stranded cryptocurrency.

While the public key is passed around openly as part of transaction data, there is nothing to link it to a real-world person or entity. As the distributed ledger is visible to all, it's important that, although transaction details such as the public keys of those involved and the number of bitcoins would be known, the real identities of the sender and receiver would be kept secret through the use of these cryptographic keys.

Digital Wallets

It is convenient to think of a digital wallet as simply an electronic representation of a physical wallet – a place where you store all of your digital assets, such as cryptocurrencies or tokenised assets like a tokenised deed to a house for example.

A wallet address represents a location on the network. This address can be the sender or recipient of transactions. Transactions can only be sent by the entity with access to the private key for that wallet address. Transactions can be received from any other wallet address on the network.

Smart Contracts and Decentralised Applications

With the arrival of the Ethereum blockchain in 2015, it became possible to write decentralised applications ("DApps") using smart contracts on the blockchain network.

A smart contract is similar to a legal contract except that the execution of the contract is defined entirely within the code of the contract including any pre-conditions. No human intervention is required (or desired).

A smart contract is technically a type of account on the blockchain, deployed as a transaction just like any other. The contract is written as executable code in the body of the transaction, using a special scripting language defined specifically for the network (such as the Solidity or Vyper programming languages defined for the Ethereum network).

Prior to deploying the smart contract, the owner must code the functions (also called *methods*) to execute the required logic using supplied or maintained parameters. The smart contract owner also defines how access to the functions is allowed, and by whom.

Once deployed, the smart contract is immutable and all of its functions (and their parameters) are visible. Later transactions can be directed at the contract to execute its functions and change its state (data). The data is stored within the blockchain's data storage area (i.e. on every node that is participating in the network). Smart contracts will follow their own logic and can also invoke other smart contracts.

Smart contracts can be used in various areas where conditions can be set out for automated execution. In supply chain management, smart contracts can help facilitate the transfer of goods between parties in a supply chain by automatically verifying the delivery of goods and triggering payment once the terms of the contract are met.

In real estate transactions, smart contracts can automate the process of buying and selling real estate. They can ensure that buyer deposits are held in escrow and automatically transferred to sellers once the title of the property is transferred.

In decentralised finance ("DeFi"), smart contracts can be used in areas such as lending, borrowing and trading where transparency and security are of utmost importance. For example, when an investor wants to buy a tokenised mutual fund, he interacts with a smart contract to complete the transaction. The smart contract includes the terms and conditions of the investment, such as the number of tokens being bought, the price of each token, and the conditions for the sale. The smart contract verifies the conditions of the investment and initiates the transaction to transfer the tokens to the investor's wallet and record the transaction on the blockchain as an "atomic swap".

The use of smart contracts increases efficiency and reduces the need for manual intervention in the execution of business rules. Crucially, smart contracts implemented in a distributed ledger environment (such as a blockchain network) ensure that all participants in the environment can view the results of that execution simultaneously, without the need for onward distribution of information.

With the growing popularity of blockchain technology, smart contracts are set to play an increasingly important role in revolutionising the various areas and provide a high level of security, transparency and automation.

Oracles

When a smart contract is invoked, it normally limits itself to data held on the blockchain. This data is called "on-chain" data. Sometimes though, real-world ("off-chain") data is needed and, in these instances, the blockchain will rely on an external application known as an "Oracle" to provide that data. A good example of Oracle data would be real-time asset price data.

Tokens and Tokenisation

With the advent of smart contracts, it was only a matter of time before different use cases for tokenisation other than for native coins (cryptocurrencies) were considered.

With a smart contract, a token could be used to represent a financial asset such as a mutual fund, a bond or an equity, or a piece of digital art-work, or even real-world objects such as paintings or real estate. The act of generating a token to represent such assets is called "tokenisation".

The executable code in the smart contract governs how the off-chain asset is represented and behaves in its on-chain, tokenised form. Functions in the smart contract allow the asset to be created, destroyed, transferred or to perform any other relevant function.

Standards

To ensure tokens with the same use case can communicate with each other standards needed to be produced.

There are many smart contract standards and most blockchains follow a similar process of approval to what is described here for the Ethereum blockchain. The Ethereum blockchain is decentralised and so the community decides which standards are formally accepted. A standard is proposed as either an "Ethereum Request for Comments" (ERC) or an "Ethereum Improvement Proposal" (EIP).

The most commonly known standard is the ERC-20, a standard used to create cryptocurrency tokens. Another is ERC-721 the non-fungible token (NFT) standard. These standards ensure a common set of fundamental functions for every token smart contract.

The ERC-20 Token Standard

To get an idea of what these functions do here are the major ERC-20 standard functions:

- Creating a number of tokens, known as "minting".
- Destroying a number of tokens, known as "burning".
- Transferring a number of tokens between two wallet addresses.
- Requesting the sending wallet address approves the smart contract to access its token balance.
- Transferring a token balance from the smart contract address to a wallet address.
- Make available the token balance of a chosen wallet address.

The smart contract address owner will have functions only accessible to them as the token creator, whilst other functions are publicly available and are usually accessed by the end user via a DApp. At its core this particular token smart contract performs simple tasks. It maintains a token balance against each wallet address it interacts with, and allows the adding (buying), subtracting (selling) and transferring of a token balance to a wallet address.

As you can see these functions are similar to what can be done by real-world banking services with fiat currencies, here though we are only concerning ourselves with the token as a digital asset.

Fungibility

Fungible tokens all have the same characteristics and so tokens can be substituted in the knowledge that each token acts in the same way. Fungibility is a core tenet of money, be it fiat currency or digital like bitcoin. When you spend physical coins to buy something, it doesn't matter which specific coins you use. As long as they add up to the value sought by the vendor, they will be happy. Coins are fungible. Money in your digital bank account is fungible, too. Cryptocurrencies are also fungible.

Non-fungible tokens, on the other hand, cannot be interchanged. Each will have unique characteristics and cannot be replaced. NFTs will differ in value and utility. Good examples of something that is non-fungible in the real world are works of art or even a person.

Tokenisation of real-world non-fungible assets allows for a publicly available record to be made, on-chain, of ownership of a real-world artefact such as a piece of art. This allows such artefacts to be more easily traded or for ownership to be shared, with full transparency on the blockchain.

CBDCs and Stablecoins

Although cryptocurrencies are widely used for the exchange of real-world goods and services, they have no intrinsic value – they are neither fiat money (backed by a sovereign state that will honour their valuation) nor representative money (relating to a real-world asset of value such as gold).

This causes an issue for consumers – if they sell their house for cryptocurrency and that cryptocurrency (which is neither backed nor insured by any reputable organisation) becomes worthless overnight, they have just lost everything they own.

The solution is to tokenise real-world (fiat) currencies on the blockchain. This allows consumers the advantages of blockchain (peer-to-peer transactions across a distributed ledger) without the risk associated with volatile cryptocurrencies.

There are two widely supported solutions:

- *Stablecoins* – a cryptocurrency that is tagged to a real-world value or to another cryptocurrency. Stablecoins can be asset-backed (where the accepted value of the stablecoin is based on a holding of a real-world asset off-chain such as cash in a bank vault) or algorithmically calculated. One of the most commonly used stablecoins is Tether which is pegged to the US dollar, although some doubts remain as to the level to which it is supported by off-chain assets.
- *Central Bank Digital Currencies (CBDC)* –a tokenised form of cash fully supported by a central bank. The digital currency "would always have the same value as a banknote".[6] Ironically, it was this system of sovereign-backed currencies that Satoshi's initial paper strove so

vehemently to topple. However, a CBDC would at least allow for peer-to-peer transactions without the need for a trusted intermediary.

It should be noted that CBDCs are sometimes further split into wholesale (wCBDC) and retail (rCBDC) versions. The financial industry is more supportive of wCBDCs as they provide for more efficient transactional flow between buyers and sellers. There is an argument to suggest that rCBDCs are less meritorious as individuals have less need for direct access to central bank money than do financial institutions.

Blockchain Networks

What Is a Blockchain Network?

A blockchain network is a collection of nodes that use distributed ledger technology (DLT) to communicate and exchange data in a decentralised way. It's like the group of scientists in our earlier example, all using the same notebooks to record transactions. Each node in the network has access to the same information and can verify transactions independently, making it impossible for any single entity to control the network.

While distributed ledgers and decentralised ledgers may sound similar, they are not the same thing.

A decentralised ledger refers to a system where multiple participants share control over the network and its operations. This involves the distribution of authority or control over the database so that no single entity has complete control over the ledger or the data stored in it. Instead, the decision-making and governance authority are shared among the network participants. Decentralised ledgers rely on consensus mechanisms to establish trust and validate transactions. Consensus mechanisms ensure that all participants agree on the correctness and validity of the ledger's contents.

It's worth noting that while all decentralised ledgers are distributed ledgers, not all distributed ledgers are necessarily decentralised. The level of decentralisation and distribution can vary depending on the specific design, governance model and consensus mechanisms employed in the ledger system.

Some distributed ledgers can have varying degrees of centralisation or rely on specific participants or entities to maintain control over the network. In these cases, the decision-making authority or governance may not be distributed equally among the participants.

Types of Networks

Not all blockchain networks operate in the same way. For example, the method used by each network to verify new blocks can vary. Some networks support smart contracts. Some are open to all participants, while others operate with a closed membership. And how the network is governed can also vary: some are open-source, operated in a collaborative way by foundations, whereas others are privately owned and operated.

There are mainly three types of blockchain networks: public, private and consortium. These types differ based on their accessibility, control and the level of decentralisation. Let's explore each type in detail.

Public blockchains are open and permissionless networks that allow anyone to participate as a node.

Some key characteristics of public blockchain networks include the following:

- Accessibility: public blockchains are accessible to anyone who wants to participate, read the data and submit transactions. No permission is required to join the network.
- Control: Public blockchains aim for a high level of decentralisation, with no single central authority controlling the network. The decision-making and validation processes are typically based on consensus algorithms, such as PoW or PoS among the network participants.
- Transparency: Public blockchains provide a high level of transparency, as the transaction history and the state of the ledger are publicly visible to all participants.

Bitcoin and Ethereum are well-known examples of public blockchain networks.

Private blockchains are restricted and permissioned networks, typically used within a specific organisation or a group of trusted entities. This might be for security reasons so that data on the blockchain is not available to the general public, or simply to limit the number of participants (and hence transactions) on the network.

Key features of private blockchain networks include the following:

- Accessibility: private blockchains have restricted access, allowing only selected participants to join the network. Permission is required from the network administrator to become a node.

- Control: Private blockchains offer higher control to the participating entities. A central authority or consortium often governs the network, determining the consensus mechanism, access permissions and rules.
- Privacy: Privacy and data confidentiality can be achieved in private blockchains, as the participating entities have more control over the visibility of transactions and data.

Ripple and Hyperledger are examples of private networks.

Consortium networks use a model that combines some of the features of both public and private blockchains.

Key characteristics of consortium blockchain networks include the following:

- Accessibility: consortium blockchains are accessible to a specific group of pre-approved participants who form a consortium. These participants collectively govern the network.
- Control: In a consortium blockchain, control is distributed among the consortium members, who often have equal decision-making authority. Consensus mechanisms can vary, but they are typically more efficient and scalable compared to public blockchains.
- Partial Control: While consortium blockchains offer some level of decentralisation, they are not as decentralised as public blockchains. Consortium members have a higher level of trust among each other compared to public blockchain participants.

Within these main types, there can be variations and different implementations based on specific requirements and use cases. Additionally, hybrid models and links between different blockchain networks are also being explored to combine the benefits of multiple types.

Layer 2 Networks and Scalability

Blockchain networks aim to be decentralised, secure and scalable. The so-called blockchain trilemma (a phrase coined by Vitalik Buterin) states that a simple blockchain architecture can only achieve two out of these three. Scalability is typically limited by the speed at which blocks of transactions can be validated and added to the end of the chain. Bitcoin transactions take an average of ten minutes to complete, while the Ethereum network processes around 15 transactions per second, rates that are not suitable for global financial transactions on an industrial scale. Networks can achieve some scalability by a process known as "sharding" where transactions are split into smaller chunks, but another approach is to take some of the activity away from the main network into another layer.

The main network is referred to as a "Layer 1" network, and the separate layer is called a "Layer 2" network. Transactions are executed (and validated) on the Layer 2 network and are then rolled up onto the main network.

These "rollups" still need to be validated on the main network, and there are two different approaches to that validation: optimistic and zero-knowledge. "Optimistic rollups" are assumed to be valid but can be challenged by the main network if deemed necessary. "Zero-knowledge" rollups supply cryptographic proof that the underlying transactions are valid, and that proof is checked by the main network.

Network Participants

The roles and participants involved in running a blockchain network can vary based on the specific implementation, type and governance model chosen for the network. The roles and responsibilities can be defined through agreements, consortium membership or technical protocols established by the participating entities.

Node operators run the blockchain network by operating the software and maintaining a copy of the blockchain's ledger. They validate transactions, store data and participate in the consensus process. Node operators can be miners, developers or enthusiasts who choose to participate in the network voluntarily.

Blockchain developers are responsible for building and maintaining the underlying blockchain infrastructure and smart contracts that facilitate the tokenisation process. They develop the necessary software, protocols and security measures to ensure the smooth operation of the blockchain network. Blockchain developers can be but are not necessarily required to be node operators.

Consortium members in some cases may come together to establish and operate the blockchain network. Consortium members can include fund managers, financial institutions, technology providers and other stakeholders who collaborate to define the rules, governance and technical aspects of the network. Consortium members can be but are not necessarily required to be node operators.

What Are the Different Blockchain Networks?

It's probably difficult to say exactly how many different blockchain networks there are, as many are private or in development. Suffice to say there are over a thousand in existence and the number is growing all the time.

It would be foolhardy (and largely unhelpful) to list them all.

But here are a few that are worthy of note (which is not to say that others, not on this list, aren't).

- *Bitcoin* – the granddaddy of them all, set up in 2009, kicking off the whole DLT revolution. Bitcoin can really only be used for cryptocurrency transactions. There are a number of clones and forks, all essentially similar in nature: Litecoin, Bitcoin Cash, Bitcoin Gold and so on. Bitcoin is governed by the Bitcoin Foundation.
- *Ethereum* – the blockchain network that first implemented smart contracts (executing on the EVM) and began shift towards the use of blockchain for DApps. Ethereum is a public, account-based network that uses an efficient PoS consensus protocol (initially PoW but switching in 2022 through a global event called "The Merge", reducing energy usage by approximately 99%.). A very large number of blockchains are based on Ethereum due to its smart contract capabilities. Ethereum is governed as not-for-profit by the Ethereum Foundation.
- A number of Layer 2 derivatives of the Ethereum network exist, which increase the scale and speed of distributed operations:
  - *Arbitrum*
  - *Polygon*
  - *Optimism*
  - *StarkEx*
  - *zkSync*

- *Tezos* – an open-source blockchain that supports smart contracts and achieves consensus using a PoS mechanism. Tezos launched in 2018 and uses an on-chain governance model to allow its community to vote on future development.
- *Cardano* – a public, open-source network using a PoS consensus mechanism and an extended version of the UTXO ledger model. It was built in 2017 by IOHK an engineering company created for the purpose and is supervised by the Cardano Foundation.
- *Tron* – an open-sourced network using PoS consensus with smart contract functionality, established in March 2014 and overseen by the TRON Foundation.
- *Solana* – launched in 2020 by Solana Labs, this is an open-source blockchain platform that uses a PoS mechanism to provide smart contract functionality and is a popular choice for building DApps.
- *Polkadot* – a network that supports cross-chain activity, with a primary blockchain named the "relay chain" and many user-created parallel chains called "parachains". Polkadot uses PoS consensus.
- *Stellar* – an open-source account-based network optimised for payments and asset issuance, set up in 2014. Stellar uses a consensus protocol known as the Stellar Consensus Protocol (SCP), which allows participants to choose which validators they trust, forming a network of trusted nodes. Stellar has limited smart contract support and uses its own language, which can make it harder to develop DApps.
- *EOS.IO* – open-source network launched in 2018, optimised for developing DApps and smart contracts. Account-based, it uses a complex consensus mechanism based on PoS. The network also supports on-chain voting for platform development.
- *Ripple* – a blockchain-based digital real-time payment network, open to banks and other financial institutions.
- *Hyperledger Fabric* – an open-source platform managed by the Linux Foundation, Hyperledger Fabric is a limited access/permissioned blockchain network with its own version of smart contracts, called chaincode, that allows specifically chosen members of the organisation to run codes very similar to a smart contract.
- *Quorum* – a customised version of Ethereum developed by JPMorgan, repackaging Ethereum into a more robust environment suitable for banks and financial institutions.

WHERE NEXT?

Blockchain is still in its infancy. If we take the first bitcoin transaction as our reference point, the technology is still in its early teen years, with all of the tantrums and everybody-look-at-me histrionics that go along with that.

Cryptocurrency prices are as volatile as ever, but the steel of a truly transformational technology paradigm is starting to emerge with smart contracts and DApps.

Industries have yet to fully embrace the potential – although there is plenty of money being ploughed into research projects (around $20Bn expected in 2024[7]), there are relatively few examples of distributed solutions running in production as yet.

As blockchain continues to mature and becomes more interwoven with the rest of the technology universe, what might the future hold? The evolution of the technology itself, along with wider adoption of the exiting capabilities, will see blockchain (and blockchain applications) become more embedded in financial and other industries, supported by standardisation and sensible regulation.

Evolution of Blockchain Technology

With the world of industry braced to spend a fortune on blockchain in the next decade, if we knew what the next big technological leap was going to be, we certainly wouldn't be writing it in a book! But one can draw parallels from the fundamentals of computer science that we have already written about.

We've seen that any computer has four basic components: input, output, data storage and a processor. Satoshi's vision of blockchain already included three of these, and Vitalik Buterin's improvements added the capability for distributed processing through smart contracts.

So, while we can be sure that there will continue to be evolutionary improvements in blockchain technology, increasing security, scalability and interoperability, there may not be much left conceptually to add to the expanding global supercomputer that is blockchain.

Overall, *security* arguably needs the most attention. The private key needed to access public blockchains and to secure one's own data is a clear single point of failure. Any solution that involves writing something down on paper and locking it in a safe has got to have room for improvement. Security of data is also paramount. In Satoshi's original paper, the implementation of privacy was through the use of the private key to hide the participants' real-world identities. But even in that paper it was acknowledged that anyone determined enough might be able to identify who was involved based on patterns of activity. For many of the potential applications of blockchain, such as in healthcare or in the tokenisation of identity, the data that has been tokenised must remain hidden at all times, visible only to the owner, while being usable by relevant participants to fulfil the desired function, through a zero-knowledge proof mechanism.

Scalability will continue to be an issue, as more and more nodes join networks, and more and more applications are added with the double impact of increasingly sophisticated DApps with commensurately hungrier data needs.

Interoperability is an area of increased interest – getting transactions on one blockchain to reliably impact data on another. Organisations (especially financial infrastructures) see this as part of the solution to the spiralling number of blockchain networks in existence.

There is already a great deal of concern over the *green* credentials of the blockchain. Vast server farms crunching through PoW consensus algorithms draw the equivalent electricity supply of a small town (mining "rigs" of 50,000 server blades are not uncommon, requiring the equivalent power of 10,000 kettles). The operators would opine that the direct cost of these mining installations is warranted financially due to the high unit price of a bitcoin, but the environmental impact is significant. One might imagine that networks will yield to pressure to move to the less harmful PoS protocol or something similarly efficient.

Adoption of Blockchain 2.0

Although we may (or may not) expect radical change of the blockchain technology supporting distributed ledgers, there is still plenty of room for wider adoption of the capabilities introduced by blockchain 2.0 – smart contracts, DApps and more effective scaling.

First, we may see a repeat of the path to commoditisation experienced in software design (where organisations initially wrote their own programming languages, then wrote their own software, then bought software packages, then contracted for software as a service from the vendors).

Today, many organisations seeking a distributed solution for their business take the first step of designing and building their own blockchain network. Perhaps in years to come, organisations will feel more comfortable using an existing public blockchain that better suits their needs. This "blockchain as a service" will provide organisations with a faster (and cheaper) route to distributed solutions. In time, DApps themselves will become commoditised, with organisations sourcing and using distributed software as they do any other kind.

Second, wider use of Layer 2 protocols should greatly increase scalability and functionality of blockchain networks. As activities move from Layer 1 blockchains to cheaper and faster networks like Arbitrum, Optimism and Polygon, high-volume activities will begin to fall within the capability of DLT to support.

And third, with the use of mainstream programming languages such as Python and Rust alongside the plethora of blockchain-specific Web3 languages such as Solidity, Vyper and Yul (all on EVM environments) as well as Cairo (StarkNet) and numerous others, the range of distributed applications available will begin to grow exponentially. The use of Oracles to provide off-chain data to on-chain applications will also grow, with a vibrant market in the provision of such data services. This will lead to more "hybrid" smart contracts – applications that combine on-chain and off-chain data.

From a business perspective, it can be anticipated that more and more problems will fall within the boundaries of a distributed solution.

Decentralised and Distributed Finance

One of the simplest things to tokenise is cash, whether cryptocurrency or stablecoin, closely followed by financial assets such as equities, bonds and mutual funds, which are already largely held electronically in centralised databases (at banks, wealth managers and custodians).

"DeFi" will rapidly increase over the coming years.

In the financial world, various issuers are already exploring and adopting asset tokenisation to digitise and tokenise their financial assets. Traditional banks and financial institutions are actively exploring asset tokenisation to digitise their financial products and services. Banks are involved in tokenising debt instruments like loans, mortgages and promissory notes.

Tokenisation enables more efficient tracking, transferability and trading of these instruments, allowing for improved liquidity and transparency.

Numerous central banks around the world are in the process of introducing CBDCs or are conducting studies within their markets. CBDCs will combine the trust and speed of peer-to-peer transactions without the risk of the wild fluctuations associated with cryptocurrencies (or even some stablecoins).

In capital markets, issuers of debt instruments, such as bonds or loans, are exploring tokenisation to enhance transparency, automate processes and enable efficient secondary market trading. Tokenising debt instruments allows for more streamlined settlement, improved market access and potential cost savings.

Real estate developers and Real Estate Investment Trusts (REITs) are embracing asset tokenisation to unlock liquidity in the real estate market. They tokenise properties, enabling fractional ownership and providing investors with the ability to invest in real estate assets with smaller amounts of capital.

Venture capital and private equity firms are exploring tokenisation as a way to enhance the liquidity of traditionally illiquid assets. They tokenise their investment portfolios, allowing investors to gain exposure to startup equity or private equity investments through security tokens.

Asset tokenisation is gaining traction in the commodities and natural resources sector. Companies involved in the production and trading of commodities such as precious metals, oil or agricultural products are exploring tokenisation to streamline trading, enable fractional ownership and increase market liquidity.

And finally, asset managers and investment firms are tokenising investment funds, including mutual funds, hedge funds and private equity funds. Tokenised funds offer advantages such as increased liquidity, fractional ownership, and automated compliance and reporting, attracting a wider range of investors.

The trend in the financial world is towards increased adoption of asset tokenisation as issuers recognise the potential benefits it offers. Although we have seen real estates, commodities, debt instruments and investment funds successfully tokenised so far, this is an early stage of that trend. Regulatory frameworks and standards are evolving to accommodate these new asset classes, providing a supportive environment for issuers to tokenise their financial assets.

As tokenisation adoption increases, consumers will begin to see consistent benefits from the "always on" nature of the blockchain. Banking customers will be able to see transactions processed in seconds, including in the evening and at weekends, even for large sums. Clearing and settlement for stock market transactions against CBDCs could be achieved in moments as soon as the trade is confirmed (a process that currently takes two, three or four days or even longer).

Currencies exchanged directly between peers may also provide more certainty for populations in countries without stable currencies or where it is less common to have a bank account, and peer-to-peer lending through the blockchain may be a more robust alternative than local providers of loans.

Not everyone believes that blockchain is a panacea for all use cases. Mainstream financial services and central banks may adopt some elements of distributed processing but use applications with more centralised control and known participants: blockchain-like, but perhaps not as revolutionary as proponents promised in 2015 when the talk was of financial services facing a "Kodak moment". Central banks in particular may look into distributed solutions for CBDCs that don't require blockchain. Many of the challenges being discussed are more to do with governance and economic consequences of CBDCs, than with technology.

Identity Management

As more of the world's financial assets are transported and stored on the blockchain by more people and more organisations, the ability to assert or validate one's digital identity will become increasingly important.

A digital identity, stored on the blockchain, will enable simpler account transfers, reduced friction when opening accounts with new organisations, or even to influence transactions based on digitally expressed preferences that can be checked by transacting organisations while remaining private and secure.

Individuals will be able to set up a decentralised identifier (DID) with a public key/private key pair. Institutions will be able to query the person's identity using the public key and the concept of zero-knowledge proof (which allows users to verify transactions or other activities by referencing stored data without the data itself being exposed). The data will be stored securely off-chain and can be accessed only by the individual using their private key.

For example, where a minimum age check is requested by an institution, the digital identifier can respond to indicate that the person has passed the check without revealing their actual age. Or, it would be possible to define any food allergies and intolerances linked to the DID. Imagine being able to attach a token to a restaurant booking whenever you make a reservation: the restaurant only needs to know that two people have a gluten allergy or that one is vegan. The identity token can be queried by the restaurant (having been given "permission" to do so by your making the booking and providing the relevant public keys).

Non-Financial Use Cases

But it is perhaps in the area of non-financial industries that blockchain may add the most benefit. To a certain extent, the financial industry is already well-versed in sharing data, whether through networks such as Swift or through hub and spoke models. Away from these more established digital markets, the ability to seamlessly share data and hand-off processes from one actor to another could indeed be transformational.

We'll take a look at examples in the worlds of healthcare, supply chain, property and voting, but there are many more.[8]

Healthcare data includes relatively static components such as the patient's conditions and historical diagnoses, as well as dynamic transactional data such as those needed to process a patient's appointments, procedures or emergency events. As it is intensely personal, the static data would need to be protected through the use of private keys. It must be possible for it to be viewed and updated by authorised health staff in the execution of their duties on the patient's behalf (but not at other times), but not by anyone else. Critically, the distributed nature of the blockchain would support this data being made available instantly and seamlessly in the case that a patient is transferred from one authority to another, or in the case that their condition changes and a new health team (such as an anaesthetist and a surgeon) need to become involved.

Healthcare data can be literally a matter of life or death for the patient. Ensuring that data is secure, available and correct (through the patient's own ability to view it directly) will go a long way to improving patient outcomes.

Managing (or at the very least tracking) a supply chain as it passes through a range of actors and intermediaries in turn is a supreme use case for the distributed ledger. Instead of data passing from one organisation's systems to another through a series of manual or inefficient interfaces, a single record of the order can be stored on the blockchain, freely available to all parties, and can be updated by each in turn to track progress. Not only can this lead to more accurate and timely invoicing and payment, it allows the parties to identify bottlenecks and choke points in a way they wouldn't be able to using their own data alone.

And the data on the blockchain, being immutable, allows suppliers to unequivocally establish the provenance and quality of their product, especially in the case of labels such as "organic" or "fair trade".

Property ownership is another example where distributed data will be beneficial. Moving the definitive property record from a central authority to the blockchain would allow for clarity on charges taken against it, and could be enhanced by surveys, valuations from estate agents, sales and other ephemeral or transactional activity. A commonly available immutable record of property ownership would also be a significant impediment to fraud.

Modern democracies have struggled to bring voting in elections into the twentieth, let alone the twenty-first, century. In an age where almost every commodity is available online, it seems curious that one is still required to physically visit a polling station and mark one's preference on a slip of paper with a cross (although there are some who would argue that this physical act has a gravitas of its own). Recent (very high profile) accusations of fraud have created a degree of distrust with the existing mechanisms. Replacing the whole paper process with a blockchain-based solution would yield immeasurable results:

- Representation – if every voter receives a personal token on the blockchain that they are required to own and maintain, the opportunity to transfer votes to someone else becomes minimised.
- Immutability – the very nature of the blockchain, and the immutability of the transactional data once recorded – would limit the opportunity for fraudulent results (and reduce the related opportunity for accusations of same).
- Security – the vote itself could be cryptographically masked, using a zero-knowledge proof counting process to accumulate overall voting numbers without revealing the individual decision of any given voter.

- Response time – with data instantly available on the blockchain, automated counting of votes would significantly reduce the delay between vote and declaration of the winners and losers, removing flashpoints and opportunities for emotional escalation.

NFTs and Cryptocurrencies

Look, we'll be honest. We don't really want to talk about this: cryptocurrencies and NFTs are far more likely to detract from blockchain's adoption as a serious business tool than to help it. They are no more synonymous with blockchain than international stock markets are synonymous with traditional computer networks: the technology enables the activity but is not defined by it.

We firmly believe that cryptocurrencies are fragile speculative vehicles – just like the wild west, it's not the person who finds the gold nugget who gets rich – "in a gold rush, sell shovels", as the saying goes. The headlong rush into crypto and initial coin offerings can be expected to diminish in time. Some cryptocurrencies (like bitcoin) have gained sufficient following and presence to survive, while many others have fallen by the wayside and the shake-out looks set to continue. Whilst they benefit from blockchain technology and its principles of trust in a distributed environment with pseudonymous actors and no central authority, the negatives in terms of environmental impact (especially for PoW), scalability and processing time are significant. Regulated institutions are likely – particularly in the light of recent developments such as the collapse of the crypto exchange FTX – to become even more uncomfortable with these pseudonymous assets.

The vast premiums spent on NFTs (over and above the intrinsic value of the real-world asset that the NFT represents) will also stabilise, once people realise that all they've done is bought a piece of art, or poetry (or in the case of digital art, not even that).

However, there remains a business model, particularly for NFTs, as a means to reach a wider market more directly than through a more traditional intermediary. Whether this replaces, or merely complements, the now "old technology" options of social media remains to be seen.

Managed properly, the NFT as a definitive, immutable provenance for the sale and resale of collectibles (whether they be priceless real-world or digital artefacts) would significantly reduce opportunities for fraud and the sale of stolen goods.

Regulation and Standardisation

Regulatory frameworks are gradually evolving to accommodate tokenised assets and other tokens. Recognising the potential benefits and growth of blockchain technology and tokenisation, regulators in various jurisdictions and industries are actively working to establish frameworks that provide clarity and oversight for tokenised financial and non-financial assets.

Key to many of these discussions is the volatile nature of cryptocurrencies, but regulators are also turning their attention to wider adoption of tokenisation throughout the financial community. Many regulatory bodies are putting together working groups and sandboxes to establish the preferred regulatory direction.

In some jurisdictions, regulators are taking a stronger hand. Recognising the benefits of DLT, these regulators are actively requiring participants in the market to adhere to (in some cases quite aggressive) tokenisation agendas.

By its very nature, blockchain and DLT impacts multiple participants in multiple industries. Standardisation and harmonisation will be key to its future adoption and growth. ISO Technical Committee 307 ("Blockchain and distributed ledger technologies") was established in 2016 and now manages 18 global standards with contributions from over 40 participating communities. The adoption and embedding of these standards is critical to successful implementation and interoperability of blockchain globally and across multiple industries.

SO WHAT?

We can be sure that blockchain will continue to evolve and to gain traction across a number of industries. Hopefully, this guide has given you some idea of where it might be heading technologically as well as highlighting some potential use cases.

It's worth remembering that blockchain is essentially software (on top of some hardware, data and interfacing aspects), so you should take a look at the questions you should be asking yourself in a software context – such as whether you really have a problem that needs to be solved, is now the right time to do it, and are you better off buying or building a product to solve it – before moving on to the blockchain-specific questions below.

And, for all the noise, it's worth bearing in mind that blockchain and DLT essentially brings you three things:

- It's a distributed database that can be accessed by multiple parties.
- It's immutable and secure.
- If you choose the right solution, it's a distributed application that can be invoked by multiple parties.

So, what should you, the business leader, be asking – specifically – about blockchain?

- Does my business include a distributed process involving multiple parties?
- Do I want to be an early adopter?
- Do I want to build a blockchain capability within my organisation?
- Do I want to contribute to the growth of the blockchain community?

Does My Business Include a Distributed Process Involving Multiple Parties?

Do you have a problem that will be solved by blockchain?

This is a key point. You may have a problem, and perhaps a software-backed solution will make things better. But is your problem one that involves a distributed database or a distributed application? Is blockchain really the answer?

We've included plenty of examples above, such as supply chains or health services.

If there is data passed from one organisation to another, especially by means of a manual process such as photographing or scanning (or even rekeying)? Might that data be shared, rather than passed on? Shared in a single, distributed, database that all the interested parties can view and update?

Do you need your customers to give you proof of their ID? Is there a shared service with competitors or partners that could be executed more effectively on-chain?

Are there already competitors in your space who are implementing distributed solutions?

A blockchain solution doesn't have to go beyond the boundaries of your organisation, of course. There might be in-house processes that you could put on-chain. But, for these use cases, it may be simpler to implement a standard software solution, with multiple applications and multiple databases liked by more conventional applications or APIs.

And there may be hybrid solutions, involving some data held on-chain and the rest more conventionally.

But before you build a blockchain solution, you should be very sure that it's appropriate to your problem.

Do I Want To Be an Early Adopter?

There is always a risk to being an early adopter of new technologies. There is a higher level of research and development spend needed, and the risk that some of the things you try won't be successful. Even success might have its downside as you may find yourself trapped into a solution that the rest of the world bypasses or leapfrogs to the next generation (as those who backed Betamax or Palm Pilots soon discovered …).

Once they are live, computer systems and applications tend to hang around for a long time – ask any bank that still runs its core overnight processing using software written 60 years ago on an emulated 1960s machine.

Specifically for blockchain, then, what are the risks for the early adopter?

- Blockchain adoption wanes: however unlikely, it's possible that blockchain is not embraced by the wider community. You may find yourself as a lone voice in the distributed wilderness and we have seen that blockchain is a solution that relies on – as well as benefits from – adoption by multiple participants.
- Poor choice of blockchain network: if you jump too soon, you may land on a network that has issues such as capacity, security or even the cost to process transactions (remember the gas?). This can be avoided by doing thorough research beforehand and making sure that you select a network that has longevity and the right operational parameters for your need.
- Rigid operational models: the way that blockchain is implemented and operated is in a state of flux – with a movement towards service

provision rather than outright build by users. There is a risk that in building your own solution, you miss the opportunity to use a different service model that would be more flexible or better suit your needs.

- Evolution of smart contracts: this technology is still very new, and new approaches are being innovated all the time (such as Oracles). If you implement your blockchain solution too soon, you may discover that something that was not possible when you started becomes achievable shortly after you have designed, built and implemented your distributed application.
- Playing solo: blockchain benefits from communities working together – building a solution on your own is unlikely to be as effective as working with your partners to cover the whole scope of your distributed processes. If you are an early adopter, you may not find the wholesale support from your industry that you need to achieve your vision.

That having been said, there are many advantages to being a first mover. Getting the first blockchain solution in your space might be a game-changer for your organisation. You know your business – that's a factor for you to decide.

Do I Want to Build a Blockchain Capability within My Organisation?

This is really just a more specialised version of the same question we asked in the software chapter. Even if you see a need (or an opportunity) for a distributed solution, should you build up a capability yourself within your organisation, or use the services of an external agent?

As for the wider software question, if the business opportunity isn't central to your strategy, or if you will be building a capability from scratch, it may be better to bring in those who have a head start on you. Blockchain may only be a few years old, but there are senior professionals at the prime of their abilities who have done nothing else since leaving higher education. Would you expect to enter a race against a top athlete who has spent a decade and a half training and be able to compete?

It's worth bearing in mind that the world of blockchain, DApps and tokenised assets is changing fast, so if you do decide to build a capability, your team will be playing catch-up while the landscape moves on. It may take some time to catch up.

Do I Want to Contribute to the Growth of the Blockchain Community?

As the world of blockchain is still so very new, with frontiers being continuously breached, and new use cases being identified with regularity, it is an area of technology that will benefit from community collaboration and collective innovation.

The lessons from the other areas of technology are there to see. Computer hardware really only began to become effective in the business space due to the IBM PC revolution, where multiple manufacturers were able to build to a common blueprint. Software and application design thrived from collective endeavour once organisations stopped writing their own coding languages as the first step of their projects. Messaging (especially financial messaging) began to become more powerful as first data fields, then message formats and finally message definition became harmonised globally.

The same will happen (and has already started happening) for blockchain. There are numerous foundations and nonprofit enterprises seeking to make blockchain a productive environment. The various standard tokens on the Ethereum network (ERC20, ERC271 and their ilk) are backed up by solid standardisation by ISO and its technical committee. Some of these organisations are funded, but others rely on the input and hard work of professionals in their community.

If you're going to play in the blockchain world, it's worth being connected to – and better yet, helping to shape – the standards that will drive its growth and successful implementation.

NOTES

1 *The Compendious Book on Calculation by Completion and Balancing* by Muhammad ibn Musa al-Khwarizmi.

2 *Summa de Arithmetica, Geometria, Proportioni et Proportionalita* by Luca Pacioli, 1494.
3 https://medium.com/unraveling-the-ouroboros/a-brief-history-of-ledgers-b6ab8 4a7ff41
4 *Blockchain Applied* by Stephen Ashurst and Stefano Tempesta, 2022.
5 *Bitcoin: A Peer-to-Peer Electronic Cash System.*
6 www.bankofengland.co.uk
7 www.statista.com
8 *Blockchain Applied* by Stephen Ashurst and Stefano Tempesta, 2022.

6

What Are the Risks?

Take calculated risks. That is quite different from being rash.

General George Patton, US Army

*Sam failed to console himself with the thought that
one day this would make a really funny story....*

DOI: 10.4324/9781003372660-6

What is a risk? In business, how does "risk" differ from "threat"? Is risk also an opportunity? Do business "risks" become less serious if we label them as "issues"? ISO Guide 73:2009[1] defines risk somewhat glibly as the "effect of uncertainty on objectives".

Do these types of definitions matter all that much? After all, surely everyone knows a risk when they see one?

Let's take a moment to illustrate some key risk concepts using an allegory about an umbrella.[2]

The Story of the Umbrella

Imagine that we're contemplating an afternoon walk in the height of spring in the British Isles. Naturally, in Britain, there is always the chance of a spot of rain.

How might we categorise this in terms of risks, issues, controls and opportunities?

The *risk*. We've already identified that it might rain. But, of course, we shouldn't stop there. We can quantify it. Take a look at the sky: is it mostly clear with a whisp of light nimbus or are there swollen storm clouds threatening?

Having identified and quantified the risk, we can choose to avoid it, reduce or mitigate it, share it or accept it. We can *avoid* the risk by deciding not to go out, after all. We can stay indoors and be dry. But assuming that we are still intent on going out, how can we mitigate the risk of rain?

Mitigation might involve reducing the risk directly by taking a shorter route or reducing its effect on us by wearing appropriate wet weather clothing or taking an umbrella. We could also hatch a *contingency* plan to stop off in the local pub to dry off in the event of rain.

As part of putting mitigations in place, we need to assess the *impact* to us of the original risk and the residual risk after mitigation. It may be that the original risk is already acceptable to us (some folk just enjoy walking in the rain), but in any case, having considered our mitigating umbrella, we may decide that the residual risk is now acceptable and go out for our walk.

Part of our risk strategy might be to regularly check the threat of imminent rain. As any seasoned British hill-walker will tell you, a nervous glance at the sky is often all you need to tell you if the weather is about to turn. This is our risk *control*.

Halfway through the walk – wouldn't you know it: it starts to rain. This is now an *issue*. Your mitigating umbrella can be deployed to full effect.

So far, so *negative*. There's another strategy we might want to consider. If we take two umbrellas with us, we might be able to sell one in the event of a shower (should we happen to encounter a hapless umbrella-free fellow walker at an opportune time). We've just added *exploit* as a key (and *positive*) strategy to use after identifying a risk. In business, we often think of a risk as a *negative* threat or an event that impacts badly on a commercial, operational or legal outcome. But the truth, as ever, is more nuanced. Some business risks could be categorised as *positive* – "blessings in disguise". Some risks are *opportunities* for a change in direction or pivot: a chance for business leaders to exploit a previously unforeseen market or product, for example. This is also referenced in the aforementioned ISO definition of risk, whereby a note clarifies that an effect is a deviation from the expected – whether positive or negative.

Strictly speaking, we could also include strategies to share the impacts of a risk or to insure against them, but we think you'll get the picture.

The key point here is that once a risk has been identified and quantified, various strategies can be put in place to manage it. The risk should only be accepted after all viable strategies have been enacted with appropriate controls to ensure their effectiveness.

In this chapter we'll look at how the world of technology contributes to the risk landscape of organisations. We'll do this broadly from two perspectives:

- How technology contributes to (or even facilitates) risk whether in an operational sense or during the risk maelstrom that is an IT project?
- How technology can help to identify and manage risks?

Organisations must contend with a great number of different risks. While we intend to try to cover most of these, inevitably there will be some that we don't address. To simplify things, we have considered three broad types of risks:

- Internal risks that are enabled or exacerbated by technology (such as software errors and user error)

- Risks from external agents that directly target the organisation's technology infrastructure (such as malware, penetration attacks and thefts of data)
- Risks from external agents that indirectly target the organisation that are facilitated by technology (such as phishing and social engineering).

In this chapter, we'll look at a brief history of technology-enabled risks, types of technology risks that may affect modern businesses and ways to manage them and the implications of developments like artificial intelligence (AI) on risk and risk management systems. As always, we'll finish off with a "so what" section to help you, the business leader, ensure that you and your team are asking the right questions.

WHY SHOULD I CARE?

As a business leader, you may or may not feel that you are the right person with the right level of seniority or specialism to be responsible for considering and mitigating the risks (or uncertainties) that impact your organisation and affect its objectives.

You might think, rightly or wrongly, that these business risks are global or macro in nature; that they affect the organisation in very defined ways and require specialist consideration and treatment in their mitigation.

This was certainly the way that many organisations traditionally operated. By assigning risks and the mitigation of risks to specialist teams, the remainder of the organisation could continue being productive whilst the risk was "dealt with". This approach may have worked in previous eras of business software, especially when networks and servers were more physical (and local) in design and deployment, and firewalls might have been more effective.

But as all businesses and organisations now use online, cloud, integrated and device-oriented business software, applications and processes across their operating model, the trend of risk leadership has changed considerably.

Risk management, prevention and mitigation are now the collective responsibilities of all members of an enterprise, including employees, third parties, suppliers, customers and specifically leadership.

At the day-to-day level, business users should all care about risk and risk management because it affects us all, constantly.

HOW DID WE GET HERE?

In the relatively short history of business risks (since the large-scale adoption of business software in the past century), there have been billions of incidental issues and several serious encounters with risks.

Initially, technology-related risks to an organisation were largely internal in nature, as most organisations built and operated their own software on machines that were housed in their own buildings.

Risks from Within

This era is neatly bracketed by two iconic examples of risks: the first-ever software bug and the notorious "Millenium Bug".

As noted in the chapter on software, early computers tended to use one-off instruction sets configured by the arrangement of switches, wires and sockets. There was no concept of a persistent and repeatable bug. However, in September 1947, a team at Harvard University "found that their computer, the Mark II, was delivering consistent errors. When they opened the computer's hardware, they found … a moth. The trapped insect had disrupted the electronics of the computer".[3]

The team included Grace Hopper who would later develop the first compiler and be influential in the design of many programming languages, including COBOL.

Debugging the first-ever recorded bug was relatively straightforward: the moth was quickly removed and taped to the (first-ever) bug report (see Figure 6.1).[4]

As software became more persistent and versatile, repeatable errors (bugs) became commonplace, elevating the importance of quality assurance and testing in the project lifecycle.

A more serious systemic bug buzzed the entirety of the world's software systems in the late 1990s – the infamous "Millenium Bug". As noted in Chapter 3, in order to save space, early data stores and software had commonly omitted the century part when storing or calculating a date (e.g.

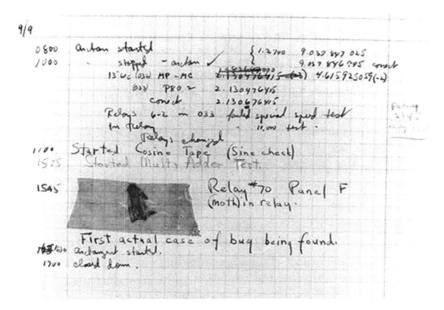

FIGURE 6.1
First-Ever Computer Bug.

saving 01/01/1970 as 01/01/70). As the end of the century approached, this began to cause operating issues.

As Martyn Thomas in The Guardian[5] noted, there were early warning signs. In 1988,

> a batch of tinned meat was rejected by a supermarket because it appeared to be more than 80 years past its use-by date. Four years later, Mary Bandar of Winona, Minnesota, was invited to join a kindergarten class because according to a computer she was four. Aged 104, she decided against.
>
> Such errors caused amusement at first but gradually businesses realised the huge problem they faced. By 1995, the New York Stock Exchange had completed a seven-year project to correct all its systems at a cost of $30m, but most organisations had hardly started: a UK survey in 1995 found that only 15% of senior managers were aware of the problem. Time was short and urgent action was needed. TaskForce 2000 led an awareness campaign, later joined by Action 2000 with a £17m government budget. Auditors started telling companies that they would not sign off audits unless those firms had credible assurance that they would survive beyond January 2000. By 1998 the G8 summit and the UN were coordinating international action.

As it turned out, aircraft didn't fall from the sky at the stroke of midnight on New Year's Eve 1999 (a popular belief at the time, showing that most people didn't understand the differences between real-time systems such as those used for aircraft navigation which had no use for recording and comparing timescales as long as years and more analytical systems such as inventory or health systems that frequently compared two dates to establish a duration or age); nuclear power stations continued to operate safely and the international banking system functioned without (software) mishap. But in the absence of the concerted effort of governments and industry communities, things could have been very different. The Millenium Bug episode also nicely illuminated to the general population (and to businesses reliant on commercial software) how dependent they had become on the design and implementation of software and data.

While the primary cause of the Millenium Bug was the space-saving efficiency employed in the early decades of the software industry, a contributory factor was the expectation by the designers and coders of the time about how long that software would remain in service.

Risks from Without

Following the Millennium Bug, the growth of the internet era saw a dramatic rise in threats from outside organisations, as global connectivity allowed almost anyone access to any system.

The global financial network predated the internet by several decades, with vast sums of digital money being moved through financial instructions, passed from bank to bank (and from country to country) through the Swift network since 1973. The role of a trusted network provider using dedicated lines, encrypted messages and rigorous non-repudiation algorithms (to ensure that any message was sent to the correct recipient once and once only and that the sender could not deny that the message had come from them) ensured that there was very little opportunity for malicious agents to intercept and benefit from such messages.

But with the internet, non-financial organisations suddenly became open to abuse by hackers and other attackers, mainly through the use of "malware".

Malware (a portmanteau combining the words "malicious" and "software") had been around for a few decades, perpetrated as often as not with educational (rather than financial or destructive) intent. Malware is a term used to describe a number of more specific threats such as:

- A *virus* – malware that is attached or embedded in a piece of software, replicating itself in other programs or files and spreading from machine to machine
- A *worm* – a piece of independent malware that is passed from computer to computer
- A *Trojan* (or Trojan Horse) – a type of malware disguised as legitimate software. A Trojan does not replicate itself, but once installed on a system it carries out its (usually destructive) purpose rather than what the user intended
- *Ransomware* – malware that locks away data or prevents access to it until the user pays a ransom to the attacker.

The very first malware is generally considered to be the "Creeper System" virus, written by Bob Thomas at Bolt Beranek and Newman Inc (BBN) in 1971. Creeper was an experimental self-replicating program that displayed the message, "I'm the creeper, catch me if you can!" and filled up the computer's hard drive.[6]

In 1975, a seemingly harmless text-based 20-questions game ANIMAL contained the world's first example of a Trojan horse. The game copied itself to a shared directory where it could be copied by other users. In itself, it was harmless, but it presaged more sinister things to come.[7]

The first major computer virus (which affected PCs running MS-DOS) was called "Brain". It was released in 1986 and would overwrite the boot sector on the floppy disk and prevent the affected computer from booting. It was written by two brothers from Pakistan (Basit and Amjad Farooq Alvi).[8]

The "Morris Worm" in 1988 was the first to gain significant mainstream media attention.

It was written by Robert Morris, a graduate student from Cornell University who wanted to use it to determine the size of the internet. His approach used security holes in sendmail and other Unix applications as well as weak passwords, but due to a programming mistake it spread too fast and started to interfere with the normal operation of the computers.

It infected around 15,000 computers in 15 hours, which back then was most of the internet.[9]

The first ransomware attack is generally regarded as the "AIDS Trojan", which manifested in 1989 after biologist Joseph Popp developed it and mailed infected floppy disks to members of an AIDS-related mailing list. After a user had booted up 90 times, the names of the user's files would be encrypted and a message would appear, instructing victims to send money to a PO box in Panama.[10]

The impact and cost of malware continued to escalate, enhanced by the global scope of the internet and facilitated by the commoditisation of software applications.

In 1999, the Melissa virus (created by David L. Smith) was the first known virus to take advantage of the macro capabilities of Microsoft Office products such as Word and Outlook.

In 2000, the "ILOVEYOU" Trojan (also known as the Love Bug or Love Letter) was created by two Filipino programmers (Onel de Guzman and Reonel Ramones). Recipients received an email with an attachment (disguised as a harmless text file) named "ILOVEYOU". Anyone foolish or curious enough to open it would not only find that their computer's files had been overwritten, but that the malware had emailed itself to every address in their contacts. Estimates for the damage caused by this Trojan are in the region of $10 billion.

More ransomware and other malware followed (such as Code Red in 2001, Beast in 2002, Zlob in 2005, Zeus in 2007, Stuxnet in 2010, Reveton in 2012 and Tiny Banker in 2016), targeting the mass market of networked computers linked to the internet running Windows and Mac operating systems. Motivations shifted, too, from seemingly random acts of destruction and the simple exertion of control to extortion of money from the victim either to make the computer usable again or to avoid being "outed" for some perceived transgression such as the viewing of pornography. Such "scareware" tactics, spread across the entire internet-using population, yielded astonishingly lucrative results for the perpetrators.

Recently, those perpetrators have become increasingly coordinated and their malware more sophisticated.

The "CryptoLocker" Trojan in 2013 was the first to be distributed by a botnet (literally a "robot" "network," a network of computers that, through the spread of malware have fallen under the remote control of a hacker, providing enormous computing power to send many spam emails or make multiple malicious attacks, all without the owners' knowing) called "Game over Zeus" which sent thousands of emails that appeared to come from a trusted source. Victims found that their documents and files had been cryptographically locked and were instructed to pay a ransom to unlock them. CryptoLocker also achieved notoriety by demanding this ransom in bitcoin.

In 2014, the "Oleg Pliss" attack bridged the gap between desktop and mobile: it used stolen Apple account credentials to log in and remotely lock iPhones, using the "find my iPhone" feature. The attacker then demanded a ransom for the phone to be unlocked.[11]

In 2017, the "WannaCry" ransomware emerged,[12] to become one of the best known cryptographic ransomwares after infecting about 230,000 computers in 150 countries, causing $4 billion in damage. WannaCry exploited a Windows vulnerability known as "EternalBlue". In a salutary lesson for enterprises across the globe, Microsoft had already released a patch for the vulnerability two months before the emergence of WannaCry, but many users and organisations had not yet updated their systems.

Around the same time, the concept started to emerge of ransomware-as-a-service (RaaS): malicious collaborations in which one group would write ransomware code and another group would identify operating system vulnerabilities to exploit.

In early 2018, a team of hackers "Team Snatch" took the new step of threatening to publish victim data (obtained through the RaaS "GandCrab") to extort money. Team Snatch "retired" in 2019 but was quickly followed by the "Maze" group which started leaking captured data through leak sites. Following this latest trend, it is now not possible to protect against the threat of ransomware simply by keeping an independent backup of sensitive data, as that data could itself be released to the public by a so-called leak site.

Risks from Insiders

While a malware attack involves a malicious agent directly targeting victims through the release of software designed to infect systems, an insider threat involves the manipulation (also by malicious agents) of someone who already has access to systems and data. This trusted insider could be an employee, a client or a third party such as a supplier (wherein it is referred to as a "supply chain attack").

Think of your technology estate as a house and your data as the family silver. Malware attacks are equivalent to a burglar trying to break in to steal your prized cutlery. In an insider attack, the burglar convinces your neighbour to pop around to your house and "borrow" a set of spoons.

This particular vulnerability was first demonstrated by an engineer called Ken Thompson in the 1980s.[13] To effect the hack, Thompson modified the Unix compiler to create a back door allowing him to log into any Unix system with the need for valid credentials. Also called the "Trusting Trust" hack and never used in anger, this theoretical exercise was intended to highlight the inherent vulnerability of computer systems to trusted parties.

One of the earliest recorded cases of an actual software supply chain attack occurred in 2003: the "Linux Kernel Backdoor Incident".[14] This involved the insertion of a backdoor into the source code of the Linux kernel, a core component of the Linux operating system which would have allowed the attacker to log on to any Linux machine. The open-source nature of the source code was partly responsible for the ease with which the hacker was able to effect the change but was also the reason that the threat was identified by another member of the community who queried the nature of the "fix" that had been made.

More commonly, an insider attack is effected by convincing the insider (a person who has legitimate system and software access) to execute an activity that is fully within their remit but to the benefit of the attacker. Most will be familiar with the term "phishing" by now. A phishing attack involves the sending of one or more fraudulent emails purporting to come from a trusted or reliable source, in which the recipient is encouraged to take certain actions, such as confirming a password, a PIN (Personal Identification Number) or other confidential information.

Phishing attacks began almost as soon as email was invented. In the mid-1990s, hackers posing as employees of AOL used email to steal users' passwords and hijack their accounts.[15] Within a few years, hackers were registering domain names similar to popular websites and sending hyperlinks to unsuspecting users who freely typed their precious credentials into web pages that merely resembled what they were expecting to see.

The arrival of Facebook and social media as a global phenomenon provided even more ammunition for these attackers. Harvesting personal information from such sites allowed them to target individuals with meaningful emails, hoping to lull the recipient into following the instructions (a practice known as "spear phishing").

In the early days of phishing, it was often very easy to spot a malicious email: spelling and grammar would be notoriously poor, while the subject matter was often vague or outlandish (featuring stranded "princes" of dubious origin or bank managers with large fortunes to impart if only you would give them your bank details). However, in recent years phishing attacks have become more sophisticated, using AI-generated text and featuring targeted information gleaned from social media sites.

But hackers don't have it all their own way. As we will see in the next section, although the range of threats is extreme, security firms and software providers (as well as effective business leadership) can combine to provide a substantial bulwark against attack.

WHAT DOES HERE LOOK LIKE?

In the previous section we looked at a brief history of internal, external and insider risks. Here, we will take a look at the most common (or impactful) of each of these and what measures can be taken to address them.

As a reminder, we are focusing on technology-enabled risks. There will be other risks that you or your organisation may face, such as market, financial or operational risks relevant to your line of business.

Internal risks are as follows:

- Software error
- Human error
- Privileged misuse
- Loss of equipment
- Technology project risk

External risks are as follows:

- Systemic vulnerability
- Malware
- Web-based attacks

- Denial of service (DoS)
- Attrition (brute force)
- Lateral movement

Insider risks are as follows:

- Phishing and other social engineering attacks
- Supply chain compromise

After providing a little more detail on each of these attacks, we'll take a look at how a risk management framework can help to mitigate the overall impact of such threats.

Software Error

As long as your organisation is running software (and let's face it – it's a rare organisation these days that isn't), there is a risk of software error. This is an evergreen risk – it's always present. The more commoditised your software the lower the risk of error, but even mass-produced office and administrative software products can have their problems from time to time. This risk is more likely (and potentially more impactful) the more bespoke your software needs. If you are configuring an off-the-shelf product, there is a risk that the configuration is incorrect or inefficient. If you are writing software from scratch, you are at risk of the most basic software bugs (but perhaps not a risk from moths...).

The impact of a software error can range from inconsequential to catastrophic, depending on the location and nature of the error. An error that causes an output report to be printed in the wrong colour may not be too disastrous. An error that exposes all of your client data to the outside world will have significant consequences.

Software errors in mass-produced products are probably difficult for your organisation to avoid, but you can plan to mitigate the impact by keeping offline backups of your data. Errors in customised or bespoke software can be mitigated by strong testing regimes during technology projects and in particular by regression testing of upgrades to ensure the existing production code is not adversely affected.

Human Error

This is another evergreen risk – as long as you have humans in your organisation taking actions, there is a risk of error. In a technology context, we are most likely to be talking about data entry errors – where an employee or agent types in the wrong data (or the right data in the wrong place).

As for software errors, the risk can have a wide range of impacts, from an inconsequential typo to sending a large payment to the wrong client or supplier. As the risk relates to an individual human, however, the impact is likely to be more localised than a software error, which could affect your entire database in a worst-case scenario.

You can never eradicate human error entirely. But mitigations will include training, role-based access (to ensure only the right people get to execute certain activities), four-eyes checking for material updates, searchable audit trails and next-day data integrity reporting. It's also worth analysing the errors that do happen, identifying the most common or those with the biggest potential impact. Then take steps to minimise or avoid those specific risks (using automation where possible).

Privileged Misuse

The misuse of privileged accounts means, in its most basic sense, where a securely logged-on (human) user of a software system acts deliberately and maliciously to damage, corrupt or amend data to such an extent that the business or organisation is negatively affected.

Despite the belief we all have about the probity of our own day-to-day actions and professional conduct, when it is considered that we all might, perhaps, act in a "bad" way (even if only once) to somehow damage a business or organisation's software means this risk is potentially everywhere, all the time and has existed since the very first abacus was invented and used.

Similarly to human error, the impact of misuse could range from the inconsequential to the severe. However, as this results from the deliberate act of a potentially disgruntled employee, it's likely to tend more towards the severe, if not caught in time.

Can businesses and organisations rule out criminals being hired by them and working for them? No. Can businesses and organisations eliminate or

mitigate this type of risk, through training, observation of activity, pro-
filing of user actions (perhaps using AI to look for patterns) and, above all,
by managing their people as best they can? Of course, the answer is yes.

But there's a somewhat sobering qualification: the business or organisation has to be right about this all the time, whereas the disgruntled employee
only has to act once for that all to be worth nought. Hoping for the best but
planning for the worst is possibly one of the optimal mitigations here, and
making data backups, using rigorous operational processes such as dual-
approval of key activities (especially around cash movement and management), is a sensible and necessary step.

Loss of Equipment

Similar to human error, this risk involves the loss (or potentially theft) of
technology equipment that contains sensitive data. This is most likely to be
in the context of a laptop being left in (or lifted from) a pub or restaurant,
or the loss or theft of a mobile phone.

Depending on the data itself, unfettered access by a third party (whether
or not the initial equipment loss was malicious) could be very damaging.
At the very least, the loss of the data could be painful if it is not backed up
elsewhere.

The mitigation here is simple – always ensure that your equipment is
encrypted and your data backed up. This applies in particular to mobile
phones which are naturally more prone to loss.

There is a further risk that whoever gains the equipment may be able to
use it to hack into your network and take more data or cause more damage.
Again, the answer is simple – ensure that your organisation uses strong
passwords with two-factor authentication (2FA) where possible and that
passwords are *never* written down.

And of course, ensure you have a clear and simple process for your
employees to report the loss or theft to close down any back doors that may
exist as quickly as possible. Why simple? Well, if your employee has just
lost their laptop and their mobile phone, how will they report the incident?

Technology Project Risk

Delivering a large IT project is inherently fraught with risk. There are
direct risks (failure of integration software to work, the risk of software

build requirements being missed, the risk of poor stakeholder management affecting decisions being made late or scope reduced etc.) and indirect risks (key supplier insolvency, legal and contractual risks, regulatory risks, a public health emergency such as the COVID-19 global pandemic, a sudden and catastrophic change in regulations).

A professional risk manager working on a major IT project will capture and categorise these risks at the outset of the programme of work in a dedicated risk plan. The risk plan will be a shared document (i.e. with open access to colleagues) complete with a schedule of risks (a risk log), RAG (Red, Amber, Green) statuses for reporting risks on a frequent basis, a series of risk mitigation plans and effectiveness calculations for each (some risks are simply unavoidable regardless of the mitigation available, others can be avoided altogether) and a governance structure for risks in general: who is told, who decides and so on.

In the evolution of the events of the IT project, it's the risk manager's task to constantly assess, report, govern and mitigate the risks as and when they occur. No two risks or indeed projects are the same, but as the project nears delivery (assuming it does deliver), the IT risk manager's risk log and other collateral become less and less relevant and useful until – based on events – the work is complete.

IT project risks tend to emerge from similar hotspots, time after time. For example, integration is a common area for IT project risks to be encountered: plumbing together two entirely different software systems is fraught with complexity and "discovery" of the to-be-integrated systems only usually starts in detail once a project has commenced. Not only that, but some fruitful risk areas in IT projects are usually not in the sphere of software at all: legal, risk and compliance colleagues can cause a hard stop to an IT project and frequently do so at the very last minute.

How would risks be measured in the example of an IT delivery project?

At a lower project level, the risk management system will need custom settings configured for risk thresholds derived from the sponsor's risk appetite; standard and specialised mitigations depending on each risk that can be predicted on a case-by-case basis, and a library of data points and language from other projects.

For example, in a global health emergency such as the COVID-19 pandemic, humans might prioritise the health and well-being of the remote-working IT project team members who are also home-schooling their children over, say, productivity or specific timekeeping. Measuring the mental health of colleagues is tricky enough for face- and body-language reading humans on Microsoft Teams. There are unlikely to be risk management systems that can overtake human oversight of risk.

Let's consider another variable in the risk management example of this fictional IT project: the pivot. In many IT deliveries, and because IT domains such as data, applications and so on can change rapidly due to impacts from external factors, there is a constant risk that a nimbler competitor emerges mid-delivery or, and perhaps even more likely, the risk of the scope of delivery being too wide, meaning a material and unexpected de-scoping has to take place in order to reach an already tough delivery landing strip.

In classic risk management terms, an IT project delivery can be put under threat by having to deliver too much with too few resources, budget or capacity as go-live approaches. The mitigation is almost always the same: de-scope to deliver a minimum viable product (MVP) and push the undelivered items to a second phase, the notorious "Phase 2".

This de-scoping is a focussing of minds and almost always reveals what were the core components of the IT project that had to be delivered (typically the functionality dealing with the flow, management and reconciliation of cash…).

But there is an opportunity to pivot here too: shorn of the "full" delivery scope it usually transpires that the core functionality works surprisingly well and allows product owners and sponsors to reflect on what actually needs to be delivered in "Phase 2" after all.

Is there an opportunity in the risk mitigation that's sometimes greater than the perceived threat to the original delivery?

There's one other aspect of a technology project (especially a large one) to consider. In most cases, a project will need the time, expertise and energy of your subject matter experts to ensure that the requirements are defined and that the project is delivering an effective outcome. Quite possibly, it will take a great deal of your own time to steer and manage the project. Necessarily, this will take some of your best people away from the coal face of the day-to-day running of the organisation. This in itself represents a risk – these are the very people you have trained and can trust to operate the business while minimising errors. In deciding who supports the project, and to what extent they commit their time and energy, you will inevitably need to balance the ongoing operation of the business against the need for the project to succeed.

Systemic Vulnerability

The systems and applications used across your enterprise are all prone to attack. Whether they are commoditised (such as popular global operating systems) or specialised (such as bespoke banking applications) they have the potential for vulnerabilities that can be exploited by those with malicious intent. This risk becomes more relevant when your core database and applications are running in the cloud.

The United Kingdom's National Cyber Security Centre (NCSC)[16] defines a vulnerability as

> a weakness in an IT system that can be exploited by an attacker to deliver a successful attack. They can occur through flaws, features or user error, and attackers will look to exploit any of them, often combining one or more, to achieve their end goal.

The NCSC defines flaws as software errors (or other unintended functionality) that can be exploited by attackers. A flaw may go undetected for some time. Once identified, a flaw vulnerability will be shared among attackers. In particular, information about a "zero-day vulnerability" (i.e. one that has only just been discovered and has therefore not yet been addressed by the relevant supplier) can change hands for considerable sums of money.

Features (intended functionality) can also be exploited, as was the case for the Melissa worm in 1999 which exploited Microsoft macros. The NCSC notes that "JavaScript, widely used in dynamic web content, continues to be used by attackers. This includes diverting the user's browser to a malicious website and silently downloading malware, and hiding malicious code to pass through basic web filtering".

User errors could be due to ineffective system administrators who fail to properly secure the system or due to operational users creating vulnerabilities such as employing weak passwords or losing their kit.

Helpfully, there are evolving and commercially available industry best practices, technological and architectural mitigations to this risk, and there is a strong chance that deploying these will help defray the danger and damage of vulnerability exploitations and lateral movement attacks. Thinking ahead, designing with the assumption of an attack – these are all recommended steps in any case and will bear fruit here.

Closing the door quickly on known flaws and vulnerabilities remains key. While a vulnerability is new, attacks may be bespoke and limited in scope. Once a vulnerability is more widely known, it may be exploited by the full range of attackers.

Malware

As we've already seen, malware is a general term covering worms, viruses, Trojans and ransomware. These software attacks masquerade as harmless files or hide inside other applications, replicating themselves and causing harm to the victim's systems or data.

The statistics around malware are startling[17]:

> In 2022, 5.5 billion malware attacks were detected around the world with the majority of these attacks occurring in the Asia-Pacific region. Among the most frequently blocked types of malware attacks were worms, viruses, ransomware, Trojans, and backdoor. Between the two main attack vectors, e-mail, and websites, the latter were used for phishing attacks more often.

The impact of a virus or successful ransomware attack can be crippling: loss of data, significant financial loss or the inability to conduct business.

This leads us to the inevitable question: is any software safe from viruses, worms, Trojans and ransomware? The overall impression is of an industry permanently under attack and staggering from pillar to post.

But consider your own business experience in the context of risks. How often have you encountered one of the above malwares? The likelihood of that in the real world is (hopefully) rare, and the reason for that is the participation of business users and leaders in the mitigation and prevention of business risk.

Malware is mitigated by up-to-date commercial security software, timely manufacturer updates, virus detectors and sweeps of the network – in short, all the best practice risk management techniques available on the market. You'll have to pay the going rate, but it'll still be cheaper than being a victim of these (often public) attacks.

Web-Based Attacks

We all use the web and the applications that run on web pages. Organisations are both users of web applications and (in many cases) provide their products and services to clients using a web application. Whilst this opens up global opportunities, it of course comes with business risk, because a website is an easy target for the malicious attacker. By inserting malicious code into the applets on your web page, an attacker can redirect unsuspecting clients to their own site, or simply track any input data.

If your website becomes compromised by an attacker, your clients may be supplying their sensitive data directly to cybercriminals.

Defence against web-based attacks runs along the same lines as for malware: up to date antivirus software and regular reviews of your corporate web pages.

Denial of Service

DoS or even DDoS, for distributed DoS, and not to be confused with the other "DOS", or disk operating system, is not named in honour of the majestic river of Egypt. In fact, DoS has far less funny origins, the inventor being an Illinois teenager with the rather more prosaic name of David Dennis. In 1974, young David, studying hard (we hope) at the august institution of the University of Illinois High School managed to write a piece of software code exploiting the "external" or "ext" command which proceeded to shut down the computer in a research lab in the nearby University itself.

Now, we can all be (and probably have been) annoying teenagers, the authors included, but this act of spite and inventiveness probably does deserve a very strict telling-off. Not only was this the first-ever DoS, it sparked a wave of successors that continue to this day. A DoS attack differs from malware in that no malicious code is ever written to the victim's systems. Instead, the attacker (or more likely the attacker's slaved botnet for a DDoS) floods the target website with a multitude of requests to connect, any one of which is indecipherable from a genuine connection attempt. In trying to answer the flood of requests, the target server becomes unavailable for those seeking to use it in an authentic manner.

While frequently initiated with political intent by "hacktivists", a (D)DoS attack could happen to any business or organisation and is hard to plan for and mitigate against. Having alternate hosting arrangements and firewalls may help, but perhaps the most effective and practical mitigation would be to have a means of continuing to run your business "manually" until the attack ceases or a replacement web infrastructure can be put in place.

Attrition (Brute Force)

"Et tu, Brute?"

In Shakespeare's play *Julius Cæsar*, the eponymous dictator receives countless knife attacks from the massed ranks of his Senatorial assassins – including a stab from his former friend, Brutus.

Brute force attacks, whilst nothing to do with spittle-flecked, greasepainted thespians declaiming drama on the stage of the Globe Theatre, do have something in common with Cæsar's bloody demise: both involve a massed or repeated attack for nefarious ends.

Attrition – or brute force – attacks involve a direct assault on a system by repeated attempts to log in to an account remotely. The attacker may use an algorithm to try a vast number of combinations of usernames and passwords, or simply a follow list of the most common passwords, often trying the same password against a large list of usernames or email addresses.

Brute force attacks often follow on from malware attacks: using stolen credentials from one database to try combinations of emails and passwords against another.

The best defence against brute force attacks is to use strong passwords that are not shared across different accounts.

Lateral Movement

We tend to think of business software and systems to be operated in a "stack", an arrangement of individual component systems and software, databases, interfaces, servers (whether physical or virtual on the cloud) etc. – and with good reason, for this is almost always the case. There are many commercial and productivity benefits to be gained from an interconnected business software infrastructure.

But, of course, this efficiency and interconnectedness comes with inherent risks too. Lateral movement is one of those and occurs when cybercriminals attack one part of a technology stack before moving deeper into the infrastructure seeking more sensitive (and valuable) data.

The old adage that a chain is only as strong as its weakest link applies here: by enhancing the overall security of your technology infrastructure, you can avoid providing attackers with such a weak spot.

Phishing and Social Engineering

Phishing (said aloud, it's an exact homophone for "fishing"...) is the process of trying to fool or trick ordinary people into responding to a flattering, urgent or otherwise compelling email or text message to the advantage of the sender (i.e. a criminal). Social engineering means tricking or grooming ordinary people to think that the scam on offer is OK, part of a socially approved conversation or activity.

Phishing is often the "thin end of the wedge", with the attacker seeking a vulnerability that can later be exploited (whether mechanical or human).

The term was originally coined in the 1990s, but as attackers become more inventive so the terminology has evolved, including:

- Spear phishing – direct and targeted phishing attacks using language or references that the victim will recognise
- Vishing – the use of phone calls (such as from a bank fraud department or a help desk)
- Smishing – the use of SMS text messages for the same purpose
- Whaling – a direct attempt to target a senior member of an organisation such as a CEO
- "CEO fraud" – where attackers manage to send an email to an employee that seems to come from a senior member of their organisation instructing them to carry out an activity (such as a payment to a specified bank account).

Phishing attacks have become increasingly sophisticated and more convincing. Typically, the language used will promote paranoia (the victim is encouraged to keep their activity secret) and urgency, inducing levels of anxiety and panic in the victim that inhibit their ability to objectively question their own actions.

Phishing and social engineering risks can be mitigated by training and by repeated "dummy" phishing and/or social engineering simulations carried out from within the business or organisation itself, with rewards or praise for colleagues and employees who spot the fakes. By stimulating curiosity and offering rewards for catching phishing attempts the mitigation becomes as dynamic as the original attempts to deceive. It's not quite gamification but has a similar energy and a proven track record of working well.

Supply Chain Compromise

You can be the best risk-managed business in the world. But very few businesses operate in a total vacuum. You will interact with suppliers and other third parties. As for a lateral movement attack, criminals will attempt to reach your technology infrastructure through that of your trusted suppliers. No matter how deeply and frequently you might do due diligence on that supply chain, there are limits.

This type of attack can also manifest through software suppliers and has been exacerbated in recent years through the use of open-source code and libraries (much as highlighted by Ken Thompson in 1984).

To secure your supply chain, we suggest mitigation in the form of practical steps, such as always (if possible) having more than one supplier of critical services or processes, always having more than one bank account (across multiple providers) and using multiple payment gateways. And, of course, regular communication with your key suppliers including security audits and reviews.

From a software perspective, it would be prudent to limit and/or monitor the use of open-source code or libraries and to ensure regression testing is rigorously enforced for upgrades and other changes.

Risk Management Framework

Risk (and risk management) doesn't operate in a vacuum. In a business or organisational sense, risk management actively monitors and assesses the world around it – importing and analysing risk metrics, including natural language, numerical data, statistics, sentiment and more into its calculations. Risk management is a practice founded on scepticism: like lawyers, risk managers frequently advise caution as a default position.

This is, in general terms, a good thing. Who would want a risky risk manager? But the naturally conservative and cautious approach of the majority of professional risk managers creates a distinct bias in the risk management systems used by them.

Risk thresholds are set according to risk *appetite*: meaning, staying on the preferred side of a risk threshold is the approach to risk an enterprise or organisation feels it is comfortable taking in a given situation, real or imagined. When challenged, most enterprises will state that they are "risk averse", meaning that when presented with a risk, they'd rather not proceed at all with an activity that might exceed their threshold and thereby simply remain as they are.

Leaving aside the question as to whether this is a viable long-term position for a commercial organisation to take (where in general the greater the risk the greater the potential return), there are issues with this approach as it entirely excludes the "risk upside" – the opportunity.

Risk appetite is a good example of otherwise almost invisible bias guardrails that are imposed by humans on risk management systems from the start. Faced with a restrictive risk appetite, and a very low threshold for risk-taking, risk managers will constantly deal down on opportunities, making other vectors of risk (the risk of failing to win new business, the risk of losing customers bored by lack of innovation etc.) more salient by comparison.

In the context of *business risk*, most established business organisations are very good at identifying the *negative* threats in a risk. That's because businesses have to be alert to bad outcomes for customers and employees alike. Gather together a group of operational people from any organisation and ask them what the risky outliers or threatening edge case risks are in their day-to-day business activities and you'll get a steady stream of examples of unlikely but damaging events that *could* happen … but rarely (if ever) do. This is the way humans are wired: we think of dangers, and we catastrophise in order to show our potential usefulness to others in spotting and calling out these threats, for collective survival.

Not many business organisations are good at the opposite: looking for *positive* opportunities in a risk. Start-ups are sometimes better at treating risks as opportunities (presumably because there's less to lose), but even then, it requires a particular set of circumstances and group attitudes to exist before such thinking can be part of the daily life of business people. It is almost always those organisations that have benefitted from such thinking in the past that can operate like that in the future.

Risk awareness in an organisation will almost always require clear leadership on risk and encouragement from senior team members for others to "fail" often, without blame or judgement.

Technology for measuring, managing and mitigating risk follows these biases because that's what people using risk tools want. They want to know the possibility of something bad happening, and they would like a way to mitigate that – ideally, for it never to happen in the first place.

It's common sense and a truism that putting in a risk management system will assist a team of people working individually or together from making silly and serious mistakes. Even if such a risk management system ultimately fails to prevent insistent human error, a risk management system can, after the fact, capture the risk signals and data that were received; the mitigation actions taken (if any) and the outcomes reached. Over time, a risk management system can assist with risk pattern analysis: what were the conditions where risk has occurred; what are the typical characteristics and features of risks *before* they happen; and what is the cost of risk – economically, reputationally and legally (to name but a few).

Risk management systems in the business world are the focus of this chapter. Where they originated from, what led to their development and refinement, how they have evolved in the age of AI and the internet and what the future might hold.

There are dangers in business people using risk management systems. Does the existence of a risk management system merely move business risk around – for example, might operations staff assume that risks are now "being taken care of" by a risk management system and therefore no longer require attention from them?

What if risk management systems highlight risks that were never before seen or considered – how are these then mitigated?

Can the effort and resource required to mitigate a risk be priced by an organisation, factored into its sales tariff and outsourced by using policies of insurance, for example?

What difference does this make to a business model, and what might be the consequences of that?

WHERE NEXT?

Business risks are significant and ever-changing, as we have seen.

The reality is that for as long as there are people, there will be criminality – and as software changes and evolves, so will attempts to exploit error, technology and processes for the purposes of theft, money laundering, ransom and other dark designs.

We've covered a brief history of risk and detailed where and how risks exist today. But what might come next?

Cat and Mouse

Since the first viruses and worms were distributed on floppy discs (look it up) in the 1980s, the countermeasures available to businesses to defend their systems and data have always lagged behind the criminals. The first antivirus software became commercially available in 1987, and since then various firms have striven to provide up-to-date patches and scanners to detect and prevent malware.

This game of cat and mouse is likely to continue indefinitely.

For the more common types of malware (adaptations of existing threats or new threats that closely resemble them), antivirus firms can often update their software quickly, sometimes within hours.

For more innovative attacks (such as the WannaCry ransomware attack), the response will take longer and may involve a degree of collaboration between the antivirus firms and software suppliers.

Risks in the Cloud

As more technology activity moves into the cloud, there will be a con-centration of risk at the cloud service providers. Applications and data will reside away from your premises and will be collected together with applications and data belonging to other clients of the same SaaS provider or even other SaaS providers.

A tempting target.

In any cloud service agreement (either directly with the cloud service provider or through a SaaS software provider) you will need to ensure that your data and services are properly segregated from others (even in a multi-tenanted operation where multiple clients use a single instance of an application with soft segregation of data). You should also check that your links to the cloud are sufficiently secure – data is always at its most vulnerable when it is on the move.

P***word Protection

The days of users having simple or default passwords (such as "Password") or using the same account credentials across multiple accounts are (hopefully) long gone. Users are seemingly perpetually and vigorously encouraged to employ "strong" passwords and not to reuse them on other accounts. Websites will now (for the most part) enforce good practice (in the strength of the password at least), and many can even suggest randomly generated super-strength passwords such as "Px65&df!xcad54$j" (hopefully, this is not your password…).

Increasingly, websites (especially financial sites) are forcing users to adopt 2FA or even multi-factor authentication (MFA) that uses three or more factors.

Strong passwords and password discipline are effective means of negating brute force attacks, mitigating phishing and other malware attacks and reducing the opportunities to exploit vulnerabilities.

Authentication using two or more factors is not infallible, but by (usually) requiring the user to have access to some physical device such as a mobile phone or at the very least to be able to log on to another related service such as email, it vastly reduces the opportunities for cybercriminals to hack an account remotely.

Authentication methods include

- Requiring the user to enter a code sent to a mobile device through SMS or email at the point of logging on
- Advising users by email or SMS when the system detects a new log-on from an unrecognised device
- Informing the user of details of their previous session when they log on
- For additional security, the issuing of a physical token for the user to use when logging on.

The typical user initially regarded password management and multi-factor authentication as a waste of time, but the enhanced awareness of cyber-crime and malware threats should ensure that users embrace stronger access governance more readily in the future.

Risks from Artificial Intelligence

AI and machine learning in the hands of criminals have the capacity to provide ever-better design and deployment in respect of all of our list of risks, but perhaps especially in the areas of phishing/social engineering (by creating and presenting us with deep faked messages and realistic-sounding calls or texts), attrition (the ability to identify, "learn" and then exploit patterns in passwords, for example) and human error (by deceiving us with messages and data based on patterns of our own behaviour).

The best mitigations against these risks remain our own alertness and credulity.

It'll always be the case that if it sounds too good to be true then it probably is. No matter how polished or realistic-looking a message, text or call might be, humans are very good at sensing danger and reacting to it.

Risks from the Impacts of Climate Change

Climate change is a fact. We can see changes in the patterns of weather and environment, and science says these will become more pronounced and the change greater as the process of climate change accelerates.

How this will affect business risk is a tricky question to answer at this stage. But examples might be more power outages, flood, fire and wind damage to infrastructure, and possibly also changes to the acceptable power consumption profiles of large cloud or server installations, for example.

Planning will be key to mitigating these new risks; and having flexibility, diversification of resources and a distributed network will rise up the list of business leaders' priorities.

Risks from Other Sources

There are always unpredictable political and social risks that flux constantly and bear down differently on businesses and leaders. War, mass migration, nationalism vs global trade – these are not new risks and perhaps are outside the scope of this book, for now.

Suffice it to say that technology used by businesses and organisations relies on innovation, collaboration and trust; and where these factors are challenged or in short supply then there will be greater friction, cost and latency in mitigation.

SO WHAT?

What is the impact of these technology-enabled risks on the business leader?

Risk isn't new. Risks existed before the widespread adoption of technology by businesses, organisations and governments. There would have been new risks arising when the wheel, gunpowder and the telephone were invented, and new ways to operate were created around these inventions.

Technology is no different, and we have to remember that a risk is both a *threat* and, potentially, an *opportunity* (although, like us, you may find it hard to see the positive opportunity in being hacked by a cybercriminal – what opportunity there is would appear to be in the hands of the antivirus suppliers).

Risk management can't mean doing *nothing* and sitting tight. The word entrepreneur, to describe almost all business activity, actually originates from the thirteenth-century French word "entreprendre" which means to undertake or to do something[18] ... to take a risk.

A calculated risk.

So, if we're in business, we need to be all across our risks, their mitigations and understand the outcomes we seek whilst living with risk.

Mitigation also includes accepting the reality of the situation: you will be under intense pressure for some of these risks, and there are occasions when risks will materialise and become issues that impact your business. What then? Having in place plans that are practised if a risk is realised and can't be mitigated might make all the difference between business survival and not.

Our view is that there are five questions the business leader should ask about risks:

- Have I got a risk governance framework in place?
- Have I done enough to prevent internal risks such as human error?
- Are my systems secure against malicious attacks?
- Are my team aware of insider risks and how to reduce them?
- Am I managing the business risks associated with my change agenda?

Good luck, and remember: it's not the falling down that matters, but how you get up again....

Have I Got a Risk Governance Framework in Place?

It's often said that self-awareness is the first step on the road to enlightenment.

If nothing else, a risk governance framework will allow you to identify, analyse and categorise your risks. At best, it will provide you with the means to monitor, control and mitigate those risks on an ongoing basis.

There's a good chance that you already have a framework in place for operational risk, but it is worth reviewing it to make sure that your technology risks are identified and appropriately mitigated and monitored.

We suggest that readers keep in mind a simple mantra, "MAART", for risk management and mitigations:

- Mitigate – have a plan or process in place to dilute risks
- Avoid – when we can see risks, they're best avoided if at all possible
- Accept – inevitably, some risks will be realised. The quicker we accept, the faster we can resolve the issues that have arisen
- Reduce – proactively (and constantly) look to reduce risks
- Transfer – this is an option for businesses, in particular, through partnership, outsourcing and insurance.

Have I Done Enough to Prevent Internal Risks Such as Human Error?

We've already said that human error is an ever-present risk. But that doesn't mean you can just shrug your shoulders and accept every mis-key.

Have your system users been properly trained? Are there refresher courses available (either through an e-learning library or with trainers on-site)? Do you have a buddy system in place to help new users understand how the various applications work?

Are you managing the errors that do happen? Can you identify the most common ones and put procedures in place (or better – automation) to prevent or reduce them? Or are the errors due to poor data architecture? Is the same field called by different labels in different systems, or – worse – is the same field used in two different ways?

Are My Systems Secure against Malicious Attacks?

You might think that this one really is squarely in the domain of the technologists. And you're probably right.

But are you doing enough to support them? When your risk manager starts to talk about data security, do you roll your eyes and sigh? Or do you recognise the vital role they are playing in protecting your data (yes – *your* data), roll up your sleeves and help them out?

Are My Team Aware of Insider Risks and How to Reduce Them?

As we noted previously, the best defence against phishing and social engineering attacks is an informed and aware user base.

Are you educating your team sufficiently? Do you have a rolling programme of simulated attacks? Do you provide an easy way for the team to report suspicious emails?

Are you helping your team to manage their security at home? Whether they are using their own kit ("bring your own device", or BYOD) through a VPN line or similar arrangement, or even just using their own technology for their private use, awareness remains the best defence.

An employee distracted by a successful phishing attack on their personal finances is not going to be delivering their best work.

Am I Managing the Business Risks Associated with My Change Agenda?

Any technology project will bring with it an increased level of risk to your organisation.

Project managers (PMs) are adept at identifying and managing risks. However, even a good PM is likely to focus on the project risks themselves (i.e. what are the risks to the success of the *project*?). They are less likely to consider the risks that just doing the project will introduce to the rest of the business.

There are broadly two aspects to consider here:

- What new risks might the project be introducing to the business?
- What is the risk to the business of running the project?

The goal of an IT project is usually to enhance the technology capability of the organisation. It might be to add a new data link to an external data vendor, or it might be to add a website that clients can use to update the information you hold on them.

As part of the project, you should ensure that a risk assessment is conducted of these new capabilities. By adding a website, for example, there is an increased exposure to web-based attacks, and clients may themselves be victims of phishing attacks or brute force attacks to obtain their passwords.

But the risk that is most often missed is the risk of running a project, especially a large project. We've seen how that will draw some of your best people away from their day's work to support the project. Have you allowed that time to be lost? Can you manage the hit on your productivity? Do you need to backfill those staff? Will the project pay for that or do you need to find the budget from somewhere?

A technology project often represents a huge change for your organisation and change never comes without risk. As a business leader, you need to make sure that the risk is identified and managed.

NOTES

1 https://en.wikipedia.org/wiki/Risk
2 Adapted from https://blog.wetrack.com/difference-between-risk-issue-and-opportunity
3 https://education.nationalgeographic.org/resource/worlds-first-computer-bug/
4 Photograph courtesy Naval Surface Warfare Center, Dahlgren, Virginia.
5 www.theguardian.com/commentisfree/2019/dec/31/millennium-bug-face-fears-y2k-it-systems
6 www.sentrian.com.au/blog/a-short-history-of-computer-viruses#:~:text=The%20first%20computer%20virus%2C%20called,and%20was%20released%20in%201986
7 www.malwarebytes.com/trojan
8 www.sentrian.com.au/blog/a-short-history-of-computer-viruses#:~:text=The%20first%20computer%20virus%2C%20called,and%20was%20released%20in%201986
9 www.sentrian.com.au/blog/a-short-history-of-computer-viruses#:~:text=The%20first%20computer%20virus%2C%20called,and%20was%20released%20in%201986
10 https://en.wikipedia.org/wiki/AIDS_(Trojan_horse)
11 https://en.wikipedia.org/wiki/Ransomware#:~:text=Ransomware%20is%20a%20type%20of,a%20technique%20called%20cryptoviral%20extortion
12 https://flashpoint.io/blog/the-history-and-evolution-of-ransomware-attacks/
13 https://medium.com/@VishalGarg1/history-and-evolution-of-software-supply-chain-attacks-6a97af8c4e19
14 https://medium.com/@VishalGarg1/history-and-evolution-of-software-supply-chain-attacks-6a97af8c4e19

15 www.verizon.com/business/resources/articles/s/the-history-of-phishing/
16 www.ncsc.gov.uk/information/understanding-vulnerabilities
17 www.statista.com/topics/8338/malware/#topicOverview
18 https://oxford-review.com/oxford-review-encyclopaedia-terms/entrepreneur-def
    inition/

7

What's a Project?

The greatest problem before engineers and managers today is the economical utilization of labour.

Henry Laurence Gantt

They're all working from home today....

DOI: 10.4324/9781003372660-7

A dictionary will tell you that project is a *"collaborative enterprise that is carefully planned to achieve a particular aim"*.

Succinct, yes? But it embraces all of the crucial elements that constitute a project.

The *collaborative enterprise* is a combination of a *project team*, who will design and "carefully plan" the project, a *delivery team* that will execute that plan and *stakeholders* who will define (and presumably benefit from) the "particular aim".

The *careful plan* is critical to the definition of the project – it is the plan that sets a project apart from a series of random activities (which may also achieve the same or similar outcome, but without the control or efficiency that a project brings).

The *particular aim* of the project is also critical. If we don't know (and agree) what the aim is, then we are unlikely to all be pulling in the same direction to achieve it. This element includes both the clarity of the aim (including how to measure success) and the level to which the project team, the delivery team and the stakeholders have committed to its delivery.

This chapter looks at a brief history of projects, and IT projects in particular, before looking at current best practices and future trends.

The chapter ends as always with the "So what?" providing you – the business leader – with a range of questions to ask yourself and your project team to ensure maximum collaboration, aid careful planning and achieve the project's desired aim.

WHY SHOULD I CARE?

A project is the most likely medium through which you, as a business leader, will interact directly with IT and IT people.

One of the things that often gets missed is that IT people do projects – that's their life. As a business leader, you don't typically do projects. They are not your BAU ("business-as-usual"). Far from being your life, the world of projects is alien and mysterious.

It's like when your car (or your body, for that matter) is due for a check-up. You take it to a mechanic (or a doctor). You are putting yourself entirely in the hands of a professional. It's what they do – it's their world and you are only briefly interacting with it before going about your daily business. In that short interaction, there's every chance that they will assume or make reference to knowledge you just don't have or use language that you don't understand.

It's the same with a project. As a sponsor or a stakeholder, you are entering the project world only briefly.

In all these scenarios, you're the one holding the pen. You have the final say on scope, priorities and timeframes, whether to the mechanic ("fix the brakes but we'll do the tyres next time"), the doctor ("here is where I'm getting most discomfort") or the project ("client onboarding is our biggest pain point"). How much better prepared will you be for your interaction with the project team if you have a grasp of the basics of how their world works?

And again, you don't need to have read the Haynes Workshop Manual (look it up if you're not sure) or *Gray's Anatomy* – an understanding of the broad concepts is all you need. You're not looking to become a project professional, but you are looking to understand one when he or she speaks to you.

Let's return briefly to our dictionary definition. A project is a "collaborative enterprise that is carefully planned to achieve a particular aim". That's the ideal. But you'd be amazed at how rarely reality reflects the ideal and how few projects actually adhere to this definition.

Let's start with collaboration. You might expect that the members of the project team will collaborate among themselves. But if you or your fellow business representatives are not fully engaged with the project, its teams, its plan and execution, then there's every chance that it will fail in some significant way. Key business impacts may be missed. The eventual users (your business colleagues) may not understand the problem or the solution; they won't be prepared for any new operating model.

Collaboration is key, in particular between the business (the people conducting the BAU affairs of the organisation) and the project team. Too often, phrases are used such as "that's the project's responsibility" or "we need the business to step up", not realising that these are themselves barriers to collaboration: there should be no concept of project and business as separate entities – the project is a single enterprise involving all parties. Granted, the business stakeholders may not be giving all their time to the project – they may spend significant parts of their day or week conducting those aforementioned BAU tasks (which are undoubtedly vital to keeping the organisation afloat or providing the funding for the project). But for the time that they are committed to the project, they are part of the project just as much as the planning and delivery teams.

Enterprise has two meanings, both of which are relevant to projects. It can be an undertaking, especially a bold one. But it can also mean a company or an organisation. It's helpful to think of the project as a small company that's been formed specifically to deliver an outcome. It has a CEO, the project manager and its own workforce. But it also has a board of directors (hint: that's you). Just as a company looks to its board for guidance and evaluation as a "critical friend" so a project will look to its key business stakeholders to ensure it remains on track to deliver their vision.

The planning of a project must be careful, and it has to be thorough. But it also has to be appropriate. Too much detailed planning too early (or indeed too late) in the project's lifecycle could lead to wasted time and effort with very little gain. Too many projects go too soon into the detailed phase and end up in "replanning hell" as they constantly try to flex and adapt their plans to internal and external stimuli (such as inevitable delays, bottlenecks and priority calls).

In terms of our definition of a project, we've left the best to last. A project only exists to achieve a particular aim. As a business stakeholder, it's most likely that the aim is one that you have put forward or by which you will be significantly impacted. You need to know what the aim is, be able to communicate it clearly and consistently across the entire project team (as well as across the rest of your organisation) and, most importantly, ensure that the focus of the project remains fully set on the original aim.

Evidence tells us that around 60% of projects fail to one degree or another. A total of 20% fail outright, while the remainder take significantly longer than planned, cost more or deliver less.

So, what are the reasons why only 40% of projects achieve their outcomes on time and to budget?

A non-exhaustive list, in descending order of incidence, might look something like this:

- Changing landscape (external factors or a change in the project scope)
- Undefined requirements
- Undefined objectives
- Communication and engagement
- Project team effectiveness

As a business leader, how many of these are your fault?

Easy. It's *all of them.*

Even the top one. Of course, you aren't in control of external factors, and many can't be predicted. Who would have thought that in March 2020 almost the entire world would enter lockdown for the best part of a year, with a resulting seismic shift in the way that organisations work together? But you can arm yourself, and your project, against even these chance events, to some degree. If the project is well-aligned to the organisation's overall goals and vision, then even external factors shouldn't force you to deviate too far from your original intentions. You may need to flex, but the project outcome can still be delivered (unless your original intention was to increase the size of the office…). Similarly, it's understandable and almost inevitable that projects come under pressure to change their scope. Again, by aligning to the organisation's core strategies, you can help to ensure that the scope is already the right size and taking you in the right direction.

Requirements are the hard currency of the project. Requirements will drive the estimating process, tell the developers what to build, the testers what to test and will drive implementation, training and readiness activities as you move to your new operating model. It's hard to get requirements 100% correct, especially early on, but it's relatively easy to get them mostly correct. The more time you spend early in the project getting its requirements right, the less time you will spend later unravelling issues and errors. The time and effort needed to fix an error during the requirements phase is a fraction of what it takes later in the project. And most of the requirements will come from you or your team. So, the more involved and engaged you and your team are with the project, especially in its early stages, the more successful the project is likely to be. And conversely, the less involved you are, the more likely the project is to fail.

At the root of every project, there's a problem (or an opportunity). Everyone will have their own idea of what that problem is, and what the project will achieve. But there is a real risk that these problems and objectives are poorly formed at best and wildly differing across the range of stakeholders at worst. Clear articulation of the problem (and agreement on it) across the entire project enterprise is critical.

Poor communication and engagement can lead to issues, both within the project team and between the project team and its stakeholders. As a business leader dependent on a successful outcome to solve your problem, you need to ensure that everyone is aligned with the project's aims and all pulling together to get it over the finish line.

And finally, while it may seem that the effectiveness of the project team is not your direct concern, remember at all times that the project is delivering a business outcome or vision for you, the business leader. If the team isn't working, you may need to take steps to address it. Whether that's training, changes to the structure or changes to the makeup of the team, you need to be that critical friend. You're there to identify issues and address them.

"Can you tell me of a time when you had to manage a difficult stakeholder?"

This is a really popular interview question for project managers and programme managers. Prospective project leaders are frequently judged on how well they handled an awkward stakeholder. The range of "difficulties" experienced is vast, from stakeholders who didn't believe in the project, or who wouldn't make themselves available, didn't deputise, changed the project scope or had their own views about how the project should be run.

After your next project has completed, and the project manager goes for their next job interview, if they get asked this question... let's try to make sure that they don't immediately think of *you*!

HOW DID WE GET HERE?

Projects are nothing new, of course.

Since the dawn of civilisation, there have been construction and logistics endeavours on epic scales, all of which were, essentially, projects. Stonehenge, the pyramids, the city of Petra, the Colosseum – none of these would have been possible without a vast amount of detailed planning and precise execution.

Sir Christopher Wren, Thomas Telford, Gustave Eiffel, Isambard Kingdom Brunel and the other great engineers of the pre-twentieth century industrial world were rightfully revered for their extraordinary vision, but it was their meticulous planning and execution that allowed them to drive their projects to fruition and realise that vision for all to see and use.

But even these great engineers tended to follow their own unique path. There was no established methodology, no best practice that was employed time and again to successfully deliver projects. And it is the methodology of project delivery that is most important to you as a business leader. It is the associated reliability that is crucial – your organisation cannot afford its technology projects – large or small – to depend on the vision, planning and execution of single person. If you're going to invest hard-earned profits in a project, you need to be sure (or as sure as you can be) that it's going to be successful and reap the anticipated benefits.

But, inevitably, the history of a reliable project delivery methodology starts... with a visionary.

The First Plans: Measuring Execution

Henry Gantt (1861–1919) was an American mechanical engineer and industrialist who worked in a number of industries from 1884, including for six years with Frederick Taylor (1856–1915) whose seminal work on the efficiency of workmen, *The Principles of Scientific Management*,[1] published in 1911, is now regarded as one of the most significant books on project management.

Taylor noted that the traditional "rule of thumb" techniques used in manufacturing for estimation and measurement of work were essentially a waste of time, leading to a lack of efficiency. He encouraged a scientific approach to estimation and monitoring, as well as the hitherto unheard-of suggestion that workers be formally trained in their trade, and in particular its efficient execution. He cited numerous examples of typical heavy labourers who would tire themselves out early in the day by "attacking" their tasks rather than pacing themselves throughout the day to eventually achieve more. He compared this to the apparently prevalent practice of workers deliberately working slowly (known as "soldiering") in order to protect their livelihoods – the "greatest evil" of the day.

Gantt took the scientific approach one step further, representing graphically on a chart the amount of work that needed to be done by a labourer and the length of time it should take that labourer to achieve the task. Gantt and his methodology were put to work in the Ordnance Department in Washington DC making munitions for World War I, mainly because "it was difficult to get a comprehensive idea of what progress was being made" in filling orders. Gantt worked on designing a chart that would show a "comparison between performance and promises".

Gantt's fundamental managing principle was that "the authority to issue an order involves the responsibility to see that it is executed". The Gantt chart's prime goal was to measure that execution against expected norms.

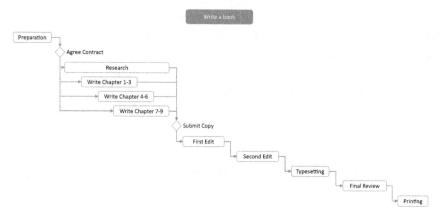

FIGURE 7.1
Gantt Chart Example.

In his 1922 book entitled *The Gantt Chart: A Working Tool of Management*,[2] Wallace Clark asserted that Gantt had "rendered an undying service" to industry. In an appendix to the same book, Walter Polakov noted that in the field of "management engineering" there had been an "almost complete absence of mathematical thinking, with the result that, instead of accurate measurement, we find vagueness, inadequacy, and looseness of meaning".

It was also noted that the mere presence of a plan, the very act of making a plan, forces the manager into a pattern of logical thought, which in itself brings about a more scientific approach to a set of tasks than simply setting them.

This management methodology focused on accurate measurement of known tasks, and although the use of the Gantt chart was adapted to help plan the execution of projects, more tools were needed before planning (as we would understand it today) could take place.

Figure 7.1 shows a simple Gantt chart for a subset of the tasks needed to write a book.

Complex Plans: Work Breakdown and Critical Path

Project management took a giant leap forward in the 1950s, when three techniques were developed and formalised which are still largely in use today.

The first of these was the critical path method (CPM), invented by the Dupont Corporation in 1957. The CPM is a methodology based on identifying those tasks in a project list that are most critical, including all dependent tasks. By laying the critical tasks end-to-end, the planner is able to identify the shortest time to complete the project. Used in isolation, CPM is most effective where the time required for each individual task is known. Dupont used it for the complex process of shutting down chemical plants for maintenance and restarting them afterwards.

The second technique was the program evaluation and review technique (PERT). This was the brainchild of the US Navy during its Polaris project.[3] PERT differs from CPM in that it defines the plan based on events such as the completion of a given task rather than purely based on a fixed task duration. Each task is allocated a "most likely time", an "optimistic time" and a "pessimistic time" and a computer is used to evaluate the most likely duration of the project.

CPM and PERT are complimentary disciplines, and most plans in the modern era are really a hybrid of the two approaches, allowing for a benchmarked "fixed" plan and flexibility as to task timescales.

The third technique went very much hand in hand with these two planning tools: the work breakdown structure (WBS). Although not given a name until a few years later, the ability to break down a larger project into a clearly defined set of tasks and dependencies was crucial to both CPM and PERT (although it was formalised as result of the latter). No doubt inspired by the old adage that the way to eat an elephant is "one bite at a time", a WBS starts with the overall outcome of the project, which it then iteratively breaks down into successively smaller components, until a series of individually manageable tasks is produced.

Figure 7.2 shows how this technique might be applied to the overall task of writing a book.

Over the next couple of decades, the tooling to support these techniques, especially on desktop computers, became more and more sophisticated. Project management began to be seen as a discipline in and of itself, rather than as simply a skill of the chief engineer on a project.

Project managers would facilitate the breakdown of the project into manageable tasks, with dependencies mapped between them. This data would be fed into a desktop software tool, producing a visual chart of the critical path through the project, likely points of failure, resource bottlenecks and other risks. Crucially, this desktop automation allowed the project manager

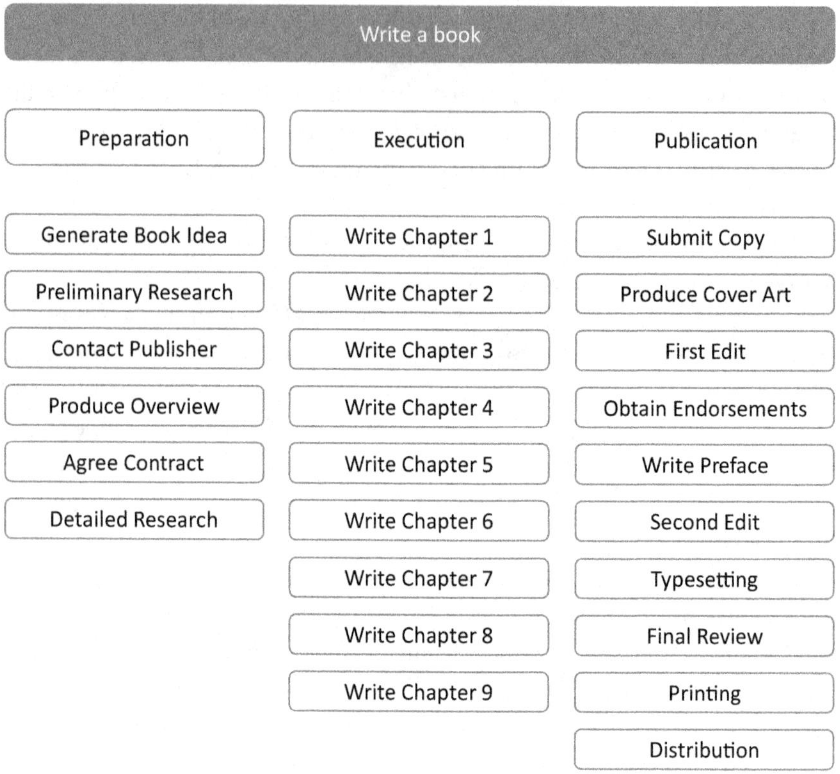

Write a book		
Preparation	Execution	Publication
Generate Book Idea	Write Chapter 1	Submit Copy
Preliminary Research	Write Chapter 2	Produce Cover Art
Contact Publisher	Write Chapter 3	First Edit
Produce Overview	Write Chapter 4	Obtain Endorsements
Agree Contract	Write Chapter 5	Write Preface
Detailed Research	Write Chapter 6	Second Edit
	Write Chapter 7	Typesetting
	Write Chapter 8	Final Review
	Write Chapter 9	Printing
		Distribution

FIGURE 7.2
WBS Example.

to adjust the plan on an iterative basis, allowing the plan to flex more rapidly based on delays or other changes.

Formal Plans: Project Management as a Discipline

This formalisation and recognition of project management as a discipline and the project manager role really took hold in the 1980s and 1990s, driven in the main by the Project Management Institute (PMI) in the United States and by the government of the United Kingdom.

The PMI was formed in 1969 to support projects in the aerospace and construction industries, and to "foster recognition of the need for professionalism in project management" as well as to provide a forum for the exchange of ideas and research and ultimately to provide guidance to project managers. The organisation began to collate and document best practice and issued a special report as a white paper in 1983 with the snappy title *Ethics, Standards, and Accreditation Committee Final Report*. These practices were refined and improved over time, and in 1996 were published as the *Project Management Body of Knowledge* or PMBOK for short.

Meanwhile in the United Kingdom, the Central Computer and Telecommunications Agency (CCTA), the government's technology agency, had developed an earlier methodology called PROMPT II (based on the even earlier PROMPT, or "Project Resource Organisation Management Planning Techniques") into a standard methodology for IT project management, called PRINCE. PRINCE (a "backronym" that eventually came to mean Projects IN Controlled Environments) was then further refined in 1996 into Prince II.

Remarkably, for a domain in which change has been fast-paced – almost revolutionary – in nature, both documents are not just still in wide use but remain the standards to which projects are governed. PMBOK is used more in the United States, and PRINCE II more in the United Kingdom, with the rest of the world a mixed bag of each. Both documents have been heavily revised, notably to account for more agile project approaches: PMBOK is in its seventh edition while the sixth edition of PRINCE II was issued in 2017 by AXELOS, a joint venture between the United Kingdom government and Capita.

Both the PMI and AXELOS offered training and accreditation to professional project managers based on their handbooks. The Project Management Professional (PMP) certification was first offered by the PMI in 1984, while AXELOS offered PRINCE II Foundation and Practitioner Training and Certification.

Two further significant concepts in project management were to emerge just before the turn of the century.

The first was called critical chain project management (CCPM), outlined in the 1997 book *Critical Chain* by Eliyahu M. Goldratt,[4] an Israeli business management expert. Based on the theory of constraints (TOC) which seeks to organise a business or endeavour around its key constraint ("a chain is no stronger than its weakest link"), CCPM focuses on resource contention and the tendency for people ("resources") to be inefficient due to a range of natural tendencies such as multi-tasking, the "student syndrome" (the tendency noted particularly among students to procrastinate and prevaricate until the last possible moment before starting an assignment, thereby depriving themselves of the opportunity to produce work of sufficient quality, while putting themselves under unnecessary pressure) and Parkinson's Law ("work expands to fill the time available", first identified in an essay in *The Economist* newspaper in 1955 on the expansion of bureaucracy, expressed as pseudo-science in the form of a mathematical equation).

Critical chain management differed from critical path management in that it sought to maximise the use of available resources rather than looking for a fastest path through a sequence of tasks.

More impactful to the world of project management methodologies was the introduction and development of agile techniques, particularly in the context of an IT development project. Traditional techniques for IT project delivery involved a software development lifecycle (SDLC) that started with the gathering of requirements, followed by build and test of the software and hardware, acceptance testing by the users and then finally an implementation at the end of the project. If this technique (known as the "waterfall" methodology) has a sporting analogy, it is that of the relay team, with each phase of the project handing the baton of progress to the next team in the chain.

Agile techniques, on the other hand, encouraged a continuous collaboration between the project team and the end users, with a series of smaller, iterative developments. Each development moved the overall output nearer to the eventual goal(s) of the project.

The waterfall method was born out of an engineering perspective: there's little point in building half a bridge. Even if the first half of the project delivered one full lane across a river, so that traffic could flow, the logistical and engineering constraints needed to add the second lane would be made significantly more complex and expensive by the constant use of the bridge.

Whereas, in a software project, half the effort may already produce an operational outcome, with very little detrimental effect on the remainder of the work. Imagine that the project is to build a phone application that allows the user to see their bank account balances and also to request payments. A viable early implementation of the application might allow the user to simply view their account balance. The later addition of the payment request capability would not be impacted significantly by the existing usage of the software.

Instead of a huge investment of time and effort that results in a momentous "Ta-da!" moment of a waterfall project implementation, an agile project delivers iteratively and often. Instead of "Ta-da!", it's "Is this OK? How about now? And now?" until the full scope has been delivered to everyone's satisfaction.

This is one of the most important concepts in project management, and we'll see a lot more of it later.

Agile project management was born out of a number of parallel initiatives in the late 1980s and early 1990s.

In 1986, two Harvard professors, Hirotaka Takeuchi and Ikujiro Nonaka, published an article in the Harvard Business Review titled *The New New Product Development Game*.[5] They coined the term "scrum" to represent a multi-functional team taking a project all the way to the end goal rather than passing the ball to other colleagues.

Elsewhere, in 1991, James Martin published his book *Rapid Application Development*,[6] itself based on a methodology used successfully to deliver projects for telecom firms. The methodology advocated prototyping and iterative development, based on the theory that prospective users of systems react better to seeing the results of their requirements working on screen than listed in a paper document.

In the early 1990s, two software developers, Ken Schwaber and Jeff Sutherland, independently employed and developed methodologies for iterative, prototype-driven development, based loosely on scrum. They collaborated in 1995 to produce a paper setting out their proposals for a new methodology.

In 2001, 17 software developers and proponents of iterative, lightweight design met in Utah to discuss aligning their various methodologies. The result was the *Manifesto for Agile Software Development*,[7] in which they declared that they valued

- Individuals and interactions over processes and tools
- Working software over comprehensive documentation
- Customer collaboration over contract negotiation
- Responding to change over following a plan

Many of the authors of the manifesto went on to form the Agile Alliance, a body that safeguards the agile principles and practices espoused in the manifesto. Although there were multiple methodologies represented at the meeting, including scrum, the unified process, extreme programming and others, these methodologies are collectively referred to as "agile".

Adaptable Plans: Project Management as a Toolkit

Since 2001, the methodologies and accepted best practices of project management have evolved gently. It's now accepted that there is a place for waterfall projects (usually where a very clear set of requirements can be defined) as well as agile projects (where iterative design and feedback may be more helpful). Many sites will use a hybrid of both methodologies (sometimes referred to as "wagile") which can be flexed in either direction as project parameters dictate.

Both PMBOK and PRINCE II now cater for agile projects as well as the more traditional lifecycle. From 2017, AXELOS has offered agile certification alongside its standard PRINCE II offering.

Failed Plans: A Case Study

One of the most high-profile project failures in history, certainly in the United Kingdom, was the London Stock Exchange (LSE) Taurus project.

Taurus (Transfer and Automated Registration of Uncertified Stock) was started in the 1980s by the LSE to replace its manual paper-based share settlement system TALISMAN with a revolutionary fully paperless electronic real-time equivalent. The project was eventually cancelled in 1993. A vast amount of money was wasted by the LSE itself (which admitted to £75m at the time) and the industry (publicly estimated at £400m in 1993 but probably far higher).

The press and industry commentators at the time were vociferous in their criticism of the LSE and the project's management. And there were problems with the approach and governance, to be sure. But if we refer back to our list of the main reasons why projects fail, the top spot is held by "external factors", which are aggravated for a large project that spans a number of years (essentially providing a longer window for the landscape to shift).

Spanning the 1980s and early 1990s as it did, Taurus was unfortunate to be conceived and built during probably the greatest decade of change in the technology industry. Hardware, software, interfacing and even data were in a state of enormous flux. Added to this, even the way projects were run was in the process of changing dramatically. In many ways, Taurus never stood a chance.

The press of the day was not so understanding. And they had a point. Taurus tried to be too many things to too many people. Some of its key stakeholders (notably the registrars who held the paper records for equities in the United Kingdom) would be out of a job had the project succeeded as initially envisaged. There was a huge distrust of electronic records, so there was a great deal of resistance to the eradication of paper certificates in the retail community. And in its later incarnation, Taurus suffered from the selection of a solution (derived from the US equivalent) that didn't meet the toned-down requirements after the first attempt at a fully paperless solution had been abandoned.

The innovation that Taurus tried to introduce may also have been its own worst enemy. As an incumbent service provider, the LSE may well have been better served by implementing a "good enough" solution. Revolution is often better delivered by disruptors who have less to lose.

In the end, the Bank of England stepped in phoenix-like with a reduced scope (that therefore created less resistance from its stakeholders) and with the benefit of improved hardware, software and project management techniques, delivered the CREST system that is still largely in operation to this day.

Sometimes, the best opportunities for success are provided by the failures of those that have gone before.

WHAT DOES HERE LOOK LIKE?

We're not going to tell you all about the different project methodologies. There are thousands of books that will do that for you, and of course you could always wade through a PRINCE II or PMI course and get the necessary accreditation.

But most of those thousands of books, and certainly the accredited courses, are targeted at project professionals.

We want you, as a business leader, to understand just enough about projects to interact with the project team and contribute effectively to the project enterprise.

So what is it you need to know?

Operating Models and Architecture

A project should have a single output. This might be a new system, changes to existing systems or a new set of processes. It might even just involve data changes, leaving the existing systems unchanged. Whatever the output is, it might be easier to think of the impact of the project in terms of a new way of working or a target operating model (TOM).

An operating model, at its simplest, defines how the people, process, technology and data within the enterprise, organisation or even department work together to deliver value.

Whether you know it or not, and regardless of the level to which you have analysed and documented it, your organisation already has an operating model. An architect (such as a business architect or an enterprise architect) will help you to define it and set it out on paper (or on screen). Inevitably, defining an operating model in this way will highlight inefficiencies, bottlenecks and manual or distributed processes that could be automated, centralised or even done away with completely. What you end up with is a target operating model: the ideal way for your organisation to operate in order to achieve its business goals.

And the way to get from a current operating model to a TOM? That's usually a project (or a programme of projects – see below).

A project will start from the current operating model and implement a new operating model through changes to one or more of people, process, technology and data. Your input in defining this target operating model will be to identify training needs for the people, map out and document new or amended processes and provide requirements for the new technology. And having defined the new operating model, you will help to prioritise, test and implement it.

Whether your organisation needs a permanent architecture team rather depends on its size and maturity. There's never a wrong time to engage an architect, but the larger you are, the more moving parts there are likely to be, with a commensurate decline in visibility of the overall architecture. In a mature organisation, there may well be entrenched inefficiencies that an architect will enable you to identify and articulate.

But whether or not you have engaged architects (permanently or as a one-off), you should make sure that you are clear on both your current and target operating models.

When Is a Project Not a Project?

Not everything needs to be a project.

A "particular aim" might be small, easily achieved or could be managed through continuous improvement of an existing state. There's an overhead to initiating and governing a project – in some cases, it's just not worth it. Even if that means sacrificing some efficiency, the end result is a net gain for the organisation.

On the other hand, some aims are more lofty or cannot be achieved in a single endeavour – in this situation, what you need is a programme.

The words "project" and "programme" are often used interchangeably, even by change professionals. This is understandable but incorrect. They are not the same thing, and it's worth really understanding the difference.

The simple mantra is that a project produces an output, whereas a programme effects an outcome.

While this sounds a little glib, it's very handy as a rule of thumb.

Need to upgrade from the Rivet-o-matic 2000 to the Rivet-o-matic 4000? That's a project. Need to overhaul the entire factory to achieve a 25% productivity gain over two years? That's going to need a programme.

More practically, a project should involve a single output, at a single point in time, whereas a programme is most likely to be delivered in a number of tranches, with each tranche incrementally contributing to the desired outcome through one or more individual projects. The programme structure provides an overall umbrella through which a series of projects are coordinated, all aimed at the eventual outcome.

All projects and programmes should have a defined end-date. Although it would also be possible to manage a rolling programme of change that incorporated a series of loosely related projects (and this is quite common in many organisations), this deviates from our ideal definition of having a particular aim in mind.

Madness in the Methodologies

As we have seen, as the process of delivering technological change through projects has matured, two broad (and apparently conflicting) methodologies have emerged, labelled "waterfall" and "agile".

This rather begs a question of why have a methodology at all? What benefit does it bring? And if even the professionals can't agree on a single flavour of methodology, is there any merit in adopting one?

The most powerful argument is that these methodologies work. Time and again, they have proven their worth by enabling project teams to manage difficult projects to successful conclusions that would otherwise have failed.

Secondly, running a project requires some structure and a plan, otherwise it becomes a string of unrelated events with a high risk of delays and bottlenecks leading to failure. You could take the time and effort to define your own structure, your own set of documents and processes, but that would all add to the project's cost and complexity.

- Running a project without a methodology would be like cooking a five-course meal without a recipe: sure, it might all land on the table, possibly even in the right order and maybe it would taste fine. But you'd be taking a risk: there's a good chance that your guests would end up with a poor dining experience – not the outcome they wanted!
- Running a project using your own bespoke methodology has a better chance of success, but think of all the extra time and effort you'd need. For the same five-course meal, you'd need to do a great deal of research upfront to get the right blend of ingredients for each course and to plan all the preparation and cooking times.
- Using one of the defined methodologies is like grabbing a menu off the shelf, lovingly perfected by a gourmet chef. All you need to do is follow the instructions. The defined methodologies likewise benefit from improvements through repeated use by industry professionals.

Another point not to be overlooked is that in all likelihood, and almost certainly for a big project or a programme of change, your organisation will need to build a project team, quite possibly using additional resources from outside the BAU supply of change professionals. You will need to recruit new employees or temporary contractors or take on the services of a consultancy as an implementation partner to ensure that your team is large enough to meet the challenge of the project. In all likelihood, the project will involve working with other third parties such as software vendors. Following a standard methodology allows those temporary and/

or external resources to start being more effective more quickly. They will already all speak and understand a common language – your project team won't need to spend a lot of time explaining how the project is structured and how it will unfold.

So, if the standard methodologies are so effective, why are there two camps?

As we've seen, the waterfall methodology derived from engineering projects, building "real world" artefacts. In such cases, it makes sense that the process of building is linear, resulting in a single defined outcome – a bridge or a building – that is only then available for use.

Whereas the agile methodology (or the broad school of agile methodologies) became possible due to the very nature of an IT project – the artefact is not a real-world physical thing. It's possible, so to speak, to build a building one floor at a time and have people living or working on the completed floors while construction goes on above their heads.

While the two types of methodology appear to be in stark contrast, they have far more in common than they have differences.

The principal goal of each is to identify and execute a plan, to identify and mitigate risks and to ensure that the project is delivered on time and at the right cost.

They just go about these in different ways.

A project following the waterfall methodology will tend to follow a strict sequence of activities, fully completing each activity before moving on to the next. For our gourmet meal, this would mean preparing all the courses before starting to cook, and then finishing all the cooking before tasting each one and finally serving the complete banquet.

An agile project, on the other hand, will complete the same activities as for a waterfall project but will deliver multiple iterative discrete packets of output (called "sprints") each of which can stand on its own. This would be akin to preparing, cooking and serving the starter course before going on to start the next course.

Aside from the obvious food-related logistics of heating food up and leaving it to cool again, why might you choose to take one approach over the other?

Well, if you have a fixed menu in mind, and you are certain it's going to be a wow for your guests, you might take the approach to prepare the meal before they arrive, confident that the banquet, once delivered, will be a smash.

But if you're not so sure about your guests' tastes, or about your own cooking skills, you might prepare the starter course only, and then take a moment to sit with your guests to gauge their feedback before taking on the next course. It is this opportunity for collaboration and honest appraisal that lies at the heart of the agile approach to projects. The project teams are able to flex the content and pace of each subsequent delivery based on the information provided by their stakeholders.

The collaborative mechanisms that are built into an agile approach do not on their own make it a more effective methodology in all cases, and of course, it's entirely possible to be fully collaborative and engaged in a waterfall project. But an agile approach does place team collaboration at its heart, and for that reason the approach is gaining more traction.

However, the downside of an agile approach is that you can never be entirely sure of what you're going to get, as the later stages of design and development will flex based on the feedback from earlier stages.

In Figure 7.3, you can see the fundamental differences between the two approaches. Although both include the same components, in the agile project, the components are processed in smaller cycles, with a review of progress after each sprint.

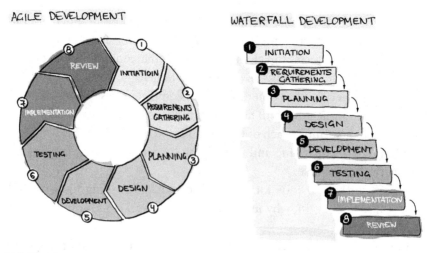

FIGURE 7.3
Waterfall and Agile.

Components of a Project

Regardless of the project methodology, there are a number of common components to a project.

Again, it's not our goal to list every aspect of a project, but what follows is a presentation of the key components with a focus on the inputs and commitments needed from the business stakeholder. In each case, we've tried to pick out why it's important, and what you need to know.

They are

- Initiation
- Requirements gathering
- Planning
- Design
- Development
- Testing
- Implementation
- Review

Initiation

The project initiation phase is the first step in starting a new project. During the project initiation phase, the collaborating project team and business stakeholders will establish why the project is necessary (the problem statement) and what business value it will deliver, as well as setting out roles and responsibilities through a terms of reference (ToR), a project initiation document (PID) or a project charter depending on the methodology.

Every project should start with a problem statement.

This is a clear and concise definition of the problem (or the opportunity) in simple terminology that everyone can understand. It defines why there needs to be a project in the first place. You might be surprised at how many projects get kicked off without a clear understanding of what they are trying to achieve (remember the "particular aim").

A famous (and almost certainly apocryphal) story goes that Albert Einstein once said that given an hour to solve a problem, he would spend the first 55 minutes thinking about it, and only the last 5 in actually solving it. Maybe not, but you get the picture.

As human beings, we are naturally prone to leaping intuitively to a solution rather than thinking about the problem itself. This reactive approach is perhaps more appropriate where there is a clear and obvious physical danger (such as an approaching avalanche) with an obvious solution (RUN!). But even in such an obvious state of threat, it might be prudent to take a short moment to assess the problem more thoroughly. What direction is the avalanche travelling? Is there suitable cover nearby? Is there a safe pathway leading you away from it?

In a modern business environment where there could be thousands of variables, it's crucial to thoroughly assess the breadth of the problem to ensure that the project team will be focusing on the right elements. Inevitably, there will not be enough time, money and corporate energy to tackle every aspect of a problem: it's critical that each component of the problem is assessed for its impact so that they can be prioritised.

As a business leader, your input to the problem statement is crucial. Although typically drafted by a business analyst or another member of the project team, it should be based on the business drivers for change.

Just as for business requirements, a problem statement should be clear, concise and unambiguous, defining the "who, what, where, when and how" of the problem. Overall, this constitutes the "why". We'll discuss business requirements more completely later.

The problem statement must categorically avoid stating the solution to the problem, even if it's "obvious". Even if you know in your heart that the right solution is to upgrade the Rivet-o-matic from version 2000 to version 4000, the problem statement should state that version 2000 is slow, no longer fit for purpose, out of support or whatever the issue actually is. Remember this could be about priorities rather than absolutes – if the product will be out of support next year, perhaps there is a more pressing issue that can be solved in the meantime.

All business stakeholders should read, understand and agree the problem statement. Ideally, this should happen before any more work is done, although that is not always possible in practice.

When you get on a plane, it's pretty clear to all concerned that it's the pilots who will fly the plane and the passengers who will sit in their seats, eat, drink and watch films.

With a project, these lines of responsibility are not so clear.

With potentially multiple stakeholders from the business, technology and elsewhere both inside and outside the organisation all interacting with a complex enterprise, it's critical that each player knows their role.

This role is defined by the ToR or sometimes in a PID.

If you'll excuse the pun, many – if not most – stakeholders and project team members find the process of drafting and agreeing these documents extremely *torpid.*

But they are crucial.

If the players on the team don't know what it is they are doing, the project is set up to fail. Imagine if, just as you are relaxing into your plane seat to watch the latest blockbuster movie with your bag of pretzels open on the table in front of you, and you glance across to find the pilot and co-pilot sitting alongside you, quaffing a beer.

Time spent getting these documents right is never wasted.

The PID goes further than the ToR, also setting out the parameters of the project such as its objectives, scope and deliverables. Ideally, it should also specify the agreed success criteria for the project in measurable terms.

As with the problem statement, your input into these documents is critical, as well as ensuring that all of your stakeholders contribute to, read and agree them. Projects are complex enterprises, with a myriad moving parts – when things go off track, the ToR or PID is often a crucial tool to bring focus back to what needs to be done and who should be doing it.

Requirements-Gathering

Once the problem has been defined, the next step is to define exactly what needs to change in order to solve the problem. This happens during requirements-gathering, and it's one of the key points of input for a business stakeholder.

This is your chance to say exactly what you think needs to happen.

It's a potentially daunting process, but a good programme team should be able to help you through it.

Gathering requirements is one of the principal skills of a business analyst – they will listen to you, document your requirements and then check them back thoroughly to help you identify any priorities.

If you type "requirements gathering" into a search engine, you will be presented with a confusing mix of pages written for or by project professionals, each providing a "definitive" five, six, ten (or any other number) step guide to the process. Clearly, with such a divergence of opinion, there is no "right" answer, but they tend to share common elements.

Broadly, these are

- Identifying the right stakeholders (hint: that's you!)
- Eliciting requirements
- Analysing and documenting the requirements
- Agreeing/confirming the requirements
- Prioritising the requirements.

Hopefully, if you paid attention during the initiation phase, the correct stakeholders have already been identified, but it's always worth making sure that the right people are engaged in the project. Of course, that can also mean checking that the wrong people are *not* engaged or that the right people are not involved in the wrong places.

Projects are curious beasts – they are new and different, a diversion from the humdrum of business-as-usual. Everyone wants to be involved. Sometimes it's because they genuinely feel they have something to offer (and they might be right!), but equally it could be FOMO ("fear of missing out"). What's that shiny thing over there? What's everyone talking about, and why am I not "in the know?"

Identifying the right stakeholders is about taking a proportionate approach to gathering requirements that will ensure the most complete set of requirements are obtained in the time available. As a business user, it's important for you to make sure you are involved where you need to be, and if you don't need to be involved – step away! Or delegate. And encourage your colleagues to do the same.

Requirements elicitation is a skill. It's important to remember that. When you're talking to a business analyst with years of experience, they may have gone through this process tens of times with different stakeholders. It may be your first time, but it's important to trust the process.

Requirements-gathering is about far more than simply writing down everything the business stakeholder (you) says. The business analyst will be carefully making sure that every requirement is a "good" requirement.

A good requirement needs to be

- Clear, avoiding jargon or loaded words
- Concise, with no "noise" words or unnecessary content
- Complete, covering the whole of the requirement
- Unambiguous, with no words or phrases open to misinterpretation

- Precise in terms of exactly what needs to happen, who will perform the action (in "active voice"), as well as where, when and how.

It's worth dwelling on the phrase "active voice". This means stating an activity as a *subject,* a *verb* and an *object.* Active voice makes it clear exactly who is performing an action. This is important for later work where the business analysis will need to map the process.

Consider the following two requirements

1. The account-opening form should be fully completed with all mandatory fields entered;
2. The *relationship manager* will ensure that all mandatory fields in the account opening form are complete.

They both seem to say the same thing, but only in the latter are we completely clear who is responsible for performing the action.

There are many ways for a business analyst to capture the gathered requirements. You may hear references to "use cases" or "user stories". Essentially, they serve the same purpose: to provide a structured way to record the requirement.

For example, a user story (which is commonly used to capture requirements in agile projects) always takes the following format:

- As a [user's role]
- I want to [perform an activity]
- So that [an outcome is achieved].

Rewriting the above requirement as a user story would give us

"As a relationship manager, I want to ensure that all mandatory fields in the account opening form are complete so that the application can be processed".

The structured approach has not only guaranteed that the requirement is in active voice with a clear owner for the task, it has also added significant information about *why* the requirement is important.

Another concept introduced and formalised in the agile user story is the "definition of done". Also referred to as success criteria, the "definition of done" provides simple tests to prove that the requirement has been met. This becomes invaluable during testing.

As a business stakeholder, either as an active user of the potential application or as an interested party in how it works or what it does, your part of the process is to be as clear and decisive as you can – the closer you can be with your raw requirements to the above ideal, the easier the job will be for the business analyst to review and document them accurately. A good business analyst will ask the right questions and make helpful suggestions to support you throughout.

Requirements are not just about activities, or stating what a process needs to do or achieve. Those are called *functional* requirements. But there are also *non-functional* requirements (NFRs). These set out some of the operational parameters of the solution – when does it need to be available, how long can it take, what are the volumes of activity and so on. They also cover operational parameters such as where and how data can be stored or how quickly the system must recover from a failure. NFRs are often overlooked, but they are as important as functional requirements, and your input – again – is critical. As with functional requirements, it will help the requirements-gathering process if you can prepare some of the necessary information ahead of time, even if you can only find indicative figures.

Another facet of requirements that are often overlooked are exceptions. We are naturally inclined to focus on the most common cases or on catering for what is called a "happy path" where everything works. But what needs to happen in a situation where the requirement is not met? In our case above, what happens if there is mandatory data missing on the form? Who is responsible for completing the missing field? How do they do that? Perhaps there are conditional fields on the form, which only need to be completed in certain (rare) circumstances. Again, a good business analyst will guide you through this process, but they are not the business expert – you are. If you know of a particularly tricky part of the process, or a special circumstance, it's your role to bring it up and make sure there is a requirement there to capture it.

As we've seen, the job in this phase is not to simply write down everything that you and your stakeholder colleagues say. In a perfect world, maybe every project could deliver every requirement (although, arguably in a perfect world there would be no need for change and hence no need for projects). In the real world in which most projects operate, a key part of the project's work is to choose which requirements can be met and which ones may have to be delayed or not delivered at all.

The selection of which requirements will be delivered is called prioritisation, and it is an essential part of requirements-gathering.

Let's say you're going to hike up a mountain, and you need to pack your bag. You lay everything out on the living room floor and realise that the bag just isn't big enough for it all. What do you do? You prioritise.

Boots – they are a must. Mobile phone, certainly. Likewise, some drinking water and a map. You probably ought to take your compass, just in case your phone loses power. Wet weather gear? Maybe... what's the forecast? The bar of chocolate might be nice to munch on at the summit but is not an essential.

It's the same with requirements. You will be called on to decide which ones are the most important and which ones could be considered at a later date.

Most projects use *MoSCoW* notation. Each requirement is annotated with

- M – for the Must haves
- S – for less critical requirements that Should be included
- C – for Conditional requirements (or for requirements that Could be needed)
- W – for things you Would like to include (or a Wish list or simply Won't be included).

So now you know that the things you must have in your bag are the boots, phone, map and drinking water. The rest you can fit in if there is space (there's always room for chocolate!).

Once all the requirements, functional and non-functional, have been gathered, analysed and prioritised, the business analyst should give you (and your fellow stakeholders) the opportunity to review and confirm that they are accurate and complete. Just as for the problem statement, it's imperative that everyone agrees and commits to the full set of requirements, although of course you can only approve those directly connected to your role.

And once you've signed off on a requirement, you should try to avoid any temptation to tinker and tweak. That doesn't mean you can't change your mind at all, or the outside world may change it for you, but often it is best to leave the project to deliver what you've asked for and then change things later if you really need to. Even in the more flexible agile approach, revisiting a requirement that has already been developed and tested incurs a cost that may threaten the rest of the project delivery. In requirements, more than anywhere else in a project, "done is better than perfect".

But as you will see in the later phases, the requirements that you help to define are the essential building blocks of the project artefacts – the developed applications, the processes and procedures, and the testing and implementation of the finished system. They are your proxy, your voice in the project for the more technical phases. If a project is a long walk in the countryside, the requirements are the map – get them wrong and no amount of bold striding will get you to the right destination.

Planning

Planning (along with governance and control of the plan) is one of the key things that set a project apart from a simple list of tasks.

Building and following a plan is one of the key skills of a project manager. Even for a small project, a plan may have hundreds of discrete tasks. For a large project there will be thousands. The project manager will build the plan based on tasks, estimates, milestones and dependencies.

But, just as for requirements, the project manager can't do this alone – they will need your input, along with that of other members of the project team.

In building a plan, the project manager needs to know every task that must be completed to deliver the project outcome. This will include tasks (such as development and testing) that aren't the responsibility of the business stakeholders, but there may well be tasks that are directly in your world, such as preparing the business users for the new operating model, learning how to use any new applications or how existing applications and processes might be impacted.

Then, for each task, the project manager will need to procure or devise an estimate as to how long the task will take to complete.

We need to talk about estimating.

Some tasks are easy to estimate. Walk to the station – 13 minutes. Catch the train to the office – 50 minutes give or take 10.

Other tasks are not so simple. Gather requirements from the Head of Human Resources on the provision of management information for the new HR system? Not so easy? Half an hour? Three weeks?

It's in the nature of technology projects that the tasks involved are unpredictable. Think of it as research and development rather than a set of easily defined activities. You wouldn't expect to be able to predict exactly when a research breakthrough will be made, and so it is with technology projects, especially in the early stages. Defining the scope of the project, understanding the exact nature of the problem and defining the requirements – these are all uncertain tasks. And there are usually people involved – people like you! People with day jobs, who are hard to get hold of. People who perhaps don't trust the project team or don't support the outcome and therefore give misleading or incomplete information. People who just don't understand what is being asked of them.

All of these factors contribute to making estimating a very fraught process.

Project professionals will have techniques they can use to make their estimates more accurate. They will be adept at breaking down tasks into smaller units of work, and they will know the sorts of issues they may face and will have methods that cater for uncertainty. An experienced project manager, backed by a solid project team, will be able to provide sensible estimates for most tasks, but the reality is that some, if not most, of these will be based largely on guesswork. As the project progresses, these guesses can be based on more concrete factors, and the accuracy of the estimates should start to improve.

Having said that, it is worth bearing in mind that these estimates are the considered opinion of an expert. It is important that you treat them as such.

Think about it. Let's say you were redecorating your house. You ask a decorator for an estimate, and you don't like the quote. You're going to challenge it. Fine. You'll have a sensible conversation with the decorator. How about if you skip one of the rooms? Does the laundry room really need three coats of paint? These are sensible suggestions. But what you are doing is prioritising or reducing the scope of the ask. What you haven't done is challenged the decorator on how fast he can work or on his competence to provide the estimate. But you'd be amazed at how often this happens to project team members.

"Three weeks to write a set of requirements for a new report? Surely that's too high? How about one week? Two weeks at most?"

No scope reduction, no consideration that maybe part of the report could be delivered later, just a clear and confident assertion that the project professional has got it horribly wrong and the stakeholder knows best. And then what happens? The task takes three weeks, and the project team gets held to account for a 50% overrun....

Of course, estimates are likely to be inaccurate, especially early on. And they are almost certainly undercooked. Humans, even project team humans, are geared to be optimistic, especially if they are inexperienced (part of the Dunning–Kruger effect whereby people with low expertise or experience tend to overestimate their ability or knowledge, while those more experienced can be known to underestimate their expertise). And we are all naturally inclined to provide good news to others. Providing an accurate estimate for a task is a constant battle between optimism and a desire to please on the one hand and the grim reality of issues and setbacks on the other. But even the most pessimistic estimate is usually light. Software developers often like to quote Hofstadter's Law: "It always takes longer than you expect, even when you take into account Hofstadter's Law".

It's important to always remember that estimates are a guideline only. But they are the best chance you have of gauging the cost of the project or when it will be delivered. Or both.

Here is another case where an agile approach can be used to advantage. By constantly delivering small components of the final product, progress through the set of tasks can be accurately measured and estimates for the remainder reassessed. At any stage, an objective decision can be made as to whether the project is complete (or complete enough), and work can stop.

Another approach commonly taken is to "time box" activities – provisioning an amount of time and effort in the plan for an activity, and then declaring that activity as "complete" at the end of its planned duration. This has a huge benefit for the plan but does risk that while a task will appear complete, the actual artefact or output remains unfinished.

But let's get back to the plan. Once it's been built, based on an anticipated sequence of tasks and those professionally sourced estimates, the project manager must track the progress of the project against the plan.

As a business stakeholder, it's unlikely that you will need to get involved with tracking at a detailed level. But you will need to understand what it's telling you about delivery dates, key milestones and where you may or may not be called upon to contribute to the project through decision-making or other activities. It's your role as the business stakeholder to give direction to the project team when things aren't going to plan (as is almost always the case).

The project manager will use a range of tools to help the team to articulate their progress against the plan.

Let's look at each in turn.

The plan on a page (POAP): Not every project will need or use this, but it's a really handy way to represent the whole project plan in a single, simple drawing. As we've seen, plans may run to many thousands of lines, and you certainly don't want to be looking into all of them. But what you do need is an easy-on-the-eye visual that tells you how the broad strokes are progressing. A typical plan on a page will show key milestones and main threads of activity (such as "requirements gathering", "development" and "testing" in the waterfall methodology and successive sprints in the agile form) as well as dependencies between them. A good POAP will draw your eye to the key issues where your input could be decisive. If you're involved in a project, and you're not sure what's happening, ask the project manager to walk you through a POAP.

RAG status: On the other hand, every project should have a red, amber, green (RAG) status, which should be constantly reviewed and updated. RAG can be used for tasks and milestones as well as for the project as a whole. The RAG status shows whether the task/milestone/project is on track (green), at risk (amber) or off-track (red). This is probably the single most important tool at the project manager's disposal. And yet it is abused horribly. For a variety of reasons, the status is often set incorrectly, sometimes deliberately so. A project manager may want to keep the project green to indicate better progress than is really being made, potentially in the hope that the situation can be recovered. Or the project manager may simply have underestimated the danger faced by the project and keeps the status green when in reality it should be amber or red. But it's absolutely critical that the RAG status is set accurately. If the project is starting to slip, then setting the status to amber is a clear indication to the stakeholders that action may be required to bring it back on track. If it has become clear that the project can no longer deliver to its agreed plan, then the red status tells the stakeholders that decisive intervention is needed. The most common reason for inaccurate RAG reporting is when the project manager (mistakenly) believes that he or she has responsibility for delivering the project. That's your job as a sponsor or business stakeholder – the project manager is your tool to make it happen. If you bought a dining room table and wanted to check that it was level, you wouldn't use a spirit level that told you it was level when it wasn't. So, you don't want a project manager to report a RAG status of green when it's really amber. If it needs to be propped up, the sooner you know about it, the better.

Progress trackers: Most project management tools will provide the capability to show a task's progress, and many project managers like to show this, as proof that the team has been working. But proof of work is not necessarily proof that the team has been effective. As we've already seen, estimating for the sort of complex tasks that constitute a technology project can be close to guesswork at times. Just because a task was estimated to be five days and the progress bar shows three days does not mean that the task is 60% done. Software developers like to refer to something called the ninety-ninety rule: the first 90% of the code accounts for the first 90% of the development time. The remaining 10% of the code accounts for the other 90% of the development time. We'll leave you to do the maths. Anyone who has tried to load a web page in a data blackspot will know what we mean here: the progress bar moves smoothly to 99% and then sits there – in reality, there is no data connection, so despite working hard, it's made no progress on loading your data: that 99% progress was just showing you some proof of work rather than proof of effectiveness.

Milestones: Before reliable maps and long before satellite navigation, travellers relied on milestones between cities and towns to tell them how far they had come and how far they had yet to travel. It allowed them to make informed decisions on their progress and on how to plan the rest of their journey. Milestones in a project plan serve the same purpose, but in a more important sense, because progress along a project plan is not linear. "We've just completed development – is that 50% of the project done?". Milestones on the plan are typically major events on which a number of other activities rely. If a milestone is delayed, chances are it will delay the rest of the project. Agreeing the milestones with your project manager is crucial, as well as understanding the impact if one of them becomes delayed.

RAID log: This may sound like a diary written by a Viking warrior, but the RAID log is a key tool for the project team to document and track a number of project parameters:

- Risks – something that might happen (usually to the detriment of the project)

- Assumptions – something that influences the project but cannot be proven
- Issues – something that has happened (that impacts the project's progress or chances of success)
- Dependencies – an activity elsewhere (for example, in another project) that impacts an activity in this project, and vice versa

As with other project tools, the business stakeholder has an important role to play in ensuring that entries on the RAID log are appropriate, accurate and meaningful. Tracking items on the log takes effort, so try not to add things that simply don't need to be there.

When the project is at amber or red status, it's a sign from the project manager that something needs to change in order to deliver the desired outcome. There's a risk that has become an issue or a dependency or milestone that's been missed or tasks are taking longer to complete than planned. Typically, the project manager will explore options to bring the project back to a green status and seek your agreement as a stakeholder.

It's important to remember that there is no magic here. Once the project is starting to slip, there is no pain-free option. Just like the decorator in our example earlier, something has to give. As the business stakeholder, your input is critical. Do you want to flex time, cost or scope?

- Time: it may be that you can delay the project to allow for external activities to complete or to align internal dependencies
- Cost: you may be able to increase the cost of the project to still deliver the full scope on time – for example, by paying the team to come on weekends to complete certain tasks
- Scope: you could reduce the scope of the project or accept that some parts of it will not be delivered exactly as you'd like.

But if you don't take at least one of these options, the chances are that the project will flounder. This is sometimes called the "project management triangle".

One last point on plans – don't flex them too often. It's worth bearing a little amount of pain if the project isn't quite to plan. Resist the urge to ask for a new plan. Too many projects end up in a cycle of constant re-planning: as soon as one plan is agreed it is already out of date as other external or internal factors have already caused a further delay. Valuable as it is, the plan is just a tool. Use the time to fix the underlying issues rather than just churning out a new plan.

Design

The design phase takes the agreed requirements as an input and produces a set of software designs as an output. As a business stakeholder or sponsor, you may or may not be involved at this stage, but that does depend on the type of project and the quality of the documented requirements.

Design documentation varies across different organisations and depending on the project methodology being used, but in general the output of this phase will be detailed technical documentation that developers can use to write their code.

Design is very much the domain of software engineers and business analysts. You may be called on to clarify a requirement, but in general the business analyst is your proxy in this phase, representing your views to the design team.

If a requirement is deemed particularly complex or expensive to deliver, it may be that you are called upon to provide a view as to whether it is worth the effort, although this should already be encapsulated in the MoSCoW priority you gave it during the requirements phase.

It's worth noting that not all requirements result in a software development. The design team may determine that a particular requirement can be met by other means, possibly by use of a manual procedure. It is during this determination that your NFRs become very important. If something must happen very quickly, or move from one location to another, it is probably not suitable for a manual process, whereas a low-volume, low-criticality and local process might be possible to be carried out manually.

Development

In the development phase, software developers write the code that will be executed in the final operational system. Again, your involvement in this phase should be minimal – the business analyst continues to act as your proxy based on the requirements you agreed in the requirements-gathering phase (You see? They really *are* important!).

Testing

Testing is the act of examining the outputs of the design and development phases to ensure they meet the stated requirements and are fit for purpose.

In the project lifecycle (whether over a number of weeks or months in the waterfall methodology or a few days in an agile sprint), testing is where business stakeholders like you will become more involved again, after leaving design and development largely to the members of the project team.

There are many different types of testing, and it can be pretty confusing – you won't be involved in all of them, and not every project will need all types.

Unit testing: This is usually planned and executed by the developers themselves on small packages of completed code. The tests are often designed to test every logical path through the code, to ensure that there are no basic logic errors such as infinite loops or undefined parameters.

Integration testing: Similar to unit testing, these tests are usually designed and executed by developers. In this case, they are testing the interfaces between applications or devices. As with unit testing, the goal is to test every parameter that can be passed across the interface. The test cases often don't bear much resemblance to a real-world business operation or situation.

System testing: This is the last phase of testing before the business stakeholders get their hands on the completed product. Dedicated test teams will test the whole system, following scripts of business scenarios prepared by the business analyst and test analysts based on your initial requirements. These tests will start to resemble actual business scenarios but will still have a more technical goal of testing every available combination of data or process. The test team will ensure they cover exception cases such as failures and incorrect inputs.

User acceptance testing: At this point, the business stakeholders and eventual users of the system get to try it out. By now, it should be working more or less as specified in the requirements. The aim of user acceptance testing is to ensure that the system (including all software applications, interfaces and even manual processes) is usable in genuine business scenarios by real users. Your role as a business stakeholder is to identify the tests needed, plan and execute them or identify subject matter experts within the operational teams who can do that for you.

Operational acceptance testing: Technical teams use operational acceptance testing (OAT) to ensure that the technical system behaves properly – does it run on the servers used by the organisation? Can it be backed up and recovered in a disaster scenario?

Non-functional testing: Remember those NFRs? Sometimes it's difficult to prove that the system can meet them all. What if the operational system needs to be available 24 hours per day for seven days a week, or needs to support thousands of concurrent users at peak times? It's unlikely that you can afford to pay an army of testers to thrash the system for a few weeks. Non-functional testing uses a configuration similar to the one that will be used in live operations (in fact, it's often done on the configuration that will eventually become the live one) and uses automation to simulate full operational volumes.

Alpha/beta testing and pilot: In some cases, it's prudent to implement the finished product for a defined subset of users. Depending on the relative size of the subset, the maturity of the system and the nature of the business, this could be referred to as alpha testing, beta testing or as a pilot.

Regression testing: A regression test suite is a sample set of tests that cover the broad range of functionality supported by the system, without being an exhaustive set of tests. The aim of regression testing is to try to catch any obvious errors introduced by successive software deliveries (which may be simply later tranches of code or new deliveries to fix defects or make changes to the application).

You may be wondering why there are so many different flavours of testing and why testing takes up so much of the project budget (typically, around 25–30% of the project spend is on testing, although arguably it should be more). Remember that software is not simple. There can be thousands (or even millions) of lines of code, thousands of variables and many different processes that can all interact with each other. In most cases, it will be impossible to test every possible combination, so testing needs to focus on the likely points of failure – "edge" cases, complex validation of user input, interfaces and data storage – as well as the most commonly used business scenarios. Imagine a system that can process 10 different kinds of transactions (each with 5 data fields), for 5 different kinds of customers across 3 regions, to be used by 3 different sets of business users (trainees, operators and supervisors). Even in such a simple model, there are 2,250 combinations to test. It's unlikely you will be able to test them all, so you will need to prioritise.

An important (and often overlooked) element of testing is what to do when you find a defect. The earlier stages of testing are usually self-contained, so the developers will tend to quickly fix any defect they find in unit or integration testing. But from system testing onwards, those executing the tests need to have a simple mechanism for raising defects, and there needs to be an efficient process for determining if the defect is already known, and if not, how serious it is. As a business stakeholder, your input may be needed during this triage process to prioritise some defects for fixing over others. "OK, the screen can be pink, not blue as specified, but it absolutely can't tell the users that they need to *lagoon* with their usernames and passwords...".

It's also worth noting that (in a project environment) there is a clear distinction between the severity of a defect and its priority. A defect's *severity* is its potential impact on the user or the organisation or the client. Its *priority* relates only to how urgently it needs to be fixed. Some defects that might be deemed severe may not in fact be all that urgent (like the lagoon case above), whereas some other defects may not have that great an impact, but if they are preventing your testers from getting access to the system and making progress through their list of test cases, it might be quite urgent. This is probably different from operational incidents where severity and urgency are more intrinsically linked.

Implementation

The last major phase of a project is the implementation. Implementations come in many flavours and sizes. An implementation may be for a brand-new application (referred to as a "greenfield" development) that will only be used by a few users initially. It may be a minor upgrade to an existing application ("brownfield") that can be implemented seamlessly with little or no impact to the existing users. Or it may be a wholesale replacement of an existing product with significant risk of disruption to the existing users and to the organisation's ability to do its business.

It's tempting to think of implementation as something that is done by the project team, but here, more than at any phase since requirements-gathering, the business stakeholder plays a critical role. Up to this point, the project has operated largely in isolation, away from the day-to-day running of the organisation, albeit with input from the business as required. But at implementation time, this separate team and the new operating model (remember: people, process, technology and data) will crash into the steady state of the organisation's "BAU" operations and teams. It's the meeting of two mindsets – the project people (who do projects) and the business and operational teams (who do business). Neither fully understands the others' world, and it is perhaps this meeting of worlds (the BAU and the project) that poses the greatest risk to the project. Despite all of the project team's hard work, it's still very possible to fall at this final hurdle if the organisation is not properly prepared.

You will need to be able to apply your full attention to the various implementation tasks: helping the project team to decide how and when to implement, preparing your colleagues for the new applications and processes (perhaps against an inevitable and understandable resistance to change on their part), ensuring that training is appropriate and complete, cleaning up any old data that may need attention, helping to plan (and possibly participate in) a data migration from the old system to the new and setting up any transitional business processes to help the organisation manage its business before, during and after the implementation.

Implementation planning: There is no right or wrong way to implement the finished applications and processes. As we've seen, projects come in all shapes and sizes, and the outputs vary from small, new applications to massive platform replacements that simply must be completed in the course of a weekend to avoid unconscionable impact on the business. Projects can be implemented in a single delivery (called a "big bang") or as small incremental deliveries (more typically under the agile methodology, but not exclusively). The choice of how and when to implement is critical and your input as a business leader will be significant. You need to consider how the implementation will affect your colleagues, your clients and the smooth operation of the business. As always, there will be conflicting factors, and the project team will look to you to help prioritise one impact over another.

Readiness: There are many aspects to preparing your business and your colleagues for an implementation. There may be some hearts and minds to win if there isn't an obvious advantage to the new operating model. Regular communications to both colleagues and clients (and third parties such as partners and suppliers) may be needed. As a general rule (similar to Hofstadter's Law above), no matter how much you are communicating, or think you are communicating, it's never enough. Your colleagues are busy with their day jobs – they don't have time to read endless memos or emails. Face-to-face sessions always work best, but videos are a good alternative and can be played again and again. You will need to create a cohort of change champions so that you are not working alone – these are colleagues who are open to the change (even if they initially needed some convincing) and will help you to spread the word. Then there's a whole host of other activities that may be needed. Is there any marketing or other printed material that needs to change? Does the corporate website need to be updated? Are there new processes to roll out internally or with your third parties or even with your clients? Remember: the project team manages change – that's their day job. But your day job (and that of your colleagues) is to manage the business. There will be preparatory tasks that need to be done that only you will be aware of. Finally, readiness is not just about preparing for the launch itself – you need to think about the next few days and weeks after implementation. How will issues be raised? Do you need floorwalkers to help colleagues to understand the system where they have forgotten their training? Many of these tasks will be driven or suggested by the project team anyway, but you have the skills and experience to help decide how these crucial tasks are approached.

Training: As a business leader, you would not be expected to train your colleagues on the new system. But your input into the training packs will be invaluable in identifying the biggest impacts and the areas where your colleagues will need the most help. The trainers will also need your help in devising the best way of rolling out the training. How many of your colleagues can be spared from their day jobs at one time? When and how should training sessions take place? And it's key to gather feedback after the sessions to gauge how your colleagues feel.

Data cleansing: As we've seen in a previous chapter of this book, the criticality of data is increasing dramatically. As more and more processes are automated, the data that drives this automation becomes ever more important to the smooth operation of the business. The implementation of a new system (or a significant upgrade to an existing system) may represent an inflection point for your business. Processes that were previously manual or involved human intervention may not have relied so heavily on the accuracy of your operational database. But if you've added new automated processing that relies on that data, you might find that the new processes don't work as well as you and the project team had envisaged. Users will complain that the "system doesn't work" and be ready to place the blame at the project's door, when in fact it's the data that's at fault. In reality, this is a shared responsibility, but as the business leader and stakeholder in the project, it's up to you to think about what data may be needed in any new automated processes and where that data may currently be compromised. Remember: you are the voice of the operational business – the project team can't uncover every data failing in the current state. Identifying poor quality data ahead of implementation is critical – as is putting in a programme of work to fix any issues. This may mean rekeying data, removing erroneous data or copying it from elsewhere in the database through a combination of your business colleagues and the project team.

Data migration: For larger projects, especially where one system (or a set of manual processes) is being replaced by another, there may be an element of data migration – moving data from the existing database to the new estate. This may be something handled automatically by the project team, or they may seek the help of operational teams. Remembering that the data in question always belongs to the business, not to the project, your role as a business leader will be to ensure that the data is migrated correctly. Data migrations typically follow three steps:

- Extract – the correct source of the data needs to be identified (especially where there is some unreliable data around) and extracted.
- Transform – not all systems treat or hold data in the same way, and the existing data may need to be converted in order to be used correctly by the new system (for example, an older system might hold an address as unstructured text, while a new system may hold it in a structured way as house number, street name, postcode and so on).
- Load – the transformed data needs to be loaded into the new system, usually by use of an automated process or set of processes.

You and your business colleagues may be called on to help with the extraction and transformation of the data, and also, crucially, to help reconcile the two sets of data following the migration.

Transitional business processes: Larger project implementations may also have an impact on the daily running of the business. Existing business processes, especially those with a complex workflow or that span several days of activity, may need to be halted or amended to cater for the change in processes before and after the implementation. Again, as the link between the project team and the operational business, it falls to you, the business stakeholder, to identify where these processes may need to be interrupted or altered. You may also need to help your colleagues to understand what they need to do and why.

These cases aren't always obvious, so an example might help.

Imagine that you have operational responsibility for a production line that manufactures widgets. The process is largely manual and many of the widgets fail quality assurance. Any rejected widgets are set to one side during the day and then their serial numbers are fed into the system the next morning.

Now imagine that the current systems are being replaced by slicker applications over the course of the weekend. For various reasons, the data from the old system will not be ported over to the new system – it will start from a blank slate. And the old system will be switched off and isolated as part of the weekend's activities.

So, on Monday morning, what are you going to do with the pile of rejected widgets from Friday? They were processed in the old system, but that's been turned off now. You are the one with the knowledge of the operational processes (old and new) and you know the team, so the solution is largely down to you. You could

- Suggest that the reject pile is processed on Friday night before the old system is switched off
- Set up a one-off process to manually process the rejected widgets on Monday morning
- Stop processing early on Friday so that the rejections can be processed during the day.

It's typical of these sorts of issues that the solution is usually down to a changed business process rather than through technology.

This is also an opportunity to make sure that client, colleague and partner impacts are understood, defined and suitably advised to the impacted parties. Impacts should be considered not just individually but also collectively, as a number of small impacts may combine to bring a level of change that the impacted party finds unmanageable.

Rollback: Not every implementation is a success. Sometimes, you need to abort to protect the organisation and its clients. The rollback plan is an integral part of the implementation plan. It will be written and managed by the project team. But, just as for the implementation itself, they are not the experts in how the business operates day to day. You are. So your input is critical. Which of the transitional business processes will need to be reversed? Which third parties need to be informed that the implementation has failed? Do clients need to be advised? All of these questions need to be considered ahead of the implementation weekend and documented in the plan. Another key consideration is the endurance of your colleagues: implementations (especially large ones with lots of data to migrate and transitional business processes to manage) can be very tiring and to reach the end only to discover that the whole thing has to be rolled back can be daunting, even if the plan has left enough time. Can alternative teams be found to perform the rollback?

Warranty and handover: Quite often, members of the project team (and in particular the business subject matter experts) are asked to stick around following a successful implementation to support the new operating model as it beds in. The support mechanisms that were prepared during readiness must now swing into action – floorwalkers to support colleagues unfamiliar with the new ways of working, extra people on the help desk to answer queries or to escalate genuine issues with the new processes and software and enhanced technical capability to fix those issues. As always, part of your role as a business stakeholder is to help prioritise to ensure the team focus on the most impactful issues. Such warranty periods are usually defined in the project approach documentation (remember the PID?), but what is often missed out is exactly how to exit into "BAU". Mostly, it's simply assumed that after x weeks, the normal infrastructure of the organisation will kick in and take over support. But this doesn't anticipate any unforeseen complexity or delay and invariably doesn't consider the *how*. It is better to state a set of clear success criteria for the handover and to be clear on how it will happen.

Review

The review phase is emphasised in the agile methodology but its value has always been recognised in the waterfall methodology too. Having either completed a sprint (agile) or delivered and implemented the whole project (waterfall), it is important for the project team and its key stakeholders to meet and discuss what went well and what went not so well.

Particularly for an agile project, where the same team will progress to the next sprint and any feedback can be immediately applied to the benefit of the project, the review allows an honest appraisal of how the team worked and whether the project is achieving (or has achieved) its particular aim.

Even for a waterfall project, where the team may disband after implementation, the review will help to improve the team's effectiveness (individually or collectively) for the next project, to the overall benefit of your organisation.

As for many other project activities, the review is something that the project team members do regularly in their day jobs – but it may be a new experience for you as a business stakeholder. An experienced project team will help set the parameters of the review, but as the agile methodology embraces reviews so wholeheartedly and places the review and collaboration at the centre of its methodology, you could do worse than following the agile ground rules for what the methodology calls a "retrospective". These are, broadly

Open mind: It probably goes without saying (but we've said it anyway) that everyone needs to come to the review with an open mind. Be receptive to the views of others, and you will, in turn, feel more comfortable putting forward your own viewpoint.

Safe space with no interruptions: Again, this may be obvious, but the review discussion needs to be a safe space for the team to air their views. Ideally face-to-face (even now), with phones and laptops away, with no interruptions from within or without. It's also important to invoke "Vegas rules" – what's said in the room stays in the room.

Encourage participation: There will be a mix of extroverts and introverts in any session, as well as a mix of project team members (familiar with the process) and business stakeholders (for whom the process may feel unfamiliar). There's a risk that one person can dominate the discussion. The meeting will be more productive (and fun) if everyone participates and contributes equally.

Avoid rabbit holes: Sometimes, a conversation can linger beyond its useful span. Only one or two people are talking. For the rest, eyes become glazed, hands start to doodle or fish in pockets for the dreaded smartphone. That's the point to stop the conversation (for now) and move on to the next topic.

Explore interests, not positions: Sometimes it can be hard to reach an agreement on a contentious topic. People can be dogmatic about their position. On these occasions, it might help to shift the discussion to principles or the interest behind the opposing positions. This may help to reach an understanding and make it easier to find common ground.

Lean into discomfort: Significant transformation typically requires us to step outside of our comfort zone. Be ready to embrace discomfort, think the unthinkable and challenge your own opinions and beliefs.

In any such review, it's so important to leave egos behind and have an honest and frank discussion. One phrase that really helps in these circumstances is to "assume positive intent". It's highly unlikely that anyone has come to the review with an axe to grind or to deliberately upset people. If someone says something that could be taken in a negative way, assume that they meant well and didn't set out to insult or demean anyone or their efforts.

Whether it's a sprint review in agile or a post-implementation review in waterfall, the key goal of the review is to make things better. If that's not working, it may be necessary to call a temporary halt and revisit with clearer ground rules.

And no matter how productive the review session, it achieves nothing if it ends without clear actions to be followed up. The goal is to ensure that the next project or sprint is handled incrementally more effectively than the one that's just completed. If actions fall to you or your team, ensure that you execute them!

Managing Changes to the Project

Inevitably, over the course of a project, something will change. This could be an external change, such as a new piece of regulation or legal requirements, or something imposed by one of your suppliers or partners. It could be an internal change, brought about by the implementation of other projects within the organisation, or by a realisation (through testing or the documentation of new processes) that there is more (or less) scope to the project than first realised.

Such changes usually have a negative impact on the project, in that they will extend the amount of work needed or add to the complexity of the final product. This will typically add cost to the project. Occasionally, a change might be to reduce scope, following some reprioritisation.

By far the most common form of change is a change to the requirements. Some technical changes are also possible, such as a change to how the solution is to be implemented, but as a business stakeholder, you are more likely to be involved with a business change, which inevitably means that requirements must change.

A well-structured project will operate a change control process that will manage the change and ensure it is considered and applied in an appropriate manner. It can get quite complex, and no one really enjoys the process, but without adequate change control, the scope (and cost) of the project can quickly creep up until it becomes impossible to deliver any benefit to the organisation.

It should be noted that the agile methodology caters for smaller changes without a formal procedure. Any minor change can be included in the next sprint of work. But even within the iterative form of the project, a large change that significantly impacts the timelines or the scope of the output should go through a formal change control process to ensure it is properly assessed for the impact it will have on the costs and benefits of the project.

For a business change, you might expect the change control process to look a little like this.

Raise change request: This is a formal document setting out the nature of the change. It will be used to track the change through the process to delivery and testing. The change request should be raised by whoever wants the change to happen. That might be you or one of your business colleagues. Unless the change is very large, or very simple, the same rigour should be put into the documentation of the change as for a business requirement. The text should be clear, concise, complete and unambiguous. The change request will pass through many hands before it is implemented, with many opportunities for misinterpretation. Leave no room for doubt or for subjectivity. You should also be clear about the reason for the change. What will break if it isn't done? How will the new operating model be deficient? It's by no means certain that the change will be implemented. The more information you can provide to help the change through the review process, the better. Once you've raised the request, a member of the project team should log it and make sure it goes forward for review.

Initial review: Most projects will operate a regular forum for changes to be discussed. Each new change request will be considered by this forum, before being put forward for more complete analysis. All aspects of the project should be represented, so as a business stakeholder you may well be part of the review. You will be reviewing your own requests and those of others. Make sure you understand every request and challenge if you don't think it's clear or where you don't see a need. Any change that can be discarded at this stage saves the project team significant work in evaluating and delivering the change.

Assessment: Once past the initial review stage, the change needs to be evaluated. Typically, this involves a mini project lifecycle of requirements-gathering and design to arrive at an estimate of the amount of development, testing and implementation effort to deliver the change. A change may also impact the benefits of the project. Every stakeholder should be involved in the assessment. Again, as a business stakeholder, you will be asked to assess other changes to determine what impact they will have on your business area. As part of this assessment, you may also need to consider alternatives to delivering the change, which may range from accepting that the project's output will be deficient in some way, to instigating manual activities to cater for the lack of an automated solution.

Decision: The change forum will decide on whether the assessed change should be implemented or not. Even a change that seems quite critical may not be implemented if the cost or impact on the project is too high. Again, your input at this point is critical. If you were the author of the change request in the first place, you may find that you need to consider the needs of the project to deliver over and above your desire for the change to be implemented. Remember that "done is better than perfect".

Planning and execution: Once approved, the change will need to be incorporated into the plan and delivered by the impacted teams. At this point, it becomes just part of the project's workload, although the change should still be tracked in the change log up to the point that it has been fully developed, tested and incorporated into the overall project output.

Steering the Ship

Most projects will operate a senior body that governs the project's progress and execution: a steering committee (also sometimes known as a project board or a project oversight committee).

It's the job of the steering committee to provide executive support to the project, solve problems and to ensure the project remains on track to deliver its goals.

The chair of the steering committee should be the sponsor (sometimes also referred to as the senior responsible owner). If that's you, great – there's some special advice for you here.

Other members of the committee could include representatives from the impacted areas of the business, technology and finance heads, as well as audit and compliance.

The committee should meet regularly (but not so regularly as to become a burden to the project), and the project manager should prepare an agenda with the sponsor, which should be sent out with supporting documentation well ahead of each meeting.

So far, so obvious.

What the steering committee should not be is a talking shop or a place where the project team simply regurgitates their progress. The steering committee is there to help, to steer, to unblock issues and to make *decisions*. It's not there to simply nod and assent to a "good job all round". In essence, its job is to steer.

The Sponsor's Role

If you're the project sponsor, you have a key role to play in the preparation and execution of each steering committee meeting.

RAG status: It's vital that you and the project manager agree a representative RAG status. In particular, setting a RAG status to anything other than green is asking the steering committee for help. It is absolutely not an admission of failure. If the members of the steering committee are prone to "shooting the messenger", then they need to be educated or replaced. In setting the RAG status, you are taking a conscious decision to either say that the project is on track and does not need meaningful intervention, or there is a problem that needs their help.

Draft and send an agenda: Make sure that the agenda and meeting pack highlight any contentious issues and are clear where help is being sought. Anything that's a simple update can be kept in the pack, but in such a way that it does not distract attention away from the key issue(s). You only have a short amount of time to get the help you need – don't waste that time by covering ground in the meeting that can be provided on paper in the body of the pack. Finally, make sure that you send the agenda well ahead of time, to give your steering committee members enough time to read it.

Support your project manager: The steering committee should be a joint enterprise between you as the sponsor and the project manager. Nothing should be on the agenda that you're not prepared to support in the meeting. Remember that this is not about shooting the messenger, so make sure that any discussion in the meeting is about unblocking and solving issues, not seeking blame.

Take responsibility: If there are actions that come out of the meeting, be prepared to take ownership of your fair share. Don't leave everything in the project manager's hands. If an action is about getting support from the business or securing more budget, then that's on you. If an action is internal to the project, then that's for the project manager to take.

A note on the difference between *accountability* and *responsibility*: The United Kingdom government (which, let's face it, probably undertakes more projects in a week than most organisations do in a year) provides two very helpful definitions[8]:

- Accountable: "required and expected to justify actions or decisions to a person or body with greater authority, from who the accountability has been formally assigned".
- Responsible: "has some control over or care for an action, or the obligation to do something as part of a wider job role".

Specifically, "a responsible person has to be responsible to someone who is accountable".

In a project, the sponsor is accountable for the success of the project. The project manager and the rest of the project team may take on various responsibilities (as indeed should the sponsor from time to time), but it is you, the sponsor, who is on the hook.

The Committee Member's Role

If you're on the committee, here are a few more tips.

Read the pack: The pack will be sent to you in advance. If it isn't, ask for it. Then, don't wait until the hours or minutes before the meeting – read it well in advance. Identify those items that impact you and ensure you are ready to speak to them. You should read the updates as part of your review ahead of time – if everyone does this, there is no need to waste time in the meeting itself covering this ground.

Look for hidden issues: Sometimes, the project manager may not draw enough attention to something you think is an issue or may not include it in the pack at all. Be ready to use your knowledge of the project to identify items that might need the committee's steer and, where possible, contact the project manager ahead of time to ensure these are highlighted in the pack.

Challenge: One job of the steering committee is to be a "critical friend" to the project. You should challenge the version of the truth put in front of you. Is it really at green status? Make a note of the things you'd like to challenge ahead of time. Ideally, let the project manager know that you would like clarity on these points – if it's just you, then perhaps that can be discussed bilaterally ahead of time.

Be prepared to help: If there are blocking issues or problems facing the project, is there any way that you can help? Can you or your team add some muscle to the project team? Is there a difficult stakeholder who works for you? Is there information you can provide? Is there a decision you can help to make?

The Project Manager's Role

Just a note on the project manager.

The steering committee meeting is something most project managers dread. It's not surprising: there's probably a history of messenger-shooting and blame-seeking.

You can help the project manager by suggesting topics for the steering committee and highlighting your key concerns ahead of time. Make sure that you have spoken to other members of the committee beforehand and are able to either start them on the journey of understanding or gather their concerns and apprise the project manager.

No one likes an ambush.

Then, in the meeting itself, support your project manager. If there's a curve ball, something neither of you have considered, take the responsibility and ensure that it's looked at before next time. If a position is challenged by a member of the committee (a position on which you and your project manager agree), don't leave the poor PM to defend it on their own. Remember that the committee members are your peers not theirs, so you probably have a better chance of understanding what's driving the question and responding appropriately.

And this may be obvious, but if you think of a curve ball yourself, don't throw it in public! Have a word with the project manager or team outside of the meeting to get it resolved. If you absolutely have to raise it in the meeting (because sometimes you just do), make sure that you do it in a way that shares the responsibility. Avoid "friendly fire" at all costs – this will impact your working relationship with the project team more than just about anything else. They need to feel that they can trust you and that you have their backs.

The Hybrid Working Model

Since the COVID pandemic and global lockdowns, organisations have moved significantly towards a hybrid workplace, where staff work from home broadly as often as they work in the office. Collaboration tools such as Zoom and Microsoft Teams have improved immeasurably in the interim, making working within a distributed environment more effective than ever.

As the world moves on, what was seen as a once-in-a-generation shift of working patterns has rebounded slightly, with patterns emerging based on company preferences and the nature of each job role.

As we have seen, a project moves from phase to phase, and the tasks (and the needs of the actors involved) are different in each phase.

Some activities (such as requirements-gathering and design) are highly collaborative and thrive on collective energy. While this remains possible using online collaboration tools, there is no substitute at present for working closely with colleagues, face-to-face.

Other activities (such as developing, testing and detailed planning) require focus, which benefits from the remote environment – time is not wasted travelling, and the team members can work in isolation for long stretches without interruption.

WHERE NEXT?

As we have seen, IT projects are almost as old as IT itself, and the project as a means of delivering a technology output isn't likely to be disappearing anytime soon.

Following rapid change in the early days of the information revolution, project methodologies are now established and we can expect to see evolution rather than revolution in the next few years.

There are a couple of dynamic factors, however, that may drive that evolution:

- Hybrid methodologies
- Collaborative working

Hybrid Methodology

As we have seen, there are broadly two schools of methodology: waterfall and agile. Waterfall is more linear and is used for projects with a more certain outcome, following a trusted path. Agile is more collaborative and iterative and is used for projects where experimentation is required or where the final outcome is less clear at the start.

The two methodologies have co-existed for a number of years and that isn't about to change.

The most likely evolution is that the edges of the two methodologies will become slightly blurred, as organisations become more adept at picking the "best of breed" for each project. Hybrid projects, which borrow a little from each methodology, will become more common and as a result more formalised.

There are real advantages in planning and control to the waterfall methodology, but the agile methodology is more collaborative with a more reliable outcome, as each iteration is built directly on the success of the previous stage. Organisations often take a hybrid ("wagile") approach of a broad plan under the waterfall methodology acting as a shell around a number of iterative delivery sprints that are conducted in a collaborative agile way.

As a business stakeholder, this gives you the best of both worlds. You are able to take comfort in the control and planning of waterfall but get to collaborate directly and iteratively with the scrum team (a multi-disciplined team of business analysts, designers and developers) to see instant results and gradual build out of the finished product.

Collaborative Working

The one genuine area of revolution that might take place over the coming years is in the area of collaborative working.

The pandemic and lockdown, like an earthquake, sent a series of seismic shocks through the established norms of working practice.

Prior to COVID, working from home was almost universally viewed with amused suspicion. "Working from home, eh?", your colleagues would say, nodding gently and offering a moderately predatory and utterly insincere smile. "Enjoy your day".

But that changed when *everyone* had to work from home.

Senior management realised that things could still get done, that most of their staff did more work (or more hours, at least) than when in the office due to the savings in travel time and that remote working had distinct advantages from a lifestyle perspective.

Since the end of the pandemic, workers have returned to offices, but in general, organisations are struggling to find the right balance. Some have issued stern edicts requiring all workers to be in the office for five days a week, others have threatened summary dismissal for not hitting a minimum three days per week target. Others are shutting down office space and sending their workforce home.

Is there a balance?

Only time will tell.

As yet, there doesn't appear to be a clear answer, despite numerous studies and a burgeoning supply of data. Some studies have reported an increase in productivity (in the region of 40%) for remote working, but these are not yet conclusive as to the type of work that would benefit from remote working. An experienced workforce following a productive, well-designed and workflow-based operating model may well achieve significant efficiency gains when the users work remotely, free from the distractions of the office.

But that doesn't really describe how a project works, in any of its phases, all of which have different needs. For projects and project management specifically, there is more work to be done before any hard rules can be defined. However, anecdotally, a few trends have started to emerge.

Collaboration

Collaboration is key, especially early on in the project, where there is a great deal of uncertainty. Project managers have now had the opportunity to run projects fully on site, fully remotely and in a hybrid model. Most will agree that the best collaboration is achieved when everyone (and this means everyone) is in a room together. There are activities that are just so much easier when everyone is physically present. There is an energy, a spontaneity and a speed of understanding that just isn't possible when some or all are only present through the screen.

Sometimes (and more often than not in the early stages of a project), it is the journey people take that matters, not the destination. Members of the project team and the various stakeholders need to understand the vision behind the project, the principles and assumptions at play. Remember that a project is most likely an alien environment to many of the business stakeholders. They need to be able to move away from their BAU day jobs and build a picture in their own mind that aligns with the project sponsor's vision. This journey is a lot easier in a face-to-face setting, with the vast lexicon of non-verbal communication that goes with it.

Standing in front of a whiteboard with pen in hand, placing and replacing sticky paper notes on the walls and windows, waving arms around and gauging body language: none of these can be fully simulated using online collaboration tools. Those tools are improving – interactive sharable whiteboards are now readily available as part of standard collaboration toolkits – but the medium of interaction remains restricted to the size of a computer screen – only in the room can you interact with everybody all at once. Sometimes, analogue is better than digital!

Focus

Collaboration isn't always the answer. Some jobs just need to be done, in isolation, with as few distractions as possible. This isn't always possible in an office environment. The hum of conversation, the close proximity to colleagues (and, yes, desks *have* got smaller since lockdown), the guy at the desk opposite you who hasn't learnt how to use his "indoor" voice, phones ringing or even just people moving around – these are all unwelcome distractions.

If focus is what you need, then you may well be better off working at home, away from the noise and bustle of the office. It may also be more productive to work in non-standard hours, to further reduce the chance of interruptions.

Development, testing and even a good deal of design are all likely to be achieved more quickly in a focused environment. There is typically less collaboration required, and any that is needed can be quickly obtained either bilaterally or with a small number of colleagues working online through cloud-based environments.

Preparation

For collaborative meetings that just can't be held in person, preparation is key. The human mind is best unlocked through visualisation, so a well-prepared presentation or graphical representation of the problem to be solved will help the team understand the issue and make progress on its resolution.

When the attendees at the meeting are less able to collaborate, it helps to have an aspirational outcome already prepared, around which ideas can accrete, rather than starting from a blank sheet of paper as might be the case if everyone was physically present in the room.

Clear agendas and objectives, along with clear ground rules for asking questions and keeping engagement levels high, are crucial to an effective meeting.

Social

Anyone who was working in a collaborative environment during the pandemic-enforced global lockdown may well have participated in the curious phenomenon of the online social events. Participants poured themselves a beer or a glass of wine and then sat in front of a screen chatting with their colleagues.

Even then, in an unprecedented period of social isolation, it all felt a little awkward, a little forced. Conversations were necessarily single-threaded (microphones and speakers aren't as selective as the human social senses), and at the end of the day, we were still drinking alone.

When the restrictions were lifted, and people were allowed to interact again, the sheer joy of being in a room with others and sharing a moment of social alignment seemed like a revelation. The world of business rediscovered the joy and effectiveness of social interaction.

No matter how much technology advances to compensate for distance, there will never be a substitute for meeting with a colleague and talking through your issues or problems or successes face-to-face.

Experience

There is also an emerging trend about the age or experience of a professional and their attitude to remote working.

Younger professionals tend to want to be in the office more.

There are probably two drivers for this. The first is simply that younger people tend to live in smaller spaces, probably living with others in a similar situation. They don't have access to a dedicated home-working environment that allows them to focus without interruptions. But there's an element of it that stems from their wanting to be present in the office, to learn from their more experienced colleagues. The human being learns through a combination of instruction, experience, observation and imitation. Even if it could be argued that instruction and experience are not diminished by the remote environment (which is doubtful), there is little opportunity for observation and imitation. How does your more experienced colleague conduct themselves during the day, what are they doing when the camera isn't on them? How do they work a room to achieve their desired outcome from a gathering be it social or professional? These nuances all require physical presence.

Flexible Office Space

Already in motion prior to the pandemic, the flexible office industry received a huge boost following the global lockdown. With reduced footprint requirements, and the need to spin teams quickly up or down, many small organisations have migrated towards a flexible office arrangement.

Bright, open offices with large collaboration and social spaces, often with a parallel social theme for evenings and weekends, are ideal for small organisations or small teams.

They also address some of the downsides of remote working – younger professionals can have a space away from their homes in which to work, and there is a mutual benefit in sharing the experience, even if those around you are not strictly colleagues.

But it's not all good news. The advantages of face-to-face collaboration may be limited by the lack of available desk spaces as organisations downsize their office footprint. You may be able to find a booth to talk to your colleague, but by far the most effective solution is to be sitting next to them throughout the day – this may not be possible if Phil from accounts has booked the desk next to you. And an unexpected (as well as deeply ironic) consequence of the rise of online collaboration is that even if a team are all in the office together, a large amount of their time may still be spent on online calls.

The Hybrid Project

So where does that leave projects?

The project is a transient organisation within an organisation. As the project moves through its phases, it places different demands on the project team and business stakeholders.

During the discovery phase of a project, when the problem is being defined and the business case being formed, the project team is small and needs constant access to business stakeholders, most particularly the sponsor.

Once the project is initiated, an absolutely critical moment is the project kick-off. Ideally, this is a single large face-to-face meeting with a social occasion afterwards. This is the opportunity to get the whole team and stakeholders together to hear from one source what the project is all about – the problem, the scope and approach, the objectives – and to meet each other. Relationships built during this meeting are vital to the successful flow of information around the project organisation in following months. Time (and money) spent on this event is rarely wasted.

Similarly, the early stages of projects will continue to benefit most from collaboration and a co-located workforce. The team will be more focused, involving a selection of business stakeholders, so this could potentially be done either onsite in a dedicated part of your office or at a flexible office space provider.

Design, development and testing (as noted above) are more focused activities and could benefit from remote working arrangements.

Project implementation will probably depend on the nature of the project. Small, focused teams working together will be able to prepare, plan and execute the implementation of most projects. Training is always best performed in a face-to-face environment (to maximise the opportunities for the trainees to learn through observation and imitation), but this will always depend on the nature of the target workforce for the new applications and processes as well as the level of change to the operating model. A small change impacting a widely distributed workforce could be managed largely by publication of training materials, videos and cheat sheets, whereas a complex change to a small, local team would benefit from direct in-person training.

SO WHAT?

So, what should you, as a business leader, be thinking about when you start or join a project?

Whether this is your first project or one of many, it's worth remembering that all projects are different, and will have different problems to solve, with different team members and stakeholders involved.

And let's just take a moment to remind ourselves of our overall purpose here – to make you an *effective business stakeholder*, either as a sponsor or as a contributor to the project. This isn't about scoring points with the project team. It's about trying to ensure that the project is a success and that your contribution to it is effective.

What, then, are the questions you should be asking?

Questions the business leader should ask at the *start* of a project:

- What's the problem?
- Do we need a project?
- Is there a clear business case?
- If the project cost twice as much, would we still do it?
- Is the outcome of the project clearly understood?
- Is my role on the project clear?
- Does the project have the right governance in place?
- Do I trust the project team?
- What's my level of certainty regarding the project outcome?

Questions the business leader should ask *during* a project's life:

- Does the project need help?
- Is hybrid working really working?
- Is the project still on track to deliver its particular aim?
- Is change necessary to meet the project objective?
- Should we just stop?
- Are we celebrating the project's successes sufficiently?
- How can I help my colleagues to accept the project's impacts?
- Are there unintended consequences of the project's launch?

Questions the business leader should ask *after* a project is done:

- Did the project achieve its aim?
- Was my contribution effective?

What's the Problem?

Douglas Adams, in his seminal work much loved by technologists everywhere – *The Hitchhiker's Guide to the Galaxy*[9] – conceived of an intergalactic supercomputer called Deep Thought which took seven and a half million years to calculate the answer to "the ultimate question". To the intense disappointment of its creators' descendants, the answer it eventually reached was 42.

> "I checked it very thoroughly," said the computer, "and that quite definitely is the answer. I think the problem, to be quite honest with you, is that you've never actually known what the question is."
>
> "But it was the Great Question! The Ultimate Question of Life, the Universe and Everything!"
>
> "Yes," said Deep Thought with the air of one who suffers fools gladly, "but what actually is it?"

Like Deep Thought, if you don't know what the problem is, how can you hope to solve it?

As a business leader involved in – or possibly initiating – a project, you need to be clearer than most as to exactly what the problem is that needs to be solved. You may already have a potential solution in your head, but that's not for airing right now. Focus on the problem (and encourage others to do so). There will time for solutions later.

And yours may not be the only voice – there may be several business stakeholders, each with their own slightly different versions of the problem. Make sure you are trying to articulate the problem and not simply talking about the symptoms. Business operating models are incredibly complex and similar symptoms may stem from wildly different root causes. Be ready to dig down. Ask iterative, probing questions of yourself and the team to make sure that you really are getting to the very bottom of the issue. What really is the problem? And how much of it do you need to solve? Can it be broken down and solved in parts? Are there components that the organisation can live with? Use the Pareto principle (also known as the 80/20 rule). Can you solve 80% of the problem with only 20% of the work?

Once you've analysed and defined the problem statement, write it down.

Then, critique it again. Is it clear, complete and concise? Check it with your colleagues. Do they understand it? Do they all agree? Check it with the business analyst: they will help you to ensure that the written statement meets all of the necessary criteria. This is what they do.

And then make sure your finalised problem statement is published and recorded in the relevant project documentation. It should be the first slide in every project presentation and shown in every workshop and meeting to remind everybody again and again what the project is trying to achieve.

This may all seem obvious, especially if the problem seems simple to define, but it is often overlooked, resulting in a project that has no certain (or universally understood) goal. Time spent early on to define and agree with the problem will be returned many times over in avoiding questioning and requestioning or in solving the wrong problem.

Do We Need a Project?

There are many reasons why projects are started, and most of those reasons are good ones. But sometimes, a project is started that simply isn't needed. The problem may not exist or may be external to the organisation. If it does exist, there may be incremental means to achieve the stated objective rather than a project-led approach. Many problems that appear to be rooted in technology can be solved with a slight change to existing business processes, or training or replacement of personnel.

There are significant overheads to constituting and initiating a project – make sure that the expense is worthwhile.

Another factor to bear in mind is the breadth and depth of the organisation's current change portfolio. If you're already stretched delivering a raft of mandatory changes, then you simply won't have the capacity to embark on another project no matter how much sense it might make in isolation.

Is There a Clear Business Case?

Most organisations operate an investment committee or project board that authorises the spending on projects. It's the job of this committee to approve the business case for any project.

As a business leader, you may be contributing to or even writing the business case, or you may simply be reviewing it. Whatever your level of input, there are a number of questions you should be asking yourself.

The main failing in writing a business case is to demonstrate positive bias, whether consciously or unintentionally. It is natural for the author or authors to be in favour of the project – they believe in it sufficiently to spend their time researching and setting out the business case and are putting their names to it. So, it's likely that unconscious bias will creep in. As a contributor or reviewer, you have the opportunity to challenge the numbers in the business case.

In building a business case, the costs are often simple to see, but the benefits are harder to find. If the author has a real or perceived need to identify a quick return on the organisation's investment in the project, then they may have got quite creative.

Are the benefits truly as stated? Is the current operating model being viewed through an overly dark lens? Are things really as they are being depicted? Or are the expected benefits attributed to the project being overstated? Could some of the benefit in fact be achieved through alternative initiatives?

Many benefits are intangible and can be hard to define in terms of monetary value. Have they been overstated? Or understated? Have they all been identified?

Some projects have an existential impact on an organisation. Failure to complete the project will directly affect the ability of the organisation to do business. If this is the case, make sure this is called out very clearly in the business case – the reader needs to experience no doubt. You can try to quantify what that means as a monetary value but only do so if it makes sense. If the project is simply mandatory (to meet regulatory or legal requirements perhaps), then the business case should say so.

If the Project Cost Twice as Much, Would We Still Do It?

We've seen how hard it is to make accurate estimates in the context of an IT project. Even the best estimates can be out by a significant degree.

Estimates for significant costs to the project (the cost of the developers' time) can be out by a factor of two or more. Typically, estimates in the early stages of the project lifecycle are padded out with 20–30% contingency, but often that simply isn't enough.

To make matters worse, a creative (and over-eager) project manager may have deflated some of the estimates in order to make the business case more appealing. Again, this may be consciously or unconsciously done.

And even if the estimates are right for the tasks identified, external factors or changes to the project scope may add more work to the stack, making the overall project more expensive.

So, the question you should ask yourself is whether you would still back the project if it cost twice as much as the estimate in the business case. It may still not make perfect sense, but do the benefits broadly still stack up and make it worthwhile? If the project has an existential impact for your organisation, you may feel that, regardless of the costs, it simply has to be taken on.

Is the Outcome of the Project Clearly Understood?

As important as it is to understand the initial problem, it's also vital that everyone understands what the project's output will be. It needs to be stated in sufficiently precise terms so that the objective of the project is clear, even if the nature of the output may not yet be defined. For example, the output might be a more efficient process, even if the precise steps of that process are not yet clear. Or the output might be a new phone application, even if the details of the application haven't yet been defined. In reality, it may not be so easy to clearly define the outputs ahead of time, but it's important to be as clear as possible.

If the output isn't clear, you will need to work with your business stakeholder colleagues and the project team to define it more accurately.

It's also important to think about whether there is a single output at a single point in time, or a succession of outputs aimed at producing an overall outcome. It may be that instead of initiating a project, you need to start a programme of change, which has a very different structure and approach.

Is My Role on the Project Clear?

Do you know what's being asked of you in your role as a business stakeholder? Is it clearly defined? Do your business colleagues know what is expected of them?

Are you the sponsor? Are you a key contributor? Are you expected to liaise with your colleagues who aren't so fully involved in the project? Is there a "hearts and minds" initiative that's your responsibility to manage? Are you involved in the project's steering committee? What specific business function do you perform that gives you a seat at the table? Are you the right person to represent that area of the business? Do you need support from one or more of your colleagues? Are there other business areas that should be represented? Are you and your colleagues able to dedicate the necessary time to the project?

The time to answer all of these questions is at the project start-up. It can be too late once the project starts, and it has a momentum all of its own.

Once the questions have been answered, and the wider stakeholder team confirmed, it should be clearly documented, ideally in the PID or similar artefact (perhaps a project charter).

Does the Project Have the Right Governance in Place?

As well as ensuring the right stakeholders are involved, it's crucial to make sure that the project's governance is appropriate. As we've seen, projects go through a number of phases during their lifecycle. The level of governance at each stage will differ, and projects themselves differ widely in their nature, so that it's not always easy to tell how much governance is "just right".

Too much senior oversight at an early stage can strangle a project. Everyone wants to be involved in the new "shiny thing" – no one wants to miss out on what could be an exciting and fun piece of work. Here is where a strong sponsor is crucial. There is a role to play in ensuring that everyone across the organisation is engaged and informed, but the number of people directly touching the project is sufficient only for the project's needs.

Once the project is up and running, and especially when it enters the design and development phases, the governance needs to be regular and reliable: managing change, intervening where needed and keeping the project on target.

Towards the end of the project, governance will need to be stepped up, as more and more people become involved in testing, readiness, training and implementation activities. But initially, it should be kept light.

Make sure you, or your colleagues, are not getting involved just because of FOMO ("Fear of Missing Out").

Do I Trust the Project Team?

This is a really important question.

You may not be familiar with the world of IT and IT projects, but your project team are. It's what they do. It's their day job. Some will have years of experience of different projects, while others may have gained hard-won certification in project management or other industry techniques.

They are professionals.

If you trust them, let them do their jobs.

Especially early on in a project, during fact-finding or planning workshops, there is a huge temptation for business stakeholders to tell the project team how to do their jobs, and, sorry to say, there are many that give in to that temptation.

Your role is to provide information about the business strategy, its data or processes. If you identify a significant milestone or a key risk, by all means call it out to the project manager. If you have a concern that certain sectors of the business may be ignored, it's your role to advise the team (and perhaps give the name of a suitable contact) so that the area can be included. But try to resist the urge to tell the project team how to manage risks, how to track milestones, how to capture and document requirements.

If you think an estimate for a task is too high in the plan, feel free to ask questions. Is there some contingency included in that figure? Is there a reason why it's higher than I'd expect? Is that a gold-plated solution or could we take a simpler approach? Don't challenge the team directly that the estimate is too high.

If they started asking you about your day job, and told you how to do it better, would you be pleased? Stay in your "swim lane", and let them manage theirs.

Of course, if you don't trust your project team, ask yourself what you are going to do about it? Can they be trained or replaced? Can you get a second opinion on their overall approach, such as from an independent consultancy? Are there other options to build trust, such as off-site sessions? Or maybe just ask them about their careers and their experience – you may be surprised at what they have achieved in the past and the level of expertise they are bringing to the team.

What's My Level of Certainty Regarding the Project Outcome?

Is the output of the project quite certain? It may be a small update to an existing application or process or a self-contained new operation. Perhaps the output of the project will be to implement some off-the-shelf software that is limited in terms of configuration.

Or is this a green-field project to buy or build a new application, highly configurable or where user input is critical to screen design?

If you've read the previous chapters, you can probably tell where this is heading....

If the outcome is more predictable, then the project might be better run using the waterfall methodology. For a less-defined output, a more agile approach may be taken, with its iterative and collaborative sprints. You may know exactly what you want and be able to clearly visualise and articulate it to the project team, or you may prefer to take the iterative approach.

The choice of methodology is likely to be made by the project team itself, but as a business stakeholder, you can at least make sure they are aware of your views and support them in making the right choice.

Does the Project Need Help?

Once the project is running, the project manager will make regular status updates to the project steering committee. The single most important item on the agenda is the project RAG status.

If you are the sponsor, you and the project manager will jointly agree the RAG status.

If you are on the steering committee, it's still your role to challenge the proposed status.

Even if you're not involved in the steering committee, you can help the project team to identify any potential bottlenecks and resolve them.

If there are issues that the project team is not going to be able to solve, then it's time to escalate to the steering committee, by setting the RAG status away from green.

The RAG status is an opportunity for complete honesty. It does not represent failure on anyone's part to set the status to amber or red. It's an indication that something has gone wrong and that the project needs help.

Imagine that you are meeting a friend.

- You leave the house with plenty of time (RAG status is green).
- The trains are all running and you catch the right train (RAG status is green).
- Then, the train stops unexpectedly. You start looking at your watch. If it stops for much longer, you're going to be late. You text your friend to let them know you might be delayed (RAG status is amber).
- The train sits for a few minutes longer, and you are now going to be late. You text your friend again (RAG status is red).
- You could ask your friend to simply wait (extending the project duration) or maybe ask them to come and meet you halfway (reducing the project scope) or you could call a taxi to get you the original meeting (adding expense to the project). Or you could even reschedule your visit for another day (reprioritising the project).

It seems really easy for such a simple scenario. Of course, projects are vastly more complicated than a train journey, but the principles above should always apply.

If you need to ask for help (or need to prepare the ground for it), be ready to set the project status accordingly.

Is Hybrid Working Really Working?

It's hard to tell if hybrid working is effective at the best of times. In order to accurately answer this question, typically one needs a control against which to compare the approach. For example, if you have two operational teams that do exactly the same work, you could operate one team on site and the other in hybrid mode and compare the outputs. Or you could change the approach for a single team from one month to the next and gather a more-or-less helpful set of statistics.

But – as always – projects are different.

No two projects are the same, and a given project can vary significantly from week to week in terms of workload and output. In the extremely unlikely event that you have the spare capacity to run two identical project teams in parallel to deliver two versions of the same project, they will necessarily compete with each other as they try to grab precious time with key stakeholders and other resources.

So, any judgement that you make as to the effectiveness of hybrid working will necessarily be subjective and only partially informed.

You could track progress against the plan, but as we now know, estimates are often light in the first place, so any slippage may be down to poor estimates or any one of a myriad external factors that could influence progress.

And other measures (such as employee satisfaction, wellbeing or turnover) are unlikely to be meaningful over the life of a project. What works for one project may not work for another.

Probably the most informative approach is to simply ask the team – make this part of your regular meetings (if the project is agile, it should be part of the retrospective at the end of each sprint). But make sure you are asking the right questions: most members of the team will have a clear preference regardless of effectiveness and impact on the team, so the conversation needs to be about the phase of the project, the level of collaboration or focus needed at that time and what's right for the team as a whole. Make sure that this is continually reviewed – we know that projects change their nature week on week, so what was right in January may not be the best approach in March.

It is probably best to avoid blanket edicts such as that everyone needs to be in for three days a week. Remember that the purpose is to be effective, not just to get people sitting at desks. If the short-term need is for collaboration, don't insist that the team come in to the office and then have them sit on video calls all day – arrange a breakfast or other opportunity for them to mix with each other and with stakeholders. Get everyone talking. Feel the buzz. Conversely, if the project is in "heads down" delivery mode and would benefit from a few weeks of focus time, let it happen but make sure you all gather together at the end to reflect and discuss the next steps.

Is the Project Still on Track to Deliver Its Particular Aim?

Sometimes, projects can lose their way. The mechanism of running and delivering a project can become all-consuming, obscuring (or at the very least drawing attention away from) the original objective(s).

Remember those PIDs and ToRs at the start? They're not "fire and forget" documents: take some time to refer back to them regularly. Remind yourself (and the team) of the goals and evaluate if you are still on track. It's vital to consider this holistically as well: don't just look at the project team. How will the project impact the organisation, its employees, partners and clients? Are these things clearer now than at the start of the project?

Is Change Necessary to Meet the Project Objective?

Managing change is a crucial aspect of running a project.

As a business stakeholder, your role in managing change is to introduce as little of it as possible!

You should always be thinking about how to achieve the project's ambitions with as little work as possible. And certainly, once the scope has been fixed at the end of the requirements-gathering phase, or an incremental delivery has been agreed for an agile sprint, you should resist changing your mind as much as you possibly can.

There will be enough risk of change to the project with unavoidable delays or external factors, without introducing more work by changing your mind on a requirement you've already agreed with the team.

Whether the driver is from outside or inside the project, it's crucial that you challenge the need for change. Your starting position should be that the change is not required. What will be wrong with the final output if the change is not included? If it materially affects the viability of the new operating model, then you can (grudgingly) approve the change, but always look for the least impact – could something be done manually for a short amount of time? Is there an opportunity to make the change to the new systems at a later date?

The later you introduce (or approve) a change, the more expensive it can be.

Early on in a project, a change may take no longer than necessary to develop the new code or design the new process. Once the project enters testing, however, the cost of making a change starts to increase dramatically. This is because the team will need to test not only the change itself but other systems and processes around it that might be impacted. This may go beyond a standard regression test and may need whole sections of the system to be retested. Even later, it may be that training needs to be changed, or printed material has to be reworked to cater for the change.

As a business stakeholder, you need to think creatively to see if you can identify a better way of reacting to the need for change, whether this is through manual processes, accepting a risk that the software doesn't work as well as it might or to stop doing the business that might cause the issue in the first place.

It can be very tempting to consider a potential change in isolation: individually, each may make perfect sense. But to do so is to risk the "death of a thousand cuts" suffered by many projects, wherein they become so overwhelmed by a tide of minor changes that they are unable to deliver any output. Think about the overall landscape of the project and the other changes that have either been approved or are in the pipeline. A handy mantra to use when considering a change request is to imagine that the project is due to go live the next day – would you pull the plug on that implementation if this change couldn't be done?

Should We Just Stop?

This is a hard question to ask, but sometimes you need to contemplate the unthinkable.

There are many reasons why it might no longer make sense to continue with a project, even one with a clear initial business case. External factors could change the economic or business landscape. Changes to scope may have rendered the project no longer sufficiently beneficial to offset further expense. There might be too much going on elsewhere in the organisation. Or the project may have turned out to be harder than initially thought.

Sometimes, it makes sense to just stop.

It's tempting to think of the cost of the project so far and to use that as an argument to continue, but that only goes so far. If the remaining cost of the project doesn't stack up against the expected benefits, regardless of the time and money spent so far, you may well be better off stopping (or perhaps pausing) the project.

Are We Celebrating the Project's Successes Sufficiently?

Delivering projects is tough.

The project team are hardworking professionals, often working well beyond the standard day to make progress in a challenging environment with thousands of variables (not that we would want to encourage this behaviour, but the reality is – especially as projects approach implementation – that a great deal is asked of the team; on the whole they are willing to do it, but the additional effort should be recognised and the team should be adequately compensated).

As a business stakeholder, they need your support, especially during the tough times. If the project isn't going to hit its deadlines, it's unlikely that it's the project manager's fault or even any one member of the team. External factors could be the cause or any number of internal factors outside their control. It could even be you! Remember those estimates? Hard to get right in the best of circumstances, they may need to be adjusted if things begin to slip.

The last thing the project team needs to feel is that they will be made into scapegoats, blamed for a lack of progress they had no way of achieving. You need to encourage them to get creative and find solutions that will help the project move forward. Is there anything you can do personally to help? Or intervene with your colleagues if they are the issue?

Be supportive in the bad times.

And celebrate the good ones.

One of the most remarkable and decisive acts of good management we witnessed recently was when a multi-million pound project that had been running for several years was delayed on the very brink of implementation – on the Friday of the launch weekend. The mood of disappointment in the project team and throughout the organisation was palpable. In response, the Chief Operating Officer (COO) gave the entire project team (some 200+ professionals) the Monday off. "Take some time," she said. "Don't think about the project. Have a day to yourself." The incremental cost was negligible but the goodwill and energy that it engendered was palpable.

Celebration and recognition are key motivators. As a business unit, you probably have small gatherings to reward monthly or quarterly targets or to celebrate a colleague's promotion. These celebrations matter and it's the same for project professionals. Except, they rarely get a chance to do it. Project teams are often viewed as expensive overheads. As soon as the project is delivered, they are moved onto the next thing, often with no break and no time to reflect.

That's why it's important to celebrate small successes along the way, while the team is still together, and there is a tangible collective benefit from the post-celebration goodwill and enhanced levels of teamwork and trust.

How Can I Help My Colleagues to Accept the Project's Impacts?

Not everyone likes change. In fact, even change professionals don't really like change when it's happening to them. Your colleagues are going to be no different.

As a stakeholder in the project, it's part of your role to help your colleagues get ready for the change that's about to happen. You can keep them abreast of project developments, hold workshops with them so that they understand the rationale and objective of the project. Walk them through the problem statement. If they see the need, they will better understand the change.

Are There Unintended Consequences of the Project's Launch?

Implementing a project will have impacts on the business of the organisation to a greater or lesser degree. Most of those impacts will have been identified by the project team, with your help, as part of the project's aims. But the team don't know your colleagues (or your job) like you do. There may be other impacts, unintended and unidentified, of the project's launch. The team will need your support and your ideas to help identify and manage them.

How is the job going to change? Which of your colleagues will be most affected by the project? What do they do now that they won't have to do in the future? What new processes will they need to follow? What won't they like? What data do they use now that is going to be more important in the new world? Is the data well-managed?

It will help to build a list of these impacts as you go through the project. Even if implementation is weeks or months away, adding something to the list when you first identify it means you will have a core of implementation impacts when the time comes. It won't be perfect, but it will be a start, and it may prompt other thoughts in the minds of your colleagues when you first get together to talk about how best to implement the project.

Did the Project Achieve Its Aim?

After the project, it's tempting to move onto the next thing. Whether that's back to the day job or onto the next project, it's almost inevitable that the last project is quickly forgotten.

All of the project methodologies will talk about the importance of a post implementation review, but in reality, a lot of organisations simply don't find the time to hold one. And even if they do, it can be perfunctory affairs rife with predictable observations.

In particular, it can be very hard to identify if a project genuinely achieved its aims. The proof may take time to emerge (months or even years), by which time the project team have long moved on to subsequent endeavours. Or other factors (internal or external) may have intervened to obscure the key metrics that would be used to measure the project's success.

For example, a project's aim may have been to streamline an accounting process to create additional capability in the finance team. But if the business has grown by the time the project is implemented, it may not be possible to categorically identify any cost savings that can be ascribed to the project.

This doesn't mean that the project hasn't been successful. It just means it's not possible to quantify it using the agreed metrics.

As a business stakeholder (or specifically as the project sponsor), it will probably fall to you to make an objective assessment of the project's success. If the originally agreed metrics are no longer valid, you will need to use creative logic to measure the project's success. Make sure that you do this, even if the project mechanism has been disbanded.

As always, the truth is more important than saving face. If the project didn't achieve its goals, it's better for your organisation to understand this and how to correct it than to believe that it was in fact successful.

Was My Contribution Effective?

It's also important to gauge your own contribution to the project. You may have a view already, but it makes sense to get a second and third opinion. Ask the team. Ask the project manager. Ask your colleagues.

And you can back up their subjective views with data.

How many change requests were there that could have been avoided? How many calls did your colleagues make to the help desk with questions that could have been included in training material? Did the project deliver on time, and deliver the original objectives? How many of the project team thanked you personally for your contributions?

Your interaction with an IT project may have been a one-off. You might be about to slip quietly back into your day job, never again to immerse yourself in the traumatic world of milestones and deadlines, requirements and change requests, testing, training and implementation. But if you think you might give it another go at some point, it would be prudent to get some feedback from the professionals as to how you did this time.

So you can do it better next time and be an effective stakeholder.

NOTES

1   *The Principles of Scientific Management* by Frederick Winslow Taylor, 1911.

2   *The Gantt Chart: A Working Tool of Management* by Wallace Clark, 1922.

3   https://web.archive.org/web/20151112203807/ www.dtic.mil/dtic/tr/fulltext/u2/735902.pdf

4   *Critical Chain* by Eliyahu M. Goldratt, 1997, ISBN 0-88427-153-6.

5   www.hbs.edu/faculty/Pages/item.aspx?num=38542

6   *Rapid Application Development* by James Martin, 1991, ISBN 0-02-376775-8.

7   http://agilemanifesto.org/

8   https://assets.publishing.service.gov.uk/media/646769cb43fe01000cac65b0/2023-04-11-V2-AFIGT-The-role-of-the-senior-responsible-owner-2.pdf

9   *The Hitchhiker's Guide to the Galaxy* by Doulas Adams, 1979, ISBN 0-330-25864-8.

8

What's Artificial Intelligence?

Human beings can do everything that AI can do. They just can't do it to scale.

Anne Marie Neatham, COO, Ocado Technology

Artificial intelligence (AI) is the capacity of computer systems to simulate human intelligence or intelligent behaviour.

Artificial Intelligence, more usually referred to as just 'AI', has been around longer than you might think.

The first steps were taken in the mid-twentieth century, and it has taken a long, slow random walk to get to where it is today. Often, that progress has necessarily had to pause, waiting for the next technological leap forward. Sometimes, economic factors or public sentiment intervened.

But suddenly, AI is everywhere.

AI sits at the heart of some of the biggest organisations in the world, shaping strategies based on their huge data models. Most of us see it on a daily basis through our smart speakers and phones, predictive text in search boxes and conversations with chatbots. *Machine learning* (ML) and the latest *large language models* (LLMs) have unlocked the power of generative AI to create music, art, poetry and free-flowing text that would fool even the most accomplished expert.

In this section we look to take a brief look at AI, to try to explain a little bit about it in everyday terms, to see where it's going and what it might mean to a forward-looking digitally enabled business.

WHY SHOULD I CARE?

AI is going to be a game-changer. There's no denying it.

But that's been the story all along. Computers were a game-changer, microcomputers even more so. The internet was a game-changer (ask Jeff Bezos). Blockchain is a game-changer.

The doomsayers are predicting the end of the world in Terminator-like robot-induced mass extinction events. Most are expecting it to radically realign businesses, lives and civilisations: whole categories of jobs will disappear to be replaced by soulless machines, while the previous incumbents find themselves washed up without skills or hope for a better life.

The same was said of computers. Most of the vast array of technology and technology-related jobs that people have today didn't exist 20 years ago.

People will still have jobs in a post-AI world. But they will have different jobs. With proper management, AI and ML will enable businesses to transform and become radically more efficient than they are now.

As Marco Iansiti and Karim R. Lakhani put it so eloquently in their book *Competing in the Age of AI*,[1] "we are no longer looking at [...] the 'new' economy. We are looking at *the* economy".

> Confronting this threat does not involve spinning off an online business, putting a laboratory in Silicon Valley, or creating a digital business unit. Rather, it involves a much deeper and more general challenge: rearchitecting how the firm works and changing the way it gathers and uses data, reacts to information, makes operating decisions, and executes operating tasks.

As a business leader, you can expect your organisation to be impacted by AI in some way over the next five years. How, and by how much, may be up to you.

HOW DID WE GET HERE?

Naturally, we asked OpenAI's ChatGPT to set out the history of AI and ML.

We gave it the following brief: "Write a history of AI and machine learning for a business reader in 2000 words or so".

Here's how it did.

QUOTE ...

Title: Navigating the Evolution: AI and Machine Learning in Business

Introduction
The dawn of the 21st century brings with it a technological renaissance, one spearheaded by Artificial Intelligence (AI) and Machine Learning (ML), terms that are often used interchangeably but have distinct definitions. AI is the broader concept of machines performing tasks in a way that would be considered "smart," while ML is an application of AI that gives the machines the ability to learn and improve from experience.

The Beginnings
AI's journey began in the mid-20th century when mathematicians and philosophers questioned whether machines could think. Alan Turing's seminal paper "Computing Machinery and Intelligence" and the subsequent Turing Test set the stage for AI by proposing a standard for a machine's ability to exhibit intelligent behavior equivalent to or indistinguishable from that of a human.

1950s-1960s: The Foundation
The 1950s saw the first programmed computers capable of somewhat independently performing tasks like playing chess. The Dartmouth Conference in 1956

marked the formal birth of AI as a field of study. In these early days, researchers were optimistic, with simple neural networks and the first AI programs developed to mimic basic human problem-solving and learning processes.

1970s: The Reality Check
This period witnessed the first of the AI Winters – a time when the promises of AI were unmet, funding dried up, and public interest waned. The limitations of existing technology became apparent; computers lacked the processing power needed, and researchers realized that human intelligence was more complex than previously thought.

1980s: The Revival
The 1980s brought a resurgence of interest in AI, thanks to the development of machine learning algorithms and the concept of expert systems – programs that answered questions and solved problems in specific domains. The Japanese government's investment in the Fifth Generation Computer Project spurred renewed interest and competition in the field.

1990s: The Internet and Increased Computing Power
The advent of the internet and significant improvements in computing power allowed AI and ML to advance rapidly. The focus shifted toward data and pattern recognition, leading to advancements in areas like speech recognition and industrial robotics. Businesses began to take notice, envisioning the potential for AI to revolutionize industries.

2000s: Big Data and Advanced Algorithms
The explosion of digital data and improved algorithms in the 2000s set the stage for modern AI and ML. The development of more sophisticated ML techniques, such as Support Vector Machines (SVMs) and ensemble methods, began to allow computers to tackle more complex tasks with greater accuracy.

2010s: Deep Learning and Business Applications
The development of deep learning, driven by neural networks with many layers (hence "deep"), marked a significant leap forward for AI. These networks were fueled by vast amounts of data and increased computational power. Businesses started to adopt AI for a variety of applications, from customer service chatbots to predictive analytics.

Major Milestones in AI for Business

- *IBM's Watson (2011): Watson's victory in Jeopardy! demonstrated the potential for AI in processing and analyzing large amounts of information faster than humans.*
- *Big Data Analytics: Companies began leveraging AI to sift through large datasets to find patterns, insights, and make predictions.*

- *Automated Customer Service: AI-driven chatbots and virtual assistants, such as Apple's Siri and Amazon's Alexa, became commonplace in customer service.*
- *Predictive Maintenance: AI algorithms could predict when machines would fail or require maintenance, saving costs and increasing efficiency.*

Challenges and Ethical Considerations
As AI technology improved, so did concerns about privacy, security, and the ethical use of AI. The potential for job displacement due to automation began to be a significant topic of discussion. Businesses and governments started to realize the need for guidelines and regulations around the use of AI.

The Role of Machine Learning
ML became the driving force of AI's success in business. Supervised learning allowed machines to predict outcomes based on historical data, while unsupervised learning helped in discovering patterns and relationships in data. Reinforcement learning, where machines learned to make decisions by trial and error, opened up new avenues for automation and optimization.

The Future of AI and ML in Business
The potential of AI and ML to transform all areas of business seems boundless. Personalization in marketing, operational efficiency in manufacturing, financial forecasting, and healthcare diagnostics are just a few areas where AI is making an impact. The move towards more autonomous systems, such as self-driving cars, and the use of AI in decision-making presents both opportunities and challenges.

Conclusion
The history of AI and ML is a tale of peaks and valleys, of winters and revivals. It's a narrative filled with technological breakthroughs and cautionary tales. For the business world, AI and ML represent a frontier of untapped potential and uncharted risks. As businesses stand on the cusp of this AI era, the lessons from history could serve as both a guide and a warning for the journey ahead.

… UNQUOTE

It's not a bad stab (although it's nothing like 2,000 words, coming in at a mere 805). It's not particularly "business focused", and we think it's maybe missed out a few key points, which we've filled in below. But it's undeniably a clear and concise description, with some creative headings and pithy interpretations thrown in. We'll take a more in-depth analysis of the text in the "So what" chapter at the end of this section.

Fantasies and Concepts

The concept of AI in one form or another had been around since mankind was able to create stories. Ancient legends and folk tales tell of magical talking statues, brazen heads, mythical creatures and other seemingly mundane objects uplifted to intelligence by gods or mortal artificers. Moreover, these creations were frequently credited with an arcane knowledge akin to omniscience ("Magic Mirror on the wall...").

As computer technology began to develop in the early and mid-twentieth century, science fiction writers began to conceive of mechanical – rather than magical – intelligences: Fritz Lang's bewitching *Maschinenmensch* in the film *Metropolis*, Isaac Asimov's *I, Robot* and other stories, the silent, menacing Gort from *The Day the Earth Stood Still* and Robbie from the Gene Roddenberry 1956 classic B Movie *Forbidden Planet*.

Alan Turing's paper in 1950, *Computing Machinery and Intelligence*,[2] was indeed seminal. Trying to address and define the concept of AI, he proposed a thought experiment based on a variation of a popular game at the time, the "imitation game" where a man and a woman, hidden in separate rooms, provided written answers to questions posed by a third person who had to guess the sex of each occupant. Turing proposed that the man (or the woman) was replaced by a computer, which would pass what became known as the "Turing test" if the observer was unable to tell the computer apart from the human, based only on the written answers to questions.

The Dartmouth Conference in 1956 is viewed by many as the birth of AI. It was organised by a group of computer scientists including Marvin Minsky and John McCarthy, who championed the term "AI".

In 1957, Frank Rosenblatt, an engineer at Cornell Aeronautical Laboratory, wrote a paper[3] describing a primitive artificial *neural network*, which he called a "perceptron", capable of learning to recognise shapes, such as circles or squares. Rosenblatt noted that the challenge (for a purely deterministic process) of recognising a complex shape such as a human being would be that the machine would need to store hundreds of thousands of pictures of humans from every angle and in every posture. His perceptron was given an admittedly simpler task of recognising either a square or a circle. The machine would be "trained" by showing it a number of squares while forcing it to reach the "square" outcome, incrementing a "weighting" value within the associated path. When left to determine its own outcome, the weighting would encourage (rather than force) the machine to reach the "square" outcome.

Theory to Reality

Throughout the 1950s, IBM computer scientist Arthur Samuel developed machine learning algorithms based on the game of checkers.[4] He advocated two methods of learning: rote learning (where the algorithm stored every iteration of the board that occurred during a game, along with a value representing the eventual chance of victory) and what he called "learning by generalisation" where a series of backups taken after each move were used to modify the value parameter. Although occasionally the algorithm taught the computer how to play badly (and had to be reset), in general, it improved with practice to become a "better-than-average novice". Samuel published a paper on his work, *Some Studies in Machine Learning Using the Game of Checkers*[5] in 1959.

The year 1966 saw the first recognised functioning AI computer program, named ELIZA (after George Bernard Shaw's linguistically challenged protagonist in *Pygmalion*). Written by Joseph Weizenbaum, ELIZA simulated human interaction by applying complex language rules to a typed input, returning a meaningful response. The program (aided by one of several "scripts") would search for keywords in the human's input, rank them and then use them to adapt and reflect the input back to the human. In the absence of a keyword, the program would use a selection of stock phrases to seek further clarity.[6] Crucially, any word typed in by the human would then be added to a growing list of keywords used by the program, and the script itself could be further enhanced through editing. It was this teaching element that led Weizenbaum to name his "translating processor" ELIZA.

The most famous interaction published by Weizenbaum is shown below (with ELIZA's responses in capitals):

Men are all alike.
IN WHAT WAY
They're always bugging us about something or other.
CAN YOU THINK OF A SPECIFIC EXAMPLE
Well, my boyfriend made me come here.
YOUR BOYFRIEND MADE YOU COME HERE
He says I'm depressed much of the time.

I AM SORRY TO HEAR YOU ARE DEPRESSED
It's true. I am unhappy.
DO YOU THINK COMING HERE WILL HELP YOU NOT TO BE
UNHAPPY
I need some help, that much seems certain.
WHAT WOULD IT MEAN TO YOU IF YOU GOT SOME HELP
Perhaps I could learn to get along with my mother.
TELL ME MORE ABOUT YOUR FAMILY
My mother takes care of me.
WHO ELSE IN YOUR FAMILY TAKES CARE OF YOU
My Father.
YOUR FATHER
You are like my father in some ways.
WHAT RESEMBLANCE DO YOU SEE
You are not very aggressive but I think you don't want me to
notice that.
WHAT MAKES YOU THINK I AM NOT VERY AGGRESSIVE
You don't argue with me.
WHY DO YOU THINK I DON'T ARGUE WITH YOU
You are afraid of me.
DOES IT PLEASE YOU TO BELIEVE I AM AFRAID OF YOU
My father is afraid of everybody.
WHAT ELSE COMES TO MIND WHEN YOU THINK OF
YOUR FATHER
Bullies.
DOES THAT HAVE ANYTHING TO DO WITH THE FACT THAT
YOUR BOYFRIEND MADE YOU COME HERE

Many users (even though they knew that they were interacting with a computer program) experienced the "ELIZA effect", imagining that the purely mechanical responses were in fact indicative of human emotions and thoughts. Reading back the transcript above, it's not hard to see why.

Expert Systems

There was indeed an "AI winter" when it was generally realised that available processing power would not support the theoretical requirements of

AI (a conclusion drawn perhaps erroneously following the publication of the 1969 book *Perceptrons*[7] which noted certain limitations). Distrust of AI was certainly rife, epitomised chillingly in Arthur C. Clarke and Stanley Kubrick's *2001: A Space Odyssey* and the traitorous HAL 9000.

A partial thaw came in the guise of "expert systems". Spurred on by the new client–server architecture that enabled business users to have more direct access to computers, many organisations and industries saw value in the creation and use of these applications that essentially comprised two components:

- A rules engine for analysing and comparing input parameters
- A knowledge base to support the rules engine with a library of conditions and outcomes

The body of knowledge could be compiled using the collective understanding of a number of experts in the relevant field. Typical applications included medical diagnosis and computer application design itself.

Expert systems did not last long as a concept, arguably because rules engines themselves quickly became embedded into software applications, no longer needing a specific name. Most modern workflow-based apps are really no different from an expert system from 30 years ago. Another factor may well have been the arrival of the World Wide Web and the ready availability of an even more vast body of knowledge, along with the means to search it.

AI in Chess and Gaming

As early as 1950, the ability of a computer to play chess was seen as a yardstick for the broader capabilities of AI. Claude Shannon posted a paper[8] setting out a possible approach to programming a computer (although the technical capabilities were not yet available for a practical demonstration). Shannon noted two options for calculating the optimum move for his theoretical chess computer: one was to calculate every possible move for white followed by every possible countermove for black (resulting in 10^{120} calculations), whereas another was to identify and store the best next move for every possible combination of pieces on the board (needing a mere 10^{43} different combinations to be held in memory).

One of the first implementations of a computer game was "Bertie the Brain", a purpose-built computer that was displayed at the Canadian National Exhibition in 1950.[9] Bertie was capable of playing Tic-Tac-Toe, beating most adults on its highest setting. Meanwhile, British mathematician Christopher Strachey wrote a draughts (checkers) program for the Manchester Baby Ferranti Mark I computer (having converted it from an earlier unsuccessful attempt on a smaller computer, the Pilot ACE).

Following further advances in computer hardware and software technology, computers began to threaten first ordinary chess players, then grandmasters and eventually reigning world champions. The series of challenges between 1989 and 1997 involving an IBM supercomputer Deep Blue (initially called Deep Thought) and the reigning world champion Garry Kasparov were the stuff of legend, with an upgraded machine eventually running out the winner of the final contest by 3½ games to 2½.

Deep Blue and its predecessors were dedicated chess-playing machines. In the following years, attention turned to a software approach as chess-playing engines (such as Stockfish) achieved superhuman levels of playing ability, using advanced algorithms to reduce the number of calculations required along with massive databases of past games. An annual AI chess tournament began to be held (the Top Chess Engine Championship or TCEC).

But, like expert systems before them, these rules engines and data libraries were relatively static. They relied on vast computational power and large memories to get through all the possible combinations available.

The real breakthrough (and literal "gamechanger") came in 2017, with Google's DeepMind and its AlphaZero gaming engine.[10] AlphaZero was entirely self-taught, using neural networks and reinforcement learning, playing thousands of games against itself to develop its understanding of winning strategies. According to the DeepMind paper announcing the results, AlphaZero took just four hours to learn to play chess better than one of the latest chess engines, Stockfish 8. To rub salt into the gaming wounds, AlphaZero then proceeded to teach itself Go and Shogi to world-beating ability.

Big Data AI

Big data also had a role to play in the development of AI. As processing speeds continued to follow the path laid out by Moore's Law and the capacity to store data likewise increased exponentially, digitally enabled organisations sought the ability to process the vast amounts of incidental data that they were gathering.

Companies like Amazon were storing a wealth of customer data on a daily basis: what customers searched for, what they looked at and what they bought. They began using AI to sift through that data and start to recognise patterns. Patterns in customer interests (customers who bought this product also bought that product), patterns in products (this product is similar to that product). These AI engines were able to use real-time updates to continually provide customers with the latest trends.

Chatbots and Language Models

Despite its limited vocabulary and relatively simple pattern-matching logic, ELIZA is widely regarded as the first "chatbot". Others followed, including PARRY (a more sophisticated attempt in 1972 that simulated the responses of a paranoid schizophrenic – the two were even put in contact with one another over the fledgling ARPANET[11]), Jabberwacky (a less serious attempt at a chatbot but with the very serious goal of storing and accessing the sum total of "everything everyone has ever said ... a conversational Wikipedia[12]") and ALICE – Artificial Linguistic Internet Computer Entity, which used a specially designed markup language (AIML or AI Markup Language) and was the inspiration for the film *Her* in which the protagonist falls in love with a chatbot.

In 2001, SmarterChild was the first union of chatbot technology and the vast array of data available on the internet. Suddenly, the chatbot could be useful, retrieving current data such as news, weather, sports scores and stock prices for users of AOL and MSN.

Within just over a decade, there would be thousands of chatbots, including all the ones you probably even now speak to through your smartphone or speaker: Siri, Cortana (replaced by Copilot) and Alexa. In 2011, IBM's chatbot Watson famously defeated two champions in the quiz game Jeopardy! These engines all had one thing in common – rather than being limited to a fixed, rules-based set of responses, the bots were capable of recognising and responding in natural language and developed through ML.

By the 2020s, virtual assistants were commonly available throughout the developed world, taking on such tasks as playing music, turning lights on and off, setting heating and alarm systems, acting as a voice search and response capability for web search engines and many others.

It seemed that chatbots were ready to – if not rule – at least manipulate the world. But even those advances paled compared to what was to follow. In 2022, OpenAI introduced the world to ChatGPT, a large language model (LLM) application that uses a range of learning techniques to simulate almost any conversation, including the ability to build on a series of prompts to fine-tune its responses. ChatGPT is able to write poetry or songs, create prose, draw images (by using the incorporated DALL-E 3 image generator) as well as retrieve and summarise information on almost any subject. Shortly after the public launch of ChatGPT, Google launched their own equivalent (Bard, now called Gemini), and the other tech giants soon began leveraging their own massive R&D budgets to follow suit.

The world's leaders and self-appointed guardians of morality had a collective hissy fit. All the predictions of the end of the world brought about by malicious machines bent on revenge against the human race came bubbling to the surface. AI was headline news (despite the horrific events being perpetrated globally by non-artificially unintelligent human beings), and AI conferences saw an uptick in famous attendees such as Musk, Zuckerberg et al.

It's been a slow burn, but AI has truly come of age.

WHAT DOES HERE LOOK LIKE?

It might be tempting at this point to dive into a deep and thorough explanation of AI and ML, along with hundreds of concepts, terms and equations.

But we're not going to do that.

Two reasons spring to mind. First, there are hundreds (probably thousands) of other books out there that will do a much better job of explaining AI and ML to any interested reader, written by computer scientists with a far deeper understanding of the genre than we have. But mostly, because this is a book about demystifying technology and technology projects to business users.

So, we're going to merely skim the surface to establish some of the basics and then spend our time looking at how AI might be used to influence a tech project or as part of a tech project to improve a business process.

If your goal is to completely and aggressively pull apart your business (or to build it from the ground up) to be fully digital, infinitely scalable and powered purely by AI, this probably isn't the book for you.

What's the Difference between Artificial Intelligence and Machine Learning?

AI is the capability of a machine to perform a task that would normally require human intelligence. This could be achieved by a set of static rules or by reference to a database of parameters. Or it could be achieved through ML, where the machine's capabilities can be increased by learning from the outcome of its operation or training.

ML is, by definition, a subset of AI. But AI is not always ML.

What's a Model?

A model is a representation of something.

A computer model is usually a representation of a real-world object or process that uses software and data to predict how the object or process will behave in certain circumstances.

Let's take a simple example: a very basic model of quarterly sales. Let's say we've just completed our first quarter and we sold 100 units.

To start with, we could simply assume that the second quarter's sales are going to be exactly the same as the first. Even though there are no moving parts, so to speak, it's still a model.

But we don't want our sales to be static – we want to see some growth. Let's introduce a single parameter (representing quarterly growth) into the model. Initially, we could set it to 4%. We could then run the model, and it would show us just under 17% growth for the next year. But maybe that growth parameter of 4% is just a guess (or wishful thinking). The important thing is to adjust it (to "learn").

Let's move on by a quarter. We now have the actual sales figures for the second quarter. We could just use our model to predict the sales for the third quarter (with a 4% growth on the second quarter's sales). But let's take a quick look at those figures first, shall we? Good news! We sold a whopping 110 units in the second quarter, so our growth was 10%. Hoping for the same success, we should adjust our simple model to show 10% growth per quarter. Using our new model, we predict third-quarter sales of 121 units. Under the old model, we would have predicted 114 units.

When we get our sales figures for the third quarter, we could adjust our model again to predict the next period's sales and so on. To keep it simple, we might simply take the last quarter's value for the next quarter, or we might decide to start introducing some rules such as taking an average, or even a weighted average, over the previous three quarters.

This feedback of the model's performance and adjustment of parameters is a key component of AI.

Of course, in reality, we will have a far more sophisticated model with many more parameters and rules. There might be seasonal or geographical factors, periodic advertising campaigns or any one of a host of reasons why sales might fluctuate. The model would be designed to apply these rules and data to derive a prediction for growth. With enough accumulated data, it should be possible to adjust the rules (or include more data) so that the model becomes increasingly more accurate.

An ontological model is another kind of computer model. It's a way of representing relationships between different concepts as well as their properties. These relationships are often obvious to the human mind but need to be explained to a computer. We all know that a bird flies or that tables have legs. The wealth and depth of knowledge to which most humans have instant access is literally mind-boggling. But for a computer program to know these things, it must be told. And the way this is done is through an ontology.

Let's take a quick look at an ontology for a book (and in the interests of clarity and brevity, this ontology is far from being complete). A book is an object. It is made up of chapters, which are made up of pages which are made up of words. It has a title and might be fiction or non-fiction. If it's fiction, it could be a crime novel. The book is written by an author (who is a person) and published by a publisher (which is a corporation) with the aid of an agent. An edition of the book is bought (thank you) and read by a reader (also a person). The author, the agent and the reader all have names. Books, persons, authors and so on are all concepts, linked by relationships, as shown in Figure 8.1. The relationship between a book and an author could be characterised as "is written by". Some of these relationships are hierarchical: a book is made up of chapters. In addition, concepts may have properties: a book has a number of chapters. It is the codification of these concepts and relationships that allows the software to make links and build language libraries.

How do machines learn?

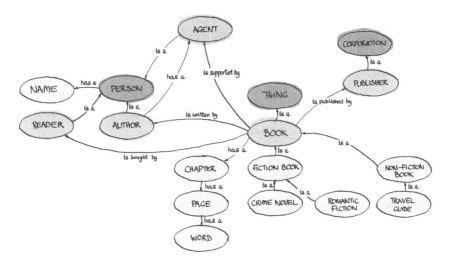

FIGURE 8.1
Ontology for a Book.

The "machine" (and here we mean a combination of hardware, software and data), also referred to as an "agent", learns by analysing the data to which it has access, referred to as the "environment".

For AI that doesn't learn, the agent is already aware of the full set of rules that it has to follow.

In ML, there are broadly three approaches:

- Supervised learning
- Unsupervised learning
- Reinforcement learning

Supervised learning provides the agent with the outcome of its action, either as a set of pre-loaded data or as feedback after each action. Think of the agent as a young child, being told "no" by a parent following every action. Eventually, the child is able to predict the likely outcome ("generalisation") even if it hasn't tried that specific action before.

Reinforcement learning is where the agent receives a reward following each action. Again, imagine a child learning to navigate from home to school or the local playground. The amount of time taken following each route is assessed, and the child naturally attempts to minimise the amount of time needed. The agent assesses the success of its choices without any external input. One additional complexity is the need for the agent to introduce new actions, usually exploiting the most efficient route of which it is aware but occasionally exploring new routes that may, in fact, further improve its effectiveness.

Unsupervised learning differs from these two methods: rather than seeking a specific goal, the agent analyses data sets (the results of actions and outcomes) to identify patterns in the data.

Language Models and Neural Networks

Language models essentially serve the purpose of predicting the next word in any given sentence. Initially, these were based on relatively simple rules, then by statistical analysis based on large libraries of words and context (called a *corpus*). In the internet age, the available language data is almost inconceivably large, leading to LLMs.

These models typically apply a statistical analysis to words in sequences, assessing the likelihood of the following word with more certainty depending on the number of preceding words.

More recently, the use of artificial neural networks has massively accelerated the learning and accuracy of language models. An artificial neural network consists of a number of nodes that act like neurons in an animal brain. The nodes are arranged in layers with input and output layers separated by a number of hidden layers. The associations between each of these linked neurons are weighted. The weighting is adjusted during a process of supervised learning whereby sample inputs and desired outputs are fed into the network and the network's output is compared to the sample.

For example, if the phrase "the cat sat on the" is provided as an input, and "mat" as an expected output. If the neural network responds with "mat", the weighting of the associations in the network is increased. If the network's output is "mouse", the weightings are reduced.

What's Generative AI?

Generative AI (or "GenAI") is a branch of AI where the agent is capable of not only learning from its available media libraries but also of reproducing work of a similar nature. This could be text, poetry, artwork, music or even software.

The most common use of generative AI is in chatbots and predictive text for word processors and other communication media. But increasingly, as it has become more sophisticated with the availability of ChatGPT, DALL-E and other engines, generative AI has been used for the creation of artistic endeavours from musical compositions to artwork.

Typically, generative AI tools accept natural language requests, which they turn into the required output. The type of output typically depends on the data that the AI uses for its learning.

For example, DALL-E, a text-to-image converter – named in homage to Disney's charming robot WALL-E and the creative genius Salvador Dali – uses pairings of text and imagery to build a picture out of its vast array of components.

What's Intelligence?

AI, especially generative AI, has been generating a lot of noise recently. There are concerns around the creation of content that will take jobs away from human beings, concerns over safety including "deepfakes" where pictures or videos featuring real people (whether celebrities or otherwise) can be fabricated with malicious intent and wider concerns over the responsible use of AI.

Amid all this furore, it's important to remember that computers are still basically idiots. That hasn't changed. They now have access to inconceivable amounts of information (recent models incorporate hundreds of billions of data points) and sophisticated neural network architecture, but a computer will still only do exactly what its software tells it to do.

AI, as we have seen, is not real intelligence, even so. It is just able to simulate intelligence by considering a huge array of parameters. There are arguments that "strong AI" is indeed akin to intelligence. On the flipside, there's an argument to the effect that so-called human intelligence is simply a mechanical response to stimuli.

In his 1980 paper *Minds, Brains, and Programs*,[13] American philosopher John Searle proposes a thought experiment that is referred to as the Chinese room. He imagines that he (a native English speaker with no knowledge of Chinese language or characters) sits in a locked room with a set of written instructions (in English) and a collection of Chinese characters that to him are meaningless. He is then fed a second set of Chinese characters.

Following the written instructions and his own set of characters, he is able to supply a response to the input. Because of the instructions and the data he has, his responses are meaningful to a native Chinese speaker. Searle then compares this to the case where he is simply fed the same input written in English to which he provides his own written responses. In this second case, his responses are meaningful to a native English speaker.

Although the outcome is the same (understandable responses), in the second case, because he understands English, he has demonstrated intelligence. A counterargument is that in the first instance, the intelligence has been provided by the authors of the instructions. Although intelligence has been demonstrated, arguably it was not by the person in the room and is thus one step removed

It's a strong argument that helps to clarify the real question. But, at the end of the day, it doesn't actually matter. Just like a front-line soldier struck by a bullet (where it makes no difference to him or her whether the bullet was fired with specific personal intent by a sniper or was part of a spray of indiscriminate enemy fire), if your job is one of the many that will be at risk from AI, you probably don't care whether the machine in question is using genuine intelligence or just a mechanical response to do your old job.

WHERE NEXT?

The future of AI is probably more open to debate than any other domain in information technology. Few would feel brave enough to make any predictions. Most of us are still in something of a head spin from the developments in the recent past.

It might be worth, however, considering some of the drivers that will have an influence.

Broadly, these are technological advances, language and model improvements, corporate activity and public debate on ethics and safety.

Regardless of the direction AI takes, we can be sure that there will be an exponential growth in the level of human and AI collaboration in both creative and executive processes, aiding in business processing, software design and artistic endeavours such as artwork, writing and musical composition.

Technology Advances

Recent developments in the field of ML can be largely attributed to more sophisticated neural network designs, such as deep neural networks and transformers. We can expect developments in specialised hardware from areas such as neuromorphic engineering to more closely mimic the human brain. Integration with quantum computing may also help to increase computational capacity and efficiency.

In addition, we can expect advances in autonomous technologies such as those used by self-driving vehicles, drones and robots. These automata will continue to improve their perception and control, advancing in leaps and bounds (quite literally) to finally realise the dream of the ancient thinkers and dreamers who wrote of intelligent and independent autonomous machines.

Language and Model Improvements

The natural language models used by public AI will benefit from the vast exposure and usage they currently enjoy. As more people across the globe use AI, the engines themselves will have access to an ever-growing corpus of linguistic data. Coupled with continued advances in ML techniques, we can expect more sophisticated chatbots and virtual assistants, with improved skills and wider vocabulary. Bots will become more sophisticated, understanding nuances and context, even emotion.

AI systems will also become better at generalising, transferring knowledge from one task and applying it to others. This will increase the versatility of AI systems, which will require less training to become productive in new disciplines (and potentially uniting hitherto disparate disciplines).

Training of LLMs may well become something of a cottage industry of its own. Specialised LLMs could be trained by experts in the relevant field (such as financial or medical) to reduce the risk of confabulation and to ensure that the model has access to the most up-to-date and accurate information.

Another aspect of this brave new world is what is called "prompt engineering". This involves an understanding of the best way to get GenAI chatbots such as Gemini and ChatGPT to respond by writing effective questions or prompts in the first place. ChatGPT accepts many thousands of characters, and by crafting a prompt in something close to pseudocode, the response can be pre-engineered both in content and format. Experts in this field will soon become sought-after professionals in their own right.

Corporate Activity

Another reason that AI has featured so heavily in the press in recent years is the level of corporate activity in the space, with AI startups being bought up (either wholly or in part) for eye-watering sums by the tech giants of the day.

Google/Alphabet (DeepMind and Waymo), Facebook/Meta, Apple (Siri), Microsoft (OpenAI and Copilot) and Amazon (Alexa) are all active, alongside IBM (with their more prosaic business-focused Watson) and even relative newcomers like Salesforce (Einstein). In addition, a number of Chinese tech giants (Alibaba, Tencent, Baidu) have heavy AI research and development agendas.

The dramatic events of November 2023 in the boardroom of OpenAI (where the CEO Sam Altman was first fired, then hired by Microsoft, then rehired by OpenAI on the threat of mass staff walkouts) were the perfect illustration of the anticipated value of the technology and the extraordinary lengths to which corporates would go to try to secure that value.

With the question of AI's applicability and usefulness now more or less answered, we can perhaps expect more volatility as these behemoths compete for the best talent and new ideas.

Ethics and Safety

Recent global summits on the ethics and safety of AI indicate the level of concern over its wider use.

Entirely practical debates over intellectual property, the threats posed by fabricated content and the need for increased efficiency and sustainability will rub shoulders with more esoteric issues such as AI-prosecuted extinction events.

We can expect AI ethics to become a hotly debated topic, addressing biases, accuracy and the right to privacy.

On the plus side, AI can be a strong force for climate change (in the positive sense), increasingly being used to model climate change scenarios, optimise energy consumption and develop more sustainable practices across more mundane but equally damaging industries.

SO WHAT?

What does AI mean for you, oh soon-to-be-out-of-a-job business leader?

First, that's not likely to happen any time in the near future.

Sure, AI is likely to put millions of jobs at risk across the globe, but as we noted at the beginning of this section, automation in general has already replaced ten times that number. The capacity of human ingenuity that will be released by such a dynamic shift of labour will result in a plethora of new jobs, all of which will need insightful management – the sort of management only you, the business leader, can provide.

AI will be a tool, no more, for some time to come.

You're already using AI when you spell-check a document or email or when you accept a predicted next word as you type. These don't feel like violations, and no one gets put out of a job as a result. There will be other uses of AI which will soon become normalised activity – gathering research, getting ideas, supporting the production of presentations and documentation. Just as every business now has a computer on every desk, and every business is connected to the internet, every business is using AI and will use it more and more.

However, there are a few questions that you might want to ask yourself.

- How effective is generative AI?
- Should I use AI to enhance productivity?
- How can I spot an AI opportunity?
- Should I use AI to replace my project team?

How Effective Is Generative AI?

There's no doubt that GenAI can be breathtakingly impressive. We've all seen generated artwork that is both stunning and convincing. The cartoons in this book (at the start of each chapter) have been generated by AI (mostly). And there's no denying that the brief history that it generated at the start of this section from a perfunctory brief was both readable and accurate.

Perhaps we've marvelled at a poem written to combine two normally unrelated concepts.

Some of these feats are indeed astounding. Others are, well, a bit like a dog playing chess. It's not that it's being done well, but it's remarkable to see it being done at all.

Here's a ChatGPT-generated haiku, combining "AI" and "business":

Machines crunching data,
Business thrives on AI's pulse,
Future merged as one.

Amusing? Pithy? Impressive? As a piece of work that we know has been generated by a machine, of course. But is it actually a good haiku? We're no judges of such things, but it does seem just a little, well, prosaic.

Let's look at the cartoons. Regardless of whether you found them gently amusing or not, now that you know they were machine-generated, you may want to revisit them and reappraise. But it's worth noting that almost none of them were generated well the first time, and it took numerous iterations in each case before something use-able was produced. Not that "iterations" is really an accurate word for the process. Even when we asked for a small tweak to the output, the next version bore almost no resemblance to the previous. And the text description supplied by the AI often bore no relation to the cartoon itself. If not to make a point, it would have been better to employ a human artist who could have applied the necessary adjustments to produce exactly what was needed. And the AI was simply terrible at producing speech or text (due to the graphic nature of the response). The captions for all of the cartoons were written by us.

The only exception is the cartoon for this section. We gave ChatGPT the brief "draw an amusing cartoon featuring AI in business". Take another look. It's quite funny and very relevant to the brief (although we'd prefer to have seen a more diverse board...). Now take a look at just one of the many "fails" we got for the same brief (Figure 8.2).

It's not just that it isn't particularly funny. It's riddled with spelling mistakes and spurious words (don't get us started on the rogue apostrophe!). And we're not entirely sure what's going on with the picture above the desk. Very much not a reliable output.

And that history piece at the beginning of this chapter? Short, quite general and missing a number of key components. Nothing in it is factually incorrect (which is a relief), but it's not entirely hitting the brief.

FIGURE 8.2
AI Cartoon Fail.

Factual correctness is itself something of a challenge for generative AI. An LLM is based entirely on input from a corpus that includes personal posts on social media (whether accurate or not), Wikipedia and other information sites. Anecdotally, therefore, responses from ChatGPT and its cohort are prone to confabulation (also known as hallucination). This can be exacerbated by prompting it with questions that are themselves factually incorrect, such as "Who won the soccer World Cup in 1066?" Sadly, in this case, ChatGPT was way ahead of us:

> The World Cup in soccer, organized by FIFA, did not exist in 1066. The first FIFA World Cup was held in 1930, in Uruguay. The 1066 date is notable in history primarily for the Battle of Hastings, which was a key event in the Norman Conquest of England. This battle had nothing to do with soccer or any sports events.

The bottom line is that generative AI will have its uses. As a chatbot for your website, especially one that you can narrow down its scope to be specific to your business, it can be relied upon to provide a first line of response to your clients. For most other business applications, you're likely to want to trust your human judgement to at the very least review and edit any AI output before putting your corporate name to it.

Should I Use AI to Enhance Productivity?

Hell yes.

This is where AI (especially LLMs) can really step into your business and up your corporate game. We're not suggesting that you invest billions in building your own AI capability. But there are plenty of AI-enabled business applications that will provide you with the potential for a step change in productivity.

Client communications could be improved through the use of chatbots on your website or through automated responses to emails (perhaps with a human to review the final copy). If a client has hand-written a letter, you could use AI-enhanced OCR (optical character recognition) to digitise it. Generative AI in the form of chatbots would be great at providing background information and educational content to your clients. Another option to avoid the potential embarrassment of a response that contains confabulated data might be to use AI to streamline the client's prompt and match it to a set of pre-fabricated model prompts, each of which will have a defined answer (a sort of "chatbot 1.5").

Converting unstructured data to structured data is a key potential use for AI. Documentation that you receive (whether from clients, suppliers or more generally from third parties) is often unstructured. Think of a letter from a client informing you of a change of address. The client isn't going to handily break down their new address into Line 1, Line 2 and so on. They will simply write their new address out. AI can scrape such communications and glean the relevant data and data fields, placing the output into a structured file that can then be fed into your database.

Central functions such as HR and finance could be improved by using AI-enhanced software to identify trends in spending and expenses or to analyse factors in staff retention or even staff productivity.

Sales and relationship management could be enhanced by being able to analyse conversion rates and the effectiveness of marketing campaigns and by tracking sales or marketing trends.

Business-specific functionality: Depending on your line of business, there may be applications and tools that include AI to manage workflows or output. And if not, there might be an opportunity for you to partner with a provider of industry applications to introduce AI capabilities. Focus on cases where text needs to be analysed or produced in significant quantities while avoiding exposing your business to the risk of unfiltered AI content.

Remember that AI is just software. You should apply all the rules you would apply for a software decision before deciding to pursue an AI solution. It's all very well installing an AI-enabled curriculum vitae or employment resume scanner for your HR team, but if you only have one vacancy a month to fill, you could probably have spent your money elsewhere.

How Can I Spot an AI Opportunity?

Opportunities for AI-enabled solutions (of the more "traditional" sort) will be all around you.

Typically, there will be a large amount of data available, making an automated solution appropriate. As with any software solution, target your least effective processes or where you have the most volume or value (although there is merit in starting small, with a less critical process initially).

Look at where mistakes happen in your organisation. Why do they happen? Is it a repetitive process that's done manually? Or is there a process that's so complex that people are called on to make difficult decisions? The first could be a candidate for robotic automation, whereas the second might benefit from some kind of expert system.

Should I Use Generative AI to Replace My Project Team?

The answer to this should be a resounding no.

Projects are very complex processes, with a large number of nuanced factors. It's unlikely that AI will become sophisticated enough to manage projects or conduct business analysis.

But there will certainly be areas where AI can help.

A large part of business analysis is understanding data. AI might be able to help analyse that data and provide a summary or a breakdown that will aid understanding.

Software development might also benefit from AI. GenAI isn't ready to write all of your code just yet, but it can certainly create templates and frameworks for the developer, allowing them to make quicker progress on the more mundane aspects of coding to get to the complex part more quickly.

Testing, and test automation, is also an area that can be made more efficient through AI. Test data can be generated quickly, and automated test packs could be built more quickly, ensuring a wider coverage of functionality and data values.

And training and business readiness could be made simpler and more impactful by the use of generative AI to create charts and graphics. But perhaps not cartoons, just yet....

NOTES

1 *Competing in the Age of AI* by Marco Iansiti and Karim R. Lakhani, 2020.
2 *Computing Machinery and Intelligence* by Alan Turing, 1950.
3 https://blogs.umass.edu/brain-wars/files/2016/03/rosenblatt-1957.pdf
4 http://incompleteideas.net/book/11/node3.html
5 *Some Studies in Machine Learning Using the Game of Checkers* by Arthur Samuel, 1959.
6 https://cse.buffalo.edu/~rapaport/572/S02/weizenbaum.eliza.1966.pdf
7 *Perceptrons* by Marvin Minsky and Seymour Papert, 1969.
8 *Programming a Computer for Playing Chess* by Claude E. Shannon.
9 https://videogamehistorian.wordpress.com/2014/01/22/the-priesthood-at-play-computer-games-in-the-1950s/
10 www.science.org/doi/10.1126/science.aar6404
11 www.computerhistory.org/internethistory/1970s/
12 www.jaberwacky.com
13 *Minds, Brains and Programs* by John Searle.

9

Who Are the People?

Once a new technology rolls over you, if you're not part of the steamroller, you're part of the road.

Stewart Brand

*Like everyone else in the meeting, Mike had no trouble
identifying the new Senior Web Designer ....*

DOI: 10.4324/9781003372660-9

In this book we've looked at hardware, software, data, interfaces, blockchains, artificial intelligence (AI) and machine learning, projects and risks of all sorts. We've encountered integrated circuits, hard drives and solid-state memory, CPUs and server racks, printers and flat screens, assembler and object-oriented languages, packet switching and the internet, tokenisation and smart contracts, agile and waterfall methodologies and many more evolutions and variations.

If you've stayed with us this far, then you should have a pretty good grasp of the IT industry and technology projects.

But like any industry, it's not just about the things, the ideas and the concepts.

It's about *people.*

And in this section, we take a quick look at the people who make up the industry.

After a whistle-stop tour through some of the historical figures who appear elsewhere in the book (and a few that didn't quite make the cut), we'll take you through a non-exhaustive list of the different *IT professionals* who are there to help you realise your business goals through technology innovation. As always, we consult our crystal ball to try to predict where these roles might be headed and what new roles might be created to support them.

And at the end, as always, we have a few questions that you might want to ask yourself or your IT project team.

███████████

WHY SHOULD I CARE?

Have you ever watched a sport where you don't really understand the rules? Who's the guy throwing the ball? Why are they all just standing around? Why does she get to pick the ball up but everyone else has to kick it? (OK, we're pretty sure you must know that last one).

If you get involved with an IT project but don't know who the team are and what they do, you run the risk of missing out on some key opportunities (at best) or making a fool of yourself.

"Data scientist? Me? No, I'm a data analyst. Surely that was obvious…? You're dead to me…".

While it's unlikely that any of your project team will feel genuinely insulted if you misjudge their exact role, we think that a lot of time (and goodwill) can be saved if you have a working idea of who is who and how *each member of the team contributes* to the overall goal. We therefore present this handy list as a reminder of the various roles we have introduced elsewhere in this book, so you have them all in one place, plus a few more we thought you might want to know about.

HOW DID WE GET HERE?

Who were the innovators and visionaries that built the IT industry? Who would be in our "IT Hall of Fame" (there is an *actual* IT Hall of Fame hosted by CompTIA)?

We're sure it won't escape your notice that the list features predominantly European and American males. That is not unique to the world of technology – societies of the eighteenth to twentieth centuries simply didn't provide the same levels of opportunity to women or to those from non-European backgrounds. But if Web3 can teach us anything, it's that the democratisation of technology is capable of reaching all inhabitants of the globe. It is incumbent on global society to ensure that any future list should contain a far more diverse mix of pioneers. Vision and the entrepreneurial spirit know nothing about skin colour, gender, credo or any other societal label.

If just one of the names on this list inspires you to find out a little bit more about the work done by the pioneers and architects of the information revolution, we'll take that as a win. If anything in the list (or the rest of this book for that matter) inspires you to go out and become a pioneer yourself, or to support others in their endeavours to push back the boundaries of technology, we'll consider that to be a triumph!

Ancients and Mathematicians

Archimedes (287–212 BC)

Ancient Greek mathematician and inventor. Among his more famous mathematical creations, he was the first person to define a number so large that it couldn't be physically counted (the number of grains of sand in the universe). As part of this definition, he also invented exponential notation and the law of exponents which is at the root of logarithmic calculation.

Archimedes died during the siege of Syracuse, when he was allegedly killed by a Roman soldier after refusing to leave his mathematical writings.

Hero of Alexandria (First Century AD)

Legendary creator of automata in the ancient world, famed for inventing a steam engine, a vending machine that dispensed holy water and temple doors that opened automatically. He was also said to have produced an entirely mechanical play driven by ropes and pulleys.

Muhammad, Ahmad and Al-Hasan ibn Mūsā ibn Shākir (Ninth Century AD)

Also known as the Banū Mūsā, these three Persian brothers were educated in the House of Wisdom in Baghdad where they translated many ancient Greek works. Part of the Islamic Golden Age, they were the prolific authors of many scientific books, including the *Book of Ingenious Devices* which contained designs for inventions and steam and water-driven automata. They were the first to propose self-regulating valves for water-driven machines through the use of a feedback loop, and their automatic flute player could be thought of as the first programmable automaton.

Muḥammad ibn Mūsā al-Khwārizmī (Ninth Century AD)

Persian mathematician, author of *The Compendious Book on Calculation by Completion and Balancing*, dubbed the "father of algebra" and whose name came to become synonymous with mathematical formulae ("algorithms"). Known for his works rather than for his life, of which not a great deal is certain. There is a suspicion that he and his namesake among the Banū Mūsā are one and the same.

John Napier (1550–1617)

Scottish mathematician and inventor of logarithms, early proponent of the decimal point and inventor of a binary notation he called *Rabdologie*.

Napier also invented Napier's bones, a "programmable" hardware solution to complex multiplications.

In his spare time, Napier reputedly wrote a paper on war machines including a "burning mirror" and an armoured metal chariot, and dabbled in the occult, keeping a rooster as a familiar.

John Graunt (1620–1674)

London hat-maker regarded as the founder of demography and often considered the father of statistics. Graunt's 1662 work, *Natural and Political Observations Mentioned in a Following Index and Made upon the Bills of Mortality*, based on data from weekly bills of mortality included findings in data tables and statistical analysis. Graunt was the first person known to use data analysis techniques in this way.

Blaise Pascal (1623–1662)

French mathematician and inventor. Pascal's works covered mathematics, philosophy and physics, but he enters our list for the invention in 1642 of the Pascaline, a mechanical calculator that paved the way for later machines.

Gottfried Wilhelm von Leibniz (1646–1716)

German polymath who made pivotal contributions to various fields, including mathematics, philosophy and computer science. He invented the Stepped Reckoner, a device capable of performing addition, subtraction, multiplication and division. Leibniz's design introduced the use of the Leibnitz wheel (a kind of stepped drum), a fundamental component that would be utilised in calculating machines for centuries. His work laid foundational concepts for binary systems, which are integral to modern computer operations and digital logic.

Leibnitz is also commonly regarded as "the last universal genius" – having proficient knowledge in nearly every field of contemporary intellectual endeavour.

Industrialists and Inventors

Joseph Marie Jacquard (1752–1834)

French weaver and inventor best known for developing the Jacquard loom, a groundbreaking mechanical loom that used punched cards to control weaving patterns. Jacquard's innovation in the use of physical cards with punched holes to represent information was adopted by a host of later inventors such as Charles Babbage, Herman Hollerith and others.

William Playfair (1759–1823)

Scottish engineer, political economist and secret agent who is widely recognised for his pioneering contributions to data analytics and data visualisation. He is credited with inventing the line graph, the bar chart and the pie chart, which revolutionised the way statistical data was represented and visualised. In introducing these graphical methods, Playfair provided a new and intuitive way to understand complex data sets, laying the groundwork for modern data visualisation techniques and tools that are fundamental in today's data analytics and interpretation.

Playfair had something of a chequered career, being at times an engineer, an accountant, a merchant, an economist, a revolutionary (taking part in the storming of the Bastille), a convict and a spy among many others.

Charles Joseph Minard (1781–1870)

French civil engineer and early proponent of the use of information graphics. Famous for the cartographic visualisation of Napoleon's disastrous Russian campaign in 1812.

Charles Xavier Thomas de Colmar (1785–1870)

French inventor and entrepreneur. Inventor of the Arithmometer, the first commercially successful mechanical calculator. This groundbreaking device could perform basic arithmetic operations, setting the foundation for the mechanical calculating industry and influencing subsequent designs and innovations in the field of computational devices.

The idea for the Arithmometer came to Colmar while he was a quartermaster in Napoleon's army, to help him with the vast number of calculations required for that role.

Charles Babbage (1791–1871)

English mathematician, engineer and inventor often hailed as the "father of the computer". He is best known for conceiving and designing the Analytical Engine, an ambitious mechanical general-purpose computer. Babbage's groundbreaking design included features found in modern computers, such as an arithmetic logic unit, control flow through conditional branching and loops and integrated memory. While the Analytical Engine was never fully built in his lifetime, its principles laid the foundation for future generations of computer hardware. Additionally, Babbage's collaboration with Ada Lovelace, who wrote an algorithm intended for the Engine, marks one of the earliest instances of computer programming, bridging both hardware and software realms.

Babbage also gave his name to a principle he noted in his paper *On the Economy of Machinery and Manufactures* (1832), namely that skilled workers typically spend time doing tasks below their skill level, whereas it would be more efficient to break the job down into more specialised tasks. The Babbage Principle is foundational to modern production methods.

Samuel Morse (1791–1872)

American inventor and artist best known for the development of the telegraph and the invention of Morse code, which enabled messages to be sent over vast distances through electrical signals. This innovation marked one of the earliest forms of digital communication and laid the groundwork for subsequent communication technologies, playing a crucial role in the evolution of computer networking by emphasising the importance of rapid and efficient information transmission of data across networks.

Morse was an accomplished artist. His masterpiece, Dying Hercules, was a commentary on the state of the relationship between Great Britain and the United States of America, who were at the time in conflict.

William Cooke (1806–1879) and Charles Wheatstone (1802–1875)

British engineers who co-invented the electric telegraph in the 1830s, operating the first commercial line between Euston and Camden Town in London in 1837.

Alfred Vail (1807–1859)

American inventor. In partnership with Samuel Morse, Vail was central in developing electric telegraphy between 1837 and 1844, significantly improving Morse's original code.

Ada Lovelace (1815–1852)

English mathematician widely regarded as the "first computer programmer". While working with Charles Babbage on the designs for his Analytical Engine, Lovelace saw beyond its arithmetic capabilities and recognised its potential for more complex tasks. She documented and annotated its workings in great detail and, in doing so, wrote what is considered the first algorithm intended for implementation on a computer. Her visionary insights are regarded as a foundational contribution to computer software and the very concept of programming.

Lovelace was the sole legitimate child of the English romantic poet Lord Byron.

George Boole (1815–1864)

English mathematician and logician, best known for his pioneering work in what came to be known as Boolean algebra. This system of algebra, in which variables have only two possible values (true or false or 1 and 0), laid the foundation for modern digital computer logic. Boole's innovations provided the framework for the design of both electronic circuits in computer hardware and logical algorithms in computer software making Boole a fundamental figure in the evolution of information technology.

Boole died of pneumonia which he caught after walking in heavy rain to deliver a lecture. Boole's wife illogically believed that remedies for illnesses should reflect their causes so she wrapped him in wet blankets with – ironically – the logical outcome.

Florence Nightingale (1820–1910)

British nursing reformer who famously used a form of pie chart to demonstrate causes of mortality in the Crimean War.

Émile Baudot (1845–1903)

French engineer, best known for inventing the Baudot code, a character set designed for telegraphy using a fixed number of bits for each letter, to simplify coding and decoding. His system improved the efficiency of telegraph transmission and laid down principles for multiplexed communications.

In his youth, Baudot served in the French Post & Telegraph Administration as an apprentice operator, where he was taught both Morse code and the operation of telegraph machinery.

Alexander Graham Bell (1847–1922)

Scottish-born inventor and (disputed) inventor of the telephone. Bell's innovative and foundational work in the field of telecommunications, and his business acumen, paved the way for both modern telecommunications and the infrastructure that would eventually support digital computer networking.

Alexander Graham Bell faced numerous challenges over his right to be identified as the telephone's inventor, notably from Elisha Gray. Bell successfully defended himself in over 600 court cases, resulting in, among other things, a reworking of the patenting process to introduce more rigour and require more substantive documentation.

Herman Hollerith (1860–1929)

American inventor and statistician best known for developing a mechanical tabulating machine that used punched cards to process large amounts of data, first used for the 1890 US Census. Hollerith founded the Tabulating Machine Company, which later became IBM. Hollerith's innovations in mechanical data processing laid critical groundwork for the development of modern computer hardware, marking him as a significant figure in the history of computing.

Henry L. Gantt (1861–1919)

American mechanical engineer and management consultant recognised for his significant contributions to project management. Gantt is best known for introducing the Gantt chart, a visual scheduling tool that displays tasks or activities plotted against time.

Dorr Felt (1862–1930)

American inventor known for his significant contributions to the field of mechanical calculating devices. He is best remembered as the inventor of the Comptometer, a key-driven mechanical calculator. Felt's prototype was built in a few days using household objects, but the Comptometer was hugely commercially successful. Comptometers were still being made right up until the 1970s.

Donald Murray (1865–1945)

Inventor from New Zealand who linked a conventional QWERTY type-writer to telegraphs using the Baudot code to enable operators untrained in Morse code to send and receive messages. Murray's modified code remained the standard for electronic telegraphy until the introduction of ASCII in 1961.

By championing the QWERTY keyboard in this way, Murray secured its dominance over other formats.

Fritz Pfleumer (1881–1945)

German engineer notable for his pioneering work in magnetic data storage through the invention of magnetic tape in 1928 by coating a strip of paper with a thin layer of powdered iron oxide. Although his intention was to magnetically record sound, the technique was later adopted for data storage.

Computer Age Pioneers

Vannevar Bush (1890–1974)

American engineer and inventor whose visionary ideas laid the groundwork for the digital age and the development of the internet. His seminal 1945 essay, "As We May Think", introduced the concept of the "Memex", a hypothetical desk-based device that allowed users to store information on microfiche, linking disparate files together with what he called "associative trails". This idea of linking and retrieving information is seen as a conceptual precursor to the hyperlink, a foundational element of the World Wide Web.

George Stibitz (1904–1995)

American mathematician and computer scientist credited with the creation of the first fully digital calculator while working at Bell Labs in 1937. Stibitz called his machine the "Model K" because he built it at his kitchen table.

Grace Hopper (1906–1992)

American computer scientist, often hailed as the "mother of computer programming". While working on UNIVAC, she identified the need for a compiler to convert human-readable commands into machine code. She developed the first compiler ("A-0"), wrote one of the first programming languages ("FLOW-MATIC") and played a pivotal role in the creation of COBOL, one of the earliest programming languages designed specifically for business applications.

Konrad Zuse (1910–1995)

German civil engineer and computer pioneer best known for creating the Z3 in 1941, often recognised as the world's first programmable, fully automatic digital computer. Zuse's machines used binary and floating-point arithmetic, laying the groundwork for many of the principles and architectures found in modern computers.

Zuse also conceptualised a high-level programming language called Plankalkül, which influenced later languages.

Alan Turing (1912–1954)

British mathematician, logician and computer scientist often regarded as the "father of modern computing". He is best known for his conceptualisation in 1936 of the "Turing machine", a theoretical construct that formed the foundation of algorithms and computation, defining the limits of what can be computed. The concept played a pivotal role in the development of the digital computer and is still in use today – modern blockchain smart contracts are deemed to be "Turing-complete". A subsequent paper in 1950 introduced the Turing Test, a measure of machine intelligence, which remains influential in the field of AI.

Turing was also a leading participant in the top-secret wartime codebreaking operation at Bletchley Park, where he constructed his Bombe machine to help break the Enigma code.

Arguably the most influential thinker and inventor of the pioneering age, Turing's concepts continue to guide even the most advanced fields of computer technology.

Hedy Lamarr (1914–2000)

Actress turned inventor who, during World War II, devised a frequency-hopping guidance system for Allied torpedoes. Lamarr's contributions went largely unrecognised during her lifetime, but her work is now recognised as a precursor to the development of modern wireless communication technologies such as Bluetooth and Wi-Fi, and she is rightly celebrated for breaking stereotypes about the roles and capabilities of women in science and technology.

John Tukey (1915–2000)

American mathematician, statistician and transformational data scientist. Credited with coining the term "bit" (a portmanteau of "binary digit") and for the first published use of the word "software".

Joseph Carl Robnett Licklider (1915–1990)

Commonly known as J.C.R. Licklider or simply "Lick", an American computer scientist and visionary who is often referred to as the "father of the Internet".

Licklider conceived of a global internet while at Defense Advanced Research Projects Agency (DARPA) in the 1960s, laying the groundwork for what would later become the internet. His seminal paper, "Man-Computer Symbiosis", emphasised the potential of interactive computing and envisioned a future where humans and machines would work collaboratively. Licklider's vision, funding initiatives and encouragement of his colleagues at DARPA (including Bob Taylor and Lawrance Roberts) led directly to the development of the ARPANET, the precursor to the modern internet.

Claude Shannon (1916–2001)

The "father of information theory" and author in 1948 of the seminal paper *A Mathematical Theory of Communication*, in which he outlined the concept of a "bit" (a term he coined as the fundamental unit of digital communication) and introduced the idea of using mathematics to quantify information. He was also a pioneer in AI and its application to the game of chess.

Edgar Codd (1923–2003)

British computer scientist, influential in the field of data and information science. Codd is best known for introducing the relational database model in 1970, revolutionising how data was stored, organised and retrieved in databases. His model remains the standard in database technology.

Jack Kilby (1923–2005) and Robert Noyce (1927–1990)

Computer engineers who independently created integrated circuits in 1958 (Kilby at Texas Instruments using germanium and Noyce of Fairchild Semiconductor using silicon). These inventions combined multiple electronic components into a single unit, marking a significant step forward in miniaturisation and efficiency, paving the way for the exponential growth of electronic devices.

John Backus (1924–2007)

American computer scientist known for the development of the Fortran programming language, the progenitor of most modern languages. Backus also helped develop the Backus-Naur Form (BNF), a notation to describe formal language syntax.

Betty Jennings (1924–2011)

American computer scientist, one of the original team of female programmers for ENIAC (known as the "ENIAC Girls"). The team tackled complex computational problems, converting mathematical equations into machine-readable code.

John G. Kemeny (1926–1992) and Thomas E. Kurtz (b 1928)

American computer scientists who co-developed the programming language BASIC. Designed for simplicity, BASIC made computer programming more accessible to the general public, thus playing a significant role in the democratisation of software and programming.

Paul Baran (1926–2011) and Donald Davies (1924–2000)

Engineers who independently invented the concept of packet switching, the fundamental model still used in computer networks today.

John McCarthy (1927–2011)

One of the pioneers of AI, credited with coining the term "AI" and organiser the Dartmouth Conference in 1956 which brought together key researchers in the fields of neural nets, language simulation and machine learning.

Marvin Minsky (1927–2016)

Another AI pioneer and co-founder of the Massachusetts Institute of Technology's AI laboratory. His work on the theory of neural networks and his advocacy for the potential of AI had a significant influence on the direction of early AI research.

Gordon Moore (1929–2023)

American engineer and co-founder of Intel. Most renowned for "Moore's Law", his 1965 predication that the number of transistors on a microchip would double approximately every two years, leading to an exponential increase in computing power and efficiency. This (perhaps self-fulfilling) observation has been remarkably accurate.

Edsger W. Dijkstra (1930–2002)

Dutch computer scientist and champion of structured programming. His famous paper, "Go To Statement Considered Harmful", emphasised the importance of control flow, urging the avoidance of the at-the-time popular "Go To" statement, leading to more readable and manageable code.

Tony Hoare (b 1934)

British computer scientist whose contributions have deeply influenced the field of software development and verification. A cornerstone of his work in software is the introduction of Hoare Logic, an axiomatic system that provides a rigorous framework for the verification of program correctness.

Margaret Hamilton (b 1936)

American computer scientist and systems engineer who played a critical role in developing the software for NASA's Apollo Guidance Computer (AGC) that controlled the Apollo moon missions. Hamilton is credited with coining the term "software engineering", emphasising the discipline and rigour required in software development.

Information Revolutionaries

Dennis Ritchie (1941–2011) and Ken Thompson (b 1943)

Computer scientists working at Bell Labs who designed two of the most enduring and influential programming languages: UNIX for operating systems and the C programming language. Many contemporary operating systems, including Linux and macOS, trace their heritage back to UNIX,

while C was the progenitor for a host of later languages including C++, C#
and Objective-C.

Larry Ellison (b 1944)

American businessman and founder of Oracle. Ellison spotted an opportunity to be a first mover in the world of relational databases having attended
lectures by Edgar Codd. Oracle v2 (there was no v1) was launched in 1979.

Robert Metcalfe (b 1946) and David Boggs (1950–2022)

Engineers best known for their pioneering work on the development of
Ethernet technology. Metcalfe went on to form 3Com and proposed
"Metcalfe's Law" which states that the value of a network grows propor-
tionally with the square of the number of its users.

Geoffrey Hinton (b 1947)

Often referred to as the "godfather of deep learning" and undertook foundational research in neural networks, including backpropagation and deep
learning algorithms. For the business world, Hinton's contributions have
facilitated the development of advanced AI applications in areas such as
speech recognition, image processing and predictive analytics.

Bjarne Stroustrup (b 1950)

Danish computer scientist and creator of the C++ object-oriented programming language.

Dan Bricklin (b 1951)

American business software pioneer and inventor of the first spreadsheet
application VisiCalc while a student at Harvard. VisiCalc almost single-
handedly transformed the personal computer from a curio to a must-have
business accessory.

Bill Gates (b 1955) and Paul Allen (1953–2018)

American computer programmers, innovators, inventors, business magnates and philanthropists. Founders of Microsoft. Together, they spotted the opportunity to bring computer programming to the masses by writing a version of BASIC for the Altair 8800 microcomputer as well as the operating system for the IBM PC. Impelled by Gates' fierce business acumen and innovation, Microsoft's success was ensured with the release of Windows in 1985 followed by Office in 1989 and Internet Explorer in 1995.

Both Gates and Allen became immensely rich and admirably championed philanthropic initiatives in their later lives.

Steve Jobs (1955–2011) and Steve Wozniak (b 1950)

American entrepreneurs, designers and co-founders of Apple Inc., their combined unparalleled vision and innovation reshaped multiple industries (and arguably the daily lives of nearly everyone on the planet). Under their leadership, Apple introduced a series of transformative products, including the Macintosh, the iPod (which revolutionised the mobile audio market), the iPhone (which virtually created the smartphone concept), the iPad (which did the same for tablets) and the entire concept of an app store.

Tim Berners Lee (b 1955)

English computer scientist best known as the inventor of the World Wide Web, the HTML markup language, URLs and HTTP. Founder of the World Wide Web Consortium (W3C). More recently, an advocate for web freedoms including the importance of neutrality and privacy.

Sir Tim was knighted by Queen Elizabeth II in 2004.

James Gosling (b 1955)

Canadian computer scientist best known as the founder and lead designer of the Java programming language.

Guido van Rossum (b 1956)

Dutch programmer best known as the creator of the Python programming language, for which he was granted the title "benevolent dictator for life" by the Python community until he stepped down in 2018.

Post-Revolutionary Innovators

Jeff Bezos (b 1964)

American businessman and founder of Amazon, in 1994. Bezos gave up his job in Wall Street to fulfil his vision of an internet retailer. Initially selling books, Amazon expanded rapidly and is now the world's largest online services company and cloud infrastructure provider through Amazon Web Services.

Bezos is famous for writing the "Bezos memo" in 2002, an email to all staff instructing them to use service interfaces for all communications ensuring that data was gathered centrally rather than distributed across the organisation, beginning the transformation of Amazon from a successful online retailer into a fully digitally transformed global organisation.

David Filo (b 1966) and Jerry Yang (b 1968)

Founders of Yahoo!, one of the first internet search engines. Initially called "Jerry and David's Guide to the World Wide Web", the website was simply a list of other web pages the two college friends found interesting.

Linus Torvalds (b 1969)

Finnish-American computer scientist, creator and lead developer of the Linux kernel and influential member of the Linux Foundation.

Torvalds' personal mascot is a penguin nicknamed Tux, which has been widely adopted by the Linux community as the Linux kernel's mascot.

Larry Page (b 1973) and Sergei Brin (b 1973)

Co-founders of Google. Page's "web crawler" software, Backrub, written for a college project, had indexed billions of web pages, making the pair's search engine more effective than any others. Google was launched in 1998.

Demis Hassabis (b 1976)

Co-founder and CEO of DeepMind, Hassabis has been instrumental in advancing AI through deep learning and neural networks. DeepMind's significant contribution under his guidance is the development of AlphaGo, an AI program that defeated a human world champion in the complex board game Go.

Mark Zuckerberg (b 1984)

Founder of Facebook (now Meta) while at Harvard in 2004 with four friends, Eduardo Saverin, Andrew McCollum, Dustin Moskovitz and Chris Hughes. Zuckerberg remains in active control as CEO and executive chairman.

Satoshi Nakamoto (b????)

Mysterious (and currently unmasked) inventor of blockchain, the bitcoin network and the bitcoin cryptocurrency. Satoshi appeared in 2007 and disappeared from posts in 2012.

Sam Altman (b 1985)

Sam Altman is the CEO of OpenAI, known for its cutting-edge advancements in AI research and for the generative AI revolution that is ChatGPT. In November 2023, Altman was first fired, then rehired by the OpenAI board in a highly publicised corporate spat that also involved Microsoft and an illustration of staff power by the majority of the OpenAI team.

Vitalik Buterin (b 1994)

Russian-Canadian computer programmer, and co-founder of the Ethereum blockchain network. Buterin's vision for a network that did more than move cryptocurrency gave rise to smart contracts and decentralised applications (DApps).

WHAT DOES HERE LOOK LIKE?

There are many, probably hundreds, of different IT job titles (one popular recruitment site claims to offer over 132 different IT roles at the time of writing). They range from the conceptually simple "developer" to the more complex "data scientist", with more roles created as new technologies and techniques emerge (such as the "search engine optimisation [SEO] specialist" or "AI safety technical researcher"). Some roles have evolved over time to cater for the ever-fluid landscape of information technology.

We present, below, a list of the more common job roles. We've tried to keep the list down to a manageable number by focusing on those roles with which the business stakeholder is most likely to come into contact. But we have kept in a couple of mavericks from left field, just to keep you on your toes….

- Governance and management roles
- Architects and analysts
- Developers and testers
- Web professionals
- Operations and servicing

Governance and Management Roles

Chief Technology Officer (CTO)

The CTO (also sometimes called chief information officer or CIO) is the senior technologist in an organisation. The CTO/CIO is responsible for technology operations, research and development. In some organisations, the CTO may also have responsibility for data management (more common for a CIO, naturally). The CTO should report directly to the CEO. Technology is too critical to any modern business for that not to be the case.

Programme Manager/Programme Director

A programme manager or programme director takes responsibility for managing a programme of work designed to effect an outcome or transformation. The programme itself is organised into tranches of delivery, each delivery potentially comprising multiple individual projects. The programme manager reports to the programme board. If you are the sponsor or a key stakeholder in a programme of change, you should ensure that you have an excellent working relationship with the programme manager or director. A programme of work is a huge undertaking, and it's easy for details to be missed or for the overall direction to be lost in constant fire-fighting. Make sure that the programme manager understands your overall aims for the programme and that you listen to them when they have issues which you may be able to help resolve.

Project Manager

A project manager is responsible for delivering a project. The project manager reports to the project governance structure (such as through a steering committee). If you are the sponsor or a key stakeholder for a project, you should ensure that you have an excellent working relationship with the project manager. Make sure that they understand your requirements for the project and ensure that you listen to them (and take action) when they have issues which you may be able to help resolve.

Project Support Officer

The project support officer is part of the project management office (PMO) team. They will help the project team to gather data about progress, take minutes at meetings, ensure that actions and dependencies are tracked and generally provide the grease that keeps the project moving forward. As a business stakeholder, keeping the project support officer onside is helpful – they will have access to the latest information (both official and unofficial) and will keep you in the loop when perhaps official channels are not so forthcoming.

Architects and Analysts

Business Architect

Business architecture is a relatively new concept. It is the blueprint of the organisation – what is it trying to achieve, and what does it need to be able to do to do that? A business architect is the custodian of the organisation's strategies and capabilities, making sure that they are aligned effectively to provide value to the organisation and its shareholders, investors or owners.

If your organisation has business architects, make sure that you help them to understand the vision and then listen to what they have to say about how you need to achieve it. In many ways, they are the closest thing you will have to a pure ally – they won't care about technology platforms or interfaces: their only role is to model the business in a structured way.

Business Analyst

A business analyst is

> responsible for discovering, synthesising and analysing information from a variety of sources within an enterprise, including tools, processes, documentation and stakeholders. The business analyst is responsible for eliciting the actual needs of stakeholders ... in order to determine underlying issues and causes.[1]

As a business stakeholder, you want the business analyst on the project to be your best friend. They are there to understand and represent your requirements to the rest of the project team. But that doesn't mean they will simply write down everything you say! A good business analyst will ask probing questions, challenge your needs and make you really think about what it is you want and in what order you want it.

Solution Architect

A solution architect will have a holistic view of the organisation's technology solution (the applications, the links between them, the hardware on which they run and so on) and will be able to map it to the organisation's business needs. They will use this understanding to define technical solutions to business problems, evolving the overall architecture as they do so. Solution architects often act as the bridge between technical and non-technical stakeholders.

The solution architect is the technologist who probably best understands the overall solution that you need. They will understand how data flows around the system, where it is stored, input and used.

Scrum Master

In agile projects, a scrum is a multi-functional team that comes together for short bursts of activity (called sprints) to achieve a set of objectives defined and prioritised by the product owner. The scrum master is a facilitator for this team, ensuring that the team understands the scrum rules and works well together.

Product Owner

The product owner is another role in an agile project. Combining aspects of a project manager and a business analyst, the product owner is expected to act as the business representative in the agile team, prioritising and setting out requirements as user stories on the product backlog.

Similarly to a business analyst, you can think of the product owner as your voice on the project team. They will want to make sure they really understand your needs, and you should give them every chance to do so. Be clear and have regular contact.

Data Steward

A data steward is a role within the data governance structure of an organisation. The data steward is responsible for ensuring the quality of the organisation's data and that it conforms to the organisation's data governance policies. If you are a data owner, you should ensure that you have regular contact with the data steward(s) in your organisation. They need to feel confident that you know and understand your data.

Data Architect

A data architect works within an organisation to help to define and document its data architecture, including data definition, as well as how and where the data will be managed, transported, stored and used. The data architect is expected to define data models, provide a common business vocabulary, maintain an inventory or dictionary of data and ensure that the organisation's data architecture supports its strategic goals. As a business leader, you should ensure that you have a good working relationship with your data architects – they should know that you take responsibility for your data and can give them a clear steer in case of conflicts.

Data Scientist

A data scientist works with large sets of data to make predictions and recommendations to an organisation. Data science involves mathematical and statistical analysis of structured and unstructured data as well as machine learning to identify patterns. Think of the data scientist as a detective, sifting through vast amounts of corporate data to find clues, patterns, insights or trends and then turning those discoveries into actionable recommendations to the business.

Data Analyst

A data analyst works with data within an organisation to solve data problems, such as poor data quality. Data analysts work on small sets of structured data, typically identifying issues in transmission and conversion between systems.

Information Security Analyst

An information security analyst is responsible for protecting the organisation from cyber threats. They do this in two main ways: operational monitoring and threat analysis on the one hand and by advising on risks and potential preventative measures.

It's in this latter capacity that you're more likely to interact with an information security analyst. They will help you to understand the risks to your data and your processes, advise on best practices and ensure your projects are following relevant company policies.

Developers and Testers

Developer (Full Stack)

A full-stack developer is a developer capable of working on code for all applications. While many programming languages are similar, some are very specialised. The logic and approach for a database-heavy analytical engine running in the background or an overnight process performing a vast number of serial calculations will be very different from a screen application allowing a user to input or manage data in real time or to navigate around a set of dashboards.

The developer is responsible for writing code that meets the detailed requirements that have been documented by a business analyst as well as initial debugging and unit testing of the completed code. You're unlikely to interact directly with them, but as the actual producer of the finished product (the working application), they are the one absolutely critical component in the project machine. You can help them (via the business analyst or the product owner) by being clear about your requirements, keeping the ask simple, and by not changing your mind (too often…).

Developer (Low Code)

A low-code developer uses low-code development platforms to design and create applications. These platforms are designed to reduce the amount of coding required by using visual, drag-and-drop components and ready-made templates.

The low-code developer may even be a business user who has specialised in the creation of business applications, as a "citizen developer". Whatever their background, they should be able to "speak your language" as they design business-friendly applications such as workflows and reports.

Test Analyst

The test analyst (also known as a quality assurance analyst or just "tester") plays a crucial role in the software development lifecycle. Testers may contribute at all stages of testing (although the first stages of testing are more often completed by the developers themselves) including planning and execution of tests, as well as ensuring that any defects are recorded and prioritised for fixing.

You may sometimes forget that testers are professionals. They understand how applications and systems are put together, and they know common mistakes and the best techniques to uncover them.

During user acceptance testing (UAT) in particular, the tester may sit alongside business users to help them to plan and execute a wide range of tests to ensure that the new or amended application is proven to its fullest extent in the time available. The tester's role is to devise a set of end-to-end scenarios and specific tests to achieve this. They may need your support and input to help prioritise their work.

Defect Manager

The defect manager has a very specific role to play in the testing cycle of a project. Once the testers have identified a defect, it needs to be analysed and prioritised (not all defects need to be fixed, remember) and then tracked through the process of design/code/test until it is cleared. Managing this process is the job of the defect manager, and it's a critical component especially near the end of a project when applications are being tested and retested (and regression tested) repeatedly. The opportunity for a critical defect to be simply dropped and never fixed is quite high – nothing rankles as much as a production issue directly impacting your business that was identified during testing but was never corrected.

Web Professionals

User Interface (UI)/User Experience (UX) Designer

A UI/UX designer will make sure that your user-facing applications are well-designed and user-friendly. UI and UX may sound like the same thing, but they are very different. The UI focuses on how the user interacts with the application ("look and feel" of screens, the layout of data and media on the page, how the page or screen responds to user input and so on), whereas the UX goes deeper and covers the overall user experience. An application can have the best, slickest interface imaginable, but if the machine hangs when the user clicks a button, or navigates to a non-existent page, the user's overall experience is not going to be wholesome.

A UI/UX designer is really just a special case of a designer who focuses on these aspects of software design. They will factor in who the user is (e.g. an experienced professional or a casual member of the public), what they might expect to see and do, how they might expect the application to behave and so on.

Again, it's tempting as a business user to think that this is simple or to take the view that (as a user yourself) you know what a user will want. If it's a professional application, sure, your opinion might be valid, but there is a science behind good design that an experienced UI/UX designer will bring to the table.

Take a look at some public websites and decide for yourself whether a professional designer was involved.

Web Developer

A web developer is a software developer who focuses on web content, typically using web-specific languages such as HTML. There are specific disciplines associated with web applications, such as interaction with browsers and the embedding of media content.

Another key difference for a web developer is that applications will nearly always be focused on the general public and so need to be significantly more resilient to misuse than a typical application designed for professional use.

Search Engine Optimization (SEO) Consultant

If you have a public website and a business model that relies on members of the web-surfing public finding it, you may want to hire a SEO consultant to help you. The SEO consultant will analyse your website and ensure it is designed to feature prominently in as many search engine results pages (SERPs) as possible. They will look at keywords used on the page, suggest content that is aligned with common searches by members of the public and provide input to the technical design of the page itself.

Artificial Intelligence and Machine Learning

The world of AI and machine learning is still developing, and many of the job roles are likely to overlap with the roles above, such as data scientist or developer. But there are a couple of roles that are worthy of note, all of which combine analytical skills with a deep understanding of the new and exciting technology.

AI Researcher

An AI researcher will focus on advancing the capabilities of AI in general, discovering and applying new techniques and developing algorithms.

AI Engineer

An AI engineer will use data science and other analytical skills to develop, optimise and deploy models and algorithms to meet specific business needs for an organisation. The engineer may also analyse data sources to ensure they are suitable to be used to drive AI algorithms.

Machine Learning Engineer (MLE)

A MLE will use their analytical skills to develop, optimise and deploy machine learning models to meet specific business needs for an organisation. This will also involve the analysis of data sources and the preparation of data to be used in the machine learning process.

AI Safety Technical Researcher

The safety and trustworthiness of AI systems is a major concern across the globe. An AI safety technical researcher seeks to understand and mitigate these concerns, ensuring that the use of AI is to the benefit of everyone.

Prompt Engineer

A prompt engineer works with AI models that generate text, such as chatbots or content creation tools based on large language models (LLMs). The main responsibility of a prompt engineer is to design and optimise prompts – the inputs given to these AI models – in order to elicit the most effective responses.

Operations and Servicing

Database Administrator (DBA)

A DBA manages the databases within an organisation. Their focus is to ensure that databases are well-designed, secure and performant. They will often be involved in application design to ensure that databases are sized and configured appropriately and will manage the data and databases in the operational environment.

Computer Operator

In bygone days, the computer operator was the technician who plugged and unplugged cables, tweaked switches and generally applied mechanical means to keep a large mainframe running. Most computer operators today will execute their craft through a laptop or desktop like any other computer user. The operator's role is to monitor the running applications to ensure that they are functioning properly. For larger organisations with overnight batch processing suites, the operator will ensure that all the jobs run correctly and that systems are ready for the next operational day.

Help Desk Support Specialist

The role of the IT help desk is to act as a first line of support for technical problems. The support specialist will need to understand all of the organisation's applications and systems, from desktops through to the most complex business software. They will know and understand the most common issues, such as access and logging on, but will need to refer more complex issues to second-line support teams (especially those to do with bespoke or internally built applications).

WHERE NEXT?

Technology roles, both in the very centre of technology and those at the periphery who act as interpreters for the rest of us, have been in almost constant flux for 50 years as the information revolution and its aftershocks have rippled ever more invasively into the world of commerce. Most of the jobs above didn't exist 50 (or even 20) years ago. Some have just been renamed. Some have gradually moved towards (or away from) the business side of the organisation. Other roles have sprung fully formed, seemingly from nowhere, to become pivotal to the modern digitally enabled business.

Even without the anticipated tsunami of change from generative AI, there are trends in the IT industry that will drive role changes: new methodologies (agile), better designed programming interfaces (low-code and no-code), a shift to a more architecture-led approach and new non-AI technologies (blockchain).

The World Economic Forum (WEF) Future of Jobs report[2] from May 2023 suggests the number of business-related tasks currently performed by machines – what it calls the "human-machine frontier" – will rise from (a surprisingly low) 34% to 43% in the next four years, with administrative jobs considered to be those most at risk. On the other hand, AI is expected to be adopted by nearly 75% of contributors to the report, with AI and machine learning specialists expected to be the fastest growing jobs across all industries.

Technology jobs won't be immune to these influences, but there is perhaps less scope (yet) for automation in an industry that is itself evolving and driving change. Whether automation in the IT industry itself is immune, or simply lagging behind the rest of the field, remains to be seen.

What Won't Change...

What is unlikely to change in the short (and potentially long) term is the set of attributes that collectively define technology professionals.

Ask a business analyst or a project manager to name their most effective capabilities, and the majority will list analytical thinking and attention to detail in their top three. These are, coincidentally, top-ranked skills across all industries, according to the WEF report. Developers, testers, architects – the story is the same: attention to detail; rational, analytical thinking.

Technologists (usually) are not business "winners". They don't go out and get clients or make strategic partnerships. But they are business enablers: without relevant technology, most – if not all – businesses will quickly flounder and lose the ability to deliver value to their stakeholders. Technologists are, and will continue to be, the lifeblood of the vast majority of organisations.

The good news, then, is that the vast majority are committed, energetic individuals, who have a passion for doing the job right (and the right job). They love to solve problems, see the complex rendered simple and make effective changes to the working lives of their business colleagues. Most, but not all, respect the Pareto Principle (aka the 80/20 rule) and will adhere to the "if-it-ain't-broke-don't-fix-it" mentality.

Almost universally, project professionals will value stakeholder management and collaboration among the most significant attributes required for their roles. Typically, what they mean is the ability to relate to their business stakeholders – that's you. If you're able to apply some of the thinking suggested within these pages, you will be taking giant strides forward in making their future jobs (and yours!) that much easier.

Where IT professionals will continue to need your input as a business leader is on the business issues themselves (not the IT issues). What's the context? What are the priorities? What else is happening that they might not be aware of? What are the internal or external constraints such as timing, budget and other initiatives?

IT Roles That Will Evolve and Flourish

Technology roles will continue to adapt and evolve as the underlying technologies improve and new (or newer) methodologies gain traction.

As more and more hardware moves into the cloud, roles that govern such operations will become more important, notably those to do with information security. When your applications and data no longer sit inside your own secure data centre but are running in a public or private cloud, they become accessible to any with malicious intent. It will become increasingly important to manage third-party providers to ensure that their data and operational security measures are sufficiently robust, as well as ensuring that data is protected as it enters and leaves your organisation's control.

Software engineering is here to stay, and as we saw earlier, the main programming languages are well-embedded and unlikely to disappear overnight. More to the point, software written 50 years ago is still widely in operation and needs to be maintained. But the skills needed to be a software developer will continue to evolve as new use cases are identified. In particular, the increased use of low-code and no-code solutions and the rise of the "citizen developer" will create an entirely new type of development capability: business users who are able to quickly (and accurately) convert their needs into operational code.

Data governance is only just starting to gain the appreciation it deserves. Roles in data management such as data architects, data stewards and data scientists will become increasingly mainstream in organisations. As data regulation becomes more widespread and more stringent, data privacy experts will become more involved in technology projects, earlier in the lifecycle.

Considering how much they have revolutionised nearly every industry, it's remarkable to think that the internet and the World Wide Web are still really in their infancy. Barely over 30 years old. The expectations that users have of how their applications and web pages will behave continues to increase, and UI and UX experts will continue to be in demand. As more functionality falls into the well of the possible, business stakeholders will be called on to provide direction and prioritisation for an ever-widening array of features.

Project methodologies will continue to merge, with more use being made of the agile approach. Business stakeholders will be asked to join small, multi-functional agile teams with constant interaction and feedback. This should lead to a more inclusive and collaborative software design process.

As software becomes more commoditised, with individual components linked by enterprise communications layers, organisations will begin to focus more on architecture than programming. Technology projects will focus less on building and testing applications and will instead spend their time considering how various off-the-shelf applications can fit together to best meet their particular business needs.

The Seismic Shock of New Technologies

Where technology roles will see the most change is in the newer and currently most rapidly evolving disciplines of blockchain and AI.

While both are essentially rooted in more traditional software engineering, they bring their own challenges and opportunities.

Blockchain specialists will become adept at writing decentralised applications (DApps) using a range of network-specific programming languages. As the use of blockchain spreads to more industries, more use will be made of oracles to pass data from the "off chain" to the "on chain" world (creating hybrid DApps). And the specifics of cryptographic security and management of blockchain data will also increase as blockchain finds use in more industries such as health and real estate.

We've seen that generative AI isn't ready to replace developers just yet, although it might begin to make their job easier as an aggregator of (largely reliable) information. While it remains a curio and creative tool, with the significant reliability issues currently experienced, GenAI will remain an adjunct to the roles fulfilled by specialists, and its output will always need to be verified. Not forever, but for now. The skills most likely to be in demand will be one step removed from the coal face, so to speak: those with the ability to train models and to frame prompts and questions to obtain the most effective responses.

It is in the application of AI to digitally savvy businesses that the next great leap will come. This is more likely to feature data architects and data scientists than AI specialists per se. The data architect will ensure that an organisation's applications are connected and able to contribute to a data lake. The data scientist will build processes to analyse that data, using it to identify patterns that can improve processes and target business outcomes that are more likely to be successful.

The Evolution of the Project Manager

Probably one of the most dynamic roles in the technology project environment is that of the project manager. Projects themselves have changed beyond recognition in the last two decades and remain in a state of flux as the methodologies continue to blend into each other. The project manager needs to deal with an ever-increasing range of technologies and needs to be able to have sensible conversations with specialists in those technologies.

A project manager is expected to be:

- Collaborative
- Motivational
- Cross-functional
- Decisive
- Innovative
- Financially astute
- Technologically aware

Add in hybrid working and the need to encourage (and monitor) collaboration within the project team across a range of project phases and approaches. Add more structured data governance and increased data regulation and information security. Add new technologies such as blockchain and AI. And it becomes clear that the project leader's role is set for some head-spinning evolution.

The most effective project managers will be adaptable and responsive to the new ways of working, able to coach and motivate a distributed team, while helping all stakeholders to understand the new technologies and associated risks. They will need to address increasingly complex problems and manage new types of players in the cross-functional team. And in such an environment, mistakes are more likely on all sides, so resilience will be key.

SO WHAT?

There are a lot of technology roles in the modern organisation. As a business leader, you may not be aware of all of them (be honest). And you probably don't get to speak to too many on a daily basis in the pursuance of your business-as-usual duties.

But what if you're asked to take part in a project? Or there's an operational issue that can be solved by the production of a low-code report or dashboard, or by the creation of a workflow? Who should you speak to first, and how should you engage them?

Here are some useful questions you might want to ask.

- Who should I be talking to?
- Do I need a permanent capability or can I hire contractors?
- How do I know my project team is aligned with my vision?
- Are people staying in their swim lanes?
- What do I do if the team isn't performing?

Who Should I Be Talking To?

Obviously, the answer to this question will depend on what stage you're at (as well as the size of the project). If you only have the inkling of an idea for a technology project or development then that's a very different prospect to a project that's in full flow and about to deliver. And of course, there are conversations that you should be having all the time, to ensure that your technology is aligned with your business on an ongoing basis.

"Always on" Conversations. You should be in constant dialogue with your organisation's architects: business architects to ensure that the business itself is aligned with its strategies, solution architects to ensure that the technology is aligned with the business drivers and data architects to ensure that your data is being correctly managed. In addition to this, you should have an open and regular conversation with your information security team to ensure that appropriate measures are in place to look after your data.

Aside from that, it's always good to keep a general level of connection with the technology and project teams. Offer to come to one of their regular meetings and tell them what the business does (or your part of it, at least), where it's going, what issues it faces and where they might be able to help. The tech and project teams will often feel that they are kept at arm's length from the business – in our experience, they are always fascinated by these sessions and get a huge amount of context out of them (far more than you might think).

Project Initiation. If you have an idea for a project or a small change to a process, your first point of contact should really be the committee in your organisation that manages the development roadmap. You may have had the best idea ever, but if the organisation can't afford to develop it, there's little point taking things further. Many organisations have just enough technology budget to meet mandatory regulatory changes. Assuming you get the go ahead, the next step is to define your idea: remember that the first thing to do is identify the problem. Best placed to help you there is a business analyst or business architect. Once you've identified the problem, you may need the help of a project manager to scope out a broad plan and identify the scope and scale of the project.

Design and Development. Who you speak to here will depend on whether the project is to be waterfall, agile or something in between. Or if there will even be a project at all (if the work is small enough). Agile product owners and scrum masters will guide you through the regular sprints and help you connect with the multi-disciplined agile team (which may include developers and testers). For a waterfall project, you will probably spend most of your time discussing requirements with the business analysts and helping the project manager with planning – what are the milestones, what's the context, what are the risks?

If there are low-code or no-code developments involved, you may find you need to speak directly to the developers, whether they are converted business stakeholders ("citizen developers") or more traditional IT professionals. Similarly, your input may be needed on UI/UX issues if the application will be heavily screen-based.

Finally, it's never too early to think about data, and for a data-heavy project, you would expect to engage with the data architect and data analysts to map out any data requirements, data migrations and any data cleansing that is needed for implementation.

Testing. Whether testing is a distinct phase that follows design and development (as in a waterfall project) or is rolled into individual sprints (for an agile project) or some combination of both, your key contacts for testing are the test analysts and the defect manager. The test analysts will help you to design effective tests and prioritise testing to ensure maximum coverage in the time available. The defect manager will help you prioritise any defects that are identified and will ensure that they are retested once done.

The defects themselves need to be fixed, of course (the priority ones, that is). Your business expertise may be needed here, too. Some are caused by bad data (which you are more likely to spot than a tester who is less familiar with the business than you are). Some defects are simply coding issues that can be fixed without your input. More rarely (but these are the ones that really hurt) a defect is raised that calls you back to the original design or the requirement. These are far harder to fix, and you'll need to work with the original team (business analysts or product owners) to address the issue.

Readying for Implementation. Getting ready for the implementation of a project can be a trying time. There's a lot going on, even if the project is being run in an agile way. The first big implementation, when the "tyres hit the road" so to speak, can be pivotal to the success of the rest of the project.

First, there's probably still some late testing going on, and some critical fixes from earlier test phases that need to pass their retest in order for the software to go live. In an ideal world, this is all done and dusted by the time you even think about launching the application, but the reality is that things slip, timescales are squeezed and the time and effort allocated for testing bleeds into the implementation window (and – ahem – even beyond it, in many cases). This testing and test management will at the very least be a distraction for the team from the huge task of getting ready for the implementation.

Second, building the release itself takes a great deal of effort. The latest tested version of the software has to be finalised, along with any final tested changes. Quite apart from the fact that this will take up a lot of the available time of some project team members, it may also mean that some of your late changes and even some defects can't be included. You may be called on to make a judgement as to whether certain aspects of the application can launch with defects, and how quickly these need to be released afterwards. This can be an area where very small margins matter. If the release is taking place over a weekend and a particular function isn't ready, but isn't needed until the first overnight batch run, maybe you can still authorise the implementation with a hotfix at some point on Monday. Close liaison with the defect manager or lead test analyst (along with an agreed alignment on priorities) will be important.

Third, preparing for the implementation weekend is a task in itself. There are teams to line up to perform all of the activities needed to complete the launch (see Chapter 7 and below). For a very big implementation, the project team may recommend trial runs and dress rehearsals to make sure that all the components and teams are in place and prepared. Your input (and participation) in this planning may be critical to the success of the launch. For a big project, there may be a specific project manager responsible for this planning, and they will be a key contact for you.

Fourth, the new users and operators of the application need to be trained. Again, there may be a dedicated training team, but it's likely that they will need to get a lot of their training material from the project team (notably the business analysts) and from you or your colleagues. Often, training on a new application is as much about what the users don't know as what they need to know. While the project team can provide information on the former, it's your role to help with the latter. Who needs to be trained? What do they know now? What do they need to know? What should the focus be? What follow-up training might be needed, and when? None of this is written down or obvious. The trainers will want to get all of that from inside your head.

Fifth: data. It should be no surprise how important data is to an implementation (but despite that, remarkably, it often is). Any new application may need to be loaded with static data from an external source or migrated from your own systems. Dynamic data may also need to be transported for any in-flight processes. The quality of that data is critical to the success of the implementation. Understanding that quality and taking the necessary steps to correct it are pivotal steps. You and your business colleagues may need to conduct intensive reviews of existing data, support the production of data quality reports and, most importantly, take steps to correct data in either the source or target systems. This can be incredibly intense and time-consuming. Typically, your interlocutors for this exercise will be business analysts and data analysts.

There's a lot going on. Just before an implementation (especially a big implementation) is probably the most stressful time for any project. As a business stakeholder, you will need to make sure that your team(s) can handle the workload and are ready for the tough days ahead. You should also be checking in with the project team to make sure they feel appreciated. This period is when divisions between the project team and the rest of the business (including other technology teams) become stretched. Feelings of resentment are rife. Accusations fly from the Business-as-usual (BAU) teams of "being done to" rather than "doing together". This is the time to remind everyone why the project exists, what it is seeking to achieve and how it will have a positive impact on the organisation. And, as a business leader, you need to take responsibility. Projects don't initiate change; they just deliver them. Make sure everyone is aware of the reasons for doing it in the first place and ensure there is a collective will to deliver. Sounds simple, no? You'd be amazed....

Implementation: The big weekend. Or maybe not. Project teams will generally try to avoid a single big implementation if they possibly can. Agile projects typically try to make regular small incremental releases. Even waterfall projects might try to spread the implementation over a number of tranches. But sometimes it's just not possible to avoid a single launch event – when a core platform is being replaced or when a new line of business is being introduced (or your business is going into production for the very first time). But regardless of the size of the implementation, it carries a degree of stress and can involve a huge team to get the job done.

There are teams to line up to perform the technical aspects of releasing the new code, rolling out access to new users, migration of data from old systems to new systems, plus any transitional business processes to prepare. Your input (particularly on the latter) will be invaluable. The project team may have been developing the new software for months or even years but quite often won't have had much time to think about how to transition from the old world to the new. What manual processes are being replaced? What about work that's halfway through a process – how does that need to be completed? For a large project, there may be business analysts and project managers dedicated to these aspects. On a smaller project, you will need to support the project team directly. Like the training needs, as the bridge between the business and the project team, you and your subject matter expert colleagues are the ones who have the vital combination of knowledge to contribute here.

Post-Implementation: The project is done. The new application or system is live and the teams are using it. Everything's great, the project team can be disbanded, and we can all go back to our day jobs, right? Wrong.

In an ideal world, all of the above. But the reality is that most projects need a great deal of aftercare in the few weeks (or months) after implementation. Remember all those priority calls? Changes that couldn't be made in time, defects that just couldn't be fixed? Sub-optimal solutions that everyone agreed could be lived with? They all come home to roost. There's an army of new users who didn't come on the project journey with you and weren't party to those decisions. They almost certainly won't understand or appreciate the pressure-cooker combination of time, money and stress that led to the compromises that have been made. You need to stand up at this point – be part of the team, take collective responsibility for anything that's not quite right. Of course, you need to help to prioritise (again) those issues that need to be fixed, but you also need to speak to your business user colleagues – help them understand why certain parts of their new world aren't perfect.

The project team will be on hand (usually) to help. It's the usual suspects again: business analysts, data analysts, product owners, maybe a developer or two for screens or processes that have been built using low-code or no-code. A good project manager is invaluable again at this time – coordinating the effort, helping you to prioritise and build an effective patch or hotfix schedule to address the most pertinent issues.

Once things have calmed down a little, and it's indeed time for the team to disband and move on, there are still a couple of key interactions for you: the project manager will want to hold a "lessons learnt" session (or a retrospective), and the handover to the business as usual support teams needs to take place (ideally as quickly as possible). For the former, you should interact with the whole project team: ensure that you understand their perspective about what went well and what went wrong (remember that it could be you!) and that they understand yours. For the handover, although this will be coordinated by the project manager, you may well need to brief members of the help desk support team on some of the likely issues with the new product.

Do I Need a Permanent Capability or Can I Hire Contractors?

The technology industry is made up of more than its fair share of temporary workforce (aka "contractors"). This stands to reason: there are a number of highly specialised jobs that by their nature can be short-lived or have a definite end-date.

The reasons could be:

- Large projects to implement new software that need a spike in project team professionals that simply aren't needed once the project is complete. This may include professionals expert in implementing that particular product or in implementations generally.
- Technologists specialising in one particular product. When an organisation no longer requires that product, it may be mutually beneficial for the professional to take their existing expertise elsewhere rather than retrain.
- "One off" analysis such as data cleansing that may require specialists.

If your goal is to spin up a project to implement a new application, or a short-term analysis exercise, you may want to hire some contractors to augment your steady-state capabilities.

It makes sense, but there are some things to think about.

Essentially, there is a payoff between transportable skills (techniques that are applicable everywhere) and what we might call local knowledge (simply knowing how things are done inside your organisation or how your business functions). These vary by job role.

Project Managers/Scrum Masters: Much of what a project manager or a scrum master brings to the table is transportable. Best practice, how to write project documents, how to run an agile scrum: these are all common enough across technology projects that a good professional should be able to slot right in. But most project managers will tell you that the majority of their job is stakeholder management – knowing and understanding who in the organisation has the power, or who can be trusted to provide unbiased information and who will try to derail the project. It works both ways: the trust of the key stakeholders is hard to earn, and a temporary or contract project manager – new in the role – may struggle to get the best out of these relationships.

This lead time can be reduced by sitting down with a new project or programme manager with an organisation chart and going through the key stakeholders explaining what motivates each and why they are good (or bad) for the project.

The other issue with projects is that although there are standard documents and methodologies, many sites have their own bespoke templates and project workflows – the more your organisation can adhere to standard methodologies (or at the very least maintain a clearly documented variation) the quicker your hired project leadership team will begin to be productive.

If your organisation can afford it, maintaining a team of permanent project managers and scrum masters will help you to get any temporary team members up to speed more quickly.

Business Analysts/Product Owners: Both of these roles use clearly defined techniques and skills, such as requirements elicitation and documentation, or business process modelling. And a really good business analyst can be dropped into any project on any subject and will ask good questions to identify the root causes of problems. But, again, much of the value of the business analyst lies in their experience, in having seen similar problems before and solved them. And a business analyst who has worked for a long time in one organisation will have developed a deep understanding of the processes, systems, data and (in particular) the people – be they users, clients or partners. This knowledge is hard-won and can't be gained quickly by any temporary staff.

Maintaining a solid core of permanent business analysts will ensure that you can build project teams that at least have access to the necessary local expertise. The one exception is when you are implementing an off-the-shelf application with minimum customisation – here, it can help to bring in a contractor who is expert in that application and can help your team to understand how the new processes will need to work.

Architects: Business, solution or data architects are most effective when they can build and mature their models over a number of years. Unless your project aspirations are truly transformational, you would be better off keeping a team of permanent architects.

Developers and Testers: The more technical roles on a project. It's here that you're more likely to benefit from hiring contractors. They require less "local" knowledge, and the documentation provided to them should be self-explanatory (if your business analysts are up to scratch). There might be economic reasons to keep a core of developers on hand, but if you need to grow the team quickly, this should not be such an issue.

Operational technologists, such as *operators* and *help desk specialists* should ideally be permanent. You're less likely to experience spikes in demand, and the accumulated knowledge of the team will be invaluable in dealing effectively with issues and incidents.

How Do I Know My Project Team Is Aligned with My Vision?

We've seen it time and again: the project team sits quietly in a meeting room (or on a video call) and the project sponsor steps up to explain his or her vision. Five minutes later – following a dizzying reel of acronyms, unfamiliar buzzwords, assumed knowledge and references to unknown people and organisations – the sponsor leaves the room in the sure and certain knowledge that the vision has been duly imparted to a fully aligned and enthused project team.

Nothing could be further from the truth.

Remember: project people do projects. You may be lucky enough to have an architect or business analyst on the team who knows and understands the business well enough, but even then, they may not appreciate what it is you want them to do.

In the early phases of a project, no one is going to object if you strip things back, start from the basics. Tech people are (on the whole) rational and sensible: they will appreciate starting at first principles and extrapolating. What they don't have is your years of experience in the business, facing off to competitors, using the applications and talking to clients.

Most IT professionals will never have used the software they have spent their lives building and customising. They will never have met or spoken to a client.

That's right. Go back. Read those two sentences again.

Project teams build or customise and then implement systems. They don't get to use them in anger, and you probably wouldn't want to sit them in front of a client anyway.

So. Keep things simple. Start from the beginning. Keep it wide and high level. Then focus on principles and vision, without jargon. Pause. A lot. Give the team the opportunity to ask questions. Talk about roles, not individuals. You may think it's inconceivable that the team don't know who Charlie is – everyone knows Charlie. But perhaps they don't, especially if they are contractors. If Charlie's the head of Client Relationships, talk about the role – what would an ideal incumbent want, not just what Charlie wants.

And then, when you're done, ask some questions back. Make sure it's really landed. Ideally, if there's a good architect or business analyst on the team, they'll step up to a whiteboard and draw you a picture. Don't resist: help the process along – tweak it where it needs tweaking. Remember, the role of the business analyst or the architect is to render your business vision into a format understandable to the technologists. They'll know best what will land with the rest of the team.

Once you're happy with the vision, it should be the first slide in every deck. As a reminder to the team of what it is they are trying to achieve.

Are People Staying in Their Swim Lanes?

We've said it before: for some reason, the project environment seems to encourage people to become experts outside their own field. Business people try to tell IT people how to run projects, and project people will try to tell the business people how to run their business.

Everyone needs to stay in their swim lanes.

Technologists need to opine on tech systems: security, ease of integration and architecture. Business analysts should be trying to find efficient and effective ways of meeting your business needs. They need to challenge you, absolutely. They should be asking probing questions about priorities and risks. But you and your colleagues set the business direction.

And this applies doubly to you. Don't be tempted to tell the team how to run a project. They know what they're doing. If the project manager wants to set the RAG status to red, you need to listen, not argue. If the business analyst wants you to prioritise a set of requirements, don't try to convince them that there's no need.

What Do I Do If the Team Isn't Performing?

You could fire them all, of course.

But, before you do that, take a moment to think about some of the aspects of this chapter.

Have you got the right people on the project? Have you got the right blend of permanent and contract team members: the core of permanent staff to bring their expert local knowledge and enough contractors to provide the necessary muscle or understanding of the target state? Do the team understand the vision? Do they know what it is they are trying to build?

And are you leaving them to it, or do you find you're always the one doing the talking, with maybe not enough listening?

By all means, if you still think it's necessary, take "executive action". But first, think that maybe, just maybe, there's another way to get the best out of the team you already have.

NOTES

1   The BABOK Guide.
2   www3.weforum.org/docs/WEF_Future_of_Jobs_2023.pdf

Conclusion

Whew.

We've covered quite a lot of ground. Hopefully, some of it (or even most of it) resonated with you. With luck, you'll get an opportunity to benefit from it the next time you are involved in an IT project or an IT conversation.

And, regardless, we hope you've enjoyed learning a little more about the world of technology.

Talking of conversations (and of covering ground, for that matter), you may remember the hot air balloon at the very start of the book.

How might that conversation proceed if the business leader in the balloon (and the technologist) applied some of the points in this book?

Initiation

"Hello", calls the business leader from the balloon to the technologist in the field. "I have a problem. Can we try to solve it together?"

"Of course", replies our technologist. "What's the problem?"

Problem Statement

"I don't know where I am".

"Is that really the problem? I don't know where I am either. But also I don't care. Why is that an issue for you?"

"I'm trying to find the recovery vehicle and I know that it's parked in a place called Little Uppington".

"And you want to know in which direction Little Uppington is?"

"Yes. Exactly".

Bingo.

Non-functional Requirements

"Do you go ballooning often?"

"No, this is my first and only time".

"So you just want a solution for today, right now".

"Yes".

Jackpot.

SaaS Solution

"I could look on my mobile phone for you".

Risk

"Thanks. I dropped mine".

Interfacing

"There is a poor network connection. But it looks as though Little Uppington is a mile in that direction".

Data

"Can we be sure? I'd like to understand the quality of the data".

"Not 100%. But there is a small wood between here and there that tallies with the map I can see on my mobile phone".

Celebration of Success and Post-Implementation Review

"Thank you. You have been very helpful".

"You're welcome. As a follow-up, can I suggest you invest in a lanyard for your phone so you don't drop it in similar situations?"

It's a little glib, but you get the picture.

A technology project or operation will always work best when it is a collaborative exercise between an informed business and a compliant tech team. Being able to articulate needs in a way that everyone can understand, taking ownership of those aspects that fall within the business domain (such as data and project sponsorship) and being able to accurately judge the appropriateness of the solutions really are key to applying technology.

This is the end of the book.

We've taken you through the components of IT and introduced you to the key concepts. Hopefully, we've given you enough of a grounding to understand how IT can help you to solve your business problems, now and in the future.

And we've asked you a range of questions (or suggested some you should ask yourself or your colleagues).

It's time for you to embrace the world of technology, to go out there and interact more meaningfully and with greater depth of understanding with your IT colleagues.

So, naturally, we have one final question for you:

- What are you waiting for?

Glossary

If you want to have an effect on other people, you first have to talk to them in their language.

Kurt Tucholsky

Now that she'd managed to log on successfully,
Lucy thought she'd try to log off

Another glossary?

Aren't there enough of those in the world already?

You may be right, but in researching this book, we were amazed at how often the technical terms involved (and there are many) are all too often defined by using other technical terms. For example, does it help to know that "RabbitMQ is an open-source message-broker software (sometimes called message-oriented middleware) that originally implemented the Advanced Message Queuing Protocol" or is it more helpful to know that it's a means to get data from one application to another?

As such, we present this glossary of the most commonly used terms referenced within the book as an aid specifically for the business professional, as opposed to the technologists.

We've also provided a "scope" for each word, phrase or acronym that might help you to place it in context.

We hope that you find it helpful.

Word/Phrase/ Acronym	Scope	Meaning
ADSL	Interfacing	Asymmetric Digital Subscriber Line: A type of broadband communications technology used for connecting to the internet. The asymmetric nature (with faster download speeds than upload speeds) enabled increased data capacity for most users compared to existing digital lines. ADSL was introduced in the 1990s and was gradually replaced by faster technologies such as fibre optic cables.
AGC	Hardware	Apollo Guidance Computer: the computer on the Apollo missions. One of the first programmable electronic computers ever built. The astronauts were able to type commands into the AGC through a keyboard and display unit.
Agile (methodology)	Project	A broad project methodology that focuses on frequent, iterative deliveries by small multi-disciplined teams. Collaboration and regular feedback are encouraged.
AI	AI	Artificial Intelligence: the simulation of human intelligence by computer systems including the use of language, reasoning and self-correction through *Machine Learning*.

Word/Phrase/ Acronym	Scope	Meaning
ALGOL	Software	Early programming language in academia (Algorithmic Language). Developed in 1958, ALGOL was hugely influential and is the predecessor of many modern languages.
AOL	Interfacing	America Online: an early internet service provider, offering dial-up internet, email, instant messaging, and web portal services in the 1990s and early 2000s.
API	Interfacing	Application Programming Interface: a defined set of messages or calls used by an application in communication with other applications. Essentially an API is what allows two applications to be linked to each other.
ARPANET	Interfacing	Advanced Research Projects Agency Network: an early US government computer network that played a vital role in the development of the internet.
ASCII	Interfacing	American Standard Code for Information Interchange: a standard for character encoding used in electronic communication and data storage.
Asynchronous communication	Interface	Asynchronous communication is a concept in interfacing where the sender of the message does not wait for a response from the message's recipient. Think of this as sending a text on your phone: the recipient may reply quickly, but it's not synchronous. A synchronous communication would be more like a phone conversation where if you ask a question you sit waiting for a response.
BASIC	Software	Early programming language (Beginner's All-purpose Symbolic Instruction Code). A simple, user-friendly language designed in 1964, BASIC was very popular with users of early microcomputers.
BBN	Risk	Bolt, Beranek, and Newman Inc.: a technology research and development company known for its pioneering work in the development of the internet (such as the development of ARPANET).
Big data	Data	Extremely large data sets (often derived from human interactions with web pages or from the *IoT*) that can be analysed to reveal patterns, trends and associations. Big data is more than just large amounts of data – it represents an approach to recording every interaction to allow *data scientists* (or *AI*) to perform their analysis.

(Continued)

Word/Phrase/ Acronym	Scope	Meaning
Bit	Data	The smallest unit of data in computing, representing a single binary value of zero or one.
Bitcoin	Blockchain	Bitcoin is both the first *cryptocurrency* and the first *blockchain network*. As a cryptocurrency (BTC), bitcoin led the way and has fluctuated significantly in value since its launch in 2009. As the first blockchain network, bitcoin is more limited than later developments such as *Ethereum* and has only a very limited capacity for *smart contracts*.
Blockchain	Blockchain	Distributed digital ledger technology in which transactions are recorded in a secure, transparent and immutable way. With *smart contracts*, blockchain technology can be adapted for a variety of business applications.
Blockchain fork	Blockchain	Caused by a disputed or erroneous change to the protocol of a *blockchain network* such that two protocols are in operation at the same time. This results in two branches of the chain starting from a common point, hence a fork. One branch follows the old protocol and one follows the new one. Some forks are temporary in nature, while others persist and effectively lead to the creation of a new blockchain network for the new protocol.
Blockchain network	Blockchain	A collection of blockchain *nodes* all running the same *blockchain* software to initiate and validate transactions in the same way. Different networks will have different rules that govern who can participate and how transactions are initiated and validated (through the *consensus mechanism*).
Bluetooth	Interface	A wireless technology standard for exchanging data over short distances using short-wavelength radio waves. Devices using Bluetooth must be individually paired with each other. The name "Bluetooth" derives from the tenth-century king, Harald "Bluetooth" Gormsson who united the kingdoms of Denmark and Norway and was himself named after his prominent dead tooth, which had turned a dark blue colour.
Botnet	Risk	A network of infected computers controlled remotely by a cybercriminal, often used to send spam emails or carry out attacks (especially *brute force attacks* or *Denial of Service* attacks).

Word/Phrase/ Acronym	Scope	Meaning
Brute force attack	Risk	A method of attack where hackers try to gain access to a system by repeatedly trying different combinations of usernames and passwords until they find one that works. Can often be perpetrated by the use of a *botnet*.
BYOD or BYD	Risk	"Bring your own Device": where organisations allow employees' own laptops, tablets and phones to be used on the corporate network as a trusted device.
Byte	Data	A unit of digital information, made up of (typically) 8 *bits* – in combination, this gives 256 different potential values for a byte (28). Modern computers use multiple bytes to store a single character allowing a far greater range of text values (see *Unicode*).
C	Software	C is a programming language. Developed in the 1970s, it is a compiled *procedural programming language* still widely used today for core programming such as for operating systems.
C++	Software	An *object-oriented programming language*, C++ was an extension of *C* released in 1983. Still widely used for real-time applications such as gaming.
CBDC	Blockchain	Central Bank Digital Currency: a *tokenised* form of central bank-issued money. CBDC is directly linked to the value of the equivalent fiat currency, unlike *cryptocurrencies* which have no intrinsic value.
CEO fraud	Risk	A scam similar to *Phishing* in which attackers use an organisation's own data to make targeted attacks on victims that are more likely to be believed due to their apparent trusted origin. So named as the attack often involves a fake request from a senior executive to carry out a specified activity (such as making an unscheduled payment).
CERN	Interfacing	European Organization for Nuclear Research: a large particle physics laboratory located in Switzerland and France, where Tim Berners-Lee invented the World Wide Web.

(Continued)

Word/Phrase/ Acronym	Scope	Meaning
Client–server	Hardware	A computer configuration that involves a mainframe or large computer as a central unit (the "server" and multiple smaller workstations (the "clients"). Common in the late twentieth century, client–server topology has largely been replaced by multiple distributed systems connected by a local area network (*LAN*).
Cloud	Hardware	"The cloud" isn't really a place. It's the name given to any servers (computers) that are connected through the *internet*. These servers may be in one location (such as a large data centre operated by a service provider) or distributed across a number of locations.
COBOL	Software	Programming language (Common Business-Oriented Language). A human-readable language designed in 1959 specifically for business processing. Although not much new development is done in COBOL, programs written in the language are still in use at the very core of some of the biggest banks in the world.
Confabulation	AI	Instances of a computer model making up or misinterpreting information, often due to gaps or errors in its data processing. A more generic term than *hallucination*.
Consensus mechanism	Blockchain	A method used by a *blockchain network* to achieve collective agreement across all participants that a given transaction or block of transactions is valid and can be added to the chain. The consensus mechanism is defined in the software that operates the network.
Corpus	AI	A large set of structured and unstructured texts used for training *large language models*. A corpus could include common websites such as Wikipedia and Facebook and may run to many billions of sources.
COTS	Software	Commercial Off-the-Shelf: a software application that is ready to run but can be customised to better fit the environment or circumstances of its operation. This customisation is usually performed as a joint project involving both the software vendor and the business.
CPM	Project	Critical Path Method: a project management planning technique involving analysis of required tasks and the fastest time to complete them all.

Word/Phrase/ Acronym	Scope	Meaning
CPU	Hardware	Central Processing Unit: the core microprocessor of a computer.
CRT	Hardware	Cathode Ray Tube: a type of computer screen common before the availability of flat screens. The inner surface of the screen was coated in phosphorus and a powerful electrode was used to fire electrons at the screen to make it glow. Modern LCD or LED screens are over 50% more energy-efficient, as well as being significantly crisper and more responsive. CRTs were also prone to ghost images where the phosphorus had been burned away from part of the screen.
Cryptocurrency	Blockchain	A type of digital or virtual currency that uses cryptography for security and operates independently of a central authority. The first example of a cryptocurrency was *bitcoin*.
Cryptographic hash	Blockchain	A function that converts an input into a fixed-size string of *bytes*, which is typically used for security purposes in data transmission.
DApp	Blockchain	Decentralised Application: an application deployed on one or more *blockchain networks* (such as an *EVM*) using one or more *smart contracts* and potentially *oracles*. The DApp is available to any users of the related network(s).
Data governance	Data	An approach to the holistic management of data including architecture, modelling, security, integrity and quality in an organisation. Data ownership and responsibility for quality is a critical component.
Data lake	Data	A very large unstructured data storage area used by organisations as a staging area for *big data*. Think of data as "sloshing around" in the lake, before it is extracted into a *data warehouse* in a more structured form for formal analysis.

(Continued)

Word/Phrase/Acronym	Scope	Meaning
Data mastery	Data	Data mastery is a concept within *data governance* whereby each datum is managed within a defined application (the master application for that data). It is best practice for data to be managed in a single place and then replicated across the organisation's infrastructure as needed rather than it being possible to update the same datum in two places, leading to data quality issues.
Data science	Data	An interdisciplinary field that uses scientific methods to analyse large data sets (including *big data*) to extract knowledge and insights.
Data warehouse	Data	A very large storage area where an organisation's data is catalogued and available for retrieval and analysis.
Defect priority	Project	In software testing, the level of urgency assigned to a software defect, determining the order in which it should be resolved. Not the same as *defect severity*.
Defect severity	Project	A classification of a software defect based on the severity of its impact on the system's operation. Not the same as *defect priority*.
Definition of done	Project	Introduced by the *agile methodology*, the definition of done is a way to clearly list the precise criteria that must be achieved for a task to be considered complete.
Digital wallet	Blockchain	In *blockchain*, a digital wallet is simply an address that is referenced in transactions (either as sender or recipient).
DIKW	Data	Data, Information, Knowledge, Wisdom: a theoretical hierarchy that helps to explain the relationships between data (at the bottom of the hierarchy), information, knowledge and wisdom.
DoS/DDoS	Risk	Denial of Service/Distributed Denial of Service: a series of cyber-attacks that overwhelm a system or network with spurious traffic, making it unavailable to legitimate users. Can often be perpetrated by the use of a *botnet*.
Dunning–Kruger effect	Project	A natural bias shown by those with lower expertise to overestimate their capabilities (balanced by a natural tendency for experts to be self-deprecating).
EDSAC	Hardware	Electronic Delay Storage Automatic Calculator: a computer built in Manchester and used by J. Lyons for their groundbreaking LEO I business application.

Word/Phrase/ Acronym	Scope	Meaning
ELIZA	AI	An early computer program created in 1966 that applied a superficial level of *artificial intelligence* to enable human–machine communication. Users noted the "ELIZA effect" whereby they believed they were conversing with a human.
ENIAC	Hardware	Electronic Numerical Integrator and Computer: the first electronic digital computer, completed in 1945.
ERC-20 Token Standard	Blockchain	A technical standard used for *smart contracts* on the *Ethereum* blockchain (and implemented on similar *blockchain networks*) in support of *tokenisation*.
Ethereum	Blockchain	A *blockchain network* that first introduced and supports *smart contracts* and *DApps* (decentralised applications). The native coin for the Ethereum network is ether (ETH).
EVM	Blockchain	Ethereum Virtual Machine: a fancy name for the *Ethereum blockchain network* in its capacity to act as a decentralised computer, executing *DApps* and *smart contracts*.
Expert system	AI	A software application that emulates (or supports) the decision-making ability of a human expert, using a defined knowledge base and set of rules.
FLOPS	Hardware	Floating point Operations Per Second: the speed at which computers perform calculations. The first computer, *ENIAC*, worked at about 500 FLOPS. Modern distributed supercomputers operate at 10^{18} FLOPS (exaFLOPS).
FORTRAN	Software	Early programming language in the scientific community (Formula Translation). Created in 1957, FORTRAN was the forerunner of nearly all modern languages.
Gantt chart	Project	A chart initially devised by Henry Gantt to measure worker effectiveness, now used in most projects to track tasks, dependencies and critical paths as well as progress.
Gas	Blockchain	A unit that measures the amount of computational effort required to execute operations on a *blockchain network*. The gas is paid (usually in the native coin) by the initiating *node* to the node that validates the transaction.

(Continued)

Word/Phrase/ Acronym	Scope	Meaning
GitHub	Software	An online *integrated development environment* (*IDE*) available to multiple software developers for version control and collaborative coding. Extensively used by modern developers for source code management.
GPU	Hardware	Graphics Processing Unit: a set of microprocessors arranged in parallel to process multiple threads, well-suited to graphics output and used more recently in large server arrays to process *cryptocurrency* mining and *large language model* training.
Hallucination	AI	Instances where a *machine learning* model generates incorrect, nonsensical or irrelevant output, often due to limitations in understanding context or to existing biases present in its training data (*corpus*).
Hofstadter's law	Project	"It always takes longer than you expect, even when you take into account Hofstadter's Law". Often invoked in the context of software development. Initially coined by Douglas Hofstadter in 1979.
HTML	Interface	Hypertext Markup Language: a standard markup language for displaying text or documents in a web browser. Codes to control formatting are embedded in the text. The browser software reads the codes and applies the appropriate formatting.
Hyperlink	Interface	A link in a digital document (usually embedded in readable text) that allows a user to jump to another part of the same document or to a different document or website.
IDE	Software	Integrated Development Environment: a software suite that provides basic tools required for software development and testing. Typically includes a code editor, a compiler or interpreter and a debugger plus libraries and collaboration tools for the developer.
Internet	Interface	A global system of interconnected computer networks ("inter" and "net") linked by the internet protocol suite (*TCP/IP*).
IoT	Hardware	Internet of Things: a network of everyday objects that are connected through embedded hardware and software through the public *internet*.
IPU	Hardware	Intelligence Processing Unit: a massively parallel processor that can process large quantities of data at the same time.

Word/Phrase/ Acronym	Scope	Meaning
ISO		International Organisation for Standardisation: organisation devoted to the development and adoption of standards internationally. Responsible in the IT context for standards relating to hardware, software (such as programming languages), data, interfacing and blockchain as well as project methodologies. Based in Geneva, ISO also operates in the French language ("Organisation internationale de normalisation"). The name "ISO" is not an abbreviation of either French or English names but rather derives from the Greek word iso meaning "equal".
JANET	Interfacing	Joint Academic Network: a network for the UK research and education community. Introduced in 1984 and played a key role in the development of the global internet.
Java	Software	Programming language for web applications. Launched in 1995, Java is known for its portability across platforms.
KISS	Software	"Keep It Simple, Stupid". Design principle championing simplicity over complexity.
Lakehouse	Data	A hybrid between a *data lake* and a *data warehouse* where data is grouped by theme or by business categories for analysis.
LAN	Interface	Local area network: a network that connects computers and devices in a limited geographical area such as an office.
Layer 2 network	Blockchain	In blockchain, this is a secondary protocol built on top of an existing *blockchain network* to improve its scalability and efficiency, through a process referred to as "rollup". Essentially, the Layer 2 network takes away volume from the Layer 1 network and provides a summarised result to be included in the parent network's blockchain.
LCD	Hardware	Liquid Crystal Display: flat screen technology that uses polarised liquid crystals to display in colour or monochrome, using reflected light or a backlight.
LED	Hardware	Light Emitting Diode: flat screen technology that uses light-emitting semiconductors to produce coloured displays.

(Continued)

Word/Phrase/ Acronym	Scope	Meaning
Linux	Software	*Operating system* released in 1991, the basis of most modern operating systems. Widely used in servers and mobile devices.
LLM	AI	Large Language Model: advanced *AI* models that use complex *neural networks* to process and generate human-readable text. They are "large" due to their extensive data sources (*corpus*) and training.
Mainframe	Hardware	A large computer, traditionally installed in organisations to fulfil centralised processing such as the primary applications run by a bank. Largely replaced by distributed computers comprising racks of server blades.
Malware	Risk	Short for "malicious software," a generic term for any program or code designed to harm or steal data from a computer. Includes *worms, viruses, Trojan (Horses)* and *ransomware.*
Manchester Baby	Hardware	Also called the Small-Scale Experimental Machine (SSEM). The first electronic stored-program computer. Built at the University of Manchester in 1948.
Message syntax	Interface	The set of rules that defines the structure and format of messages in data communication. Syntaxes must be agreed between sender and recipient (or ideally follow an internationally agreed standard).
MFA	Risk	Multi-Factor Authentication: a type of security that requires more than one method of independent authentication (such as via both a password and a code sent by email or SMS) to verify the user's identity before granting access.
Microprocessor	Hardware	A microprocessor is a computer processor where all necessary computer hardware components (input, output, processing and storage) are contained in a single integrated circuit. First launched in 1971 (as the Intel 4004) and a core component of computer hardware ever since.
Mining	Blockchain	The process by which *nodes* in a *blockchain network* are rewarded (in some *consensus mechanisms*) for validating transactions.
ML	AI	Machine Learning: a subset of *AI* that involves the use of data and algorithms to imitate the way that humans learn, gradually improving accuracy based either on observable outcomes or on human supervision.

Word/Phrase/ Acronym	Scope	Meaning
Modem	Interface	Short for "modulator-demodulator". A device for converting digital data into analogue signals for transmission along standard telephone cables. First freely available as the Bell 103 in 1962, modems became critical to *internet* and other communication in the late twentieth century but have now largely been phased out due to the widespread use of optical digital networks.
Moore's Law	Hardware	A prediction made in 1965 by Gordon Moore that the effectiveness of microchips would double every year (later revised to every two years). The "law" has remained largely accurate ever since.
MQ	Interfacing	Message Queuing: a mechanism for sending messages from one application to another. Messages are queued, allowing for *asynchronous communication*.
MSN	Interfacing	Microsoft Network: a collection of internet services provided by Microsoft, originally introduced in 1995.
MUMPS	Software	A programming language developed in the late 1960s, designed for the healthcare industry but used in financial applications too (Massachusetts General Hospital Utility Multi-Programming System).
MVP	Software	Minimum Viable Product: in software delivery projects, this is the smallest build/effort that can be implemented and operated. Often vilified (sometimes appropriately) as a cost-cutting exercise, used properly an MVP can introduce an interim operating model ahead of time, building familiarity and potentially realising early benefits.
Neural network	AI	A highly complex software algorithm that mimics the way the human brain operates by building paths of association between inputs and outputs, reinforcing successful associations and de-emphasising unsuccessful ones.
NFR	Project	Non-Functional Requirements: these are requirements that govern how an application or system should behave. But instead of things that the user can see, NFRs define capabilities such as volumes, timing, availability and so on. NFRs are critical to development of software applications but are often overlooked.

(Continued)

Word/Phrase/ Acronym	Scope	Meaning
NFT	Blockchain	Non-Fungible Token: a *token* on a *blockchain* that represents a unique asset or good, as opposed to a generic type of assets or goods. Cash is fungible (it doesn't matter which particular coin you are spending) whereas a piece of artwork is not fungible.
NoSQL database	Data	A non-relational, scalable database used for storing large amounts of data, such as *big data*.
Node (blockchain)	Blockchain	Any computer that connects to a *blockchain network* and supports it by validating and relaying transactions.
Node (network)	Interface	A connection point within a network that can receive, create, store or send data along distributed network routes. Most often a computer or server but could also be a printer, modem or other network infrastructure.
Object-oriented programming (OOP)	Software	A programming approach that uses "objects" (such as windows and buttons on screens) to design applications and computer programs.
OEM	Hardware	Original Equipment Manufacturer(s): makers of large or distributed computer systems.
OLAP	Software	Online Analytical Processing: software that performs analytical tasks.
OLTP	Software	Online Transaction Processing: software that supports transaction-oriented tasks (such as data entry and transaction processing).
Operating system	Software	Software that controls a computer environment such as its memory, input and output (e.g. screens and keyboards) and processing (the software that it can run). *Linux* and *UNIX* are examples of operating systems for mainframe computers, while *Windows* and iOS are examples of operating systems for PCs and smartphones.
Oracle	Blockchain	In a *blockchain network*, a *smart contract* can typically only interact with data that is available within the network itself. An oracle is a mechanism whereby the smart contract can interact with external data.
Packet switching	Interface	A method of data transmission where messages are broken into small units called packets, sent independently over the network and reassembled at the destination.
Parkinson's Law	Project	"Work expands to fill the time available". Coined in 1955 by C. Northcote Parkinson as a commentary on bureaucracy.

Word/Phrase/ Acronym	Scope	Meaning
PERT	Project	Program Evaluation and Review Technique: a project management planning technique involving analysis of required tasks and the time necessary to complete them.
Phishing	Risk	A scam in which attackers send fake emails that appear to be from trusted (or plausible) sources to trick people into giving away personal information such as passwords, PINs or bank account details. Similar to *Spear Phishing*, *Vishing*, *Smishing* and *CEO Fraud*. In most attacks, the scammer will attempt to induce a sense of urgency and secrecy to inhibit the victim's rational thought processes.
PICNIC	Software	"Problem in Chair, Not in Computer": technology help-desk slang for a "user error".
PID	Projects	Project Initiation Document: a document that sets out the scope of a project as well as its deliverables, objectives, constraints and approach. These can also often be found in a Terms of Reference (ToR) or project charter.
Pilot ACE	Hardware/ AI	The ACE (Automatic Computing Engine) computer designed by Alan Turing in 1954 was never built, but a smaller version (Pilot ACE) was built in 1950.
PMBOK	Project	Project Management Body of Knowledge: the collected best practice for project management as defined by the Project Management Institute (PMI).
PMI	Project	Project Management Institute: global industry body for project management to define best practices and provide a forum for open discussion.
PRINCE II	Project	PRojects IN Controlled Environments: version 2 of the framework for project management as defined by the UK government (and now managed in conjunction with AXELOS Ltd).
Private key	Blockchain	A secure digital code known only to the owner of a *digital wallet* that allows them to access their *smart contracts* and to send transactions.
Procedural programming language	Software	A procedural programming language is one that supports the use of procedures (also called functions or methods) that can be defined and invoked.
Proof of stake (PoS)	Blockchain	A *consensus mechanism* in a *blockchain network* where participants validate transactions based on the number of coins they hold and are willing to "stake" as collateral.

(Continued)

Word/Phrase/ Acronym	Scope	Meaning
Proof of work (PoW)	Blockchain	A *consensus mechanism* in a *blockchain network* where *miners* compete to solve complex cryptographic puzzles in order to validate transactions.
Public key	Blockchain	A publicly available digital code linked to the owner of a *digital wallet* that allows others to decrypt transactions.
Python	Software	A high-level interpreted programming language launched in 1991. Human-readable and versatile, very widely used in web development to data science.
RaaS	Risk	Ransomware as a Service: a "business model" for cybercriminals where the creators of ransomware sell or lease it to other criminals, who then use it to carry out attacks.
RAG status	Project	A project management tool that uses traffic lights (Red, Amber and Green) to indicate project status.
Ransomware	Risk	A type of *malware* that locks your computer or encrypts your files, demanding payment (ransom) to regain access.
RFP	Software	Request For Proposal. A document or process used when an organisation wants to procure a product, application or service, inviting suppliers to bid.
RPG	Software	IBM's proprietary programming language (Report Program Generator) created in 1959. Used extensively on IBM mainframes for business applications.
SaaS	Software	Software as a Service: a software distribution model in which applications are hosted by a vendor or service provider and made available to customers over the internet.
SDLC	Project	Software Development Lifecycle: the process used within a project environment to design, develop and test software and applications. SDLC may be waterfall, agile or a combination of both.
Semantics	Interface	The meaning (or interpretation) of the characters and codes in a data transmission. Semantic meaning should be established and agreed between sender and recipient (or ideally follow an internationally agreed standard).

Word/Phrase/ Acronym	Scope	Meaning
Smart contract	Blockchain	A digital contract stored on the *blockchain*. The smart contract includes one or more functions coded in a defined programming language specific to the *blockchain network*. The contract can be executed by any transaction that correctly invokes these functions.
Smishing	Risk	A scam similar to *Phishing* in which attackers send SMS messages that appear to be from trusted (or plausible) sources to trick people into giving away personal information.
Spear phishing	Risk	A scam similar to *Phishing* in which attackers use data scraped from social media or other sources to make targeted attacks on victims that are more likely to be believed due to their personal content or context.
SQL	Software	Programming language designed in 1974 for accessing relational databases (Structured Query Language). Embedded SQL features in many other programming languages to manage database access.
Supply chain attack	Risk	A cyber-attack where hackers infiltrate a company through a trusted third-party supplier or service provider.
TCP/IP	Interface	Transmission Control Protocol/Internet Protocol: the foundational protocols that enable communication over the *internet*. IP (internet protocol) deals with routing and delivery while TCP (Transmission Control Protocol) ensures the reliable interpretation of data.
Token/Tokenisation	Blockchain	Tokenisation is the process of representing a real-world asset digitally in a *blockchain* (as a token) through the use of *smart contracts*.
Transformer	AI	A type of extremely complex *neural network* used to process natural language.
Trojan (Horse)	Risk	A deceptive type of *malware* that masquerades as a legitimate program but, once executed, can give attackers control over your system.
Turing complete	Hardware	A system is deemed to be "Turing complete" if it could in theory perform any computational task (given enough time and resources). The test was put forward by Alan Turing at a time when computers were very limited in their capabilities.

(Continued)

Word/Phrase/ Acronym	Scope	Meaning
Turing test	AI	A theoretical test devised by Alan Turing along the lines of a game show, The Imitation Game, to test whether an artificial intelligence (*AI*) could be distinguishable from a human being. If a "normal person" could not tell the difference (based on written responses to questions) then the AI is deemed to have passed the test.
UAT	Project	User Acceptance Testing: a form of software testing in which ultimate users of the application run through a number of simulated business scenarios to prove that the application achieves the correct business outcome. Unlike earlier stages of testing, UAT focuses only on business inputs and outputs – it does not look at interim states, messages or other non-visible data.
UI	Interface	User Interface: the means by which a user interacts with a computer application. Typically, this refers to input screens and their design but can also refer to any method of communication (such as a mouse or pen). Not to be confused with *UX* (User Experience).
Unicode	Interface	A standard for representing text in computers supporting multiple languages and non-Latin characters.
UNIVAC	Hardware	Universal Automatic Computer: a range of early mainframe computers produced between 1951 and 1986.
UNIX	Software	*Operating system* first developed in 1969. Multiuser and multitasking, UNIX influenced many other operating systems, including *Linux*.
URL	Interface	Uniform Resource Locator: a unique reference (an address) to a page, document or other content on the *internet*.
USB	Interface	Universal Serial Bus: design for sockets and leads that are universally accepted by all manufacturers and interface protocols. The latest version (USB C) also carries power, allowing laptops to connect and charge using a single standardised port.
Use case	Project	A means of capturing a business or user requirement for a software application. Similar to a *user story*.
User story	Project	A structured way to capture a business or user requirement for a software application. "As a … I want to … so that …". Similar to a *use case*.

Word/Phrase/ Acronym	Scope	Meaning
UTXO	Blockchain	Unspent Transaction Output: a means of tracking how much of a digital currency the sender has remaining after the execution of a *cryptocurrency* transaction.
UX	Interface	User Experience: a user's overall satisfaction when using a particular product or application. This includes the *UI* (User Interface) but also goes beyond to include the overall experience for the user.
Virus	Risk	A type of *malware* that attaches itself to a legitimate program and can replicate itself, spreading from one file to another and from one computer to others.
Vishing	Risk	A scam similar to *Phishing* in which attackers make phone calls that appear to be from trusted (or plausible) sources to trick people into giving away personal information.
VisiCalc	Software	The first spreadsheet computer program for personal computers, revolutionising business accounting and data analysis. Bundled with the Apple Mac.
Visual Basic	Software	Graphical programming language designed by Microsoft in 1991.
VPN	Interfacing	Virtual Private Network: a technology that creates a safe and encrypted connection over a less secure network, such as the internet.
Waterfall (methodology)	Project	A linear project delivery methodology that involves the completion of one phase before moving to the next. Each phase uses the output from the previous phase. Often criticised as the end user or sponsor is seen to be involved only at the start and end, creating an opportunity for the project to deliver an output that does not meet initial requirements.
WBS	Project	Work Breakdown Structure: a method of reducing a large task into groups of smaller, related tasks. A common tool in project management.
WiFi/Wi-Fi	Interface	A technology for wireless local area networking with devices based on IEEE 802.11 standards. As a local network, WiFi supports conversations between multiple devices. The term "WiFi" was proposed by a marketing firm as a user-friendly label.
Windows	Software	*Operating system* developed by Microsoft initially for personal computers. One of the most widely used operating systems globally across a range of devices.

(Continued)

Word/Phrase/ Acronym	Scope	Meaning
WordPerfect/ WordStar	Software	Early (1980s) word processing applications.
World Wide Web	Interface	A vast library of information accessible via the *internet* where each "page" is identified by a unique *URL*. Pages on the web are mutually connected using *hyperlinks* and *HTML*.
Worm	Risk	A type of *malware* that can spread itself without attaching to a program (unlike a *virus*). It exploits vulnerabilities in software to infect systems.
WYSIWYG	Software	"What You See Is What You Get". A largely redundant term now, but revolutionary in the 1990s when it was more typical for applications such as word processors to show a much-simplified view on screen compared to what would eventually be printed.
XBRL	Interface	eXtensible Business Reporting Language: a standard for codifying business information in text documents, mainly used for financial reporting.

Index

Note: Page numbers in *italics* indicate figures on the corresponding pages.

Printed in the United States
by Baker & Taylor Publisher Services